PENG[illegible]

DISCOVERI[illegible]

Frits Staal wrote about language, philosophy and [illegible] is scientific pursuits encompassed diverse areas and disciplines. Born in Amsterdam in 1930, he studied several languages, including Greek and Arabic, but concentrated on physics and mathematical logic before a Government of India scholarship took him to India, Indian philosophy and Sanskrit. He travelled on both sides of the Himalayas, taught and did research for extended periods in Europe and Asia, but spent most of his life in the departments of philosophy and of South and Southeast Asian studies at the University of California, Berkeley, where he was professor emeritus. His most well-known books are *Agni: The Vedic Ritual of the Fire Altar*, *Universals: Studies in Indian Logic and Linguistics* and *Rules without Meaning*. After retirement, he moved to Thailand, having long predicted that civilization would return to Asia under the intellectual guidance of India and China. He passed away in 2012.

PRAISE FOR THE BOOK

'This is a remarkable book. It untangles the many complexities of the Vedas and combines Staal's scholarly respect for the texts, with explanations that are lucid and occasionally witty. His insights are thoughtful and perceptive'—Romila Thapar

'Frits Staal's thoroughly researched *Discovering the Vedas* throws new light on these mysteries. . . . An exhaustive volume . . . Staal writes with rare literary skills, vibrant prose, and tops it up with humour. . . . This book would add fresh insights to our understanding of one of the most important epochs in Indian history'—*Tribune*

DISCOVERING THE VEDAS

Origins, Mantras, Rituals, Insights

FRITS STAAL

PENGUIN BOOKS
An imprint of Penguin Random House

PENGUIN BOOKS

USA | Canada | UK | Ireland | Australia
New Zealand | India | South Africa | China

Penguin Books is part of the Penguin Random House group of companies whose addresses can be found at global.penguinrandomhouse.com

Published by Penguin Random House India Pvt. Ltd
7th Floor, Infinity Tower C, DLF Cyber City,
Gurgaon 122 002, Haryana, India

Penguin Random House India

First published by Penguin Books India 2008

Illustration 9, Sanchi Stupa I: East Gate, south pillar, front phase, lower panel, courtesy Archeological Survey of India.

Illustration 12, Procession cart with solid wheels from a temple at Kumbakonam, courtesy National Museum, New Delhi.

14 13 12 11 10 9 8 7

ISBN 9780143099864

Typeset in Bembo by Eleven Arts, New Delhi
Printed at Replika Press Pvt. Ltd, India

For
Saraswathy,
Parvati Jeannette
and
Frederik Nanoo Staal

Contents

List of Illustrations*

*Except for the map, these illustrations appear after page 348.

List of Tables

Preface

He who studies understands, not the one who sleeps.
Rigveda 5.44.13

The beings of the mind are not of clay.
Byron, *Childe Harold*

The Vedas are often regarded as abstract and mysterious sacred books. If there is one thing the Vedas are not, it is books: they are oral compositions in a language that was used for ordinary communication; and were handed down by word of mouth like that language itself. Though the Rigveda is said in English to consist of ten 'books', it is a misleading mistranslation of Sanskrit *maṇḍala* which means 'cycle'. The expression 'sacred book' is also an erroneous appellation. It is applicable to the Bible or Qur'ān and was insisted upon by missionaries and colonial administrators who could not imagine anything else. It is less easy to explain why this misleading construction has been thoughtlessly embraced by moderns. It is true that the Vedic poets were regarded as inspired and their speech was considered a powerful agent. The Rigveda says: 'Soma unpressed has never elated Indra, nor its pressed juices unaccompanied by sublime language (*bráhman*)' (RV 7.26.1). It nowhere says that the Veda is *revealed* or *śruti*, literally 'what is heard.' It is heard only in the sense that it is transmitted from father to son or from teacher to pupil. The Vedas are an Oral Tradition and that applies especially to two of the four: the Veda of Verse (*Rig-veda*) and the Veda of Chants (*Sāma-veda*). Another anachronistic idea is that the Vedas are *apauruṣeya*, 'of non-human origin'. They never regard themselves as such. The idea comes from the Pūrva Mīmāṃsā, a philosophical system that arose several centuries after the end of the Vedas. The Rigveda was composed by poets, human individuals whose names were household words even before there were households: Viśvāmitra, 'Friend of All', Bharadvāja, 'Bearing Strength', Dīrghatamas, 'Seeing Far Into Darkness'. These poets were not *addressed* by gods. They used the *bráhman* of Vedic invocations to *address* gods. I have translated *bráhman* as 'language' and not 'speech', a common rendering, for reasons that will become increasingly clear in the course of this book.

My book will demonstrate that the Vedas are not one or all of a piece. It is easier to say what they are not than what they are. The Vedas had no founder or supreme authority, no popes or pontiffs, and neither were they associated with temples or icons. They refer to a variety of priests with distinct ritual tasks (sixteen in the classical *Śrauta* ritual), but no hymns or prayers, English words often met with in translations. There are gods, on earth and in heaven, but they do not dispense grace (with the possible exception of Varuṇa, who came from Bactria). They do not expect loving devotion or *bhakti*. The Vedas are not a religion in any of the many senses of that widespread term. They have always been regarded as storehouses of 'knowledge', that is: *veda*. But they are more than that. They embody a *civilization*.

The idea of writing a book about the Vedas that addresses both the scholar and the interested lay reader came from Romila Thapar. It was also inspired by Wendy Doniger's *Rigveda* selections published in Penguin Classics, a book that was written 'for people, not for scholars.' That selection of 'one hundred and eight hymns', a tenth of the Rigveda which is the first and earliest of the four Vedas, contains beautiful translations and a mass of scholarship.

* * *

The Vedas are often puzzling; sometimes abstract or mysterious; they may also be muddled; but those are the exceptions, not the rule. They overflow with information, much of it concrete. Part I of my book extracts such information from the Oral Tradition but also from archaeology. It deals with Vedic people and their language, what they thought and did, and where they went and when. Part II, almost twice as long as any of the others, provides essential information about the canonized four Vedas as we know them. It includes selections and translations. Part III seeks to discover and understand not only the facts and where they come from, but what they mean. It is analytic and attempts to shed light especially on mantras and ritual, about which many absurd statements circulate (*iṅgayanti* as the Rigveda puts it: like words moving around in a sentence). Mantras and rituals are the main channels through which Vedic contributions entered what came to be known as Hinduism.

Part III does not arrive at definite conclusions because I do not believe that we know and understand enough. Part IV tries to answer a rarely asked question: what can we learn from the Vedas? I do not advocate a Vedic lifestyle, but believe that there are things the composers of the Vedas knew and we do not. They include the original forms of the Vedic sciences and the meaning of *bráhman*. Part V, the concluding part, puts the Vedas in perspective in a wide-ranging comparison with Indic philosophies and religions, primarily Buddhism.

* * *

Before going further, I should say something about myself and my work. In the realm of non-fiction, creativity thrives on specialization, yet I have always been convinced that the distinctions between letters, sciences and other man-made subdivisions and disciplines are arbitrary. The seeds for these beliefs were planted during World War II in Amsterdam. Though I count myself as a citizen of the world, and not a native of any particular country, it is in this cosmopolitan city that I attended a Gymnasium. We did do gymnastics there though we were not naked (Greek *gumnos*), but concentrated on mathematics, physics, chemistry, biology, history, geography and several languages. Our teachers were not only teaching us these subjects, they were lively and eccentric men and women who were interested in developing our minds. The number of languages we learnt might baffle an Anglo-American, but not an Indian. In addition to Dutch, we were taught English, French, German, Greek, Latin, with optional Italian and Hebrew.

To this I added Arabic which I continued to study at the universities of Amsterdam and Leiden.

Languages are the gateways to civilizations. I did not care for literature, but languages may be studied for a variety of reasons. The primary appeal of Arabic had been the beauty of its flowing calligraphy. Without it, I would not have read al-Khwārizmī's treatise on algebra under the tutelage of a famous scholar. When I was younger, I had played about with Chinese characters; but did not continue, perhaps because I sensed that it might take a lifetime to learn them. The first three languages we learned to read and write at the Gymnasium were English, French and German. The last was the easiest but was not popular because of the German occupation. At the university, its horrors stayed fresh in our minds; but now we began to see similarities with the Dutch colonial empire. These acts might have been of a milder sort, but were detailed where necessary by the Indonesian students in our midst. The classical languages, five years of Latin and six of Greek, belonged to a more idealized world. But not one of dreams, because it gave access to ancient civilizations and especially to Greek philosophy which became my favourite. I continued with Greek philosophy at the University of Amsterdam, where I combined philosophy and mathematics which led to the first subject I studied in greater depth: mathematical logic. It was the time of L.E.J. Brouwer in intuitionistic mathematics, Kurt Gödel and Alfred Tarski in logic and foundations.

Amsterdam itself was, of course, 'a center of culture', though no one called it that. If I now try to remember how that quality appeared to me when I was young—a flavour that has evaporated in the course of more recent visits—I recall only the facts. When I walked from my home to the Gymnasium, I passed the Concertgebouw and sniffed the dusky air beneath the large passage gateway of the Rijksmuseum. I had been at home in the Concertgebouw since I was five years old. My violin teacher took me there during rehearsals when I was allowed to sit on a podium chair. I heard and saw all the great conductors of Europe before my legs could reach the floor. All of it prepared me to play the violin and viola in the student's orchestra and in string quartets and quintets. These are perhaps the ultimate reasons that I added a fifth part to a book about the four Vedas.

The walk to the university was in the same direction as that to the Gymnasium but twice as far. I crossed the bridges that spanned the four concentric canals of the ancient city. It never occurred to me that the old buildings at their very centre would not be my future home. I was not interested in being a teacher or educator. 'Scientist' isn't a special label in any language but English. French *science*, Dutch *wetenschap*, German *Wissenschaft*, Japanese *gaku*, Sanskrit *śāstra*, etc., refer to any serious discipline. We paid no attention to practical applications such as technology, politics, economics, civics or business administration. Only basic sciences were taught and I was interested in all of them. Research and the search for truth, that was me.

In 1948, the year I became an undergraduate, the Tenth International Congress for Philosophy was held at Amsterdam. Three lectures fired my imagination. The first was by the intuitionist mathematician L.E.J. Brouwer, the greatest Dutch mathematician since Christian Huygens. Brouwer put a long quotation from the Bhagavad Gītā in the middle of a forest of mathematical symbols. The second was by I.M. Bochenski, a Dominican logician and historian of logic, who was Rector of the University of Freibourg in Switzerland and an expert on Marxism. The third was by T.M.P. Mahadevan from the University of Madras. He ended his talk with a quotation from Ānandagiri: 'An enlightened person does not become a bondslave of the Veda. The meaning that he gives of the Veda, that becomes the meaning of the Veda.' T.M.P. is the first of three Mahadevans that are mentioned in this Preface.

After the war, we were free to travel, not only in our own country but all over Europe. Hitch-hiking, mostly in trucks that transported wine, was fashionable. The driver refilled his bottle at every stop from the tank behind and did the same for us. Virtually all students went south. Some of us lucky survivors reached Paris, the Côte d'Azur from Marseilles to La Spezia, Rome and the Greek temple at Paestum in southern Italy. My French and Italian were fluent. There were no tourists. A few of us, including two Arabs from Indonesia, crossed the Mediterranean on the deck of a small cargo boat. We were a few weeks in Algeria until the French police became suspicious and ordered us out of the country.

* * *

Halfway through my graduate studies, a friend handed me a newspaper, the kind of thing he knew I never read: 'Something for you!' The Government of India was offering a one-year scholarship to a Netherlands student. I applied and was selected, much to my surprise, until I discovered that the Indians preferred a student who might have done something else and had an open mind, to a professed India expert. The Indian embassy told me that I had to choose a university forthwith. Since I knew only one, it became the University of Madras, at Madras, now Chennai. It was an almost blind but fortunate choice. My first Mahadevan, T.M.P., left me entirely free but corrected my English and forwarded from his own pocket my monthly stipend of two hundred rupees that generally arrived late. After three years, one spent at Benares, I obtained a PhD from the University of Madras for my thesis on *Advaita and Neoplatonism: A Critical Study in Comparative Philosophy*.

Fortunately for me, Indian philosophy was taught in Indian departments of philosophy through the medium of English. I knew, however, that one cannot study such a subject without Sanskrit. I could not follow the classes of V. Raghavan, one of the world's great Sanskrit scholars, for beginning students already knew the language. But he found me a pandit who taught Sanskrit to little children using Pāṇini's grammar through the medium of Tamil; and was willing to use the same method for me but through English. Thus, I was taught Pāṇini's method before I learned Sanskrit. How did I do it? Again, I recall only some facts. First, I had to correctly pronounce my teacher's name: R. Sankarasubrahmanya Ayyar. Second, I walked daily, under a large black umbrella, from the Victoria Student Hostel in Triplicane to the Kuppuswami Research Institute in Mylapore. During holidays, my two hundred rupees enabled me to travel all over India, including Sri Lanka. The amount astounded the Dutch ambassador in New Delhi who arranged for the embassy to buy me a copy of Monier-Williams *Sanskrit-English Dictionary*. It is still within arm's reach from my desk. Study and travel—they were good beginnings and have continued through my life.

Here I should mention that, though a student of Vedānta or 'end of the Vedas,' I never learned anything about the Vedas. Outside academia I did discover that there are many Indian ideas about the Vedas—just as there is a German Greece, a French Greece, an English Greece, images that are all quite different from each other, as W.H. Auden had observed. I knew only one thing: that one should study Vedic as I had studied Latin and Greek. It is then that I discovered another entry to that apparently unknown realm. I heard the vigorous varieties of Vedic recitation not only in Madras and Tanjore, but in Dikshitar houses surrounding the temple of Śiva Naṭarāja in Chidambaram. It opened my ears and gradually led to the study of Vedic ritual, not from books or Sanskrit texts, but on the terrain and especially among Nambudiri brahmans in Cochin and South Malabar. I began to make tape-recordings all over India. Some of my rarest recordings of Vedic recitation and chant were made during a ride across South India on an old Royal Enfield. The complete collection is now being digitized at Berkeley and will be housed at the Archives and Research Center for Ethnomusicology at Gurgaon.

At Banaras Hindu University (BHU), T.R.V. Murti had not only taught me how to study Indian philosophy, but introduced me to a pandit in the old city under whose tutelage I nibbled at Navya Nyāya, the modern logic of India. But my three years in India were beginning to come to a close. I also had to look for a job. I returned to Amsterdam, expecting to do more work on logic, but obtained instead an assistant lectureship in Sanskrit at the School of Oriental and African Studies at London. Subsequently, I taught philosophy at the University of Pennsylvania and returned to Amsterdam to be given a title that was the result of long deliberations: 'professor of general and systematical philosophy, including comparative philosophy.' I was locally famous which proved to be stifling, a golden cage from which I escaped occasionally. In 1962, at the Stanford International Congress of Logic, Methodology and Philosophy of Science, I met Noam Chomsky and discovered that his linguistics was a straightforward combination of Pāṇini and logic. I understood immediately what a packed auditorium of linguists failed to grasp. It led to a year of teaching the Sanskrit Grammarians at MIT and publication of my *Reader on the Sanskrit Grammarians*.

Throughout the following decades, while teaching at Tokyo, Kyoto, Paris and other places, I continued to work in India. At BHU, Murti introduced me in Sanskrit as Abhinava Kautsa, a new Kautsa, not because he agreed with his thesis (see Chapter 8), but because he loved to discuss it. In the meantime, I had settled at the University of California at Berkeley with an appointment in Philosophy and an assignment to set up a new department of South Asian Studies to which, in due course, I added Southeast Asian. I continued to give lectures and do fieldwork in many Asian countries though my colleagues in philosophy never learned the difference between South and South-east Asia. Other Berkeley colleagues knew that, on one occasion, I had trekked across the western Himalayas into Zanskar and Ladakh; and on another, reached Mount Kailas and Lake Mansarovar via Peking and Lhasa. My publications began to pay attention to Thailand, Indonesia, Central Asia, China and Japan, where the wooden ladles used to make oblations in the Shingon Buddhist fire ritual have the same shapes as the Vedic.

The University of California allowed me to embark upon a decade of ritual studies, going up and down between Kerala and my California desk. A 1975 performance of the Agnicayana Vedic ritual in a small village was documented with the help of Harvard anthropological film-maker Robert Gardner and several others, including Romila Thapar and Adelaide de Menil. One outcome was the film *Altar of Fire*. The chief result was *AGNI, the Vedic Ritual of the Fire Altar*, published in two volumes, and in collaboration with the two ritual experts who had been in charge of the performance, C.V. Somayajipad and Itti Ravi Nambudiri (see Bibliography). Most of its 130 plates, in colour or black-and-white, come from Adelaide de Menil, including Figure 18 in this book and the one on the cover which depicts how one of the Vedic accents is taught, namely the 'resounding' (*svarita*) accent. When the pupil is about to recite the syllable on which it occurs, the teacher bends his head to the right. Other head movements are used for two other Vedic accents.

I should stop writing about myself and my work. But I cannot fail to add that in the meanwhile I moved to Thailand, having long predicted that civilization would return to Asia under the intellectual guidance of India and China.

* * *

I started writing these pages in Thailand while supervising the construction of a house. Both tasks were foolhardy but are now finished. I could never have completed the first if I had always stayed in my own library. Every other book would have looked at me with a reproachful mien as if I had forgotten that it existed which, more often than not, was true. The reader should not rush to the conclusion that I have been writing off the top of my head. I had access to books and papers that emerged from ten boxes of luggage. They had been marked with red labels before I left California and before I knew that I was going to write about the Vedas. Some boxes contained Vedic: one was occupied by *AGNI*, another housed the five large volumes of the Poona edition of the Rigveda which includes its word-for-word analysis of the Padapāṭha and Sāyaṇa's commentary. Other boxes contained other primary sources, translations and secondary sources that had become classics in their own right, like the works of Willem Caland (1859–1932) and Louis Renou (1896–1966). One box was stuffed with recent offprints, some embodying what, in 2000, I had called a 'Breakthrough in Vedic Studies'. That recent advance in knowledge is due to Michael Witzel and several others, including George Thompson, who helped me with a Soma hymn from the Rigveda; Arlo Griffiths, who rendered assistance on Atharvaveda and gave permission to quote from his translations; and my second Mahadevan,

'T.P.', who gave me access to his forthcoming studies on the arrival of Vedism in South India.

By the time my drafts were finished, I had moved to my new home, 150 boxes that had been waiting were unpacked and their contents ordered. I now had my library which enabled me to make corrections and add precision without changing the outline of the course of action upon which I had embarked. The year 2006 was meant to be devoted to the completion of this book; but took me away for lectures, conferences and rituals in Thailand, India, Europe, China and Australia. It may explain some eccentric excursions that must be due to pitfalls of travel that are incompatible with the concentration needed to write a book. But *pitfall* also means: *cunning device designed to catch someone unawares*. The OED adds: now *rare*.

* * *

In 2006, I stayed for a month at the National Institute of Advanced Studies (NIAS) on the Indian Institute of Science Campus in Bangalore. It is one of those rare institutes where scholars are free to devote themselves entirely to their own work. I spent part of my time on Vedic and hunting for Vedic publications I did not have at home. It also enabled me to discuss with eminent scientists of which I mention two: Roddam Narasimha, with whom I had fruitful exchanges on many topics, and Vidyanand Nanjundiah who, among other things, told me about recent researches in Indic genetics. Another similar visit took place earlier this year. I owe these generous opportunities to K. Kasturirangan, Director of the Institute, who welcomed me warmly and invited me to all the programmes and facilities of the Institute. At NIAS, K.S. Rama Krishna assisted me with computers and general IT under the benign supervision of Captain Joseph. My second visit to Bangalore was also supported by the *Śrauta Prātiṣṭhāna* and the Organizing Committee of the *Āptoryāma Somayāga*, a Vedic ritual that was performed near the Sanskrit College. I lectured at both 'venues', as they are called in India, having been encouraged to build a bridge 'between science and ritual'.

After Bangalore, I went via another Vedic ritual in Trichur to New Delhi where the idea of my book had been born. Romila Thapar introduced me to Kunal Chakrabarti of Delhi University. He had not only read but studied every page of my first draft and returned it to me with copious annotations which we discussed for days. Throughout my preparation of the final draft, these notations have been at my side. My indebtedness to Kunal is enormous. Let me mention two results. Kunal had read all my comments on *mantra* but asked: why don't you discuss one mantra in detail, for example, the Gāyatrī? It resulted in the final section of Chapter 11. He wrote a note on a short chapter I had inserted on Buddhism: 'this is not "introductory"; it is, in fact, original.' It emboldened me to write Part V.

Later in 2006, I spent another month in Leiden and Amsterdam, where I organized a workshop on artificial languages (since published with a sequel in the *Journal of Indian Philosophy*) and attended and participated in other meetings that left their traces in this book (especially in Part IV). I owe this opportunity to another generous invitation for which I am indebted to Wim Stokhof, then Director of the International Institute for Asian Studies, of Leiden and Amsterdam, and his successor, Max Sparreboom, whose book on *Chariots in the Veda* had already provided me with much that I needed. Again I was assisted in all my endeavours. An especially warm word of thanks is due to Marloes Rozing who was in charge of the Institute's seminars and publications.

At Amsterdam, I renewed my acquaintance with an old friend and former colleague, the renowned Hittitologist and expert on Anatolian languages, Philo Houwink ten Cate. He told me everything I needed to know and gave me access to a rare and sumptuously illustrated catalogue of an exhibition on *Rad und Wagen* ('Wheels and Wagons') held at the Museum of Oldenberg in 2004. Some of my best illustrations in Part I come from that source.

When the text of this book had already been finalized, I had an opportunity to participate in a major Vedic event: The Fourth International Vedic Workshop which was held at the University of Texas at Austin from 24 to 27 May 2007. It was attended by scholars from Australia, Canada, several European countries, India, Japan and the United States. Needless to say, I learnt totally new things. I hope to refer to some of these in the source notes to this book. And I am waiting, like many others, for the first reliable and up-to-date translation into English of the entire Rigveda by Stephanie Jamison and Joel Brereton. It will be a publication the absence of which I have often deplored in this book.

* * *

Many of the savants I mentioned exemplify branches of Orientalism, traditional and modern, that are based upon the firm foundation of the Oral Tradition which Vedic Indians, and in due course the brahmans of India, preserved with astounding precision and more or less faithfully over a period of more than three millennia. The most remarkable feature of that preservation is that fathers taught their sons and teachers their pupils how to recite, chant, and apply mantras to ritual, without concern for meaning but by emphasizing *form*. There is, in fact, as Kautsa pointed out, 'a tradition for mantras to be learnt by heart, but no corresponding tradition to teach and thereby preserve their meaning.' It should be noted that that very fact helps to explain not only that much is known about Vedic languages and dialects, but why we possess the Vedas at all.

My book could not have been written without any of the scientists I mentioned. There are, however, many others who have helped me and deserve my sincere gratitude. First among them is Wichai Kampusan, my other self, without whom neither the house, nor the book could have come into existence. I have already referred to some of the teachers, collaborators and friends from whom I learned most. Many are no more: R. Sankarasubrahmanya Ayyar of the Kuppuswami Sanskrit College at Mylapore, my first Mahadevan, T.M.P., of the University of Madras; V. Raghavan and his student Chengallur Madhavan Nambudiri of the same university; T.R.V. Murti of Banaras Hindu University; E.R. Sreekrishna Sarma of Kaladi and Tirupati Universities; K. Kunjunni Raja of the University of Madras; and especially Cherumukku Vaidikan Somayajipad, M. Itti

Ravi Nambudiri, Madamp Narayanan Nambudiri and many other Nambudiri teachers, ritualists and friends.

Let me end with a list of the many people who helped me with generous advice, books, literature, illustrations, copyrights, warnings, comments and critique. Some made one or two luminous suggestions, that shine all over the book. Others spent a great deal of time on it, especially the third Mahadevan who comes at the end of the list. Special mention should be made of my computer expert Peter Vandemoortele, who helped me negotiate the virtual space of Thailand and tame the user-unfriendly monster behind my screen. I am unable to put the others in significant groups or combinations and cannot even make use of the rational order of Indic syllabaries such as *KA, KHA, GHA*, etc., that start in the back of the mouth (see 'The Sound Pattern of Language' in Chapter **14**). I therefore resort to the irrational order of the alphabet or *ABC* to which there is no rhyme or reason: Prapod Assavavirulhakarn (Bangkok), Kamaleswar Bhattacharya (Paris), Vinod Bhattatiripad (Kozhikode), Johannes Bronkhorst (Lausanne), Sucitra Chongstitvatana (Bangkok), Josée C.M. van Eijndhoven (The Hague), Louis Gabaude (Chiang Mai), Robert Gardner (Cambridge, Mass.), Sarath Haridasan (Palakkad and Chennai), J.C. Heesterman (Leiden), J.M. Hemelrijk (Wanneperveen and Amsterdam), J.E.M. Houben (Leiden), Yasuke Ikari (Kyoto), Stanley Insler (Yale), Jean-Luc Jucker (Lausanne), Adelaide de Menil (Paris and New York), Alexander Lubotsky (Leiden), Victor H. Mair (Philadelphia), Gananath Obeyesekhere (Princeton and Sri Lanka), Richard Karl Payne (Berkeley), Jeffrey Riegel (Berkeley and Sydney), S. Settar (Bangalore), Robert H. Sharf

(Berkeley), Peter Skilling (Bangkok), Ivan Strenski (Santa Barbara), Abram de Swaan (Amsterdam), Stanley Tambiah (Cambridge, Mass.), Peter Tindemans (The Hague), Toshihiro Wada (Nagoya) and Akira Yuyama (Tokyo). I am greatly indebted to the Archaeological Survey of India and to the Superintending Archaeologist of the Bangalore Circle. The time has come to add my third Mahadevan: consultant editor at Penguin India, Kamini. All three have greatly deepened any knowledge of English. Heartfelt thanks to you all!

* * *

I have not been shy about my classical background which was instilled in me when I was still young and should have started on Sanskrit. Actually, this has not proved to be a limitation. The Rigveda is composed in a language so distant even from classical Sanskrit, that only Europeans who were familiar with the critical analysis of their own classical languages could have begun to crack its forms and codes. That was two centuries ago and does not imply that they were in a superior position to divine its meaning. My writing may reflect some of their findings and many of their failures and shortcomings. The field has grown vastly and there is now no single person who can have a total view, let alone control it. The remaining parts step on shakier ground where there are no academic guidelines and the end is not in sight. In both areas there is much to discover that is relevant and new.

Frits Staal
Berkeley/Chiang Mai
June 2007

Attested Locations.
7–8 Vedic
7–6–5–4–2 Buddhist

1. Sintashta 2100–1800
2. Indo-Aryan > 2000
3. Iranian
4. Khotan
5. Muztagh Ata & Oxus
6. BMAC 2100–1900
7. Khyber Pass
8. Bolan, Pirak & Kachi 1700
9. Western IA < 1380

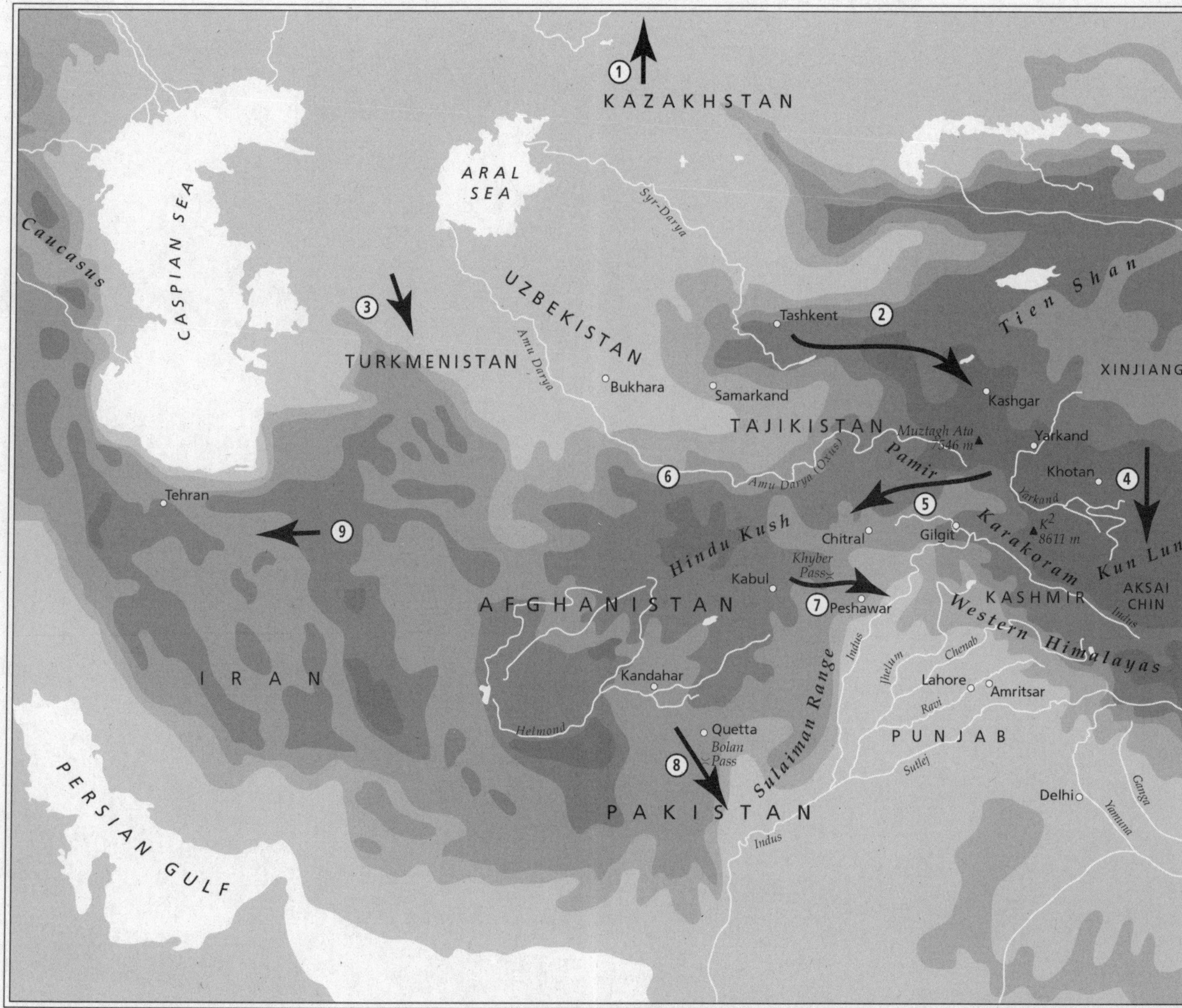
KAZAKHSTAN
ARAL SEA
CASPIAN SEA
Caucasus
Syr-Darya
UZBEKISTAN
TURKMENISTAN
Amu Darya
Tashkent
Tien Shan
XINJIANG
Bukhara
Samarkand
Kashgar
TAJIKISTAN
Muztagh Ata 7546 m
Yarkand
Pamir
Amu Darya (Oxus)
Khotan
Yarkand
Tehran
Hindu Kush
Chitral
Gilgit
Karakoram
K2 8611 m
Kun Lun
Khyber Pass
Kabul
Peshawar
KASHMIR
AKSAI CHIN
Indus
AFGHANISTAN
Western Himalayas
IRAN
Kandahar
Jhelum
Chenab
Lahore
Amritsar
Ravi
Helmond
Quetta
Bolan Pass
Sulaiman Range
PUNJAB
Sutlej
Delhi
Ganga
Yamuna
PAKISTAN
Indus
PERSIAN GULF
1
2
3
4
5
6
7
8
9

Transliteration of Sanskrit

Unlike English, Sanskrit is written as it is spoken; but in the Roman alphabet, diacritics have to be used. The vowels *a*, *i* and *u* are long (*ā*) or short (*a*), etc.; *e*, *o*, *ai* and *au* are always long. 'Long' lasts twice as long as 'short'. Thus we have: *a* as in *mantra*, *ā* as in *father*, *i* as in *Indra*, *ī* as in *police*, *u* as in *Viṣṇu*, *ū* as in *pūrṇam*, *ai* and *au* as in *my cow*.

Many consonants are pronounced as in English: *k*, *g*, *j*, *p*, *b* and *m*. Most of these come in two forms: unaspirate and aspirate: unaspirate *c* as in *candra* or Churchill; aspirate as in church-hill but without a pause. Dentals contrast with retroflexes where the corresponding English sounds are more or less in between. A glance at Figure 24 shows how they are produced in the mouth: the dentals *t*, *th*, *d*, *dh* and *n* by making the tip of the tongue touch the upper teeth; the retroflexes *ṭ*, *ṭh*, *ḍh* and *ṇ*, placed in a box, by turning the tip of the tongue or flexing it back and make it touch the palate. Thus the dental *n* in *mantra* or *candra* contrasts with the retroflex *ṇ* in *Viṣṇu* and *pūrṇam*. Dental *s* as in *singing* contrast in the same manner with retroflex *ṣ* in *Viṣṇu*. A third sibilant sounds like the *ś* in *Śiva* or *Shiva* or *sheet*.

The other consonant signs are almost obvious: *ṃ* as in *haṃsa* or *humming*, *ñ* as in *jñāna* or *España*, *ṅ* as in *aṅga*, *ng* or Bangla Desh. The sound *h* is as in English, but *ḥ*, which sometimes occurs only after a vowel at the end of a word, may in South India sound like an echo: *Indraḥ* like *Indra*[ha], *Viṣṇuḥ* like *Viṣṇu*[hu].

PART I

ORIGINS AND BACKGROUNDS

One or Many?

Part I extracts concrete information from the Oral Tradition and archaeology about Vedic people and their language, what they thought and did and where they went and when. It shows that, contrary to what is often assumed, the Vedas are not one and all of a piece. They were composed on Indic soil, in different parts of North India and Pakistan, over a long period. That also holds for the so-called 'schools' of the Veda to which we return in Chapter 4 of Part II. But some features of the Veda do not come from the subcontinent itself. They include language, some mythologies and technologies, ritual altars and the cults of fire and Soma. It turns out to be a large puzzle which consists of many different puzzles, some of them large themselves. Part I puts them together for the first time and a consistent picture of historical development and chronology appears.

In geographical terms, Part I explores ancient links between the northern subcontinent, the Near East, the Indus civilization, Central Asia, South-east Asia and the extreme west of what is now China. It ends with a review of the various itineraries and routes that some ancestors of the Vedic Indians took and that were later taken, but in the opposite direction, by Buddhist pilgrims. India's openness to other peoples and cultures is nothing special. If we exclude a few isolated pockets, it is a common feature of Asian and European civilizations or what has been called the Old World. The uniqueness of the subcontinent seems to lie in the fact, that some outside influences were imported by a small number of people. The discussion of this issue will continue and an explanation will be given in the section on Rathakāra in Chapter 3 of Part II.

ONE

~

GEOGRAPHY OF THE VEDAS AND THEIR LANGUAGE

Yājñavalkya, a Vedic sage, taught his wife Maitreyī that after death there is no awareness of specifics and 'that's all there is to immortality.' This secret teaching or *upaniṣad* presents a problem, perhaps not for Maitreyī, but for us. Would it help us to discover what Yājñavalkya may have had in mind if we knew who he was, what language he spoke, where he lived and when? These are questions we can answer. Yājñavalkya was an eccentric thinker, skilled in debate. He spoke Vedic, an archaic language, fairly well understood nowadays. The name Yājñavalkya comes from *yajña,* 'ritual', but he was a thinker, not a ritualist. When we say he was a 'sage', we use a customary interpretation of Vedic *ṛṣi*, literally 'seer'. Maitreyī means 'Friendly One'. Yājñavalkya was a native of Kośala (part of modern Uttar Pradesh). Together with Videha (roughly Bihar), that was the eastern fringe of the Vedic area and signalled, around 450 BCE, the end of the Vedic period. If we knew where, when, how and why it began, we might be ready to learn something new.

The Vedas, then, did not originate suddenly, all of a piece, like Athena emerged fully armed from the head of Zeus according to Greek mythology. This is demonstrated by the Rigveda which is not revealed by gods, but invokes them through its poets who are known by individual names we have already met in the Preface: Viśvāmitra 'Friend of All', Bharadvāja, 'Bearing Strength' and Dīrghatamas 'Seeing Far into Darkness'. They are the *dramatis personae* behind the lines. Viśvāmitra was an irascible seer. Bharadvāja, like some contemporaries, was fond of the term 'exciting' (*niśiti*). Dīrghatamas did as his name says. The Sāmaveda chanters were masters of long breath (*dīrgha-prāṇa*). In the Yajurveda, their place is taken by priests/scholars and master ritualists like Baudhāyana, 'Concerned With Insight', a scientist who organized and clarified complex structures. All of them conveyed knowledge and insights.

We now come to some basic facts about the four Vedas.

RIGVEDA

The Rigveda is the earliest because its language is the most archaic and because the other three Vedas presuppose, depend on, quote or refer to it. It consists of verse (*rig-*). Many of its invocations ask gods for long life, riches, sons, cattle and victory in battle. Other compositions tell stories or refer to myths, familiar to their audience but not known to us. They discuss sex with the same attention to detail as rites. They contain speculations about the universe and much else.

The Rigveda contains 1,028 poems called *sūkta* from *su-ukta*, literally 'well said'. The shortest poem consists of one verse, the longest of fifty-eight. The average is ten and the total number of verses is 10,462.

SĀMAVEDA

The Sāmaveda is the Rigveda set to music. Almost all its verses are taken from the Rigveda but its melodies (*sāman*) are older. Two of them are mentioned in the Rigveda, one called Rathantara 'Excellent Chariot'. Others have unfamiliar names.

The Sāmaveda is larger than the Rigveda because it lists all the modifications the Rigvedic verses undergo when they are chanted or used in ritual.

YAJURVEDA

The Yajurveda is the Veda of ritual. Its composers are priests. The term *yajus* refers to a ritual formula. The bulk of the Yajurveda comes again from the Rigveda. These verses are referred to as *mantra*. They are accompanied by prose sections which interpret the mantras in terms of ritual, often in a muddled fashion. These sections are called *brāhmaṇa*, a term which also refers to their composers, the hermeneuticians of the day. Baudhāyana, already mentioned, sorted them out by concentrating on *ritual form*.

The Yajurveda is also larger than the Rigveda because it consists of numerous schools, often repeating each other with differences large and small. A simple count of words would not do justice to the size of either Sāma- or Yajurveda.

ATHARVAVEDA

The Atharvaveda is in some respects similar to the Rigveda. About one-seventh of its verses are the same or more or less the same. The collection reflects a different social background. Instead of poets, singers or priests, we meet with physicians and magicians who use drugs and spells to cure diseases, mental as well as physical. The

Atharvaveda exists in two recensions, each containing almost 6,000 verses.

It is clear from the earliest compositions that they were the prized possessions of small tribal groups, families or clans, hunter-gatherers and pastoralists who avoided the forests and followed the course of rivers before they settled down. The geography of the Vedas may be largely reconstructed from the names of these rivers. They are shown on the map in Figure 1 (see end of book) which is reproduced from Michael Witzel's 1989 study on Vedic dialects. The reader will recognize most rivers: *Sindhu* is, of course, the Indus after which India has been named. *Kubhā* and *Suvāstu* are the Kabul and Swat Rivers, *Vitastā* the Jhelum, *Asiknī* the Chenab, *Paruṣṇī* the Ravi, *Śutudrī* the Sutlej and others should speak for themselves as does *Himavant*, the Himalayan range.

The Vedas often mention the names of tribes. Figure 2 depicts another map from Witzel, based upon these data which identifies the region of the Rigveda, the white area to the west (north and west of the 'desert tribes'), not including any part of Rajasthan or Gujarat. This area contrasts with a large dotted area to the east which marks the places of origin of the bulk of compositions that make up the other three Vedas. Names of tribes often correspond to Vedic 'schools' to which we return at the end of Chapter 4.

We now know something definite, we know where the Vedas were composed, that the Rigveda is the earliest because it is presupposed by the others and we have an inkling of their relative chronology. What about absolute dates?

The Rigveda and the Indus Civilization

Extraordinary claims have been made and are being made with regard to the dates of origin of the Vedas. In the past, such claims were difficult to evaluate because little was known about the Vedic language or prehistory of India. I shall have more to say about language, but the latter deficiency was made good by the discovery of the Harappan or Indus Civilization. It turned out to be the third major early culture of humankind after Egypt and Mesopotamia. By 'early' I mean that the Early Harappan or pre-Harappan civilization started in the late fourth millennium BCE, more than five thousand years ago. Were the Vedic Indians perhaps inhabitants of those famous brick-built cities, Harappa, Mohenjo-Daro, or some of the numerous other sites that have been excavated? It seems unlikely because the Rigveda does not refer to towns and does not even have a word for 'brick'. It refers to forts with mud walls and later Vedas mention ruins. And yet, the Rigveda is not oblivious to its surroundings.

The names of many rivers and their tributaries are mentioned as we have just seen. It gave to some Indic rivers the names of streams in Afghanistan which the poets or their ancestors had known before. In that respect the rivers resemble New York, which my ancestors had already called New Amsterdam before the British name prevailed. A much discussed example is a river called *Harax'aitî*, now in Afghanistan where it is called Helmand. The Rigveda gave that same name to a river in the Punjab: *Sarasvatī* in Vedic.

Harax'aitî or *Sarasvatī* means 'provided with ponds.' The river ended in the desert, a fact attested by Vedic sources as we shall see in Chapter 9.

Relevant in the present context is another fact of geography: the areas of the Indus Civilization and of the early Vedas overlap in part: they overlap in the Indus Valley as Figures 1 and 2 clearly show. We should, therefore, be more precise about the geography of the Indus or Harappa Civilization as well. Figure 3 depicts a map of its final period, ca. 2100 to 1600 BCE. As we see at a glance, Late Harappan included Sind and Gujarat which were not known to the Rigveda.

Our map comes from a reputable source—Joseph Schwartzberg's *Historical Atlas of South Asia*—but does not shy away from injecting civilization into geography by pictures of stone-blades, pottery and a 'Mother' Goddess who might be a queen or an otherwise distinguished woman. Why does it not include the famous Harappan clay seals with their even more famous inscriptions? Schwartzberg devotes two sentences to them in the extensive account of the Indus or Harappa Civilization that follows his maps after 146 pages. There he writes that many attempts have been made to read the script, but 'none of the putative decipherments has been generally accepted. There is, however, agreement, that the script is ideosyllabic, and the currently preferred working hypothesis is that it represents an early Dravidian language.'

Evasive caution or wise words? As a matter of fact, starting in 1877, over a hundred claimed decipherments of the 'Indus Script' have made it into print. I have seen only a few but must confess, that I have always been convinced that these symbols have nothing to do with writing. However, this is not my field and I did not enter the fray. As a boy, I had dabbled in Egyptian hieroglyphs. I was familiar with the discovery of the Rosetta Stone and its decipherment by Champollion. I knew that prior to that famous event, there had been hundreds of 'putative decipherments'. But once the key was found, everything clicked and fell into place. Nothing was heard of the early theories again. Scientists may be stubborn and stupid, but everyone accepts a theory that explains and makes sense of *everything*. That is what we have with regard to hieroglyphs and lack with regard to Harappa.

What these symbols are and what they are not has been stated only recently in clearer terms. Steve Farmer, Richard Sproat and Michael Witzel explain the main reason why these scribbles cannot be a script: they are too short. The four to five thousand inscriptions that are now known occur on a variety of materials but mostly on clay. The longest consists of seventeen symbols and less than a hundred have as many as ten. The average length of the 2,905 objects listed in I. Mahadevan's standard concordance of 1977 is 4.6 signs. No known written language consists of inscriptions that are that short.

Short symbolic expressions exist, but they are markings of a different sort. Many are known from early civilizations. Those from the Near East are similar to the Harappan and have been studied in great detail. They link families, clans, offices, places, professions or festivals to deities or other celestial or mythological figures. Their purposes may be magical, but governments can make use of them for tax purposes. To associate such functions with the Indus seals would be consistent with many of the pictorial representations of deities, celestial beings and mythological figures found on the seals.

Romila Thapar summarizes: 'They could have been tokens identifying civic authorities, supervisory managers of long-distance trade, merchants or those bringing raw materials to the cities, or clan affiliations.'

I conclude that the Harappa 'script' does not exist and cannot therefore assist us in dating the Vedas. We know that the Harappa Civilization and the Rigveda overlapped in space. Since everything else seems to be different—a feature to which I return—they cannot have overlapped in time. I conclude that the Rigveda must be older than the late fourth millennium or later than, say, 1800 BCE. Why not both?

It is here that we come face to face with a basic feature of human evolution: it includes language because languages evolve. Just as mammals came after saurians and birds after fish, Hindi or Marathi came after Sanskrit and French or Italian after Latin. The Vedic language itself changed within the Rigveda and between the Rig- and Yajurvedas. The Late Vedic of the Upaniṣads, the language of Yājñavalkya, has evolved further: it is close to classical Sanskrit. It is out of the question that the language of the Rigveda, then a living language, was the same during the fourth and second millennia BCE.

Mitanni Vedic and Indic Genetics

As it happens, the question does not arise because we are fortunate in possessing precise chronological evidence that throws light on the matter and is as astonishing as it is conclusive. It has been known for about a century, albeit to a handful of specialists, that three Vedic gods, Indra, Mitra and Varuṇa, are referred to in a treaty between a Hittite king, who ruled over a large part of Asia Minor or what is now Turkey, and a king from Mitanni, an equally large empire in what is now Syria and northern Iraq. The Hittite king spoke Hittite, an Indo-European language, and the Mitanni king was a speaker of Vedic or a language very close to Vedic that has been called Mitanni Vedic. That remarkable piece of information is recorded on a cuneiform clay tablet dating from about 1380 BC.

Other tablets of the same period mention Vedic numerals and terms that refer to the training of horses and the construction of chariots. Kikkuli, a Mitanni expert whose language was also identical with or extremely close to Vedic, knew a great deal about how to tame, rear, yoke and harness horses, their temperament and colours—an important and entirely new technology. He wrote a treatise on these topics, which was transliterated into the cuneiform script that was used for Hittite. Two 'pages' are illustrated in Figure 4. It is a syllabic script that gives us a good idea of the way Kikkuli pronounced his words:

CUNEIFORM	RIGVEDA
a-as-u	*aśva* 'horse'
a-as-u-us-sa-an-ni	(?) 'horse-trainer'
a-i-ka-wa-ar-ta-an-na	*eka* 'one' and *vartana* 'turn'
ti-e-ra-wa-ar-ta-an-na	*tri-vartana* 'three'
pa-an-za-wa-ar-ta-an-na	*pañca-vartana* 'five'
ša-at-ta-wa-ar-ta-an-na	*sapta-vartana* 'seven'
na-a-wa-ar-ta-an-na	*nava-vartana* 'nine'
p/babru-nnu	*babhru* 'deep-reddish-brown'
p/barita-nnu	*palita* 'grey'
p/binkara-nnu	*piṅgala* 'tawny yellow'

Kikkuli's treatise explains the essentials of his training programme. It prepared horses for the drawing of chariots that were used for hunting or ceremonial purposes but primarily for fighting in battle. The horses were made to run distances three times a year: during winter, autumn and spring. It involved various courses at the end of which a turn (*vartana*) had to be made. All the Mitanni transliterations are very close to Vedic words with the exception of the numeral for 'one' that appears as '*a-i-ka*'. Vedic has *eka* but '*a-i-ka*' confirms the older form of the numeral 'one' that linguists had postulated for proto-Vedic. It is not found in Iranian, the language of ancient Iran, which is closely related to Vedic but has *aiva*. These correspondences show that the few Vedic Indians who moved west did so at an early period, probably just before the stage of development of the Vedic language with which we are familiar. It suggests that there was a linguistic development from an earlier language which split into two: Iranian developed *aiva* and Vedic *aika* which turned into *eka*. It also shows that Vedic, which was later located *east* of Iranian, is more closely related to the language of Kikkuli which was located to the *west*. It is an apparent paradox but there is a perfect explanation at which we shall arrive when we will discuss the relationships between Vedic and the Iranian Wedge.

The close connections between the language of the Rigveda and that of Kikkuli's treatise solve an important historical problem but that need not be the end of the story. Science is never final and new evidence accumulates all the time from other lost Southwest Asian languages such as Kassite, Hurrian, Luwian and Emar; and also from Austro-Asiatic, Dravidian, Tibeto-Burman and other language families that left traces in Vedic as we shall see. But whatever happens, and whatever their itineraries, to which we shall return as well, the recorded dates of these Vedic names and words are firm and establish beyond doubt that the Vedas cannot be earlier than the Indus Civilization but must be later.

This conclusion pertains not only to history but sheds light on society. Kikkuli's treatise was obviously regarded as a valuable document that transmitted practical knowledge from a distant civilization. It carried prestige and may help to explain that some speakers of Mitanni Vedic became rulers of the Mitanni Empire during its formative period. Something similar happened in India on a smaller scale: speakers of

Vedic became chieftains of Indian clans and these chieftains learned to speak Vedic through close associations that were, centuries later, referred to as *brāhmaṇa/kṣatriya* alliances.

At this point of our story we have to record another astonishing fact that comes from a very different source. The circumstance that Kikkuli was a single informant or one of very few is in unexpected accordance with the most recent information on the genetic composition of the population of the subcontinent of South Asia. The first genetic research findings were interpreted as supporting the traditional theories of extensive movements or 'invasions' by peoples from Central Asia into the subcontinent. Much more careful recent investigations by Denise R. Carvalho Silva, S. Sengupta, C. Tyler-Smith and many others have shown that the genetic origins of the large majority of present-day Indics go back some 9,000 years during which period they have continued to live within the subcontinent. These indigenous lineages remained widespread in both tribal and caste populations. Those who entered from elsewhere during the first half of the second millennium BCE cannot have contributed more than a few Y-chromosomal lineages. This is consistent with the facts about Mitanni Vedic: new knowledge and even a new language may be introduced by very few people, provided there is a powerful incentive. What were the incentives and major differences at the receiving end between the ancient Near East and the subcontinent of South Asia?

The Near East counted many early civilizations that were embodied and transmitted in *written* form. Suppose a Mitanni Vedic poet had composed Vedic verse in such a situation, it would be done orally and transmitted orally as a matter of course. It would be an ephemeral event amidst powerful scriptural traditions, soon forgotten without leaving a trace behind. The Vedas would in any case not have much future with the eventual emergence of Judaism, Christianity and Islam, the three 'religions of the book' as the Qur'ān calls them, that are intolerant even of each other.

The Indus Civilization was different. Roughly as old as its Near Eastern cousins, it left no script or scriptural tradition behind. It was weakened and exhausted by the time the first so-called 'family books' of what was later called the Rigveda appeared on the scene. Of course, these 'books' were not *books*. They were oral compositions, later assigned to 'circles' (*maṇḍala*). They would not have attracted anyone's attention had not the Indus Civilization left a large gap into which anything could fall and disappear. Thus was Vedic added to many Indian languages already spoken—but it did not disappear. On the contrary, its impact deepened and the seeds were sown to produce what with hindsight we have come to regard as 'Vedic civilization', a new *Oral Tradition*.

What I have just sketched is no more than a nutshell account of the import of horses and chariots along with the appearance of another language on Indian soil. It does not explain the success of the Vedas in India. But I have not yet mentioned a different, perhaps unique and decisive factor. It became apparent that the few families and groups that trickled across the mountains possessed a mysterious power different from that of language: the power of mantra. That power was attributed to their seers who were also their poets and sages. Vedic mantra power was different from the 'spiritual' power assigned to them by fashionable modern, postmodern and post-postmodern constructions. It also has better credentials. One of the ancient hymns of a family circle (RV=Rigveda 7.33) speaks about the credentials of Sage Vasiṣṭha, the 'Most Excellent'. Fathered by two gods, Mitra and Varuṇa, he was born not from the womb but from the mind of a nymph named Urvaśī, 'Widely Extending' like Dawn. In due course, Vasiṣṭha became the domestic priest of King Sudās who was the victor in the War of the Ten Kings (*dāśarājña*), a struggle between tribal chieftains who spoke different languages. Sudās's victory was due to Indra's intervention, which was in turn based upon Vasiṣṭha invocation with mantra power. In its first pangs of birth, the Rigveda already has many such stories.

The power of mantras is a large topic. Not yet understood, I believe, it must be left for further discussion in later chapters. It certainly played a major part in the multiple processes of reciprocal acculturation between indigenous lineages and those few speakers of Indo-European who had entered from elsewhere.

Even without including mantras, our brief sketch gives short shrift to a ridiculous idea of long standing: the supposition of large numbers of people invading the subcontinent with their fighting chariots and horses, crossing the high mountains that shield India from the rest of Asia. That supposition is correct in one respect: there is no doubt that horses were introduced from elsewhere. They are not found or depicted in the Indus Civilization. Their earliest traces in South Asia come from Pirak, southeast of the Bolan Pass, and date from the seventeenth century BCE as we shall see in Chapter 2.

Horses have always been rare in India. They do not thrive on Indian soil and the climate does not smile on them. But they are rampant in the Vedas. In the Rigveda, I counted 792 occurrences of the word *aśva* in various forms. The word for chariot, *ratha*, is equally common; but there was no need for chariots to be carried across mountains. It was the *idea* of the chariot and the precise knowledge of how to construct one that were transmitted across the mountains by a handful of experts. That knowledge was enough.

Transmitting the idea of the chariot may be a peculiar feature within the much wider perspective in which our topic must be placed. Light horse chariots with spoked wheels replaced traditional carts with solid wheels, pulled by oxen, not only in the Near East and South Asia, but also in southern Europe and other parts of Eurasia. It happened in most of these places during the first half of the second millennium BCE; in China slightly later. What may set the Indus Valley apart from these other areas is that such chariots were imported there by a small number of people *through their minds*.

What about actual numbers of people? The population of the lower town at Mohenjo-daro, more dense than the citadel, has been estimated at 42,000 or more. That of the entire subcontinent at the middle of the first millennium BCE has been put at around twenty million. Let us assume that the population of all of 'Vedic India' (that is, not only speakers of Indo-European) as depicted on the map of Figure 2, more than half a millennium earlier, was around half a million or 500,000. Assume that half of those were tribes: 250,000. The map mentions fourteen tribes mentioned in the Vedas. Assume there were fifty in all, that is 5,000 people per tribe *on an average*. But that number is far too large for our hunter-gatherers and pastoralists at any given time. They may have moved over the same terrain, but came trickling in over many centuries. Conclusion: We know far too little to make reliable guesses about numbers but they must have been small.

These tribals did not invade or conquer, as has long been assumed. They mingled and settled with others already there. There were battles as well as alliances, the latter between tribes as well as persons. There was the exchange of information, some of it of a specialized nature. We shall study one case at the beginning of Part II: that of the *Rathakāra* or 'chariot-maker'. He had not crossed the high passes on a chariot and did not arrive on a chariot: but he *knew* how to make chariots with spoked wheels just as the Mitanni experts knew how to train horses. Over time, both acquired high social status and lived in palaces. What did the indigenous tribes and later settled populations contribute? Mantras of their own, chants, rituals, sciences, insights, structures and patterns of thought—the bulk of what we find in the Vedas and shall study in this book.

In the remaining sections of Part I, we shall try to explain what happened before and why it happened. If we exclude the chants of the Sāmaveda to which we return in Chapter 6, we know nothing of pre-Vedic oral traditions on the subcontinent, e.g., of the Harappans. There might not have been any connections with the Vedic oral tradition in any case. But with regard to language and other specific matters, including Agni and Soma, much is known about Vedic origins and backgrounds from outside the subcontinent.

Some scholars have stressed outside influences. Others have de-emphasized them. We should always remember that in any process of acculturation both sides have to be taken into account. This leads us to an answer for a contemporary problem.

The United Nations has recently issued a 96-page report on international migration that calls for 'the immediate establishment of a high-level-inter-institutional group to define the functions and modalities of, and pave the way for, an Inter-agency Global Migration Facility.' Such an inter-agency might learn from the Vedic experience if it would be willing to accept—but for political reasons will not—that immigration is successful when both sides have something to offer, try hard to understand what makes the other side tick and establish close personal alliances. The latter includes not only marriages, but what in South Asia is sometimes called *sambandham* or 'relationship'. The status of a person, who is about to be born from an inter-tribal alliance, may depend on complex rules that vary from tribe to tribe. We know little about such matters during Vedic times until we come closer to the end of the Vedic period.

Geography and Indo-European

In recent years, Indian politicians and expatriate engineers have claimed that everything Vedic hails from India. It is true that the Vedas were largely *composed* in what are now India and Pakistan, but it does not follow that all the ideas, composers and their ancestors came from there—just as all of Spinoza's philosophy does not come from Holland though he found comfortable settings and published his books there.

The opposite theory, that everything Vedic comes from outside India is equally absurd. Bal Gangadhar Tilak's famous assignment of the Vedas to an 'Arctic Home' has never been demonstrated. We have to look carefully at each feature about which a claim is made that it hails from elsewhere. Do these claims hang together? We need precise and exact answers, and to specify the geography, the paths taken, the chronology—in other words we must arrive at a consistent picture of development in which everything fits.

Most traditional theories of large-scale invasions have regarded Central Asia as their area of origin. None of the evidence presently known is consistent with the hypothesis of invasions, but all of it continues to point to that region, taken in its widest extension. So let us start with language.

Readers may have noted that Kikkuli numerals *tri* and *sapta* look like English *three* and *seven* or resemble the names for '3' and '7' in other Indic or European languages. We need not confine ourselves to numerals. The relevant linguistic evidence goes beyond names and words. The language of the Rigveda has a definite structure that belongs to a particular family of languages which has been called Indo-Aryan. The other three Vedas exhibit that same language family at later stages of its development.

Indo-Aryan is a subfamily of the large family of Indo-European (IE) languages. Their relatedness was discovered by Sir William Jones, founder of the Asiatic Society of Bengal. In a famous lecture in 1786, Jones defended the thesis that Sanskrit, Greek, Latin and several other languages were related. He did not invoke vague analogies but 'a stronger affinity, both in the roots of verbs and in the forms of grammar, than could possibly have been produced by accident; so strong indeed that no philologer could examine them' (that is, the languages) 'without believing them to have sprung from a common source, which, perhaps, no longer exists.'

Although 'one common source' may be a simplification, two centuries of research and a large accumulation of facts have confirmed Jones's hypothesis. Relationships between words are illustrated by basic parts of the vocabulary: numerals as we have seen (*sapta* is related not only to English *seven* but to Greek *hepta* and Latin *septem* from which we have *September*); body parts (*pada*, *pedon*, *pedis*, *foot*); common verbs (*asti*, *esti*, *est*, *is*); conjugations and declensions (Sanskrit *agnis*, *agnim*, *agnibhyas*, Latin *ignis*, *ignem*, *ignibus*). Syntax is illustrated by Rigveda 1.32.1: *indrasya nu vīryāṇi pravocam* is similar in structure to *of Indra I shall now proclaim the heroic deeds* and means the same. The *nu* is the same as Greek, Old Irish, Lithuanian and Old English *nu*, modern English *now*. Indra's *vīryāṇi* are English *virile* deeds from Latin *vir*, 'man'. *Pra vocam*, 'proclaim', literally 'speak forth', is related to Latin *pro* 'forth' and *voco* 'I call'. English *provoke* has the same form though the meaning has become different. *Pro* is common in Greek, Latin, French, English *produce*, *protect*, *provide*, etc. *Vāc* and *voc*—correspond to Latin *vox*, French *voix*, English *voice*, *vocal*, *vociferous*, etc. Thousands of such facts and the sound laws that relate them to each other determine the place of Indo-Aryan within Indo-European (IE).

There is an intermediate stage between the two language groups: Indo-Iranian, one of several subfamilies into which IE split. Indo-Iranian itself split in due course into Iranian and Indo-Aryan. I shall concentrate on Indo-Aryan, the language of the Vedas, but continue to refer to Iranian on a few significant occasions:

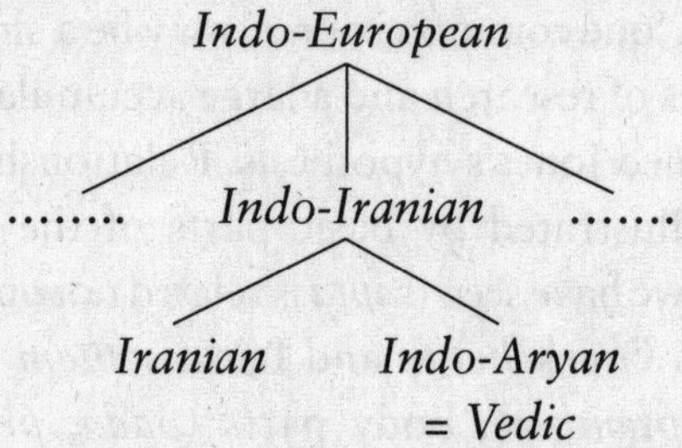

The Iranian Wedge and the BMAC

What are the paths the words, phrases and structures of these languages could have taken through history and geography? The map of Figure 5 presents us with a number of facts, some we have discussed and others we are about to explore. The two thick arrows explain the paths that Mitanni and Indic Vedic followed. The treks may have been followed by few people, but the arrows are thick with ideas. What explains their bifurcation? It is widely accepted that this is due to a powerful *Iranian Wedge* which came from the north and pushed them in opposite directions. That happened somewhere in the area labelled on the map as 'BM'. That label is based upon the name *BMAC* which refers to another recent discovery: a highly developed urban civilization on the Oxus river. I shall discuss it first because it provides some facts that explain the Iranian Wedge.

The BMAC or 'Bactrian-Margiana Archeological Complex' was discovered during recent decades of archaeological excavation and research in Russia and the Central Asian Republics of the former Soviet Union. Large fortified and walled structures from kiln-fired bricks were unearthed and reconstructed (see Figure 6). The dates of the mature phase of that civilization are 2100–1900 BCE. Such dates are close to what we would expect if we were looking for influences on early Vedic. No inscriptions or texts have been found but that is not surprising: why should the BMAC people at that early period have arrived at a system of writing when the earlier Indus Civilization with its kiln-fired bricks, from which the BMAC certainly derived theirs, did not have a system of writing either?

At this point, closer inspection of the language of the Vedas extends a helpful hand. About 300 words that occur in the Rigveda are not Indo-Aryan or Indo-European but come from elsewhere. Many come from Munda, a group of languages still spoken in parts of India, or proto-Munda. It accounts for words starting with *ka-* (e.g., *kapardin*, 'with hair-knot'), *ku-* (e.g., well-known *kumāra* and *kumārī*), or *ki-* (especially tribal names such as *Kīkaṭa*). Munda belongs to the large group of Austro-Asiatic languages that include Khmer, Mon, Vietnamese and seventy-five others in South-east Asia.

Dravidian words in the Veda, which become more frequent later, include *nīr*, 'water,' *mleccha*, 'foreigner' and perhaps *vrīhi*, 'rice', though a Munda origin was proposed by Suniti Kumar Chatterji. Other Vedic words come from Tibeto-Burman or isolated languages, still spoken by small groups of people in the Himalayas or Central India. The process of mutual influences and interpenetration continued. Madhav Deshpande has shown how such contacts and convergences caused a gap to develop between the spoken Indo-Aryan dialects, living and constantly changing, and the language of the oral tradition of the Vedas which was more or less fixed.

A clearly identifiable group of non-Indo-European words belongs to a lost language that must have been spoken in Central Asia because it includes words for camel, donkey, panther, hemp and mustard. Some speakers of Indo-Aryan must have trekked through this area or through regions under its influence. Space and time suggest that it is the lost language of the BMAC, which linguists have begun to reconstruct, and is non-Indo-European as is obvious from its linguistic structure and supported by its semantics. It left traces in the Vedas and in Vedic ritual.

But how does one reconstruct a lost language? It is like asking, how does one reconstruct a dinosaur? We have to put pieces together with great care. Some may come from, or have moved, elsewhere. An interesting BMAC word is the term for 'brick' that was missing from the Rigveda. The Yajurveda has such a word: *iṣṭakā*. It refers to kiln-fired bricks from which large Vedic fire altars were constructed. It looks like Sanskrit and there is a cognate in Iranian, but its structure is not Indo-European and it does not occur in any other IE language. Its formation resembles that of the other words from the BMAC that have been grouped together. Some return in the Sāmaveda. They are like a jawbone missing from an excavated skull but found on the other side of a rock. It is not easy to put a skeleton together. Everything must fit, including the dates.

We are now in a position to explain what the map further depicts and implies. Speakers of Indo-Aryan came from the north and picked up some BMAC words. Some of these were passed from Indo-Aryan to Iranian as A. Lubotsky has shown. That explains the Iranian Wedge which forced Indo-Aryan to go in two opposite directions: west to the Near East and east to India. It explains at the same time the remarkable fact we met with before: West Asian Vedic is more closely related to Indian Vedic than to Iranian for the simple reason that they were one before Iranian came and pushed them away from each other in opposite directions: the Iranian Wedge.

The Tarim Mummies

The last piece of the puzzle comes from another story so far unrelated to the others: that of the 'Tarim Mummies of Xinjiang'. Not as recent, but as topical as its oil boom status, both stories have paved the way for the fame of the Uighur Autonomous Region. But the mummies require a wider perspective.

Prior to the BMAC excavations of the previous section, archaeological research in Russia and the Central Asian

Republics of the former Soviet Union had made it increasingly likely that the traditional theory of the Eurasian steppes being the original home of speakers of Indo-European was correct. But there was no proof. The elements were at hand, but they came from further east, a region unknown to most students of Indo-European, where Chinese and Uighur archaeologists had since the late 1970s exhumed scores of desiccated corpses and hundreds of skeletons in the dry regions of the Yarkand–Tarim Basin of Xinjiang. Their most noteworthy feature demonstrated in the 1990s, through DNA analysis, is that they belonged to Europoid or Caucasian peoples who are elsewhere known to have spoken Indo-European. The earliest of these Tarim mummies date from approximately 2000 BCE and the latest from the second or third century CE. The early dates fit our context like a glove.

They do not fit the prevailing hypothesis about the language of the mummies. All authors of publications I have been able to consult (many of them articles edited by Viktor Mair) have unquestionably assumed that Tocharian, an extinct and isolated Indo-European language, was the language of the mummies. This is a far-fetched and unlikely assumption since the only dates of Tocharian that have been attested come from Buddhist manuscripts found in the northern part of the Tarim Basin and dating from the sixth and seventh centuries CE. That is roughly two-and-a-half millennia too late for us. The 'T' on the map of Figure 5, therefore, does not refer to late Tocharian but to 'Tarim', *tout court*.

There are many arguments to show that Tocharian was an ancient Indo-European language. But the languages it resembles most closely are early languages spoken in Europe such as Celtic, Italic (which is older than Latin) and Prehellenic (which is older than Greek). It must have branched out to the Tarim Basin at some date or other, but during that extended period of almost three millennia, its speakers could have moved, settled or disappeared almost anywhere in Eurasia or even in Alaska or California without leaving a trace behind. How many people become mummies that are preserved and discovered because the region is so excessively dry? What then was the language of these mummies before they were mummies?

If we put the facts together, it becomes clear what happened around 2000 BCE. Speakers of Indo-Iranian were roaming the steppes south of the Ural Mountains, northeast of the Caspian Sea. All went in southern directions but the south-west was blocked by the Caspian Sea. Some went due South and ended up speaking Iranian. We shall return to them in a moment. Others went in the south-eastern direction through what is now Kazakhstan and entered the Tarim Basin. They went the only way one could go: passing through the famous gateway of the Tien Shan mountain range known as the Dzungarian Gates. It is located between what are now called Tashkent on the west and Kashgar on the east. More than two millennia later, Chinese Buddhist pilgrims went through those same gates in the opposite direction to Tashkent and Samarkand, a city with which Xuanzang (Hiuan-tsang), having crossed the deserts and despite his monastic status, fell in love. He was a great scholar about whom we shall learn more towards the end of this book.

Moving in the opposite direction, our speakers of Indo-Iranian may have had different feelings when they entered the desiccated Tarim Basin where some of them became mummies and where not only their bodies and tattooed skins, but their clothes survived in excellent condition. Colour illustrations would be needed. Some mummies wear knee-high socks of matted wool fibres in the rainbow colors of the gay flag.

Tarim mummies have been found in two areas, north and south of the Taklamakan Desert, subsequently the northern and southern Silk Roads. In the north, most discoveries come from the eastern end, close to China proper. Along the southern branch, a series of finds, going from east to west, leads to Khotan, close to the source of the Yarkand–Tarim Rivers, the Pamir Ridge where Muztagh Ata towers at 24,757 feet. It is a colossal mountain and it was a long trek to get there through the deserts. It is not surprising that the Indo-Iranian language of the speakers had changed by the time it got there. It had become what is now called Indo-Aryan. It was then and has always remained the easternmost Indo-European and Indo-Iranian language.

The conclusion at which we are arriving is confirmed by Rigvedic information about the Soma, a rare hallucinogenic plant that grew in the high mountains and to which we return in Chapters 5 and 7 and more often. The best Soma comes from Mount Mūjavat which means 'the Mountain that possesses *Mūj*'. It reminds us of the name of the colossus Muztagh Ata which means 'Father of *Muz* Mountain'. *Mūj* and *Muz* are both unexplained but Witzel related them to each other and identified the two mountains accordingly.

It implies that speakers of Indo-Aryan, who passed through the Pamirs on their way from the Tarim Basin to what is now Afghanistan, picked up the original Soma there. Witzel's hypothesis is consistent with my emerging conclusion.

So far I have concentrated on the slow development of Indo-Iranian into Indo-Aryan but what happened to those who became speakers of Iranian? They were larger in number and moved more slowly through the steppes and into the deserts. We know that they proceeded from south of the Ural Mountains and that their language eventually changed into the language of the Avesta which includes the Gathas of Zarathustra. It supports the suggestion that they had gone due south, before acting as a wedge, receiving some BMAC words from the Indo-Aryans and ending up in Greater Iran.

That those who became speakers of Iranian went due south is demonstrated by another and more extraordinary fact. Speakers of Iranian referred to the Vedic *soma* as *haoma* but they knew numerous *haoma*s which grew in common places, even along the roadside. The effects of ingesting those plants were slight. The Rigveda knows only one Soma which grew in the high mountains and was rare. The effects of drinking its juice were described in ecstatic terms as we shall hear in Chapter 5. If speakers of Indo-Aryan discovered Soma when passing through the Pamirs, it follows that the Iranians never went there. Their many *haoma*s were substitutes.

Meanwhile, what happened to the horse? It does not thrive in the sandy deserts of the Tarim Basin, as Victor Mair has pointed out. It prefers steppes like Mongolia, from where it reached China, and Kazakhstan, from where it reached India. This explains that horses did not go via the Khyber Pass as some speakers of Indo-Aryan did, but went from the BMAC region straight south with other groups, crossed the Bolan Pass and reached Pirak and Kachi, the earliest places in South Asia where traces of horses have been found.

One horse has been found at Gonur in Turkmenistan and much was made of it. According to David Anthony, it was not domesticated there but was a trade item, as Victor Mair explained on the Indology Internet in October 2006.

TWO

~

ARCHAEOLOGY AND THE ORAL TRADITION

Diversities of Reliability

So far we have looked at the geography and history of the Oral Tradition. We have also seen that the language of the Vedas is Indo-Aryan, a branch of the large family of Indo-European languages, which has undergone some influence of many other languages and language groups, some of them located within the subcontinent, others from other areas of Asia, including Central and South-east Asia.

Next, we should confront the Oral Tradition with the findings of archaeology. And we need to address more basic issues. We have a partly empirical question: to what extent will archaeology and the Oral Tradition be able to assist us in our search for the Vedas? And we have another that is, at least in part, theoretical in nature: what are the strengths and weaknesses of oral traditions and of archaeology? Where do they fail and how can they complement each other and come together? And what role is played by that third unspoken tradition we take for granted, the written tradition to which we as readers and writers belong ourselves?

Archaeology provides us with information on localities and dates that are often precise. Its information on civilization may be patchy and it tells us nothing about language unless it includes inscriptions that have been deciphered or languages, or parts or features of languages, that have been reconstructed. The Vedic period left no inscription because there was no writing.

Oral traditions provide us with information on localities and civilization that may be precise. Their dates may be patchy or worse. In an oral tradition, all depends on the fidelity of its transmission.

A written tradition is in these three respects like an oral tradition. But *we*, readers and writers of books, have little faith in oral traditions. That is our natural and professional opinion, a modern predicament that recent communication technologies have not yet sufficiently challenged. In so far as it derives from ignorance of oral traditions, our opinion is based on prejudice. That prejudice explains the persistent search for ancient scripts. This results in our failing to pay attention to two well-known facts: writing appeared very late in the development of human language; and even at present, the large majority of languages spoken on our planet have never and may never be written down. The reader, then, should keep in mind that we will not be able to understand the Veda unless we understand the strength and reliability of which an oral tradition is capable.

The Vedic Oral Tradition was exclusively oral until its end. Inscriptions on stone or metal do not refer to it until later. Manuscripts of the Veda belong to the Common Era and are at most as reliable as the Oral Tradition on which they depend. Part of that tradition is still alive though there are uncertainties and errors in the transmission; indeed, as there have always been. There are now for the first time printed editions and handbooks, carrying their own uncertainties and errors. None of it would exist without the Oral Tradition and the extreme care with which is has been transmitted. This is a topic that we met on the cover of this book, in the preface, and shall discuss in Chapters **4** and **14**, and revert to again and again throughout this book.

Is it unfortunate, then, that what the reader holds in hand is a *book*? Not necessarily for readers, author and publisher; all of them are users and perhaps even lovers of books. But there are diversities of reliability and we should return once more to the archaeology of the Indus Civilization.

Carts, Chariots and the Mind

Figure 7 illustrates small models of toy carts, excavated at Harappa sites and dating from from 2100 to 1600 BCE. The first fourteen are made of terracotta, the last three are bronze. One shows draught animals (cattle) and all have solid wheels. Items number 13 and 14 do not show that there were wagons with four wheels as had been originally assumed (by Mackay and Wheeler). Figure 8 shows wheels from the side. They are all terracotta and belong to the period from 2600 to 1900 BCE. Some are painted in black and number 15, of which only a small part survives, is painted on both sides. All these wagons that were pulled by cattle show the only type of wagon with which the Indus Civilization was familiar. Similar carts were found in the Near East during the same period, but it is now assumed (by Kenoyer and others) that the Harappan development was autochthonous.

The Rigveda provides us with a different picture. Its chariots (*ratha*) are pulled by horses and have wheels (*cakra*) with spokes (*ara*): 4, 6, 8, 12 or more. The term *cakra* is a well known Indo-European word: it is related to Greek *kuklos* from which comes English *cycle,* Latin *circus*, Anglo-Saxon *hveohl* and English *wheel*. It is combined not only with numerals but with words such as *kāla* 'time' in *kālacakra*, a powerful ritual; with *Viṣṇu* in *Viṣṇucakra*, referring to the god's wheel or disk; with *dharma* in *dharmacakra*, the wheel of *dharma*, etc. It is often combined with forms of the verbal root *vṛt*-'turn', 'revolve', 'set into motion'. Compare Kikkuli's *vartana* and Latin *vertere*, German *werden*, English—*ward* in 'toward', 'outward', etc. Vedic has related nouns such as *pravartana* and *parivartana*, 'turning' and 'setting into motion,' *dharmacakra* 'the wheel of dharma' (Chapter **16**) and *cakravartin* 'turner of the wheel' = 'ruler'. It will not surprise us that the Rigveda possesses in addition a detailed technical vocabulary with terms for 'felloe' (*nemi*), 'rim' (*pavi*), 'nave' (*nābhi*), 'linch-pin' (*āṇi*), 'hollow aperture' (*kha*), and so on.

The Vedas are, of course, familiar with the distinction between the old cart (*śakaṭa*) with solid wheels, used for transporting goods, and the new chariot or *ratha* with wheels with spokes, used for fast movement. And yet, the term *śakaṭa*, in its feminine form *śakaṭī*, occurs once in the Rigveda (RV 10.146) where a traveller is lost in a forest. He is alone and frightened. He imagines familiar sounds and sights that are not there: someone calling his cow, someone cutting wood, someone crying out, 'You think you see cows grazing; you think you see a house; you think a cart (*śakaṭī*) is rumbling' (translation Doniger).

The poets of the Rigveda have an obvious preference for the term *ratha* which refers to the more fashionable and recent discovery. Their coveted knowledge of its difficult construction earned them respect and high prestige. It enabled members of the clan to win the chariot race. They use the term even to refer to an old cart. All of this and more seems to play a role in the fantastic story of Mudgala (RV 10.102), an old sage who hopes to win a chariot race but only owns an old wagon. He asks Indra to transform his faulty old cart into a chariot. Indra needs to do a great deal more to complete this magical transformation, but the goal is reached: Mudgala on his old wagon, with his young and nimble wife as charioteer and pulled by the unlikely pair of a bull and a mysterious wooden club, wins the race and a thousand and one hundred cows.

The Rigveda derives from the terminology of chariots and spokes some of its most sublime puzzles: RV 1.164, in which verse 11 declares: 'The wheel of time (*cakraṃ ṛtasya*) with its twelve spokes turns around and around [in] the sky and never ages. Here stand, O Agni, the sons in pairs, seven hundred and twenty.' The phrase I have translated as 'turns around and around' is a rare mode of the verb *vṛt-* which expresses an intensive act: *varvarti*. The medieval commentator Sāyaṇa explained it correctly as: *punaḥ punar vartate* 'turns again and again.'

The Rigveda contains many riddles, some of them profound and difficult to explain. The present verse is straightforward: it refers to months, days and nights. The

Vedas inherited these subdivisions of the year from Mesopotamian astronomy which also influenced China and the modern world, together with other sexagesimal subdivisions such as minutes and seconds. The riddle shows that the Rigveda did not only know chariots with spoked wheels, but that its poets had started to muse about them and explore their imagery.

The tribes who spoke Indo-Aryan imported such chariots into the subcontinent through their oral tradition that is: *through their minds*. The Rigveda provides plenty of evidence supporting such mental imports. This will give the reader further inklings of Vedic poetry and the playfulness of its poetic imagination. The terms most often used in these contexts are *manas* 'mind' and its declined forms such as *manasā* 'with' or 'in the mind'. They will engage our attention again in later chapters.

Here are three examples of chariots in the minds of poets. In Rigveda (RV 7.64.4), after invoking Mitra and Varuṇa, the poet describes himself as 'he who constructs the high seat of the chariot in his mind' (*manasā*). RV 10.85, a poem that was later recited during marriage ceremonies, relates how Sūryā, daughter of the Sun (Sūrya), travels in a chariot made of mind (*manas*), whether it is to her future husband, immortality or the abode of Soma. RV 10.135 is a dialogue between a son and his dead father. The son says: 'I did not like him looking back at his ancestors and take the evil path. I want him back.' The father responds: 'The new chariot without wheels, which you boy have made *manasā*, which has one draught pole and goes in all directions, standing on it you are seeing nothing.' The father's sarcasm has been interpreted as making little of the boy's play though it is, in fact, concerned with imagination and reality both.

The power of the mind is applicable to the charioteer himself. RV 6.75.6 says: 'Standing on his chariot, the excellent charioteer leads the horses wherever he wishes. Praise the power of reins: the ropes follow his mind.' Verse 8 refers to a cart called *rathavāhana*, a movable platform on which the much lighter chariot (*ratha*) is transported. It could not be done across a mountain pass, but would be useful in the plains, an idea also transported by mind.

The word *manas* is often translated as 'thought'. The uses of *manas* we have met in our Rigveda contexts point unmistakably to 'mind' as the correct translation. 'Mind' is a faculty, an inborn capacity of our species. Thoughts are passing things, like the wind.

Indic Representations of Spoke-Wheeled Chariots

The Indus Civilization did not have a script but our information on the Vedas is lacking in another respect. The Vedas left no temples, friezes or icons as we have seen. It had ritual enclosures, but they were made of perishable materials and generally used only once. Connections have been sought between the Vedas and a type of grey-ware pottery, but these pots do not provide pictorial representations, let alone of spoke-wheeled chariots which are common, for instance, on Greek vases. The oral tradition speaks loud and clear, but for visual representations we must wait for the Buddhist era, after the Vedic period.

It begins with the columns or pillars erected by the Mauryan emperor Ashoka who reigned from 268 to 231 BCE. The one with lion-capitals from Sarnath, where the Buddha first turned the *dharmacakra*, 'the wheel of Dharma', display wheels with spokes and there was originally another large *cakra* on top. Solid enough reasons for it to have become the emblem of modern India. Figure 9 is more specific. It comes from one of the gateways of the Sanchi Stupa and dates from the early first century BCE. It depicts a horse chariot's procession with clear details, some we have discussed and others we have not: for example, the tying up of the tail of the horse to a strap connected with the neckstrap which is found elsewhere in Sanchi as well. The chariot that is depicted here is used ceremonially, not for hunting or fighting as was frequently depicted in the Near East and Egypt. Ideas behind representations like these are transmitted orally which is likely to have continued during later periods even when writing had become common.

Figure 10 illustrates a hold-up and may be even earlier than Sanchi: it is a rock painting from Morhana Pahar in Mirzapur, dated to the last centuries BCE. It provides again a wealth of detail. The picture on top is taken, more or less, from above. It shows how the draught pole is connected with the yoke and how the reins run separately to the heads of four horses. The axle is at the end of the chariot box and there are six spokes. The traveller is met by two armed men: one who is about to shoot an arrow and the other who stands ready with club and shield. The picture below is taken more or less from the side and is more sketchy.

After these early representations, spoked wheels become abundant in Indic art. A famous example is illustrated in Figure 11: a wheel of the Sun Temple at Koṇarak, built by Narasimha Deva of the Ganga dynasty between ca. 1238 and 1264. It depicts erotic positions that have to be imagined on this illustration but are said to be common in the Sun's celestial realm. Some have been provided with Tantric interpretations.

India has preserved the chariot with spoked wheels for almost three millennia. Spoked wheels survive on bi-cycles (*dvi-cakra*) and rickshaws. But the even older carts with solid wheels from Harappa and other pre-Vedic civilizations have never died out. They are represented on stone temples (at Hampi, for example) and Figure 12 depicts a wooden procession cart from the temple at Kumbakonam. It is called *ratham*.

Sintashta

Where do we find the origins of the spoke-wheeled chariot? In Central Asia, the earliest known excavations take us to its northern rim: the Sintashta–Arkaim culture which flourished between approximately 2100 and 1800 BCE. It was situated near the source of the Ural River, southeast of the Ural Mountains and northeast of the Caspian Sea. It is, or was, a border zone between the forest and the treeless steppe. Some twenty-five years ago, Russian archaeologists started excavating grave sites there of tribal chiefs who were buried together with their weapons, horses and two-wheeled chariots. The most widely discussed site is illustrated in Figure 13. The numbers 1 to 3 denote ceramics and a halter, number 4 is a knife, number 5 and number 6 are arrow and spearheads. The horse and human skulls are close to each other and the wheels, which had spokes, stood upright in small trenches as is shown on the left and below, indicated by the Russian letters Z and E. Dimensions are given in centimetres.

It is often taken for granted that the language of the Sintashta–Arkaim people was Indo-European; but there is no evidence and the leap from archaeology to language is not that easy. All we have to assume is that speakers of Indo-European, who may already have possessed horses, learned about chariots with spoked wheels here or in this neighbourhood before 1800 BCE.

It is possible that they knew about similar chariots already because there is a similar grave excavated far to the west that falls within the same period and has more precise dates. It comes from Krivoe Ozero which is north of Odessa on the Black Sea and has calibrated midpoints between 2032 and 1990 BCE. Perhaps speakers of Indo-European who came from there did not have to travel to the Sintashta–Arkaim region. Future discoveries or present ones about which I do not know may tell us more. In our present context we do not need it: we know from where north or northwest of Central Asia the spoked chariots came.

Attested Locations on the Way to India

We are now ready for a conclusion which summarizes and recapitulates what is presently known about the origins and backgrounds of Vedic civilization insofar as it came from outside the Indic subcontinent, that is, India and Pakistan. That conclusion will put the pieces together in chronological order and fill some gaps. I shall do this with the help of the map of the Frontispiece, following the attested locations that are numbered there and indicated by arrows. The map has been placed at the beginning of the book, so that the reader can refer to it when studying the following more specialized notes.

The first thing that strikes us about this map is that it is obviously an idiotic and far-fetched idea to try to invade India from the northwest with anything like an army. The goal is the lush Indus Valley of the Punjab. The barriers are a cluster of the highest mountains on the planet: the Hindu Kush, the Pamirs, the Karakoram and the western extremities of the Himalayas. Via the Khyber one might move with camels, elephants hardly, but most horses would certainly die. Via the Bolan it is easier if one comes from western Afghanistan or is already there. Horses like grasslands as still exist in Kazakhstan, but dislike the deserts further south and certainly the mountains. There is, in this respect, a significant contrast with both west and east. In the west, horses could almost gallop from the southern Russian steppes to Greece. In the east, they easily went from Mongolia into China, avoiding the Gobi Desert. It is not even very far.

From Kazakhstan to India along the tracks of the map of the frontispiece is about a thousand miles.

I call the numbered locations on the map *attested* because they are dictated by geography. The few adventurous ancestors of the speakers of Indo-Aryan *must* have trekked through the passes, passages and 'gates' on the east or right of the map—2, 5 and 7—because there were no other ways to go unless they were trained mountaineers. The attestations of these locations are confirmed by the itineraries of Buddhist monks coming from India or Chinese, Korean, Japanese and other pilgrims coming from the east more than a millennium later. They are also the old trade routes, including much more than the over-exposed Silk Roads that economic historians of Asia have begun to study.

The map shows that 2 and 5 were pre-Vedic, but 7 Vedic, following the directions of the arrows. The same 2, 5 and 7 were Buddhist, in either direction. Buddhist movements *mirror* Vedic movements. One might describe the entire process with the help of double arrows, not in terms of our cherished labels ('Vedas,' 'Buddhism'), but as a continuous movement and exchange of people, ideas, rites and goods over the centuries and millennia. I have adopted single arrows pointing to India which is my topic.

When I emphasize geography, I could have used the more fashionable term ecology, but it is mostly mountains that I have in mind. They are the most unmoving features of our terrestial environment. Oceans are not, as we are painfully becoming aware. Rivers flowing through plains change their courses through human history. It does not apply to mighty rivers like the Indus that have cut steep gorges through the mountains. Humans, the most destructive species, have tried to cut gorges but have not been able to move mountains. They have been successful in destroying themselves and each other and are efficient in doing away with rivers, not only by constructing dams that are like people in not giving a damn about others, but by milking them dry for excessive irrigation. They have almost finished off the Oxus, now called the Amu-Darya, famous in Antiquity, forgotten in the Rigveda and later rediscovered by Indian Buddhists. The Oxus used to flow into the Aral Sea which has now been split into two mineral stews that unleash and spread poverty and disease.

Mountains can be moved but not by humans and it takes time. The Himalayas were pushed upward by the chunk of land that drifted across the Tethys Sea, collided with the Asian Plateau and became India. The Indus, which had been flowing directly into that sea, adapted its course and started to flow around the mountains. So did the Tsangpo/Brahmaputra, also starting from the Kailāsa region, but flowing to the east before it turned south. All of it took place during the Tertiary Age, long before India, let alone humans had arrived. But geography continues to determine our life.

We shall discuss the arrows of the Frontispiece one by one. Each of them is special and that applies to **1** which primarily points to Sintashta, 2100–1800 BCE, more than 300 miles north of the map. Perhaps it indicates the approximate movement of some Indo-European speakers in both directions: for we have seen that they might have picked up the chariot wheel from the Sintashta–Arkaim culture. We have also seen that speakers of Indo-European may already have been familiar with *cakra* and not have had to travel to Sintashta all the way. In that case we erase **1** from our map and proceed to **2–9**.

The arrow **2** leads into the Tarim Basin of which the map shows the western half of Xinjiang. It is there that the earliest Tarim mummies of 2000 BCE were found. It is around the time that speakers of Indo-Iranian arrived and began to change their language into Indo-Aryan. The 'T' on the map of Figure 5, instead of referring to Late Tocharian, is the 'T' of Tarim.

At roughly the same time, speakers of Iranian, indicated by arrow **3**, moved in southern directions but much further west, closer to the Caspian Sea. Their arrow is smaller and thicker, denoting the slow movements of larger numbers of people, some of them moving in the direction of **6**. These easier itineraries through the steppes, inviting leisurely stops or settlements, contrast with those of the more adventurous few who went further east, following arrows **2**, **4** and **5** and always on the move.

The arrow **4** has not been discussed so far. Together with arrow **5**, it is of great intrinsic interest and strongly supports our general argument about the geographical origins of Indo-Aryan. Located south of the centre of Khotan, a flourishing centre of civilization at various periods of history, it is one of the points from where it is possible to reach India more or less directly. These tracks seem to have been used throughout history and could have been used by Indo-Iranians who had begun to speak Indo-Aryan. It is likely, but there is not much evidence and the reason is that none of these paths are easy to follow. One first has to cross the Kun Lun Mountains and then almost impassable areas such as the freezing and desolate Soda plains of Aksai Chin, the area of India's China war in 1962. Another trail from Khotan goes via the Karakoram Pass, formidable at 18,290 feet. Skirting the southern extremities of the Karakoram Range, it reaches the Indus in the Valley of Ladakh after which it becomes a wide tract of land at an altitude of about 12,000 feet, easy by comparison. It does not change much between Leh, still on the map, and Mount Kailāsa, which is not. All there is left to do is cross the Himalayas and one is in India. A third possibility, going southwest from Khotan, is almost impossible because one has to cross the Karakoram Range over a pass of more than 19,000 feet next to K2, the world's second highest mountain. The only people who did it, as far as I know, are Sir Francis Younghusband and his Balti guides. After slaughtering many Tibetans, Younghusband turned into a mystic (which he may always have been beneath his colonial face) and peacenik (which he had never been).

Arrow 5 passes Muztagh Ata and reaches the Oxus. It marks the preferred route between South and East Asia and is often referred to as the Wakhan Corridor. South of the Pamirs and north of Swat, Hunza, Gilgit and the Karakorams, it is a grey valley with a bitter wind blowing over the grasses, the only things that grow there. From there one might go straight south and cross the Indus, but I have not marked it because it was a very much worse, in fact a dreaded route, 'where iron chains serve for bridges suspended across the void,' as the Chinese Buddhist pilgrim Sung-yün put it in 519 CE. Nowadays everything is easy, if not disrupted by wars, because of the Karakoram Highway.

Arrows 4 and 5 combined may shed light on a group of small languages and cultures of exceptional interest because they have preserved elements and structures that are as old as or older than the Vedas and may be related to them in unexplored ways. All are located in the mountains, some of them in secluded and inaccessible valleys. They are either Indo-Aryan or Indo-Iranian which, in that case, may not have split into two (as depicted on *page* 22) but into three branches like this:

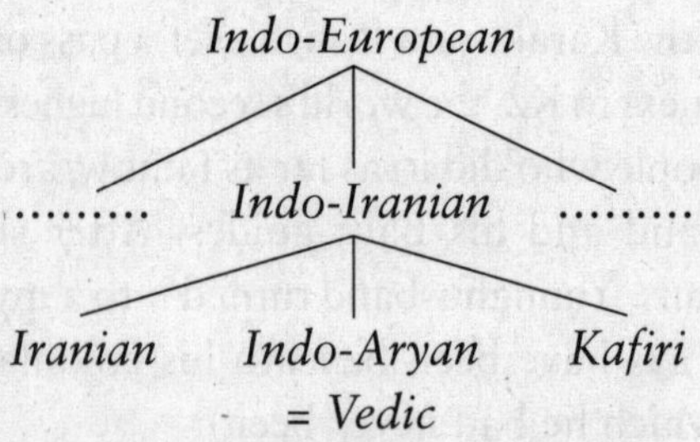

Either hypothesis is consistent with the emergence of Indo-Aryan in the region of arrows 4 and 5 though it must be added, if one wishes to maintain an unclouded perspective, that non-Indo-European languages may have to be included. To come to grips with any of these languages and cultures is not easy. The few researchers who knew them have called them by almost equally many different names. I have referred to them as *Kafiri*. A great deal of work should be done on those that are still spoken before it is too late.

I shall mention two of these languages and cultures here. The first is Kafiri itself, located in north-east Afghanistan, but seriously threathend. Like Lithuanian in Europe, it has retained words that have not changed their form in some 3,000 years as the comparative linguistics of Indo-European shows. Kafiri culture has priests, bards and shamans. They stress purity and their seers are half-grown boys, seemingly similar to *brahmacārin*s, 'going with brahman', i.e. students of the Veda before marriage. The Kafiri are different in that they tend goats during the summer months. Kafiri left traces in Vedic, e.g., the word for 'pearl'.

The other language is Kalasha, until very recently spoken by some 3,000 people in the valleys south of Chitral which is south of arrow **5**. It retained its original culture to some extent. Purity is again emphasized but women play an important part. Men and women dance, separately and together, and as transvestites. All undergo purification ceremonies. There are fire and other rituals that might shed light on the Vedas, and the opposite holds as well since ritual and purity are closely connected.

Speakers of Indo-Aryan who emerged from the deserts of Xinjiang following arrow **5** were close to the source of the Oxus which they continued to follow. They met inhabitants of, or passed through area **6**, the BMAC, which flourished there between 2100 and 1900 BCE. Asko Parpola found about 340 camp-sites of people from the steppes surrounding practically all known BMAC sites and dating from the Final Bronze Age, ca. 1550–1350 BE. If they were speakers of Indo-Aryan, it shows that they could not easily enter the BMAC forts. It is roughly in that area that they were pushed in two opposite directions—7 and 9—by the Iranian Wedge coming from arrow 3. Some went east and crossed the area 7—the Khyber Pass, where the first speakers of Indo-Aryan crossed the Indus and entered India.

Arrow 8 takes us to an area we have touched briefly: the Bolan route which was the most important link between India and the regions to its west during the early periods, more so than the romanticized Khyber. Bolan is also the name of a river near Quetta in Baluchistan, marked on the map. Northwest of the Bolan lies the *Harax'aitî* river, now called Helmand. Bolan may reflect the name of the Vedic tribe *Bhalāna*, a BMAC word, which was defeated in the battle of the Ten Kings. After crossing the Bolan Pass in the southern direction, one reaches Pirak and Kachi, the earliest places in South Asia where traces of horses have been found. Pirak is remarkable for another reason. It is there that Jean-François Jarrige and other French archaeologists excavated altars that resemble early altars of Vedic ritual which are depicted in Figure 20 and described in Chapter 14. In the same neighbourhood lies Mehrgarh, a Neolithic village in the sixth millennium BCE, and a continuous settlement of population that exhibits the gradual evolution from agriculture to urbanization.

Arrow 9 refers to the speakers of Vedic who went west to reach Mitanni Syria before 1380 BCE. We started with them and they end the story I have tried to tell in Part I.

Note on Aryan and Race

We cannot conclude Part I without a word about the linguists' unfortunate but continued use of the term *Aryan*. 'Indic' would do just as well. I sometimes use 'Indian,' which parallels 'Iranian' and is still very common in these studies. There is some justification for that usage in cultural contexts, though it is odd in terms of modern boundaries since much of the area of the Indus Civilization and where the Rigveda was composed overlap with Pakistan.

The use of 'Aryan' is a more serious matter that transcends the frontiers of nations and affects all of humanity. I wish I could simply have dropped it, but it would be confusing to the reader who might come across it elsewhere. Perhaps a Vedic workshop, now a flourishing and trend-setting event, will appoint a committee to look into the matter. While the committee does its work, the term should be avoided as much as possible.

In Vedic or Sanskrit, the distinction between *arya* or *ārya* and *anārya* has never been a racial or ethnic distinction. Madhav Deshpande has shown that it expresses claims to moral, social and spiritual status, tending towards exclusion in so-called 'Hindu' legal texts and epics, but inclusion and transformation among Jainas and Buddhists. Even at the time of the Rigveda, when many clans and tribes where fighting with each other, terms that refer to enemies such as *dasyu* or *dāsa*, which also means 'slave', lack racial overtones. Skin colour attracts or repels humans but who would have related it to race, a modern concept that is only at present beginning to acquire a scientific meaning?

PART II
THE VEDAS

Constructing an Edifice

Almost twice as long as any of the others, Part II provides essential information about the Four Vedas as they were canonized and as we know them. It includes selections and translations. It examines not only the two earliest Vedas, the Rig- and Sāmavedas of which the melodies of the second are of indigenous origin; but also their constituents: the Saṃhitā collections that are the source of the later mantras, the voluminous prose Brāhmaṇas and Āraṇyakas that are replete with speculation on the meaning of rituals.

The story of the Yajurveda is different from that of the Rig- and Sāmavedas and led in other directions that will be further explored in Part III. The Atharvaveda is also rather different but its chief theoretical contribution, the thesis of Kautsa, will be included here.

Part II ends with the Classical Upaniṣads, sometimes similar to the speculative poems and puzzles of the late Rigveda. They developed the art of public debate and include the beginnings of Indian philosophy.

Construction of the edifice of the Four Vedas coincides with the movements in the eastern direction of some of the composers from the Indus Valley to the Gangetic Plains. The earliest Brāhmaṇas and Āraṇyakas were composed in the Kuru region, not far from modern Delhi, the latest as far east as what is now Bihar.

THREE

~

CIVILIZATION AND SOCIETY

Absence of Caste in the Vedas

The Vedas depict a small civilization, beginning to settle on Indic soil. The small groups of which it consisted kept their Indo-European language, together with its poetic techniques, mythologies, the cults of fire and Soma and the knowledge of horses and chariots. That latter knowledge had been carried along with language across the mountain barriers that separate Central Asia from the Indic subcontinent. It was carried not by hordes of invaders, but in the minds of small groups of men who established alliances with local women. Language and ritual were transmitted from father to son. Fathers insisted that sons learned Vedic until transmission became ritualized (as illustrated by the Gāyatrī mantra at the end of Chapter 11). We hear little about the mother or the institution of marriage until the end of the Rigveda. Women came from many sections of the indigenous population and spoke various languages. They may have been 'widely extending' nymphs like Urvaśī, but at first they did not know Vedic and rarely, or ever, composed Vedas. Though matriarchal and matrilineal clans and tribes must have existed, it is not obvious that the general Indic pattern of dependence of women on men was in existence also. That pattern was formulated explicitly in post-Vedic times by the code of Manu or *Manu Smṛti* of the second century CE: as a child, a girl must remain under her father's control, as a woman, under her husband, and when her husband is dead, under the sons. None of these restrictions may have existed or imply that a caste system existed in the Vedas.

That the indigenous population contributed substantially to the Vedas follows from the fact that the names of indigenous families, clans and tribes, became the names of Vedic *schools* (*śākhā*). Those subdivisions are the social units into which the Vedas came to be divided. There is not much of a hierarchy between them apart from the widely accepted fact that the Rigveda comes first. These units had no chieftains, not to mention bishops; but there were experts (*brāhmaṇa*s) of the language (*bráhman*) who included members of indigenous groups that had started using Vedic as a second, third or another language. Thus arose a vast edifice with undefined boundaries because it depended on ritual and other specialists with independent origins and independent minds. It was canonized only later as described at the end of the next chapter and depicted in Table 1.

Until we reach the latest stages, there is no evidence for any kind of caste system in the Vedas. It begins to be visible in late Vedic works and the post-Vedic *Dharma Sūtra*s. And is fully developed as a theory in the law book of Manu.

The hypothesis of caste being a Vedic institution is based upon the idea of invading hordes of Aryans who conquered indigenous lineages. There were no such invading hordes as we have seen. We know that nomadic or semi-nomadic tribes were looking for booty but that was not confined to speakers of Vedic. Nor is there evidence for 'free Aryans and subjugated indigenous people', the kind of phrase still used by modern historians of India such as Kulke and Rothermund. The genetic picture assigned both tribal and caste populations to indigenous lineages going back some 9,000 years. I do not know how much light DNA can shed on these matters, but that picture does not contradict anything we have gathered so far. Part I showed that they were no more than the adventures of nomadic pastoralists on the way to India and beginning to settle there.

To sum up this brief introduction: the interactions of a handful of Vedic speakers with indigenous groups, themselves speaking many languages and of great diversity in so far as we can reconstruct them, could not possibly have led to anything grand like a 'new social system'. Post-Vedic India was and still is obsessed with caste and continues to attribute that idea to the Vedic Indians, whether they were regarded as scapegoats or as its semi-divine originators. But do the Vedas not use terms such as *brahman*, *kṣatram* and *viś*? They do and it has been the cause of great confusion. The mistake of the large majority of writers has been to imagine that these terms refer to the names of the later castes, *brāhmaṇa*, *kṣatriya* and *vaiśya*. What do the Vedas themselves say?

Vedic Evidence and Scholarly Discussions

Three lines of an early Rigvedic invocation of the Aśvins, divine twins who travel through space in their horse-drawn chariot, provide a picture of early Vedic civilization in a nutshell. In so doing, they make use of three of the four terms that underlie the later social system:

> 'Promote the *bráhman* and promote poetic inspirations. Slay the demons, drive away pain and illness. Drink the pressed Soma in harmony with Sun and Dawn, o Aśvins!
> 'Promote the *kṣatram* and promote able-bodied men. Slay the demons, drive away pain and illness. Drink the pressed Soma in harmony with Sun and Dawn, o Aśvins!
> 'Promote cows and promote the *viś*. Slay the demons, drive away pain and illness. Drink the pressed Soma in harmony with Sun and Dawn, o Aśvins!' (RV 8.35).
>
> We meet here with three basic concepts:
>
> *bráhman* or 'language', later connected with *brahmán*, 'learned man' or 'priest' (note the accent difference);
> *kṣatram* which means 'power' or 'dominion';
> *viś* which refers to 'the people' in the sense of those who are settled on the soil. It may also refer to milk bearing cows.

Sometimes we come across passages that evoke a united front of *brahma-kṣatram*. It refers to alliances between priests and chieftains directed against *viś*. It is likely that *viś* refers to indigenous groups that were sedentary. The three terms also occur in later prose compositions of the Yajurveda such as the Brāhmaṇas but it proves nothing: for we shall see that there is little that the composers of these works do *not* say. These same compositions mention the derived terms *brāhmaṇa*, *kṣatriya* and *vaiśya*, which later will refer to the three highest castes, but there is no fixed hierarchy among them and it sometimes looks as if order does not matter at all. An example from a Yajurveda Brāhmaṇa: 'The seers of yore say that the *vaiśya* is born of the Rigveda, the *kṣatriya* of the Yajurveda, the *brahmán* of the Sāmaveda.' A composition in prose from the Sāmaveda mentions three boys who were reared by hyenas. Each was given a boon and they chose, in order of seniority, *kṣatram*, *bráhman* and *viś*. When hierarchies display so much variation, even if it is due to hyenas, the only thing that remains is the number three.

Composers of the Vedas are fascinated by many numbers, but three is the number they seem to like best. It is the one uncontroversial feature of the vision defended, half a century ago, by Georges Dumézil. He believed in a grand Indo-European tripartite scheme of *fonctions*, as he called them. They apply to many things, including deities and social classes, not only among ancient Indians but among Iranians, Celts, Greeks, Romans and others. The French word *fonction* is even vaguer than its English cognate *function*. It means, apart from 'function', also 'post', 'office' or 'occupation'.

Dumézil's ideas continue to be widely discussed, especially by religious scholars and students of religion in the United States and France. Dumézil started with the Iranian, but its society is different from the ancient Indian. Vedic society itself is much more complex than the simplistic triads of Dumézil suggests. I shall not try to summarize the extensive discussions that have followed but make an exception for the critique of John Brough, which is not only thorough and authoritative, but also entertaining. He has shown that

Dumézil's arguments apply equally well to the Hebrew monotheism of the Old Testament as to Indo-European mythology.

The alleged specificity of the three *fonctions* is applicable to Biblical monotheism because any divinity has various aspects. In the Rigveda, Varuṇa is an ancient and ambiguous deity on whose nature scholarly opinions vary. Dumézil stresses his wrathful features though he is sometimes willing to 'untie' the sins committed by his worshippers. Twelve invocations of the Rigveda, out of over a thousand, are addressed to Varuṇa and twenty-three to a dual-divinity called Mitra–Varuṇa, in which Mitra is not only, as his name indicates, a friend but also a personification of contract, another meaning of the word. According to Dumézil, Varuṇa and Mitra–Varuṇa exemplify the Brahman class.

Brough shows that Dumézil's argument equally applies to the jealous god of the penitential psalms of the Old Testament, who is, like Mitra, the god of a covenant. The Hebrew god is also mighty in battle, which is the *kṣatriya*'s domain. He furthermore 'causeth the grass to grow for the cattle, and herb for the service of man: that he may bring forth food out of the earth' (Psalm 104.14). It sounds like a translation of a Vedic phrase on *viś* which refers to the life of farmers after which the *vaiśyas* were named.

The small number of invocations of Varuṇa and Mitra represents a cult that is more ancient than the cult of Indra which pervades the entire Rigveda. According to R.N. Dandekar, Varuṇa was a deity of the early Indo-Aryans of Bactria. I have used this cult with its puzzling features because it is relatively small and manageable.

Brough's chief arguments are concerned with Indra, but they are extensive and detailed and I cannot pursue them here. Brough concludes that the three *fonctions* are so elastic—and therefore useless—that 'any sufficiently extensive and diversified body of literature might be expected to produce significantly comparable results.'

None of these savants pay attention, and for good reasons, to another Vedic poem that is invariably quoted in general books about India to make a point about the caste system. I am referring to the 'Hymn to Puruṣa' (RV 10.90). Puruṣa is a primordial male and the poem assigns the terms *brahmán, rājanya, vaiśya* and *śūdra* to his mouth, arms, thighs and feet. Brahmán does not refer to caste but to a learned man or priest (see above *pages* 55–6). The place of the term *kṣatriya* is taken by *rājanya*, which refers to a person of princely status. There are factual and analytical anomalies about this poem. The first are that it is the only place in the Rigveda where the late term *śūdra*, and therefore a four- instead of a threefold division of social classes occurs. The analytical anomaly is: why should this poem support the idea of the later caste system, when its main point is to describe how that primordial male was dismembered and killed? Does it imply that castes are dismembered limbs and therefore dead?

The Puruṣa myth looks like a late addition to the Rigveda. It does not resemble any other Rigvedic myth and is not in accordance with any other Vedic reference to social distinctions. The only common features are negative. Puruṣa recurs in later Vedic compositions and still later, and in a different sense, in the philosophical system of the *Sāṃkhya*.

That system has ancient roots but is concerned with enumerations and lacks structure. As for the term *jāti*, which long after the Vedas began to refer to caste by birth and applied, in due course, to hundreds of castes and sub-castes, the word is not common in Vedic and only used for 'birth'. We have seen about birth that the status of a person, who is about to be born from an inter-tribal alliance, may depend on complex rules that vary from tribe to tribe.

Last but not the least, Vedic has no general term for social class such as the later word *varṇa*, which, in the Veda, exists but refers to 'colour', 'outward appearance' and especially 'form'. In the epic, it means 'caste' but to attribute any such meaning to the Vedas is anachronistic.

Varying Terminologies and the first 'Vedic Villages'

The mere occurrence of terms such as *brāhmaṇa*s or 'brahmaṇs' proves nothing about caste or caste distinctions. The Rigveda speaks of them often, but the term refers to various kinds of learned people, including 'sages', 'poets' and 'priests'. The term *kṣatriya* has no settled meaning either, neither in the Rigveda, nor in later Vedic compositions. The Taittirīya Saṃhitā of the Black Yajurveda mentions *kṣatṛ* which is a chamberlain or doorkeeper. The Tāṇḍya Brāhmaṇa of the Sāmaveda refers to 'eight brave persons that hold up the kingdom'. The list ends with *kṣatṛ* and *saṃgrahītṛ*. According to P.V. Kane, they are the names of high officers of some sort. Similar observations could be made with regard to other names that became caste names in the later hierarchy. But the chief difficulty is not that we would get entangled in a fruitless and abstract discussion of social systems. What we have to know first is who were the speakers of Vedic and the composers of the Vedas. We know that composing Vedas took place almost entirely within the continent, and that the Vedic language was a branch of Indo-Iranian that had come into existence a little earlier and further to the north. Those earlier peoples may have composed 'Vedas', but they are at best the precursors of the Vedas as we know them. The latter were composed by descendants of those precursors, as well as others and a variety of intermediaries as we have seen.

The alliances we have discussed include battles and one of these is mentioned specifically in the Rigveda: the Battle of Ten Kings who were, obviously, tribal chieftains. According to the Rigveda, the battle was won by the Bharatas. Their victory was due to the mantra power of their priest whose name was Vasiṣṭha, the 'Most Excellent' sage whose aristocratic pedigree connected him with Dawn (*page* 16) and who is associated with the seventh circle of the Rigveda. The Bharatas, who gave their name to what is also called 'India', settled eventually on the banks of the Yamunā river.

'Settling' means settling with cattle, animal husbandry and increasing wealth. Cows were as important as horses, but horses remained rare and only the number of cows plays a role as a measure of wealth (*page* 131). The development of Vedic terminology reflects other changes, such as the gradual replacement of the barley cultivation of Early Vedic pastoralism by the agriculture of rice. Civilization and society became gradually village-based.

Three stages of this process may be distinguished with the help of the semantic development of the term *grāma* as Wilhelm Rau has shown. In the Rigveda, it denoted a train of herdsmen, roaming about with cattle, ox-carts and chariots in quest of fresh pastures and booty. Subsequently, it came to refer to a temporary camp for such a train, made of bamboo poles and reed mats that could be quickly assembled. Towards the end of the Vedic period, *grāma* began to mean 'village'. It continues to be used in that sense to the present day.

Concepts of civilization that seem to be 'Vedic' are more difficult to capture. I use 'civilization' rather than 'society' (which is too narrow) or 'religion' (which is seriously misleading) but all are very imprecise concepts. Features of civilization vary not only in different Vedas, but in different compositions within each Veda. We shall pay attention to more specific and useful concepts such as mantra, chant, knowledge, meditation and language, *brahman* and *brāhmaṇa*. Each of them has its own history. We cannot pursue these exercises in semantic history but it is difficult to make a meaningful generalization that goes beyond them unless we are happy with bland statements such as: the Vedic period was a period of dynamic change in civilization and society both.

Rathakāra and a Note on Women

From what we have mentioned in Part I about the great prestige of experts who knew how to train horses or construct chariots with wheels with spokes—both specialized tasks that reflect a high level of technology—we would expect them to occupy an important, or at least a special place in early Vedic society. They might be assigned to a high caste had the notion of caste then existed. Would the chariot-maker give us an idea of Vedic society *before* the caste system? It should not be difficult to find information about this since there is a common term that refers to that chariot-maker: *rathakāra*.

The term *rathakāra* does not occur in the Rigveda. There is no other specialized term that refers to a professional who constructs a *ratha*. Does the term just happen to be absent, or is the Rigveda more concerned with the imagery and symbolic significance of the chariot? These questions are difficult or impossible to answer, but late explicitness of a term proves little. In the long poem about the battle of the ten chieftains (Rigveda 7.18), the term *ratha* does not occur. But there exists a technical terminology for many parts of chariots in the Vedas and especially in the Rigveda. They include terms for its various beams, axle, side-pieces, interior, seat, yoke, etc., and especially for the parts of its wheels: axle-pin, nave, felloe, spokes, etc. (*page* 34). There must have been professionals who were able to put these things together and should be referred to as 'chariot makers'.

The term *rathakāra*, which becomes prominent later, is more interesting and puzzling than one might expect. I begin again with P.V. Kane who has some significant information, primarily from post-Vedic sources. I quote him *verbatim* (*History of Dharmaśāstra*, Vol. II, Part I, 1930: 45–6):

The Taittirīya Brāhmaṇa (I.1.4) after stating that the *brāhmaṇa* should consecrate sacred fires in the spring, the *kṣatriya* in summer, the *vaiśya* in autumn, ordains that the *rathakāra* should consecrate sacred fires in the rainy season. The question arises whether the *rathakāra* is a member of the three higher castes who has taken in economic distress to the profession of making chariots or is a person belonging to a caste other than the three higher *varṇas*. Jaimini in his Pūrva Mīmāṃsā Sūtra (VI.1.44–50) discusses this question and establishes that the *rathakāra* is a member of a caste other than the three higher *varṇas*, that he has on account of the express words in the *śruti* the privilege to consecrate sacred fire with Vedic mantras, that the mantra for the consecration of *rathakāras* is *ṛbhūṇāṃ tvā* (*Tai.Br.* I.1.4) and that the *rathakāras* are the caste called *Saudhanvana* which is neither *śūdra* nor one of the three higher ones, but is slightly inferior to the three higher *varṇas*. Viśvarūpa [a commentator on another *dharmaśāstra* work] notices that in some *smṛti* the *rathakāra*, though not belonging to the three higher *varṇas*, was allowed the privilege of *upanayana*, but adds that this dictum of the *smṛti* is due to mistake, it being misled by the fact that he is allowed the privilege of *ādhāna* (consecration of sacred fires). In modern times, the members of the carpenter caste in certain parts of the Deccan at least are in the habit of performing the *upanayana* and wearing the sacred thread.

Here speaks a lawyer (Kane was an advocate at the Bombay High Court and a senior advocate at the Federal Court of India) and an expert on medieval and modern technical Sanskrit texts and treatises on a number of disciplines, including not only law and ritual but also the ritual philosophy of the *Mīmāṃsā* and the commentatorial literature on all these works. His terminology is replete with post-Vedic concepts, which does not affect the value of his work, but should be kept in mind when we are enquiring into the status of the original *rathakāra*.

Kane refers to many Vedic compositions by name, and I shall do the same in this *rathakāra* section. The reader is requested to chew on these names as if they were tobacco, a practice he or she may regard as refreshing or repulsive. Some will be explained later and I have retained them here only in case someone knows the names already, or wants to refer back to this section after they have become familiar. As for the other terms that Kane uses: *brāhmaṇa*, *kṣatriya*, *vaiśya* and *varṇa* do not have their post-Vedic meanings in the Rigveda, and *śūdra* occurs only in the so-called Puruṣa Hymn as we have seen in the section on 'Absence of Caste in the Vedas'. The terms *śruti* and *smṛti* acquired the specific meanings used here only in the *dharmaśāstra* literature and have lasted until the present day: *śruti* refers to theVeda itself which came to be regarded as a supernatural revelation of non-human origin; and *smṛti* refers to Vedic or post-Vedic sources (such as the Bhagavad Gītā), based upon and therefore second in authority to *śruti*. The term *ādhāna* designates the consecration of sacred fires which is a basic feature of Yajurveda ritual; and *upanayana* is the initiation of the student which involves, among other things, investiture with the sacred thread. In sum, Kane's paragraph is a straightforward expression of the Indic obsession with the caste system of the last two millennia. I am not saying that during that period it was always defended or adhered to, or that Kane himself was advocating it: but it is his frame of reference and is *not* applicable to the Vedas.

Kane's long sentences combine the style of legal documents and that of the classical Sanskrit treatises and commentaries. The paragraph I quoted belongs to what scholars and students of Indian civilization will continue to regard as Kane's greatest contribution: the monumental *History of Dharmaśāstra* in five volumes with several more parts, one of the great works of scholarship of the modern world. But his learned paragraph throws light on many more problems than the author is aware of and deserves close reading. So after clearing up the terminological jungle, let us take a brief look at Kane's sources and what is known of their chronology.

The Taittirīya Brāhmaṇa was composed towards the end of the Vedic period, after 800 BCE, in Pañcāla from where it went south. It is clear from Kane's quote that it accepted and advocated a system of three castes: the composers were beginning to act as legislators and their acceptance of caste would continue for millennia to come. Whether it was accepted by 'Vedic society', which by then had settled in many schools and independent villages, is another question. The most likely answer is that traces of something like it might have existed in some (like the later Taittirīya compositions) and remained unknown to many. One matter is clear: the position of the *rathakāra* caused problems for this system wherever it was beginning to raise its ugly head. His status must have been high *before* anything like the system of castes had been thought of. That is what we would expect if the first *rathakāra*s possessed knowledge that came from elsewhere and was new to the Indic subcontinent. Kane can envisage the *rathakāra* only as a village craftsman, not the owner of mysterious insights and technologies that he carries in his mind.

Other scholars have added new information, sometimes illustrating the high position of the *rathakāra*, but they have generally followed Kane's line. Wilhem Rau tells us that during the Brāhmaṇa period, the *rathakāra* owned palatial residences because during the *aśvamedha* or horse sacrifice, the horse attendants stayed with him and what is more, there were four hundred such attendants according to the Śatapatha Brāhmaṇa. Hertha Krick makes the same mistake as Kane: she is aware of the *rathakāra*'s high status, but assumes that he came from the 'lowly indigenous people who had been conquered'—a straightforward restatement of the outdated, traditional view. Following a commentary on a Śrauta Sūtra, Gonda believes that 'this artisan' was given almost *kśatriya* status because it had become easier to achieve such status in later times.

I conclude that the *rathakāra* occupied a high social status in some Vedic circles long before anything like a 'caste system' existed. It doesn't follow that his ancestors entered South Asia on a chariot, or carried chariots across the mountains, unless it was in their heads (*manasā*). All of the section on 'Carts, Chariots and the Mind' at the outset of

Chapter 2 applies to him and is relevant to our understanding of his position.

The position of women in the Vedas is instructively similar to that of the *rathakāra* in some respects. Different in being subservient to fathers, husbands and sons, women are entitled to be *brahmavādinīs*, 'speakers of *brahman*,' which P.V. Kane translates, appropriately vaguely, as referring to 'sacred lore'. It requires the initiation of *upanayana* and prescribes the wearing of a sacred thread and the keeping of a fire. Later commentators, mystified, explain the wearing of the sacred thread as 'wearing the upper garment in the manner of the sacred thread' though the original wording is unambiguous. According to Manu's post-Vedic book of laws, women are eligible to perform rites but without reciting the accompanying mantras. It makes sense: the ritual use of mantras presupposes that they are already known but there is no tradition for the Vedas to be taught to women.

Having said that much—or little—it bears repeating that we should never look upon 'The Vedas' as a unit. Their riches and deficiencies are due to a great variety of people of different backgrounds and origins, living in different regions and interacting during an extended period of time. We shall see in the next section that composing poems in the early Vedic language, making a selection, putting it together and looking upon it as 'The Rigveda' took very roughly half a millennium. Something similar holds for two of the other three Vedas though much of their earlier histories are now lost. The only Vedic units to which we are able to assign more definite places of origin and less vague beginnings in time are the schools of the Yajurveda as we shall see.

FOUR

~

THE FOUR VEDAS

Yājñavalkya is said to have received his mantras directly from the Sun. This captures the notion of timelessness that is not interested in 'early' or 'late' and is blind to historical development or evolution. I shall make limited use of that synchronistic and analytical perspective because it is a helpful abstraction when using language as a writer must do: it assists our discourse because it looks upon the four Vedas as a kind of transcendental idea that had not yet descended to earth. In actual fact, we shall see that each of the Vedic schools developed in a different place and at a different period. A survey of these schools is a straightforward continuation of the maps of Figures 1 and 2. They show that the Rigveda was composed in the Indus Valley in the west and the other three Vedas originated around the upper and middle courses of the Ganges further east. A closer look reveals that 'upper' Ganges refers to Kuru and Pañcāla (parts of the eastern Punjab, modern Haryana and western UP north of the Ganges) and 'middle' Ganges to Kośala and Videha (eastern UP and Bihar north of the Ganges). If we add approximate dates we have a framework for the present chapter. If we add the Vedic compositions themselves, the four Vedas are in hand. To help capture that the next four chapters, 4 to 8, will treat each of them separately.

The reader may wonder how we can be precise about such ancient history especially when our sources are oral. Part of the answer is that the transmission of the Vedas has been remarkably accurate. The rest of it is due to the history and evolution of the Vedic language, which is now fairly well established though it tends to be ignored or neglected by most archaeologists and historians. Alas, when disciplines isolate themselves from each other, progress will soon come to an end. Languages change though not necessarily at the same pace. Just as Chaucer, Shakespeare and W.H. Auden exhibit three stages of the development of English, our tripartite division of the Indus Valley, upper Ganges (Kuru-Pañcāla) and middle Ganges (Kośala and Videha) corresponds to three stages of development of Vedic, conveniently known as Early, Middle and Late Vedic. I shall use these labels and other variables and treat the three periods one by one, trying to illustrate to what extent the Vedas were connected with each other and to what extent they were artificially put together. On Early Vedic, we can be brief since I have partly dealt with this before.

Early Vedic

This form of Vedic was spoken in the Indus Valley, ca. 1700–1200 BCE, by families and clans, the Vedic Indians by definition, whose language was adopted by others along with their mantras partly because of the power or alleged power of the latter. We are already familiar with some of its features because it is the period of the Rigveda. It resulted in verse that described sublime language (*bráhman* as well as *vāc*) as all-knowing (*viśva-vid*), a compound derived from *viśva* and the same verbal root *vid-* 'know' or 'see' from which the noun *veda* derives. It restricts that power to seers, poets and priests (*brahmán*, accented differently, or *brāhmaṇa*).

Early Vedic was originally the language of the Indo-Aryans but was gradually adopted by indigenous inhabitants of the subcontinent who had spoken and continued to speak many different languages. Apart from contributing to the composition of the Vedas, they inherited simple fire rituals that their ancestors or predecessors had performed on the steppes of Central Asia.

The Bharata chieftains are portrayed as practitioners of a multilateral policy. They combined poetic compositions from different tribes in an authoritative collection that was used to boost their morale and strengthen their hegemony. This early collection of 'family books' corresponds, how roughly we may never know, to the core of that part of the canon that was going to be established as 'the Rigveda'. The period of Early Vedic ends with power using language and knowledge for political ends.

Middle Vedic

This form of the language belongs to the period of Kuru and Pañcāla on the upper Gangetic plane between ca. 1200 and 700 BCE. The name Kuru is the name of a clan. The geographical regions where clans settled were generally called after them. In the case of the Kurus, this region was the district of Meerut and the territory situated some 100 miles north of Delhi called Kurukṣetra. That general area saw not only the codification of the Rigveda, but the putting together of three other collections that, together with other compositions, became the Sāma-, Yajur- and Atharvavedas. 'The Kuru realm,' as Witzel put it, 'became the center of Brahmanical culture, with Kurukṣetra as the traditional heartland of Brahmanical orthopraxy'—that is, ritual.

Leading historians of India are not in full agreement about what kind of structure that Kuru centre possessed. Burton Stein (1998) called Kuru a *mahājanapada* which he translates as 'great community', skirting around the then fashionable interpretation of *janapada* as 'republic'. According to him, some of the 'great communities' became states but that was after Kuru. According to Hermann Kulke and Dietmar Rothermund (1998), *janapada* referred first to the 'place of a tribe' and then to the territory of 'a people', using a term that is inoffensive and a little vague. Vagueness is not inappropriate when the evidence is as meagre as it admittedly is; but it does not resist generalization which is often more vague, not less. *Mahājanapada* accordingly became 'great territory of a people' (like 'great hall of the people'). Romila Thapar (2002) refers to the Kuru–Pañcāla territories as confederations, accepts their inclusion among *mahājanapada*s and adds some precision: 'The linchpin of the *janapada* had been the ruling clan, after which it was named, and this in turn ensured some linguistic and cultural commonality. But the *mahājanapada* was also incorporating varied cultures.'

'Varied cultures' is undoubtedly the *mot juste*. It adds substance to received wisdom and contributes to our understanding of the Middle Vedic period by recognizing, that composing Vedas should no longer be looked upon as an outpouring of Indo-Aryan sentiment and preoccupations, but reflected a variety of languages and cultures. It had been true of the Rigveda as we have seen in Part I and again at the beginning of Part II, but applies with greater clarity and force to the composers of the Yajur- and Atharvavedas. The Sāmaveda undoubtedly came from an indigenous, non-Indo-Aryan lineage. With the Yajurveda, composing Vedas became something like a job. The Atharvaveda is replete with local cults.

The Kuru started a confederation through alliance with the lineage of the Pañcāla clan. It does not follow that the Kuru were alien immigrants and the Pañcāla indigenous inhabitants of South Asia. It does not even follow that Kuru males took Pañcāla wives. We do not know much about 'wives' until we come to a marriage ceremony in the tenth circle. It is true that the Rigveda emphasized the male lineage. Throughout the Vedas, ancestors are referred to as *pitṛ*, 'fathers'. Transmission of the Vedic tradition was and remained patrilineal. Wendy Doniger's statement on the Rigveda remains valid for the early compositions of Middle Vedic: 'The Rigveda is a book by men about male concerns in a world dominated by men; one of these concerns is women, who appear throughout the hymns as objects, though seldom as subjects.' Whether as subjects or objects, they became instruments, i.e., mothers of sons. But *male* is not the same as *alien immigrant*.

We shall return to goddesses, but the chief result of the Kuru–Pañcāla alliance from the perspective of the four Vedas is that it led to several Yajurvedas and explains the increasing importance of the concept of 'school' or 'branch' (*śākhā*). Each school goes back to the clan, tribe or community of a particular area. The Kaṭha or Kāṭhaka school of the Yajurveda represents the tradition as practised in Kurukṣetra. The Taittirīya of the Yajurveda and the Jaiminīya of the Sāmaveda started in Pañcāla from where they went south. A selection by Kuru–Pañcāla compositions from these and other schools, combined into one vast collection, became 'the three Vedas' of the early Vedic canon. By the time of its first establishment, various communities started speaking Vedic and using the phrase 'our own people'. The Yajurveda invokes Soma as a guide against 'hostilities committed by our own people and by others'.

During the Middle Vedic period, Soma, like Agni, a material substance as well as a deity, was *ritually* combined with Agni in vast and complex rituals. Its juices are extracted from the Soma plant which is 'pressed' or rather, beaten with stones. The structural features of these ceremonies and their ritual significance will be addressed in Chapter 12. Such activities should, if possible, be seen and heard for they are an essential feature of Vedic civilization. Describing ritual combinations and interactions between Agni and Soma in language is not only difficult but tedious. It helps to explain that those who composed Middle Vedic prose were no longer poets, let alone seers, but had become scholars. The vision of the Rigveda is replaced by a measure of pedantry. It explains similarities in interpretation between contemporary scholars and these early predecessors. Vision would return with the Upaniṣads when contributions were made by birds of different feathers.

During the latter parts of the Middle Indic period, a large number of Yajurveda compositions were composed, especially in the school of Taittirīya, named after the partridge (*tittiri*) which acted as a patronymic bird. Among the sub-schools of the Taittirīya, the *Āpastamba*s lived on the banks of the Yamuna in the region of Mathura. They produced what became a popular ritual manual, the Āpastamba Śrauta Sūtra. It describes, like other manuals, large Soma rituals, performed for the benefit of a *yajamāna* or patron. At a culmination point in the ritual, the Adhvaryu priest of the Yajurveda arrives at the main altar with a long cloth tied around his head and dragging behind him. Underneath, the *yajamāna* and his family are hidden. They are about to take up residence in a new abode and the Adhvaryu proclaims the *yajamāna* as king. The participants shout: 'Soma is the king of us brahmans!' At this point there appears a rare allusion to what may well have been historical events. Āpastamba explains that the subjects of the king are Bharatas, Kurus, Pañcālas, Kuru–Pañcālas and others. It expresses at the same time and in the clearest of terms the brāhmaṇs' wish to wrest control from kṣatriya lineages. It does not follow that brāhmaṇs were descendents from speakers of Indo-Aryan and kṣatriyas were not. It suggests that both were interested in acquiring the power or alleged power of Vedic civilization.

Kuru–Pañcāla was also the region from where the construction or reconstruction of the Atharvaveda came.

Its contents came from all over the place and some may be older than the Rigveda. It took a long time before the collection was accepted by scholars and other authorities, and the collocation of 'Three Vedas' was accordingly replaced by 'Four Vedas'. Buddhism never seems to have realized that there were four Vedas and not three. The *Avadānaśataka*, a collection of legends or 'glorious events' (*avadāna*), mentions three Vedas and Buddhists have asked me: 'What fourth Veda are you talking about?'

Late Vedic

Late Vedic characterizes the confederations of Kośala and Videha, ca. 700–450 BCE. During this period, the White Yajurveda was compiled or extracted from the Black (as will be explained below and more fully in Chapter 7), other Kuru compositions were modified or reworked (like the important Aitareya Brāhmaṇa of the Rigveda), but the chief event of the period from our Vedic point of view was the final canonization of the four Vedas. The paradigm of canonization was the fixation of the precise form of the Rigveda, based upon a linguistic analysis that separated the words (*pada*) in each sentence from each other. It dissolved the *sandhi* of continuous speech (*saṃhitā*): the linking of the sounds of words with those that precede and follow in the sentence and in nominal composition, often discernible within words, that Vedic shares with later Sanskrit. English *sandhi* is exemplified by the difference between 'a mango' and 'an apple'. Here are the *Saṃhitā* and *Padapāṭha* of Rigveda 10.127.2:

Saṃhitā 'continuous speech':
orvaprā amartyā nivato devyudvataḥ/
'The immortal Goddess has pervaded wide space, depths and heights.' (1)

Padapāṭha 'word-for-word analysis':
ā/uru/aprāḥ/amartyā/ni-vataḥ/devī/ut-vataḥ
'per/wide (space)/vaded/immortal/depths/goddess/ heights.' (2)

The reader who is so inclined will be able to derive underlying *sandhi* rules (though not their formulation) by combining the corresponding 'words' from Saṃhitā and Padapāṭha. It is not simple when three forms (*ā/uru/aprāḥ*) are combined into one by following one of two paths that may be symbolized as '(1–2)–3' and '1–(2–3)' (*page* 283).

The Padapāṭha was the work of a great scholar and scientist, the first great linguist in human history, known as 'clever' (*vidagdha*) Śākalya. Like Yājñavalkya, he lived at the eastern extremity of Vedic India but they were not friends. The Bṛhad-Āraṇyaka Upaniṣad describes, at roughly the same time, a series of questions they asked each other. When Yājñavalkya answers a question, Śākalya says, sarcastically, 'Yes, of course', and asks the next. But in the end he loses and his head shatters apart which suggests that *vidagdha* may have been a sarcastic epithet as well. Whatever the stories, Śākalya was not only clever but conscientious. He faithfully preserved early forms of the language that were no longer in use at his time. He did not treat them as 'early'; but attributed them to the different regions from where, in fact, they came. Nor did he know that his Padapāṭha was creating a paradigm; but his analysis stands at the core of the third and final stage in the centuries-long process that led to the Rigveda collection or *Ṛk-Saṃhitā* as we more or less know it, and was adopted in due course by most of the other Vedic *Saṃhitā* collections.

The view of a modern philologist (as distinct from a linguist) is *historical*. It starts with the Saṃhitā and derives the Padapāṭha from it. That is what happened in history and this is how I have described it. Śākalya's perspective was a-historical, systematical and *analytic*. He was the first linguist.

The Apotheosis of Schools

The combination of the four Vedas with all their auxiliary texts into a single canon was inspired by Śākalya's analysis and his separation of words. It took place, likewise, in the eastern territories and is associated with the name of king Janaka of Videha, who attracted learned men from the west to introduce Kuru orthopraxy to his court. A great debate is said to have ensued, in which Yājñavalkya, the local celebrity, defeated these alien experts. The old Yajurveda was now called Black Yajurveda and found its ultimate refuge in South India. The White Yajurveda was established in the north where it continues to the present day.

According to post-Vedic myths like the *Vāyu Purāṇa,* the Yajurveda was first taught to twenty-seven pupils, one of them Yājñavalkya. The latter offended his teacher as was his wont. Ordered to disgorge what he had been taught, other pupils took the form of partridges and swallowed the soiled pieces, hence named 'black'. A less fanciful explanation is that the White Yajurveda was called white because it separated mantra and brāhmaṇa portions which in the earlier Yajurveda *Saṃhitā* collections had been mixed, thus returning to the purity of the Rigveda which consists of poetry only. By the end of the period, the corpus of Vedic compositions was closed though it had one open end: many Upaniṣads were added later and artificially attached to the Atharvaveda.

The chief subdivisions of the Four Vedas are the schools or branches (*śākhā*). They constitute an impressive edifice which is depicted in Table 1 on the following pages. On the left, its first column lists, from top to bottom, the four Vedas. The second column, immediately to its right, lists the forest of branches or schools.

To understand the table we must jump across it in two dimensions—without losing the threads (*sūtra*) that bind the pieces together. The second column depicts what should be our point of departure if we wish to understand 'The Four Vedas': the edifice of schools which was the great achievement of Middle Vedic. A glance at that column shows that it was created by the Yajurvedins, the followers of the Yajurveda. They created more schools than the other three

Table 1: The Four Vedas

	Schools:	Saṃhitā:	Brāhmaṇa:	Āraṇyaka:	Upaniṣad:	Śrauta Sūtras:
Ṛgveda	Śākala Vāṣkala	Ṛk	Aitareya Kauṣītaki or Śāṇkhāyana	Aitareya Kauśītaki or Śāṇkhāyana	Aitareya Kauśītaki	Āśvalāyana Śāṇkhāyana
Atharvaveda	Śaunaka Paippalāda	Atharva	Gopatha		Muṇḍaka, Māṇḍūkya, etc.	Vaitāna
Sāmaveda	Kauthuma-Rāṇayāniya	Sāma	Pañcaviṃśa Ṣaḍviṃśa		Chāndogya	Lāṭyāyana Drāhyāyaṇa
	Jaiminīya or Talavakāra		Jaiminīya		Kena Jaiminīya-Upaniṣad-Brāhmaṇa	Jaiminīya

(contd...)

(*Table 1. continued*)

	Schools:	Saṃhitā:	Brāhmaṇa:	Āraṇyaka:	Upaniṣad:	Śrauta Sūtras:
Yajurveda	Kṛṣṇa (Black):					
	Taittirīya	Taittirīya	Taittirīya	Taittirīya	Taittirīya	Baudhāyana Vādhūla or Bādhūla Bharadvāja Āpastamba Hiraṇyakeśin Vaikhānasa
	Kāṭhaka	Kāṭhaka	Kaṭha	Kaṭha	Kaṭha	Kāṭhaka
	Maitrāyaṇī	Maitrāyaṇi			Maitri	Mānava Vārāha
	Śukla (White):					
		Vājasaneyī	Śatapatha		Īśā and Bṛhadāraṇyaka	Kātyāyana

Vedas together. It is they who created the concept of school: the other three Vedas followed their lead not by *creating* compositions (they were already there) but by *assigning them a place*. From then on the Rigveda was no longer the leader. It too was assigned its proper place. The assigner was the Yajurveda which came to occupy the centre and in so doing marks, more than the semi-alien Rigveda, Vedic civilization as it continued to be known.

How did the Yajurvedins do it? With the help of ritual. The Yajurveda priests acquired power through the power of mantras, ritual and organization. A telling illustration will be treated at the start of Chapter 7 and in Chapter 13.

The Table of the Four Vedas will enable us to follow much of the development of the Vedas. The trick is not to try to memorize the many names, but to get some idea of the structure.

With this caveat we return to the third column which is labelled Saṃhitā: it refers to the continuous recitation of the initial and main part of each of the four Vedas. It is the linchpin of the system, the *ratha*-derived metaphor used by Romila Thapar, but we must take care not to confuse it with the first column. That first column lists the four Vedas which includes all the accretions as enumerated in the four columns to the right.

We are now in a position to explain the headings of those four remaining columns, some of them already familiar to the reader.

Column 4 lists the Brāhmaṇas. They are prose sections but were composed orally like all of the four Vedas. They are crucial to the development of the Yajurveda because of its division into two: the Black Yajurveda incorporates the Brāhmaṇas in the 'Saṃhitā' metrical sections on which they are commentaries and to which the Yajurvedins refer as mantra. The White Yajurveda separates its Brāhmaṇas from the mantras, thus attaining its alleged purity. It also explains some apparent anomalies which pertain to the fourth, fifth and sixth column of the White Yajurveda but cannot be pictured by the table because it is only a two-dimensional device: the Īśā Upaniṣad of the White Yajurveda is part of the Vājasaneyi Saṃhitā, and the Bṛhad-Āraṇyaka Upaniṣad of that same Veda is the concluding section of the Śatapatha Brāhmaṇa.

Column **5** lists the Āraṇyakas. They are 'forest' (*araṇya*) sections which does not mean that they are for ascetics though they may be concerned with meditation. Forests are places where powerful mantras or ideas may originate. It is not yet the third stage (*āśrama*) of life which was combined with caste (*varṇa*) in the *varṇāśrama* system, a product of the post-Vedic Dharma literature.

Column **6** lists the Upaniṣads that are 'secret teachings' in a special sense to which we return. They end with 'etc.' because it is an open category. We shall mainly be concerned with the so-called Classical Upaniṣads, those that fall within the Vedic period and are largely pre-Buddhist.

Column 7 lists the Śrauta Sūtras, structural descriptions of the Śrauta ritual with the help of *sūtra* rules to which we return in Chapter **14**. They are in many respects different from any of the other categories of the Table. First, they deal with Śrauta ritual which we shall explore in Chapter 12. It is connected with the Soma rituals on which we touched briefly. Second, these sūtras were orally composed and transmitted; but their transmission was not confined to recitation and chant but practised by application (*prayoga*) in the field, that is, in the ritual arena. Performances of large Vedic rituals are, among other things, large rehearsals for the priests, for the junior priests especially, but also for all the others who sit around. They include the youngsters that will be the ritual experts of tomorrow. The Śrauta Sūtras, therefore, are concerned with the continuity and survival of the Vedic tradition. Recitation of mantras and singing of Sāmans are their fuel as are the altar fires into which the oblations of ghee or Soma are offered.

The earliest and most important of the Śrauta Sūtras is that of Baudhāyana who lived, like Śākalya and Yājñavalkya, at the eastern extremity of Vedic India but a little later. He was not only clever and conscientious but a great scientist who analysed, organized and explained structures of formidable complexity. He deserves a place in Chapter 14 where, for the sake of simplicity, I shall quote from the work of his younger colleague Āpastamba who is also listed under the Tattirīya Black Yajurveda in the last column of our Table.

We shall return to many of these topics in Chapters 5 to 10. As for the forest of names, they are like any other names: they originate from various backgrounds and I shall explain some of them later only if it seems relevant or interesting in some respect or other. We need not recall most or even any provided the Table of *pages* 80–81 is at hand. But we should remember that some of the schools may be late reflections of tribes.

The Table, finally, is not complete. Omitted are the Gṛhya Sūtras, which deal with domestic rites that will be touched upon in Chapters **8**, **11** and **12**; the Prātiśākhyas and Śulba Sūtras, which treat linguistics and geometry, respectively, subjects of Chapter **14**; and a few others.

I can summarize our chapter on 'The Four Vedas' in simple terms. I have tried to show that The Four Vedas were cast into One Large Unit, but that is not what they were to begin with. The Vedas are not one of a piece. History shows this; and our summary shows in turn the relevance of revolutionary developments.

I can do no better than end with a quote for no one has amplified that summary better and is more qualified to place it in a wider perspective than Octavio Paz who was not only Mexico's great poet but her ambassador to India:

> India was always in communication with other peoples and cultures of the Old World: first with Mesopotamia, and later with the Persians, Greeks, Kuchans, Romans, Chinese, Afghans, Mongols. The thought, religions and art of India were adopted by many Asian peoples; in turn, the Indians absorbed and transformed the ideas and creations of other cultures. The Mexican peoples did not experience anything like (that) . . . . They lived in an immense historical solitude; they never knew the essential and common experience of the Old World: the presence of the Other, the intrusions of strange civilizations

> with their gods, technical skills, visions of this world and the next.

Multiculturalism, until recently the correct fashion in the USA and Europe, treats Arabs, Chinese, Euro-Americans and Indians as if they inhabited separate cognitive worlds and were as isolated as were the Meso-American cultures. That idea is not supported by South Asia and not by the Vedas either.

FIVE

~

RIGVEDA

I shall let the Vedas speak for themselves as much as possible, making use of existing translations, always acknowledged, but sometimes changed whenever I find what I think is a better translation or a happier phrase. I am not a Vedic specialist and have especially avoided translating Rigvedic poetry. I believe this should be done by a native speaker of English or Sanskrit, which I am not.

The reader is literate by definition, but I must continue to state that the Vedas are oral compositions that have been transmitted orally. They do not consist of *texts*. The Sāmaveda, moreover, consists of melodies. It should be heard and if studied it must be, it should be done by someone who is at least in part a composer or musicologist. Other Vedic compositions are concerned with rituals about which Renou wrote: 'One cannot grasp even the outward meaning from reading the text unless one is gifted with the rare virtuosity of a Caland.' Fortunately, one can still hear recitations and study living Vedic rituals in India. One should be aware that not everything one sees is Vedic. In Kerala, for example, large brass lamps with wicks are better than electric bulbs but neither are Vedic. Nor are priests who study published texts of Vedic works instead of following the oral tradition (which may be extinct where he lives). Caland was aware that abbreviated forms of domestic rituals (e.g., birth or marriage rites) continue to be performed in India, but did not know that large Soma or Śrauta rituals had survived as well. I hope my book will help to determine questions of the authenticity of such performances whenever and wherever they arise.

Gods, Composers and Metres

The Rigveda is an anthology of poems, selected from the early traditions of families and clans and then gradually expanded. The reader is already familiar with some lines and phrases quoted in preceding chapters. We must now pay attention to a few topics that are practical and somewhat technical for us though they were of great significance to the composers.

The first is of our own making: our numerical references such as '7.64.4' or '10.135'. In the first, '4' refers to a verse (*ṛk*) or line of a verse, '64' to the poem and '7' to the 'circle' (*maṇḍala*) of the Rigveda. If there are only two numbers as in '10.135,' they refer to a circle and a poem. Recall that there are ten circles so that the first number should always be one of these. The early 'family traditions' are mostly of circles 2 to 7, the core of the Rigveda. Metaphysical speculations such as '1.164', occur in circles 1 and 10 which contain the latest parts of the Rigveda and additions of various sorts such as 10.90.

There are 1,028 poems in the Rigveda as we have seen, but the poets and transmitters of the Veda did not think in terms of such numbers. They knew the Vedas by heart and if references were needed, they would quote the beginning words followed by *ādi*, 'etc.'. 'Promote the *bráhman* etc.' would refer to the poem I quoted at the beginning of Chapter 3. The later tradition provides indices, but the early reciters needed for each poem additional information only on three points that were of equal significance to them: the deity, the composer and the metre, for example, 'Indra, Viśvāmitra, Triṣṭubh'. We may be surprised by the attention to metre, but the Rigveda has sophisticated metres, strikingly different from the *śloka* monotony of the epics. There are about fifteen different types, each defined in terms of the number and length of its syllables. The three most common are: Triṣṭubh (4 x 11 syllables), Gāyatrī (3 x 8) and Jagatī (4 x 12). That the poets looked upon them with the same awe as the gods is consistent with the fact that they sometimes identified the two: the Triṣṭubh with Indra, the Gāyatrī with Agni, the Anuṣṭubh with Soma, the Virāj with Mitra and Varuṇa, and 'Jagatī entered all.'

Vedic, like ancient Greek, Chinese or Thai, but unlike Sanskrit, possessed an accent. *Bráhman* is different from *brahmán* as we have seen. The original accent was probably a stress accent but the oral tradition often preserved it as a tonal accent, rendered differently in different parts of India. These recitations with their varieties continue to fascinate Vedic brahmans and illustrate a characteristic emphasis on *form* to which we frequently return.

Many of the riches of the Rigveda (RV) are now understood, but there remain unexplained words, names and phrases. To understand everything in a civilization, one might need anthropological, botanical, ethno-mycological, folkloristic, gender-oriented, geographical, historical, linguistic, literary, mythological, phenomenological, philologic, philosophic, religious, ritual, sociological, theological and other approaches. The best thing is immersion in what has now been made accessible in print and become a *text*. The anthology by Wendy Doniger remains the most accessible but covers only about a tenth of the whole. The reader who wants more and knows German, can do no better than plunge into Geldner's translation. Renou has also translated most of the hymns in French but has put everything in a different order, emphasizing deities which may not be such a good idea. No one can find anything without the concordance published by Wilhelm Rau in the *Orientalistische Literaturzeitung*. The essential readings are listed in the 'Readings' on *pages* 352–3, just before the Source notes and Bibliography where full particulars are given for every publication I have used. There is new information on almost every topic in more recent publications.

Taking my cue from the traditional recital—'Indra, Viśvāmitra, Triṣṭubh' on the previous page, I shall in this chapter concentrate on three deities and then provide an example of a famous speculative poem. Much is known about the former because the poets address them but they often presuppose familiarity with qualities or stories that were only known to the audience. My selection of deities is not subjective because 'most common' is measured in numbers. But should I follow numbers when there must be poems about the Creator God with whom we *ought* to begin?

The answer is, No. Wendy Doniger's selection is a cultural construct due to religious prejudice in that it starts with *creation.* It is a concept that pops up automatically in the mind of a Euro-American, religiously minded or not, as well as many other speakers of English, because it is well known that the sacred books of Judaism and Christianity start with the creation myth of *Genesis*. RV 10.129, with which Wendy begins, is accordingly referred to by almost all scholars as a 'creation hymn' as if it were the foundation of a creed, but it is not. It simply *wonders* like the famous speculative poem that follows.

Aren't there infinitely many gods? The number of gods in later so-called 'Hinduism' is infinite because that is what it is sometimes said to be. There are also various lists that seem indefinitely long. The number of Vedic gods is finite but fairly long. It is not laid down by an 'authoritative' poem because there are no such poems in the Rigveda. We have met with a goddess who pervades space, but several goddesses and gods are impersonal. Male gods struggle with the Asuras, a group of supernatural beings that are often referred to as demons. The Asuras may also be gods, but of a world of darkness.

The most important Vedic gods are Agni, Indra, Soma, Uṣas, Rudra, Bṛhaspati, the Aśvins and the Maruts. Viṣṇu survives as a god with more personal traits. Śiva means 'auspicious' in Vedic where his predecessor is Rudra. The Rigveda dedicates more than forty hymns to the *Viśve devāḥ* or All-Gods, to make sure that none is left out.

Agni and Soma have much in common. They are impersonal divinities but concrete as well: Agni is fire and Soma refers to an invigorating juice that is extracted from the stalks of a plant. Agni and Soma are increasingly ritualized. Indra has more personal traits. He is a hero, always willing to assist in battle and fond of adventures. He is referred to as king of the gods, the function best remembered after the Vedic period and in Buddhism, for example.

AGNI

The first poem of the Rigveda, *RV* 1.1, invokes *agni vaiśvānara*, 'Agni who is common to all men'. It starts with: 'I praise Agni, minister and divine priest of the ritual, who as invoker brings most treasure.' Agni is fire and, as receiver of oblations, a link to all the gods. He is addressed in about 200 hymns and makes a brief appearance at the beginning of the final poem of the collection which is in praise of unity. It may have been especially composed to mark the successful completion of the entire corpus which, by that time, was regarded as a single gigantic composition. The poem is on the theme of unification, a theme with variations on the key word *sam-*, 'together':

1. You, bull Agni, take all treasures including those of able-bodied men. You will be lit on the offering altar. Bring those treasures to us!
2. Go together, speak together, let our minds come together, like the gods of old sat together at their offering.
3. Unify the mantra, unify the meeting, let your mind and thought be unified. I recommend to you a unified mantra, I offer to you with a unified offering.
4. Unified be your intention, unified your heart. Your mind should be unified so that there is a good connection!

A typical hymn to Agni is Rigveda 5.11:

1. Guardian of the people, vigilant, clever; Agni was born for new prosperity. Face touched with butter, he shines bright with great sky-touching flame for all the Bharatas.
2. On the triple altar, men have kindled Agni, banner of the ritual, first domestic priest. Let him ride the chariot with Indra and the gods; let him be seated on the sacred grass as a skilful invoker for the ritual.
3. Impure, you are born of your parents; bright, you came up as the joy-bringing seer of Vivasvant. With butter they made you strong, Agni, to whom the offering is made.
4. Agni . . . may he come at once to the ritual; Agni, whom men carry in every house; Agni became the messenger, the bringer of offerings; Agni they are choosing, shocking one with a seer's power.
5. For you, Agni, these sweetest words; for you may this invocation be a blessing to the heart. You are the one these songs fill with power, as the great rivers fill the Indus, you are the one they make strong.
6. The Aṅgirases found you in a secret place, Agni, resting in every wood. So are you born, when stirred up with great force; you are the one they call 'Son of Strength', O Aṅgiras!

Aṅgiras refers to a sage and sometimes to Agni. Agni is touched with butter, the main oblation into the fire, and rests in every wood because he is born when two pieces of wood are rubbed together.

INDRA

Indra is invoked in all his splendour in an early hymn, translated by me largely after Doniger and with the help of Geldner, Macdonell and Renou: RV 2.12. The composer seems to be concerned that the cult of Indra is weakening:

1. The first, the wise god who from the moment he was born, surpassed the gods in power, before whose hot breath the two worlds trembled at the greatness of his manly powers—he, my people, is Indra.
2. He who made fast the tottering earth, who made still the quaking mountains, who measured out and extended the expanse of the air, who propped up the sky—he, my people, is Indra.
3. He who killed the serpent and loosed the seven rivers, who drove out the cows that had been pent up by Vala, who gave birth to fire between two stones, the winner of booty in combats—he, my people, is Indra.
4. He by whom all these changes were rung, who drove the Dāsa peoples down into obscurity, who took away the flourishing wealth of the enemy as a winning gambler takes the stake—he, my people, is Indra.
5. He about whom they ask, 'Where is he?', or they say of him, the terrible one, 'He does not exist,' he who diminishes the flourishing wealth of the enemy as a gambler does—believe in him! He, my people, is Indra.
6. He who comforts the weary and the sick, and the poor priest who is in need, who helps the man who harnesses the stones to press Soma, he who has lips fine for drinking—he, my people, is Indra.

7. He under whose command are horses and cows and villages and all chariots, who gave birth to the sun and the dawn, the leader of the waters—he, my people, is Indra.
8. He who is invoked by both of two armies, enemies locked in combat, on this side and on that, he who is even invoked separately by two men standing on the same chariot—he, my people, is Indra.
9. He without whom people do not conquer, he whom they call on for help when they are fighting, who became a match to every opponent, who shakes the unshakeable—he, my people, is Indra.
10. He who killed with his weapon all those who had committed a great crime, even when they did not know it, he who does not pardon the arrogant for their arrogance, the slayer of the Dasyus—he, my people, is Indra.
11. He who in the fortieth autumn discovered Śambara living in the mountains, who killed the violent serpent, the Dānu as he lay there—he, my people, is Indra.
12. He the mighty bull, who with his seven reins let loose the seven rivers to flow, who with thunderbolt in his hand hurled down Rauhiṇa as he was climbing up to the sky—he, my people, is Indra.
13. Even sky and earth bow low before him, even the mountains are terrified by his hot breath. He who is known as the drinker of Soma, thunderbolt in hand, thunderbolt in his palm—he, my people, is Indra.
14. He who helps with his favour the one who presses Soma and prepares, who praises and completes, he

for whom sublime language is nourishment, whose is Soma, whose is this donation—he, my people, is Indra.

15. You who eagerly grasps the price for the one who presses Soma and prepares, you are truly real. Let us be dear to you, Indra, all our days, and let us as heroes speak with wisdom.

Rauhiṇa, here a demon who attacks Indra, became a stellar constellation. Dāsa and Dasyu, terms used of enemies, servants and slaves, are generally taken to refer to indigenous tribes or clans which is likely; or to an earlier group of speakers of Indo-Aryan. Śambara has been interpreted as an Austro-Asiatic name and linked to early excavations in Bactria. He survives in Buddhist Vajrayāṇa Tantrism—or so does his name.

SOMA

Here is a famous hymn of the tenth circle (10.119) as translated by George Thompson:

1. Yes, yes, this is my intention.
   I will win the cow, the horse. Yes!
   Have I drunk of the Soma? Yes!
2. Forth like raging winds
   The drinks have lifted me up.
   Have I drunk of the Soma? Yes!
3. The drinks have lifted me up,
   As swift horses lift up the chariot.
   Have I drunk of the Soma? Yes!

4. Inspiration has come to me,
Like a bellowing cow to her precious son.
Have I drunk of the Soma? Yes!
5. I, as a craftsman the chariot seat,
I bend around in my heart this inspiration.
Have I drunk of the Soma? Yes!
6. Not even a blink of the eye
Have the five tribes seemed to me!
Have I drunk of the Soma? Yes!
7. Neither of these two worlds to me
Seems equal to one of my two wings!
Have I drunk of the Soma? Yes!
8. I have overwhelmed heaven with my greatness,
I have overwhelmed this great earth!
Have I drunk of the Soma? Yes!
9. I myself, I myself will set down this
Earth, perhaps here, perhaps there.
Have I drunk of the Soma? Yes!
10. Heatedly will I smash the earth.
I will smash it, perhaps here, perhaps there.
Have I drunk of the Soma? Yes!
11. In heaven is the one of my two wings.
The other I have dragged down here below.
Have I drunk of the Soma? Yes!
12. I myself, I am become great, great,
Impelled upward to the cloud!
Have I drunk of the Soma? Yes!
13. I go forth a home that is well made,
A vehicle of oblations to the gods!
Have I drunk of the Soma? Yes!

Soma is the juice pressed from the stalks of a plant growing in the mountains. The best Soma comes from Mount Mūjavat which Witzel located near the source of the Oxus. Soma stalks are without leaves or flowers. The term *soma* is not a name. It comes from *su-* which means to press the dry stalks or extract the juice. The entire ninth circle of the Rigveda is concerned with the preparation of the Soma. All the activities that are described there are regarded as effective only if they are accompanied by mantras. The effect of drinking is not discussed but drinking Soma often occurs in the Vedas as in 10.119, just quoted. The effect is described by forms and derivatives of *mad-* (which has nothing to do with English 'mad'). It may mean delight or inspiration and refers to the heavenly bliss of gods and ancestors. In the context of Soma, it is best understood as rapture or elation.

It is clear from the Brāhmaṇas and other Vedic and post-Vedic compositions, that the original Soma was lost at an early period and substitutes were used. What was the botanical identity of the original Soma? Though some have claimed that it is unimportant to the philologist, as if the referents of words did not matter, the majority of Vedicists have been puzzled by that question. Doniger enumerates more than 140 theories, published between 1784 and 1967, not in her *Rig Veda* but in her chapter in R. Gordon Wasson's magnificent book entitled *Soma. Divine Mushroom of Immortality*.

Wasson introduced a fresh and new approach to the study of the Rigveda that might lead to a solution of the problem. He had been a New York banker but his wife, Valentina

Pavlovna, turned his attention to mushrooms. It became a hobby and, after his retirement, a vocation. He became a leading ethno-mycologist, an expert on the religious and social uses of mushrooms. With full control of the rapidly increasing information about psychoactive plants among botanists, chemists, pharmacologists and others, Wasson argued that the Vedic Soma was the fly-agaric mushroom, *Amanita muscaria*, familiar from the birch forests, alpine meadows and folklore of the cooler regions of Eurasia from Western Europe to Siberia.

The Rigveda describes Soma as emerging from the soil as a little white ball. It bursts its white garment, fragments of the envelope remaining as white patches on the red skin underneath. Those are the white spots of the fly-agaric. Wasson's illustrations are often inspired by poetic descriptions of Soma such as 'the hide is of bull, the dress of sheep'.

Wasson's work was reviewed by anthropologists, botanists, mycologists and the leading Vedicists of the day: Sir Harold Bailey of Cambridge (*see page* 119), Daniel Ingalls of Harvard (*see page* 101), F.B.J. Kuiper of Leiden—all positive with qualifications—and John Brough of London (*see pages* 57–9), whose review was the most substantial and entirely negative. Brough writes about the poem of our *pages* 96–7 that it could not have been composed by a poet under the influence of the Soma: 'the artifice of its structure excludes this.' It is true that it may not have been composed under its influence, but it certainly was composed by someone who was familiar with the effects of drinking or digesting Soma, as Thompson's translation shows. Brough discusses the colour of the plant and objects to Wasson's theory because the fly-agaric is, according to him, but not to Wasson, a depressant.

The next major contribution was a monograph by D.S. Flattery and Martin Schwartz. It took account of Vedic but also of hallucinogens and the Iranian evidence on Haoma, the equivalent of the Vedic Soma. Although it mentions that, in Iran, there were many *haoma*s, it defended the thesis that the original Soma/Haoma was *Peganum harmala*, the mountain rue. Since then and for no good reason, the mainstream opinion among European and Indian scholars has been that Soma was Ephedra, a mildly psycho-active plant that prevents sleeping. Like the mountain rue, 'a common weed available from the nearest rubbish heap' as Flattery and Schwartz describe it, Ephedra is ubiquitous and therefore an unlikely candidate because Soma was rare and grew in the high mountains as on Mount Mūjavat. Its rarity contrasts with the numerous Iranian haomas which must have been substitutes. They explain geographical and other differences between Indo-Aryan and Iranian.

No unanimous conclusion has been reached with regard to the identity of the original Soma. Those Vedic scholars who had declared that it does not matter, making a virtue of necessity, could not deny that Wasson was undoubtedly right, that the identity of the Soma plant is not a problem that Vedic scholars can solve by themselves: 'Let the Vedists leave off feeding exclusively on the Rigveda and each other.' I don't believe that Soma was the fly-agaric but Wasson's new perspective was a great step forward and his recommendation sounds to me as sane advice.

A few Vedicists (George Thompson among them) have paid attention.

Ingalls, who sided with Wasson, observed that the Agni hymns seek for a harmony between this world and the next, but are always aware of the distinction. Soma poems are different: they concentrate on an immediate experience: 'There is no myth, no past, no need for harmony. It is all here, all alive and one.' Ingalls's characterization is apt and I would only add that the Agni hymns are concerned with a beneficial but dangerous entity that must be controlled by mantras and ritual. Memories of one of man's greatest discoveries, how to make fire, seem to reverberate in Agni. The Soma hymns are as Ingalls described them: though an entire circle dealt with the preparation of the Soma substance, they aim at ecstasy and insight. Ritual (*karma*) continued to dominate the Sāma- and Yajurvedas and the Brāhmaṇas. The search for insight or knowledge (*jñāna*) was brought to fruition in the later poems of the Rigveda and in the Upaniṣads.

A Speculative Poem

I shall now fulfil a promise: RV 10.129 which presents itself without deity or poet. The poem belongs to the late Rigveda when the Veda reflected a great variety of ideas, cultures and sections of society. It mentions its metre: Triṣṭubh. It is not a puzzle or riddle like some other long poems of the same period, belonging to the first or the tenth circle. I would rather describe it as thinking aloud. I shall quote its most recent and reliable translation, that of 1999 by Joel Brereton, adding Wendy Doniger's sage comment on poems that puzzle: 'Good. They are meant to puzzle.'

1. The non-existent did not exist, nor did the existent exist at that time.
   There existed neither the midspace nor the heaven beyond.
   What stirred? From where and in whose protection?
   Did water exist, a deep depth?
2. Death did not exist nor deathlessness then.
   There existed no sign of night nor of day.
   That One breathed without wind through its inherent force.
   There existed nothing else beyond that.
3. Darkness existed, hidden by darkness, in the beginning.
   All this was a signless ocean.
   When the thing coming into being was concealed by emptiness, then was the One born by the power of heat.
4. Then, in the beginning, from thought developed desire,
   Which existed as the primal semen.
   Searching in their hearts through inspired thinking,
   Poets found the connection of the existence in the non-existent.
5. Their cord was stretched across:
   Did something exist below it? Did something exist above?

There were places of semen and there were powers.
There was inherent force below, offering above.

6. Who really knows? Who shall here proclaim it?
From where was it born, from where this creation?
The gods are on this side of the creation of this world.
So then who does know from where it came to be?
7. This creation—from where it came to be,
If it was produced or if not—
He who is the overseer of this world in the highest heaven,
He surely knows. Or if he does not know . . .?

I have retained the words of the translator but would prefer to render *visarjana* as 'emission' and *visṛṣṭi* as 'production', not 'creation', because the latter term evokes a personal creator and verse 6 says that the gods are 'on this side of it'. It is moreover in line with 'produced' in the last verse though the Sanskrit term used there is different. Geldner has 'Schöpfung' but Renou senses a difficulty and wonders: 'création secondaire?'

This poem recognizes genuine problems of philosophy at a level most religious poetry does not even touch. Since it can speak for itself and speaks well, I need only add that no translation can do full justice to the sounds of the original. Brereton's translation is ringing ('deep depth death—deathlessness then', etc.), but the original sounds can be heard only in the original. Tatiana Elizarenkova has quoted them: Negations as expressed by *na*, *a-*, *an-* supported by constant repetition of *mā*, *ma*, *am*. Existence as expressed by *as-* 'exist' and its conjugated forms *āsīt*, *sat*, *asat*, reflected by echoes: *tamasā*, *asya*, etc. Questions as marked by interrogative pronouns starting with *k-*: *ka* 'who?', *kim* 'what?' *kutas* 'whence?', *kuha* 'where?' The 'polyphonic nature of the sound symbolism', as she has called it, is not inferior to Kalidāsa or Paul Valéry.

The Scientific Study of the Veda

In the last two chapters, we have looked at two controversies between Euro-American scholars about the Vedas. One is concerned with Vedic society, the other with the Soma. Both might seem to illustrate the irrelevance of infighting between Americans, Britons, Dutch- and Frenchmen to our august topic. But those inclined to think so would miss the point. The differences of opinion rest at least in part on categories that transcend contemporary national or political boundaries and are universal features of knowledge. Dumézil exhibits not nationalism but rationalism, Wasson combines rationalism with empiricism in another discipline, Gonda empiricism, and Brough comes closest to combining both. Of course, a good rationalist respects the facts and a good empiricist respects logic, otherwise they would not be scientists or thinkers—in any civilization.

If the rationalist Nyāya system of logic and the empiricist Vaiśeṣika—before they combined into the Nyāya–Vaiśeṣika—had paid more attention to the Vedas, they would have defended similarly different positions as Dumézil, Wasson, Gonda and Brough. The one philosophical system that is concerned with the Veda and to which I have already referred for that reason, the Mimāṃsā, combines rationalism and empiricism. Its theory of *apūrva*, offered as a causal explanation for the mechanism of karma, is rational. Its attention to Vedic *minutiae* is empirical. Although the data of the Mimāṃsā pertain exclusively to ritual, based as they are on the Śrauta Sūtras, they are concerned with facts. The Mimāṃsā may have little to say about history, but it has evolved an original theory about the facts of Vedic syntax.

Indian sciences pay attention to Vedic facts as Chapter **14** will demonstrate. The small number of Pāṇini's rules that apply to the Vedic language are marked by the expression *chandasi*, 'in the Veda'. They are far from exhaustive, and if omitted would not affect the system. I include Pāṇini in our discussion, though he does not belong to the Vedic period, because he would not have existed without it and adds fuel to my final observation: each of my few examples of rational and empirical approaches help to demonstrate that the Vedas have always been the subject of serious study. They are worthy of it and I hope they will remain so, that scholars and scientists will continue to pay attention to the facts, as we know them, and to rational argument in order to make sense. In these respects, the scientific study of the Rigveda and the other Vedas proceeds like any other science. We must know what the composers had in mind before we invoke the Vedas in support of a pet theory or deep conviction.

The present chapter has been concerned with some of the characteristics, including composers, subdivisions, metres and accents, invocations of gods and speculative poems of the Rigveda. I have discussed different points of view on the identity of the Soma plant and try to adjudicate between them. Has it been 'a scientific study' as I advocated just now? It is not because that would take more time. If we combine it with our earlier discussions pertaining to the Rigveda in Chapters **1** to **4**, it may be looked upon as an introductory exploration.

SIX

~

SĀMAVEDA

Having paid much attention to the Rigveda, I shall be relatively brief on the other three Vedas. This is as it should be for several reasons. The Rigveda is the earliest, the most venerable, obscure, distant and difficult for moderns to understand—hence is often misinterpreted or worse: used as a peg on which to hang an idea or a theory. The Saṃhitā portions of the Yajurveda are in some respects similar. The Sāmaveda takes all its words from it. The Atharvaveda is also similar but stands apart from the other three.

The Sāmaveda or Veda of Melodies or Chants (*sāman*) consists almost entirely of verse of the Rigveda set to music. There are variant 'readings' but the Sāmaveda has to be *heard*. The melodies were held in extraordinary awe and it looks as if they might not have been created for the sake of the verse, but were in existence already. The reason is not that two melodies are mentioned in the Rigveda by name, but that many of the words do not fit the melody. There were reasons, often ritual, for their selection and incorporation. Sometimes we have a series of chants in which the words fit the music in the first instance but less closely, or hardly at all, in those that follow. It shows that the words for the first had been carefully selected to fit the melody; after which others, different in length and number, were forced into the same format as if confined in a straitjacket. When words do not fit, they are changed or transformed and embellishments called *stobha* are inserted. They are meaningless like the sounds of a lullaby. According to a commentator, the term *stobha* is used even in daily life to refer to a meaningless string of sounds, something that may be uttered by a joker for killing time. Much more systematic study is needed, but I believe the melodies were originally sung to the words of another language and that Rigvedins or proto-Rigvedins and Sāmavedins or proto-Sāmavedins worked closely together. As for that other language, there are many candidates as is obvious from Part I. A good phonologist with much *Sitzfleisch* could deduce the phonology of that language from the changes made in the underlying language of the Rigveda.

The first song of the collection is derived from a Rigvedic verse that starts as: *agna ā yāhi vītaye*, 'O Agni, come to the feast.' It is sung in the Jaiminīya Sāmaveda from which I take most of my illustrations as:

o gnā i / ā yā hi vā i / tā yā i tā yā i /

It is not possible to translate this, but it is obvious that there is a formal correspondence between the original sentence and its Sāmavedic transformation: some vowels are changed, others are added, and some phrases are repeated. No attention is paid to what was originally a word and one suspects that some of the chanters who created these forms may not have understood the language from which they came.

Among the meaningless syllables that are inserted are OM and other famous *stobha* sounds that anticipate the equally mysterious mantras of Tantrism. Insertion and transformation may have happened on several levels, as in the Rigveda verse: *abhi tvā śūra nonumo 'dugdhā iva dhenavaḥ / īśānam asya jagataḥ svardrśam īśānam indra tasthuṣaḥ*, 'we cry out for you, hero, like unmilked cows to the lord of this living world, to the lord of the unmoving world whose eye is the sun O Indra!' It has been turned into a famous chant called Rathantara, 'Excellent Chariot'. It is one of the two that the Rigveda mentions. Its Sāmavedic form is: *obhitvāśūranonumovā / ādugdhā iva dhenava īśānamasya jagatassuvārdrśām / īśānamā indra / tā sthu ṣā o vā hā u vā / ās //*

The *stobhas* are *o vā hā u vā* and *ās*. They may occur almost anywhere but have here been put at the end. In the Bhakāra-Rathantara, 'Excellent Chariot with *bha* syllables', there is a more radical transformation into something more powerful and effective: syllables are replaced by others that keep the same vowel but replace the initial consonant by *bh*. The result is: *obhitvāśūranonumovā / o bhu bhā bhi bha bhe bha bha bhī bhā bha bha bhi bha bha bhā bha suvārdrśāmoyi / sānamā yindrā / iḍā o sthū ṣā o vā hā u vā / ās //*. We may translate/literate as: 'we cry out for you, hero, *bhye bhu-bhi-bhow bhu-bhe-bhoo bho-bhi-bhi-bhi-bho . . .*'

Wayne Howard has transcribed some of these forms in musical notation which gives those who are familiar with it a more realistic idea of how they sound and how long they last. *Pages* 111, and 112 provide two pages of his transcription. It is clear that chants like these should be studied not only by students of the Vedas but by musicologists. It has been claimed that the Sāmaveda stands at the origin of Indian music. All we can say is that it preserved its earliest surviving form. That such forms are sometimes similar to later forms (such as the *Ābhogi* raga) is unavoidable, given the great variety of *sāman* melodies that have survived.

The core of the Sāmaveda consists of ritual chants. They are ranked in the order of the Śrauta rituals we have mentioned but will examine a little more closely in Chapter **12**. Famous among them are songs that are called *stotra* or *stuti*, a term that also means 'praise'. Each *stuti* consists of five portions. The names of three Sāmaveda priests who sing them are based upon the names of three of these chants. The following illustration comes from a Rigvedic verse that addresses Soma and begins: *upāsmai gāyatā naraḥ* 'Gentlemen! Join us in chant to him!' The meaning of the remainder is lost in the remaining four sections that have been replaced or transformed into something else:

1. Prelude (*prastāva*): *upāsmai gāyatā narom* (chanted by the Prastotā priest facing west);
2. Chant (*udgītha*): *om oooooooooo* (chanted by the Udgātā facing north);
3. Response (*pratihāra*): *huṃ ā* (chanted by the Pratihartā facing south);
4. Accessory (*upadrava*): *oo* (chanted by the Udgātā);
5. Finale (*nidhāna*): *sā* (chanted by all three).

The reader will have noted that the beginning of the Rigvedic verse has been modified slightly at its end, and

Table 2. The 'Excellent Chariot' with *bha* Syllables I

Table 3. The 'Excellent Chariot' with *bha* Syllables II

that the rest is hidden by other sounds. Such hidden sections are called *aniruktagāna* 'unexpressed chant'. Hidden texts like these must be in the *minds* of the singers for otherwise it is difficult or impossible to chant such long sequences of meaningless syllables. I can learn to sing: *bhā bhu bhā bhi bha bhe bha bha* when *ādugdhā iva dhenavaḥ*, 'like unmilked cows', is in my mind. Similarly in English. I can learn to sing *bhye bhu-bhi-bhough bhu-bhe-bhow'* if and only if I think of: 'like unmilked cows to the lord'.

The difference between sound that is 'expressed' (*nirukta*) and language that is 'ineffable' (*anirukta*) is a large topic in Vedic discourse to which we shall return in Chapter **15**. It is related to the distinction between sound, which is limited to what is audible, and language which is not. In the final analysis, language and melodies are infinite but speech is not.

Each of the *stuti* sections has to be sung in one breath. It is not easy because the chants are long and the chanting of o's is extraordinary long. Good chanters are trained like opera singers but in a different style. Both need to inhale deeply and produce long breath. Others have to wait for the singers to finish before they can continue with their own recitations and ritual acts. They could easily get lost in oceans of sound that seem to continue for hours and sometimes do. To help them keep on track, the Prastotā gives at the appropriate times signals such as: 'This is the middle!' to the Adhvaryu priest of the Yajurveda, general manager of the ritual to whom we return in the next chapter.

Numerous other special chants, recitations and rites

surround these songs. At the beginning, the three chanters have already intoned an extended *ō hṃ*. Udgātā, leader of the Sāmaveda team of three, often has to sing a long sequence of chants with his two colleagues. For each chant he winds blades of grass around his fingers. He will attach them to a pole when the chant is over. These attachments mark the number of chants that have been completed so that nobody gets lost. Prior to the beginning of a *stuti*, which is the beginning of a series of ritual activities, the Adhvaryu hands the blades of grass to the chanter with the recitation: 'You are the bed for coupling Rik and Sāman for the sake of procreation!' Found only in the ritual sūtras, it is a significant statement, as the reader can guess and Chapter **12** will confirm.

Each Sāmaveda chant is followed by a Rigveda recitation called *śastra*, literally 'weapon'. It is also ritualized but not hidden: the originals are easily recognized by ritualists and other experts though their order is not the same as in the Rigveda and, when translated, do not make sense. Large ritual performances are defined by the number and identities of such sequences of chants and recitations that take place in the Sadas, a ritual enclosure at the centre of the ritual proceedings where the officiants 'sit' (*sad-*): Sāmavedins to chant their *stuti*s, Rigvedins to recite their *śastra*s, and both to drink Soma. We shall return to all of these in Chapter **13**.

Like the Rigvedic *śastra* 'weapons', Sāmavedic chants are powerful. When enemies attack with raised weapons, they should be recited in the mind which is another way of saying that they should be meditated upon. The

Yajurveda says: *mano vai vācaḥ kṣepīyaḥ*, 'mind is swifter than speech.' In the Soma ritual, the 'Outdoor Chant for the Purified Soma' is preceded by offerings for the selection of the priests. If the Udgātā hates the patron, he should meditate on *vāc* during those offerings.

Seemingly endless repetition is a characteristic of all ritual chants. Repetitions may be indicated by stage directions. Such directions are marked by *iti*, 'thus', like the end of a verse in the Padapāṭha. Stage directions should not slip into the recitation. Once I recorded a mantra recited by a priest when he gave a stick (*daṇḍa*) to a boy. The recitation included the final words of a rule: *iti daṇḍaṃ dadhyāt*, 'thus he should give the stick.'

Sometimes the opposite happens: something is left out. I traversed South India on an old Royal Enfield. My tape-recorder was packed in a padded aluminium box fixed to its back. The bike often needed repairs and I had to spend time in a garage. Once I arrived late for my recordings of Sāmaveda chants. On the next morning, one of the singers told me that he had omitted one round of repetitions. I made a note of it.

The Sāmaveda possesses meaningless syllables, unexpressed chants and chants with non-Indo-European names, some of them identified as BMAC words. It also reflects the structure of the Yajurvedic *Śrauta* ritual. The organization and fixation of its chants in one large collection during the Kuru period must have been undertaken in close cooperation with the Yajurvedins, many of them indigenous inhabitants of the subcontinent like the Sāmavedins themselves.

Singing in Villages and Forests

The Sāmaveda exhibits two types of chant: *grāma-geya-gāna*, 'to be sung in the village' and *araṇya-geya-gāna*, 'to be sung in the forest'. The former are accessible and relatively popular. The latter are complex and regarded as extremely powerful. *Araṇya* is sometimes translated as 'wilderness' for that reason. The Sāmavedic perspective of the forest as something dangerous, alien and replete with powerful chants, supports the idea that they belonged to an indigenous lineage that had long been settled. Did they picture the Rigvedins, who had given them the words for their songs, as alien beings that had emerged from the forest where they were roaming about with their powerful mantras? Or was it the other way round, since even a Rigvedic composer evoked the image of a traveller, isolated and frightened because he was lost in a forest (*pages* 34–5)? That Rigvedic poem, however, belongs to a late circle (the tenth) and merely shows that by that time the Rigvedins were just as settled as the Sāmavedins. All we can say is that those were golden times (subsequently called the *Satyayuga* or 'Age of Truth') at least in one respect: our planet was still replete with forests.

Charles Malamoud related *araṇya* to *ari* and *alien*, both meaning 'the other'. He could not have known that Octavio Paz was to write later, that the essential and common experience of the Indic, and of the entire Old World, was the presence of that *Other*: 'strange civilizations with their gods, technical skills, visions of this world and the next'. Paz contrasted India with the New World of the Americas, which had lived 'in an immense historical solitude (*pages* 85–6)'. Malamoud was writing about Vedic Indians, Paz included them in a generalization about the entire history of the subcontinent.

'Other' depends, of course, on who is speaking or singing, which, in the present chapter, is the Sāmavedins. The fact that they sang in the village as well as in the forest suggests that they had already incorporated 'the other'. But 'the others' were not the only 'Vedic Indians'. The Sāmavedins were themselves Vedic Indians. Their melodies were probably pre-Rigvedic though the majority, including all the village songs, had already Vedic names (such as *Rathantara*, 'Excellent Chariot'). That does not hold of the forest songs. Some of their names are non-Indo-European (IE), and some of these non-IE names have the structure of the vocabulary of the reconstructed BMAC language (Staal 2004, with the assistance of Lubotsky). I conclude that the Sāmavedins belonged to indigenous lineages that had originally spoken languages that were non-IE and that may have included the extinct language of the BMAC. Features of Vedic ritual point to the BMAC as well as we shall see.

'Forest' or 'wilderness' also characterize the Āraṇyakas which follow upon the Brāhmaṇas or are appended to them, and precede the Upaniṣads (see Table I, *pages* 80–81). One of the earliest Upaniṣads is called 'Great Āraṇyaka' (*Bṛhad-Āraṇyaka*). Renou characterized all these 'Forest Compositions' as 'meta-ritual esotericism', stressing their secretive character as well as the fact that they are still pervaded by ritual technicalities and often exhibit ritual structures. Village and forest are the two sides of Vedic life.

SEVEN

~

YAJURVEDA

The Role of the Yajurveda

The Yajurveda is not simply the next Veda. Sāyaṇa, a scholar with a deep and wide-ranging knowledge of the Vedas, described the Rig- and Sāmavedas as the pictures (*citra*) and the Yajurveda as the wall (*bhitti*). If he is right, the reader has been reading about beautiful things—Rigveda poetry and Sāmaveda chants—and should now get ready for the study of what supports and holds them together. These supporting structures must refer to ritual, the domain of the Yajurveda, which is concerned with complex activities. How to understand these structures? Must we wade through masses of ritual descriptions?

Stephen Lindquist is right that we should sometimes pay attention to traditional interpreters who may preserve something a modern scholar cannot know. Sir Harold Bailey did not agree with it, as we shall see in a moment, but it certainly applies to Sāyaṇa, who was chief minister of Harihara II, one of the rulers of the Vijayanagar empire which controlled a large part of South India in the fourteenth century CE. Together with his equally gifted brother Mādhava, who wrote on philosophy and also served Harihara II, Sāyaṇa contributed to the fame of the empire in the areas of arts and letters by writing extensive commentaries on the Vedas. Sāyaṇa knew Vedic ritual well because the

Vijayanagar period was a period of Vedic revival as had been the Chola period earlier and the Gupta period earlier still.

I played records of Veda recitation in the rooms of Sir Harold Bailey at Cambridge which were also his library. The reader will remember him as one of the reviewers of Wasson's book on Soma (*page* 99). Bailey had the habit of putting pamphlets, offprints, booklets and books into other books rather than next to each other. With few students in attendance, he used a carton board to which he attached large sheets of paper. Each time I had filled a sheet with the help of a crayon, he tore it off carefully. We discussed the meaning and etymology of words and I asked Bailey whether he took Sāyaṇa's interpretations into account. He raised his bushy eyebrows whimsically and said that Sāyaṇa, when he does not know the meaning of a word, says that it means water. Bailey, who was familiar with all the early languages of the Indo-European family and many others, was an etymologist at heart. He once made a passing suggestion, perhaps because of his liking for Wasson (*pages* 99–101), that *soma* should not be derived from the root *su-* and the suffix *ma-*, but analysed as *som-a* in which the first element corresponds to German *Schwamm*, Latin *fungus*, Greek *spongia* = English *sponge* and other Indo-European terms for mushroom. No one took it seriously. Having come this far we should recall what Voltaire said about etymology: it is a science where vowels count for nothing and consonants for little. Yes, etymology is more speculative than old-fashioned philology but not as speculative as string theory in modern physics.

Geldner in his Rigveda translation mentions Sāyaṇa often. According to Renou, we should look at what he says but not forget that there is a gap of thirty centuries between him and the Rigveda and the tradition that connects them has been interrupted often. Each gap lasted many centuries. One between the Vedic period and the Gupta (more than a millennium), a second between Gupta and Chola, a third between Chola and Vijayanagar, a fourth between Vijayanagar and the present. Plenty of time to forget again and again. But there is strength in the Oral Tradition and assiduous training in schools and on the ritual grounds. The Upaniṣads know what preserves it and remind us: Revere Memory!

We may get an idea of what Sāyaṇa imagined when he declared that the Yajurveda constructed a suitable space for Rig- and Sāmaveda to display their beauty. He was thinking of murals that were fashionable during the Vijayanagar period. I have seen one that relates to our story. Like Sāyaṇa and Mādhava who were in the service of Harihara II, the latter's predecessors, Harihara I and Bukka, were also brothers. During a war with the Sultanate in Delhi, they were captured and taken not to an undisclosed place, but to Delhi where they embraced Islam which stood them well with the Sultan. In due course they were freed and dispatched back, this time to quench a revolt. It was not a wise decision on the part of the Sultan, though there are different versions of what happened. According to one, the two brothers fell under the spell of Vidyāraṇya, not only a scholar who wrote on philosophy but a great sage.

Fired by his teaching, they returned to the Hindu fold and continued to pursue schemes of conquest and consolidation. According to another version, Vidyāraṇya was an insignificant ascetic who was Jagadguru or Śaṅkarācārya of the Śṛṅgeri Maṭha, stronghold of the Advaita Vedānta.

The large and beautiful painting that I saw comes from the ruins of Hampi and depicts Vidyāraṇya being carried in procession on a palanquin (see Figure 14). He looks like a great sage rather than an insignificant ascetic. I prefer that version of the story, but the significant point in our context is that it is a ceiling panel painted behind walls. Sāyaṇa was, of course, familiar with this painting. His simile seems to refer to the walls of the Sadas in which Sāmavedins sing their *stuti*, Rigvedins recite their *śastra*s and both drink Soma. I have not found the term *bhitti* used with reference to the Sadas, but it is used in similar contexts in the Śatapatha Brāhmaṇa and the Maitri Upaniṣad.

The Ritual Arena

There is more to it as we shall see in Chapter **13**, but I am afraid we must return from Sāyaṇa to the Yajurveda and the Yajurvedins. The Adhvaryu priest of the Yajurveda was a typical product of Kuru *orthopraxy*, that is: he was concerned with 'right action' rather than 'right opinion' or 'right belief', the meanings of the term *orthodoxy*. His home was the ritual arena, especially as it is constructed for the performance of Soma ceremonies.

Its origins lie in 'the ancient hut' (*prācīnavaṃśa*) and is depicted in Figure 15. There are three altars: on the left or west is the circular domestic or kitchen altar on which the oblations are cooked; on the right or east the square offering altar on which they are poured or thrown into the fire; and in between them, facing the south, a semi-circular altar which protects the officiants from sinister and dangerous influences emanating from the south.

To the east of the 'ancient hut', bottom right in Figure 16, a new enclosure is constructed, the Mahāvedi or 'Great Altar Space'. It has a much larger roof and is made especially for ceremonies and other activities connected with Soma. On its western side, closest to the 'ancient hut', the *Sadas* is situated. It is surrounded by walls. It is the place where Rigvedins and Sāmavedins sit, recite and chant but also where they sip the Soma juice. To its east is the Havirdhāna where Soma is prepared and kept. At its eastern end is the new square offering altar where Agni will be carried in a pot and Soma and other oblations are offered to the gods.

The Yajurveda Adhvaryu was manager of the ritual, showing the path (*adhvan*) as his name indicates. He managed, perhaps manipulated the priests of the two older Vedas, who did not always see eye to eye, and put them together at the centre of the ritual arena which is called Sadas from *sad-*, 'sit', because it is the place where the priests sit. The central position of the Sadas is clear from Figure 16 and we shall return to in Chapter **13**.

The Figure tells us a few more things. The rectangular area on the left or west, which has its own roof and is surrounded by low walls, represents the domestic arena that speakers of Indo-Aryan had taken with them from the steppes of inner Asia.

The rest of Figure 16 is a historical map which includes the ritual arena of the Soma ceremonies. Robert Gardner, the anthropological film-maker who was in charge of the documentation of the 1975 performance of the Agnicayana ritual (see Preface), called it the playpen.

This ritual arena contains several structures and altars, three of them within the Sadas, that are called or addressed by the priests with names that are non-Indo-European. As in the case of the chants discussed at the end of the previous chapter, some of these are BMAC words or names.

I have led the reader via a circuitous road to the ritual arena which is the centre of the Yajurveda just as the Sadas is the centre of the ritual arena. To see what the Yajurvedins exactly caused to happen inside the Sadas will become more transparent when we know a little more about ritual (Chapter 12) and, with special reference to the Sadas, in Chapter 13. The remainder of the present Chapter is an examination and discussion of specimens of *yajus*, Mantras and Brāhmaṇas from the Yajurveda.

Yajurveda Mantras and Brāhmaṇas

The Adhvaryu and his three assistants do not only recite Mantras and Brāhmaṇas of their Yajurvedic school. They mutter brief formulas referred to as *yajus*. These accompany ritual acts and the Yajurveda is named after them. Many are muttered in a low voice: *upāṃśu*, 'articulated (within the mouth) but inaudible'. Uttering them in a low voice strengthens them so that they will strengthen the mutterer as the Śatapatha Brāhmaṇa puts it in its sacerdotal fashion. The meaning of the word is more interesting: it comes from *aṃśu*, the stalk of the Soma plant and *upa* which means 'close' (as in *upa-niṣad*, 'sitting close'). The Soma drink is obtained from pressing these stalks which are, therefore, the essential part of the plant. In Soma rituals, prior to the main pressing, there is an *upāṃśu-graha* or small pressing before sunrise. It takes place without recitation; the Adhvaryu keeps silent ('restrains his voice') as on many other occasions. But the Śrauta Sūtras display variations: breath may be taken or not, different deities are involved, etc. It is a somewhat mystifying and flexible word: it may occur as a noun, adjective or adverb.

Upāṃśu occurs in other ritual contexts and rites. Brereton has studied its uses in the 'New and Full Moon Rituals' (*darśa-pūrṇa-māsa*, which according to Gonda should be translated as 'Full and New Moon Rituals'). He has reported much variation in its description by the Śrauta Sūtras. He refers to the view of the Taittirīya Saṃhitā that *upāṃśu* originated in the Full and New Moon Rituals, which is unlikely since there is no Soma pressing there. Brereton's most important conclusion is that the *upāṃśu* provides an inaudible centre around which the recursive structure of ritual is organized. He had already emphasized the importance of such structures in 'Why is a Sleeping Dog like the Vedic Sacrifice?' The similarity is that the beginning and end are the same. The sleeping dog has no centre, but other structures do and many are recursive, that is, they can be applied to themselves, again and again. I shall return to these topics in Chapters **11** and **12**.

Apart from inaudibles, there are silences. The most common is called *tūṣṇīṃ*, 'in silence' or *tūṣṇīṃ-japa*, 'muttering silently'. I shall return to them in Chapter **15**, but our present context is *yajus* recitations. One repeats structures of the form A B B A, e.g.: 'Agni (is) light, light Agni; Indra light, light Indra.' Another is recited by the ritual patron, on whose behalf and for whose benefit the ritual is done: it is his 'abandon' (*tyāga*) after each oblation, e.g.: 'this is for Agni, not for me!' (*agnaye idaṃ na mama*; and similarly for other gods). The statement is ungrammatical: the correct form is: *agnaya idaṃ na mama*—a feature that is of no ritual relevance.

The *yajus* 'ritual formulas' are different from Yajurveda Mantras and Brāhmaṇas. The Mantras are often taken or adapted from the Rigveda into Middle Indic and collected in the Yajurveda Saṃhitā which is also in poetry but followed by or mixed with prose Brāhmaṇas, interpretations of the Mantra sections in ritual terms. The mixture is typical of the Krishna or Black Yajurveda. Reacting to this, the Śukla or White Yajurveda Vājasaneyī Saṃhitā consists in its entirety of Mantras, a return in this respect to the Rigveda. Its Śatapatha Brāhmaṇa is separate and in prose.

During the Kuru period, composing Vedas no longer reflected an inspired vision but had become a job. The change may be due to the occupation or occupations of the Yajurvedins before they became Yajurvedins, but we know nothing about it.

Many of the accompanying changes are reflected by the new or widened uses of the term *brāhmaṇa*. The reader may have picked them up along the way:

1. a learned man, expert, priest or professor, who occupies a fixed niche in a community but does not speak for it, unlike the poet whose language gives it a voice;
2. a composition in prose that accompanies and interprets the mantra portions composed in verse that are recited during the ritual (in the earliest Yajurvedas);
3. a separate work, also in prose, that is similarly concerned with the interpretation of mantras and rites (in the White Yajurveda and the other Vedas).
4. a member of the highest caste (post-Vedic).

The Yajurveda ritualized deities-cum-substances of the Rigveda such as Agni and Soma. Early rituals were expanded, new ones added and all combined and organized in a new form called *śrauta* (from *śruti*, 'what is heard', i.e. 'learned'). The ceremonies were performed under the direction of four priests: Hotā for the Rigveda, Udgātā for the Sāmaveda, Adhvaryu for the Yajurveda and Brahman, assigned somewhat theoretically to the Atharvaveda. Each had three assistants. The Four Vedas became the sound foundation—in two senses of 'sound'—of Kuru orthopraxy. Through the Adhvaryu, chief manager of the Śrauta ritual, the Yajurveda became the core of the tradition, maintaining the walls which concealed its greatest treasures as Sāyaṇa described them.

One of the most highly developed and famous Śrauta

rituals of the Kuru era, allegedly first performed around 1,000 BCE, was the Agnicayana or 'piling of Agni'. Its defining feature is a large offering altar constructed in the form of a bird in five layers from a thousand kiln-fired bricks. It is piled in the place of the small square offering altar depicted at the extreme right of Figure 16, at the eastern end of the Mahāvedi. The configuration of bricks in the first layer will be explained in Chapter **14**.

Numerous rites are unique to the Agnicayana ritual. At its beginning, fire is placed in a clay dish with eight breasts or udders around its circumference. Its preparation is accompanied by long recitations. The following are taken from the Taittirīya Saṃhitā, based upon Keith's translation. The mantras include a few from the Rigveda, with variations. Savitā is the sun, especially before rising:

MANTRAS (Taittirīya Saṃhitā 4.1.1)

1. First harnessing the mind, Savitā,
   Creating thoughts and perceiving light,
   Brought Agni from the earth.
2. Harnessing the gods with mind,
   They who go with thought to the sky, to heaven,
   Savitā instigates those who will make great light.
3. With the mind harnessed, we are instigated by god Savitā
   For strength to go to heaven.
4. Priests of the lofty wise priest harness their mind, harness their thoughts.
   He who alone is possessed of knowledge distributed the priestly duties:
   Great be the praise of god Savitā.

5. I harness with honour your ancient hymn.
The verse go like Sūras on their way.
All the sons of immortality who have ascended to divine abodes are listening.
6. Whose journey the other gods follow, praising the power of the god,
Who measured the radiant regions of the earth,
He is the great god Savitā.
7. God Savitā, impel the ritual!
Impel for good fortune the lord of ritual!
Divine Gandharva, purifier of thought, purify our thoughts!
Today may the lord of speech make our words sweet!
8. God Savitā, impel for us this ritual,
Honouring the gods, gaining friends,
Always victorious, winning wealth, winning heaven!

The Taittirīya Brāhmaṇa begins with identifications based upon identical numbers ('four oblations'/'four feet'), a favourite mode of interpretation, but the Taittirīya Brāhmaṇa asks a straightforward question: why should the Agnicayana ritual, which is dedicated to Agni, start with mantras that invoke Savitā? The answer is that Savitā is the sun which is invoked for 'instigation' (*prasūti*). The Brāhmaṇa is lengthy and I select a few passages only:

BRĀHMAṆA (Taittirīya Saṃhitā 5.1.1)

He (the Adhvaryu) offers the Savitā offerings, for instigation. He offers with an oblation ladled up four times, cattle have four feet; thus he wins cattle; the quarters are four; thus he finds support in the quarters. . . . He abandons prosperity at the beginning of the ritual when he departs from Agni as the deity. These offerings to Savitā number eight, the Gāyatrī has eight syllables, Agni is connected with the Gāyatrī. Therefore he does not abandon prosperity at the beginning of the ritual, nor Agni as the deity . . . . With four verses he takes up the spade; the metres are four; thus he takes it up with the metres. 'Instigated by god Savitā' he says for instigation. Agni went away from the gods, he entered a reed; he resorted to the hole which is formed by the perforation of the reed. The spade is perforated to make it his birthplace. Wherever he lived, that became black; the spade is stained, for perfection of form and colour; it is open at both ends for the winning of light both from here and the other world. It is a fathom long; so much is the strength of man. It is commensurate with his strength and unlimited in girth to win what is unlimited. That tree which has fruit is strong among trees, the reed bears fruit, the spade is of reed to gain strength.

The four-ladled oblation and the ritual spade belong to the vast ritual knowledge of the commentator. The hole of the reed which marks Agni's birthplace does not stand in need of a Freudian interpretation. It would first need to be shown that sexual associations of holes, that may have been repressed by the Viennese before Freud, were repressed by the Vedic Indians, an effort that is unlikely to meet with success. Passages that we would regard as sexual or erotic occur almost anywhere in the Vedas. The ways we react to them throw light not on them but on us. The Rigveda tells us about Apālā, a young woman who was rejected by her husband because she had a skin disease. The Jaiminīya Brāhmaṇa of the Sāmaveda continues: she found a Soma stalk in a river and chewed on it. Her teeth sounded like pressing stones and Indra came running, but she recited her own story from the Rigveda. Indra then sucked the Soma from her mouth: 'it verily becomes like a Soma drink for him who knows this when one kisses a woman's mouth' (translation Hanns-Peter Schmidt).

The Bṛhad-Āraṇyaka Upaniṣad of the White Yajurveda (BĀU 6.4.3) equates the sexual act with a Soma ritual: 'Her vulva is the sacrificial ground; her pubic hair is the sacred grass; her labia majora are the Soma-press; her labia minora are the fire blazing at the centre. A man who engages in sexual intercourse with this knowledge obtains as great a world as a man who performs a Soma sacrifice' (translation Olivelle).

That the Rigveda does not repress sex is amply illustrated by Wendy Doniger's selections and is not confined to what some moderns regard as 'straight.' Indra is fond of all adventures. The majority were with women, but he wanted to experience sex from the other side and became the wife of Vṛṣaṇaśva, 'Bull Horse Man', who was so strong that he used for his chariot bulls instead of horses (RV 1.51.13). It would be far-fetched to classify Indra as a closet *paṇḍaka*—a term for a '(passive) homosexual' in later Sanskrit (*pages* 323–24). Indra liked variety, that much is clear.

The Yajurveda contains a series of mantras recited by the patron that contain long enumerations of very large numbers. It occurs after the construction of the Agnicayana altar from a thousand bricks has been completed:

> May these bricks, O Agni, be milch cows for me, one, and a hundred, and a thousand, and ten thousand, and a hundred thousand, and a million, and ten million (10^7), and a hundred million (10^8), and a thousand million (10^9), and ten thousand million (10^{10}), and a hundred thousand million (10^{11}), and a thousand thousand million (10^{12}), and a hundred hundred thousand million (10^{13}) (Taittirīya Saṃhitā 4.4.11 p).

After a million, the powers of ten have been added since English has not been very good at generating names for such large numbers—an undeveloped language compared to Vedic that has separate terms for each of them. Powers of ten would be needed in any case if we were to describe the large numbers introduced by the ancient Jainas, that went up to 10^{23}, or the Buddhists and the Ramayana, each going up to 10^{60}.

The patron has not completed his recitation and adds another round with a variation:

> May these bricks, O Agni, be milch cows for me, sixty, a thousand, ten thousand, unperishing (Taittirīya Saṃhitā 4.4.11 p.)

The large numbers that occur in Vedic have nothing to do with the universe. They belong to mathematics; and might in contemporary terms be interpreted as a manifestation of corporate greed. The mysterious sixty is put in context in the section on Vedic mathematics in Chapter **14** (*pages* 270–71). The non-Vedic numbers refer to years that measure the age of the cosmos; and express its immense size.

A few pages ago we came across quarters or four-somes such as 'four oblations' and 'four feet'. These will also be put in context in the section on Vedic mathematics. The majority of Brāhmaṇa interpretations wander around without arriving at a conclusion. The *yajus* recitation 'Agni light, . . . light Agni . . .,' has a technical name: *puroruc*, literally 'light in front'. The Brāhmaṇa interprets:

> Now, the *puroruc* is he yonder who gives out light (i.e., the sun; for he shines in front). Now the *puroruc* is the vital breath, the words, the body or the person himself. (Or) the *puroruc* is the body, the words offspring and cattle.

Other Brāhmaṇas are similarly rambling. A few interpretations are straightforward, some obvious and many trite. The large majority appear to be entirely arbitrary. The simple truth is that there is little that the Brāhmaṇas do *not* say. It explains their continued fascination for those who wish to prove a point by invoking an ancient authority.

If all that is true there must also be much or at least something in the Brāhmaṇas that is valuable and valid. There is indeed, but it must be ferretted out. Unintended as such by the composers, there is information about ancient

India, its inhabitants, society, history and other matters of fact. Here is an illustration, beginning with the Mantras:

MANTRAS (Taittirīya Saṃhitā 1.5.10.3)

O Agni, lord of vows, I shall perform this vow; may
I accomplish it; may it be successful for me.
Agni, the priest, I summon here.
The gods who are worthy of ritual, whom we invoke,
Let these gods come in kindly mind.
Let these gods enjoy this oblation of me.

BRĀHMAṆA (Taittirīya Saṃhitā 1.6.7.2–3)

He takes fire; he appropriates the gods in their own abode; to them he sacrifices when the next day comes. When about to undertake a vow, he should say: 'O Agni, lord of vows, I shall perform this vow.' Agni is the lord of vows among the gods; therefore, after announcing it to him, he undertakes his vow. At full moon he undertakes his vow with the spreading of grass, at new moon by driving the calves away, for that is their abode.

People say that the fires, in front and at the back, must be covered; men indeed desire what is covered with grass, how much more the gods whose dwellings are new. The gods dwell with him who peforms the rites on the next day, who knowingly covers the fire. People say that the ritualist should take animals both domesticated and wild. If he desists from eating domestic animals they increase in number; wild

> animals are only useful if eaten (?). If he were to fast without eating, the ancestors would be his divinity. If he eats wild animals, he bestowes their power upon himself. If he were to fast without eating, he would be hungry; if he were to eat, Rudra would plan evil against his cattle. If he partakes of water, it is neither eaten nor not eaten; and Rudra would not do evil to his cattle. The ritual is a thunderbolt, the enemy of man is hunger. If he fasts without eating, he immediately slays with that thunderbolt the enemy which is hunger.

The commentary declares that the gods should enjoy the oblations, because they can be eaten and there is hunger. Not edifying messages perhaps to us, but they show that also in Vedic times, many were hungry. Perhaps the composers of these lines were the first poor brahman priests—a topos of Sanskrit literature—speaking the Vedic language that had become the language of many. It tells us something about life in the Ganges Valley during the period of Middle and Late Vedic, that is from roughly 1000 to 450 BCE.

We have completed our survey of *three* Vedas. There are good reasons for keeping them together. The Rigveda is the first and most ancient. It incorporated local elements, but was a fresh apparition on the Indic scene. Largely composed within the subcontinent, it included features from elsewhere such as its language and all that it entailed. The Sāmaveda refers to the Rigveda but was an indigenous priestly tradition with its own language or languages as well as ritual structures. It incorporated verse from the Rigveda and inherited a few names from the BMAC. We know virtually nothing about its origins. The Yajurveda refers to Rig- (RV) and Sāmaveda (SV) both. It incorporated RV verse and SV chants in its ritual framework that may have developed from other rites and prototypes about which we know nothing except that there are links with the BMAC. The Yajurveda was the *locus* of the concept and the edifice of the Vedic schools as depicted by Table I (*pages* 80–1), which was adopted by the other two Vedas. 'The Three Vedas' are still the only ones mentioned in Buddhist texts and in the law code of Manu (second century CE). Four Vedas are mentioned in the Mahabharata epic and in later literatures. They include the Fourth or Atharva Veda to which we shall now turn.

EIGHT

~

ATHARVAVEDA

The Atharvaveda consists in its entirety of poetry and therefore, in the Kuru terminology, of Mantras. It survives in two schools. The earliest is the Paippalāda, called after its teacher Pippalāda whose name is derived from *pippala*, the sacred fig tree, *Ficus religiosa*. Some compositions of this school remind us of the Rigveda, but they are in linguistically younger forms, refer to the Kuru kings and their origins lie in the Kuru region. The second school, Śaunaka, arose a little later and further east in the land of the Pañcālas. It is less similar to the Rigveda. The composer-priests were Āṅgirasas and Bhārgavas, sometimes excluded from the 'Three Vedas' into which they were officially incorporated when the 'Four Vedas' were established. All of it combines to show that the Atharvaveda consists of early compositions that developed on their own and were incorporated in the edifice of the Three Vedas to turn it into Four.

We shall see in the next chapter that the main varieties of Vedic ritual are the *gṛhya* 'domestic' ritual and the *śrauta* ritual which is less easy to explain. The Atharvaveda consists chiefly of sorcery invocations (black and white magic), speculative or mystical poetry, fragments of *gṛhya* 'domestic' and royal ritual, as well as more specific compositions such as those that are linked to the arts of healing. It was originally excluded from the *śrauta* ritual.

I shall not be able to do full justice to the Atharvaveda, which continues to be a specialized subject within Vedic studies. It illustrates an attractive feature of these studies that deserves to be known by anyone interested in the study of human civilization: it is still possible to make important fresh discoveries in the field of Vedic traditions and open up new avenues of inquiry.

In 1957, Durgamohan Bhattacharyya made an 'Announcement of a Rare Find': the discovery among Orissa brahmans of palm-leaf manuscripts of the Paippalāda recension of the Atharvaveda of which parts had been available only in a single and notoriously corrupt manuscript from Kashmir. These were spectacular finds and it took the few people, who were able to make use of them, much time and work to make them accessible to the outside world. Durgamohan published one large volume in 1970 and his son Dipak Bhattacharya another in 1997. In the mean time, others went to Orissa in search of more. They include C.G. Kashikar of Poona, Michael Witzel of Harvard and Arlo Griffiths of Leiden.

Here is Griffith's translation, done together with Alexander Lubotsky, of a poem that illustrates the importance of the Atharvaveda for the study of Indian medicine (Paippalāda Saṃhitā 4: 15). It deals with the healing of an open fracture with the help of a plant. The translation is literal and supplies within square brackets additional clarifications:

1. Let marrow be put together with marrow, and your joint together with joint, together what of your flesh has fallen apart, together sinew and together your bone.

2. Let marrow come together with marrow, let bone grow over [together] with bone. We put together your sinew with sinew, let skin grow with skin.
3. Let hair be put together with hair. [The Rohiṇī-plant] shall fit together skin with skin. Let your blood grow with blood; let flesh grow with flesh.
4. Grower [are you], healer, grower of the broken bone. You are born on the Rohiṇī-day, you are grower, o plant.
5. If broken, if inflamed is your own bone, your flesh, Dhātar shall fix it whole, he shall put together joint with joint.
6. If a thunderbolt that has been hurled has hit you, or if there is an injury due to falling into a well (?), or one that is there [due to falling] from a tree: the ten-headed one shall remove [it]. I put together your joint as Ṛbhu [the parts] of a chariot.
7. Stand up, go forth, your joint has been put together. Let Dhātar put together the injury of your body. Be steady in this way, as a chariot goes with good wheels, with good felloes, with good axle-holes, with good naves.

Many references call for a further explanation. Rohiṇī, a red cow, is also a plant and the name of the Rauhiṇa day of the lunar calendar. Dhātar, the arranger, is a creator, not in the monotheistic sense but one of several architects or fashioners of the universe or some of its regions, similar to the *demiurge* of the ancient Greeks. The Ṛbhus are a group of divinities and Ṛbhu is a builder of chariots, patron deity of the Rathakāra of Chapter 3. One question about this poem is to what extent its recitation may have been accompanied by actual surgery—a question that touches the heart of Vedic studies: to what extent are mantras, that often *accompany* activity, meant to *replace* it?

A different hymn (Paippalāda Saṃhitā 6: 14) is directed at various noxious creatures and is replete with even more unsolved puzzles. Yet, or precisely because of them, it is worth quoting. Here it is, as translated by Griffiths in his forthcoming edition, uncertainties and all:

1. The one with a large neck, born from dung, the one which is not a proper offering, eating bowel-contents—and the *koka*-faced Lip (?): these we cause to vanish from here.
2. The dark-toothed Splitter, the snake-nosed Striker, the Approacher (?) *balāhaka*, the *khela* that brays like an ass, the vulture that moves like an elephant: these do we cause to vanish from here.
3. The Grabber that eats what must be groped for, the Groper with a horrible hand, the Shuddering-eyed One with soft fingers, the Nail-strong One with force in the teeth: these do we cause to vanish from here.
4. The constantly approaching . . ., the phantom that tries to win (food); and also the slimy one with quills: these do we cause to vanish from here.
5. The Beater with a snout in front—the *alimṣa* and the *vatsapa*; the Slipping one whose knot is as [tight as] that of a cord—the one belonging to the jungle, and the one belonging to *armas*: these do we cause to vanish from here.
6. The knee-hairy Asurian demon that roams here, that

seeks out the absent-minded one; the Arāyas that are . . ., that are . . ., and on the hair, the ones that are *Śvakiṣkin*: these do we cause to vanish from here.

7. The Asurian fiend who eats a man's young boys, the hairy, dreadful Arāya who slays and eats men: him do we cause to vanish from here.
8. The one of the Arāyas, called Vein-eyed, who is in the house, killing where the sun does not reach: him do we cause to vanish from here.
9. The chewing, robbing Vitūla, and the ever climbing (?) Forest-Shriek(er); the eater of raw [flesh], that seeks out the absent-minded [person]; the one running around, wet all over; the deep howling of a wolf: these do we cause to vanish from here.

The unexpected discovery of these Paippalāda hymns focused attention on another surprising fact: manuscripts written in the Oriya script had hardly ever been used in Vedic Studies before. That has not been true with respect to other Indic so-called 'vernacular' scripts. Many important Vedic manuscripts from South India, written in Grantha or Malayalam, have been known for almost two centuries.

The Atharvaveda provides much information on ritual, especially domestic. Connections with the Śrauta ritual, from which it was originally excluded, are less firm. Speculations on ritual and ritual interpretations remind us of the Brāhmaṇas, but they occur in verse form. The Atharvaveda knows *rig*, *sāman* and *yajus*, the latter in a form that seems closest to the Taittirīya Yajurveda. It evinces wide knowledge of the Sāmaveda and some of its technicalities. There is specific information on how to chant *stuti*s. The principal composers of the Atharvaveda were closely related to chanters of *sāman*s as Stanley Insler has shown. Perhaps some precursors of Atharvavedins knew a form of Sāmaveda that was not yet entirely pervaded by the language of the Rigveda.

There is one topic left that may belong to the realm of the Atharvaveda though it is only known from post-Vedic sources.

The Thesis of Kautsa

One much neglected thinker probably belonged to the Atharvaveda school of Śaunaka: Kautsa. The name is uncommon but not unknown. An early treatise on phonetics and phonology of the Śaunaka school is sometimes referred to as 'Kautsa's Grammar'. It is available in a recent critical edition with translation into English and extensive notes by Madhav Deshpande. The same name is associated with a work that has been lost but that presented a thesis that is well known. It has been much maligned but plays a major role in the history of ideas. In our present context, it occupies a special place: for as I am winding up my account of the four Vedas, we are approaching a more analytical treatment of some of the facts that have been assembled and the author of the thesis combined a vast knowledge of linguistics and mantras with an analytical mind.

The second Kautsa was a grammarian-cum-ritualist and keenly aware of the *difference* between language and mantras. His thesis was that, unlike language, of which meaning is the defining characteristic, 'mantras are without meaning': *anarthakā mantrāḥ*. Kautsa may have articulated these views during the period of the middle Upaniṣads, say, around the fifth or fourth century BCE. It could be the same date as that of the Kautsa Grammar of the Śaunaka school though the latter does not even contain the term *mantra* and there are no indications, as far as I know, that the two Kautsas were the same. The name has an ominous ring. Though it is directly derived from Kutsa, the name of a seer, it is ultimately derived from a verb *kuts-* which means 'despise' or 'revile'. Not to encourage prejudice, I shall call him 'Kautsa'.

The period I mentioned was a revolutionary period during which many radically new perspectives were voiced. The second Kautsa was a revolutionary, but unlike many Upaniṣadic sages, he gave reasons for his views. It reflects his background, training and familiarity with early stages of Indic linguistics as well as the Rigveda.

It is not surprising that Kautsa works have been lost. Fortunately, some of his arguments have been preserved by his main critics in two different sources: the Nirukta, a treatise on etymology that is still assigned to the Vedas as a special science, and the Sūtra manual of the Mīmāṃsā school of ritual philosophy, composed some two centuries later, around the second century BCE.

It is unfortunate that all our information on Kautsa comes from opponents, but it is counterbalanced by an attractive feature of Sanskrit philosophical and scientific works: it is not uncommon for authors to provide fair summaries of their opponents' theses. This commendable habit need not be entirely due to fairness: at the time of the earliest preserved opponents, the composers of the Nirukta, Kautsa works may have still have been around in the Oral Tradition. It would narrow down their own date to roughly the fourth century BCE, sealing off the Vedic period.

According to the Nirukta, Kautsa provided six arguments for his thesis, each except the first accompanied by two or more illustrations from the Rigveda. The manual of the Mīmāṃsā quotes a few others without referring to Kautsa explicitly. I shall mention the most perspicuous and give the clearest examples I can find, sometimes from a commentator:

1. In the Veda, the order of words may not be changed as is generally the case in Vedic or Sanskrit which are languages in which word order is basically free: since the inflected endings of the words convey their function, changing the order of words does not affect the meaning. It is different in the case of mantras: *agna āyāhi vītaye* (*page* 108) may not be replaced by *āyāhi vītaye 'gne* (with a difference due to sandhi) though both mean exactly the same: 'O Agni, come to the feast!'
2. The *sound* of the mantras may not be changed: words may not be replaced by synonyms, other words that mean the same as is common in ordinary language: the mantra *agni āyāhi vītaye* may not be replaced by *vibhāvaso āgaccha pānāya* 'O fire god, proceed to the drinking!'
3. Vedic mantras sometimes address inanimate objects such as stones or herbs, or things that do not exist,

e.g., a being with four horns, three feet, two heads and seven hands.
4. If mantras were meaningful, it would have to be admitted that they sometimes contradict each other: one mantra asserts that there is only one Rudra, there never was a second, and another refers to 'the innumerable thousands of Rudras'.
5. There is a tradition for mantras to be learnt by heart, but no corresponding tradition to teach and thereby preserve their meaning.

Since ordinary language exists for the sake of conveying meaning, Kautsa concluded that mantras are unlike the statements of ordinary language. This should not be interpreted as a form of scepticism or positivism. It is a purely ritualistic stance that limits mantras to their ritual use just as language is for the sake of meaning. Since the *Śrauta* ritual of the Yajurveda is performed for its own sake, it would be anachronistic to interpret Kautsa's views in terms of later views, such as the more philosophic Upaniṣadic or Buddhist emphasis on knowledge (*jñāna*) or wisdom (*prajñā*) as a means toward enlightenment, or the more religious preaching of loving devotion of the later bhakti cults in which the soul is lifted up by the grace of a personal divinity. Even India's greatest philosopher, Śaṇkara, an unquestioned follower of the Upaniṣads, quotes with approval a brāhmaṇa that declares: 'he who teaches a mantra or officiates at a ritual with mantras without knowing their composer-seer, metre, deity and brāhmaṇa, will run his head against a pole or fall into a pit.' In this list of requirements, Śaṇkara does not include knowledge or meaning: all he demands are formal data transmitted together with recitations. The triplet deity-composer-metre consists of recited names, as we have seen in Chapter 3. The brāhmaṇa itself is another recitation.

In Indic usage, mantras are meaningless from which it follows that they cannot be true or false. In modern English, 'mantra' is used in a different manner: it refers to a statement that is not meaningless but hollow, false and cynical. If an editorial in the *International Herald Tribune* says about the Bush administration's statement 'the economy is strong and getting stronger' that it is a mantra, it means that it is a lie and that the opposite is true. In another respect, English and Indic mantras are the same: they are effective if and only if they are repeated incessantly.

With the Atharvaveda we seem to have come to the end of our survey of the four Vedas. We have seen that the Atharvaveda stood apart from the others though there are undoubted links; and that it probably gave rise to a philosophical thesis that affects the heart of the Veda. But we have not really come to the end. A glance at the table on *pages* 80–81 demonstrates that we have so far mainly treated the Vedic Saṃhitā sections which constitute the core and are the oldest parts of the collections. There are several other important categories of Vedic works, including the Brāhmaṇas, Āraṇyakas and Upaniṣads. We have looked at Brāhmaṇas of the Yajurveda because they are sometimes mixed with Mantra Sections, but there are Brāhmaṇas elsewhere. They will be combined with the Āraṇyakas and discussed in Chapter 9. The Upaniṣads are the topic of

Chapter 10 but their list is open: Table 1 shows two names of Upaniṣads under the category of the Atharvaveda that are followed by 'etc.'. Some other Vedic and many post-Vedic Upaniṣads that were looking for a home have been artificially attached to the Atharvaveda. The one remaining category of the Table, the Śrauta Sūtras, are the topic of Chapter 12.

NINE

~

BRĀHMAṆAS AND ĀRAṆYAKAS

Villages, Forests and the Ecology

In Chapter 1 I have referred to a hypothetical period of 9,000 years during which the indigenous lineages of the subcontinent of South Asia remained widespread in both tribal and caste populations. Whether it was actually 9,000 years or more or less is irrelevant from our Vedic point of view. Other facts are more significant in our present context: Chapter 3 showed that caste was assigned to the Vedas by a post-Vedic and caste-obsessed society. Sedentary villages, on the other hand, pre-dated the Vedas. One such village with a history of some 5,000 years is well-known: the Neolithic village of Mehrgarh (Frontispiece, near 8).

The civilization of the Brāhmaṇas and Āraṇyakas or 'Forest Books' is certainly sedentary but illustrates at the same time that *forest* continued to be contrasted with *village*. Chapter 6 showed that the Sāmaveda distinguished, probably at an earlier period, between songs sung in the village and the more powerful and secret chants that were reserved for the forest or wilderness. It supplemented Chapter 3 which had detailed the interesting history in Vedic of the modern term for village, *grāma*: its meanings ranged from 'trains of herdsmen' to its modern denotation. As for *araṇya*, it was a frightening place and replete with power: hence 'wilderness' as well as 'forest'. Vedic has also an intermediate term, *vana,* which refers to 'woods' where villagers went to collect wood along with herbs and medicinal plants. The *araṇya*, forest and wilderness as well as desert, was further away. What we call cities and states (*nagara*) do not seem to have come into being before the early Upaniṣads, in the Ganges valley, sixth to fourth centuries BCE.

Speaking of forests, deforestation has always been around the corner. Deforestation by fire may have started soon after its discovery. Copper and bronze appeared in due course but it took a few thousand years for them to be replaced by iron, between 1,000 and 500 BCE. Now strong weapons and tools assisted fire in clearing forests north of the Ganges. A well-known story of the Śatapatha Brāhmaṇa depicts Agni setting a path of flames going from west to east. He could not cross the Sadānīrā (*nīra*, a word for river from Dravidian) which is now called Gaṇḍak (a Munda word, like perhaps Gaṇgā itself), and the other side (Videha, Sanskrit 'without body') was regarded as inferior and uncultivated though it is likely that flourishing cultures existed. Not long thereafter, Vedas were composed there, including the Śatapatha Brāhmaṇa itself. All these transitions were accompanied by conceptual changes. The Śatapatha exists in two versions as the Table of *pages* 80–81 showed. 'Breath' (*prāṇa*), still preponderant in the Mādhyaṇdina recension, is replaced by *brahma* in the other, the Kāṇva recension.

New ideas appear when people cross mountains and rivers, meet others and begin to settle down.

Brāhmaṇas and Āraṇyakas

We have seen that the term *Brāhmaṇa* is used in several senses. The meaning with which we are concerned in this chapter is one of them: a Vedic composition in prose. In the Yajurveda, that composition is mainly concerned with interpretations of mantras in ritual terms. In the Rig-, Sāma- and Atharva-Vedas, a Brāhmaṇa is more like a separate unit—what we have in mind when we think of a 'book'. But all these compositions continue to be oral and orally transmitted, sometimes with the old accents. To be a composer one now had to be not only a ritual expert, preferably a priest, but also a scholar, familiar with the tradition. No wonder that such people were called *Brāhmaṇa*. They were no longer sages, they were specialists who composed Brāhmaṇas or pieces thereof, and liked to be the advisers of rulers or chieftains. In all these capacities, being specialists did not prevent them from holding forth about anything that took their fancy. Like authors of successful books, they could count on an audience. They are in many respects like *authors*, only they did not write; but they expressed their opinions forcefully, putting themselves in their compositions, and they became *authorities*. That is what brahmins, as I may now call them, always remained, in India as elsewhere where we find them during the post-Vedic periods. Khmer, Javanese, Balinese, Thai and other brahmans remained ritual experts and advisors to rulers or chieftains.

In the Black Yajurveda, the Brāhmaṇas that these *brāhmaṇa* authorities composed, were still relatively closely attached to the poetry, now called Mantra, which they interpreted in ritual terms. But what they say is meant or intended there, has often nothing to do with the Mantras they followed. We have already met with these Brāhmaṇas in Chapter 7 on the Yajurveda. I shall not repeat any of this here but *pages* 125–6 would fit in the present chapter precisely at this spot.

The White Yajurveda, a reform movement, returned to the structure of the Rigveda: it consists in its entirety of verse. So does the Atharvaveda, and the Sāmaveda in a similar manner but here the verse are chants. Āraṇyakas which are 'Forest' or 'Wilderness' compositions are the final parts of Brāhmaṇas or attached to them in the Yajurveda. In the Rigveda they are transmitted as separate compositions.

If we look at Table 1 on pp. 80–81, these differences are expressed as follows. In the Rig-, Sāma-, Atharva- and White Yajurveda, Saṃhitā and Brāhmaṇa are distinct and have different names. In the Black Yajurveda, there is one continuous series of compositions that starts with sequences of Mantras and Brāhmaṇas and to which Āraṇyakas and even Upaniṣads are attached. Āraṇyakas occur in the White Yajurveda also but are attached to the Śatapatha Brāhmaṇa. This includes the Bṛhad-Āraṇyaka Upaniṣad which is an Āraṇyaka as its name says. The only other Āraṇyakas are listed under Rigveda where they belong.

So much for the forms. What about the contents? I have already alluded to the fact that almost anything may be put in a Brāhmaṇa. That applies to the Āraṇyakas as well. In the Yajurveda chapter, I heaped much adverse comment on both 'literary' genres—if that is what they are. Although both contain valuable information and insights, the modern student has to ferret them out. 'Ferreting' does not imply that we impose extraneous criteria on a composition that is constructed in accordance with a well-thought-out scheme; for that is not what the Brāhmaṇas and Āraṇyakas are. They are large depositories of interpretations, comments and observations that sometimes follow the order of ritual proceedings, elsewhere interrupt their course and shift to other rites or reflections on an almost unlimited range of topics. They are mixed or put together with etymologies, stories, speculations, and a great deal of what we may call magic but is better, more truthfully and less condescendingly or insultingly described as simple superstition. It is the kind of thing with which authorities can get away.

We need not accept 'multiculturalism', but should we not be charitable? We should be, but there is a limit even to charity. We do need to distinguish between valuable and valueless; without this nothing has any value and 'discovering' or 'analysing' is idle. From that point of view the two large Brāhmaṇas of the Rigveda are the most attractive. Most suspect is the Śatapatha Brāhmaṇa, 'Brāhmaṇa of the Hundred Paths' of the White Yajurveda, a veritable encyclopedia of meandering opinions on ritual and other matters. A simple example is its discussion of the term *upāṃśu* in the sense of 'indistinct' (rather than the more technical 'articulate but inaudible' to which we return in Chapter 15). The Śatapatha regarded it as the appropriate form of invocation when addressing the 'ineffable' (*anirukta*) creator god Prajāpati, 'Lord of Creatures'. The Brāhmaṇa declares that the indistinct is appropriate to Prajāpati 'because the indistinct is the ineffable, the ineffable is the whole and Prajāpati is the whole world.' Why does it not make sense? Because it is parallel to a declaration that is palpably absurd: 'blue is green because everything is green and cheese is everything.'

The Śatapatha is one of the largest Brāhmaṇas, accessible through the five volumes of Eggeling's translation into English that was published in the *Sacred Books of the East* between 1882 and 1897 and has been reprinted often. It continues to enjoy great popularity because of its availability and because it contains enough material to support *any* theory.

Eggeling must have spent a good part of his life translating the Śatapatha Brāhmaṇa. He speaks with authority, therefore, when he declares in the third sentence of his Introduction to the first volume:

> For wearisome prolixity of exposition, characterized by a flimsy symbolism rather than by serious reasoning, these works are perhaps not equalled anywhere; unless, indeed, it be by the speculative vapourings of the Gnostics . . .

The Gnostics were a variety of Christian and non-Christian teachings, written in Greek during the first centuries CE in the Near East.

Keith and other translators of the second half of the ninenteenth century and the beginning decades of the twentieth agree with these harsh judgements and so do I as the reader will have noted. Some Vedic scholars have subsequently tuned down the purple prose to a watery rose. Jan Gonda, author of roughly a hundred volumes on Vedic and related matters, has tried to place the facts in a wider context of an ethnography that is now rather dated, but without expressing similar feelings of distaste. Should we or should we not be charitable?

We should take our sources seriously, for to do otherwise is merely an insult to the composers. The difficulty is that they make no sense as a statement in language, whether it is Vedic or English. For a statement to make sense it must obey the minimum of logic that lies at the core of every human language. Children are at first unaware of it, but it is already part of their mental structure. They become conscious of and familiar with it when they pick up a language. If a mother says to her child, in any language: 'blue is green because everything is green and cheese is everything,' the child asks: 'What do you mean, Mama?'

It is in that same spirit that we must ask the same question from the Brāhmaṇas, Āraṇyakas and Upaniṣads.

Locating Obscurities, Esotericism and Irrationalities

Parokṣakāmā hi devāḥ: 'The gods love what is out of sight!'

I don't know what the gods love, but we have to widen our perspective if we wish to understand, not only who were the brāhmaṇa authors of these early prose compositions of the Veda and to what kind of society they belonged, but what was in their minds insofar as it is distinct from what is in our own. Some people say: we cannot know, and stop there. I say: we must explore the unknown. This implies that we must begin to tolerate uncertainty. We want to find out what our Brāhmaṇa composers know but we are also aware that they do not know what we know. One thing we find is that they had different ideas about *conveying* knowledge.

The composers of the Rigveda initially composed for family or clan members. That is why much remains obscure to us, as it would be to other outsiders—but that was not the special intention of the creators. The audience they had in mind was their natural sounding board. When we come to the Brāhmaṇas and Āraṇyakas, the audience as well as the contexts have changed. It is clearly visible in the Śatapatha Brāhmaṇa. We can speak here of esotericism or the keeping of secret doctrines. But what is secret here? Should we remain satisfied that it remains 'out of sight?'

Some of it we can only understand too well. The mystic equivalences we find in the Brāhmaṇas and Upaniṣads, referred to as *bandhu*, are often connected with pseudo-etymologies and sometimes it is enough for them to share a sound (e.g., the consonant *p* as in *puroruc* is *prāṇa*, 'vital breath'). They may be based on loose semantics, as in the Śatapatha's repeated declarations: 'Ritual is language' or 'Ritual is man.' They are explained by fancy reasons that point at existing connections which do not, however, establish that the two members are *identical*. Thus, 'Ritual is language' is explained by saying that utterances of language accompany ritual; and 'Ritual is man' by explaining that ritual measurements are based upon the size of the ritual patron. But ritual is neither and what is gained by spreading confusion? It may keep outsiders out and insiders in which is where they already are. Since they perform no other function and there is neither content nor literary flavour in any of these games, they can only be described as puerile.

I am not saying that the authors of these nonsensical phrases are stupid. They know the intricacies of ritual—a complex topic—and the grammatical rules and properties of their language. As for irrationalities, these are common worldwide and possess a certain straightforwardness. They are ultimately reduceable to contradictions of the form, '*A is not–A*.' They make no sense and do not convey anything because the function of the particle *not* is to deny what follows and one cannot at the same time affirm and deny in the same respct. Contradictory knowledge is not knowledge. It is another way of saying that Brāhmaṇas are not veda.

Rational insight is a rare commodity compared to the vast universe of irrationalities that people and language produce. Knowledge, therefore, is the ferreting out of what is of value. This was clearly explained by Āryabhaṭa, the greatest Indic mathematician before Srinivasa Ramanujan, who described one of his discoveries as 'a precious sunken jewel from the ocean of true and false knowledge'. Al-Bīrūnī, equally great as a scientist and also a student of Indic civilization, characterized Indic science in similar terms as 'a mixture of pearl shells and sour dates, or of pearls and dung, or of costly crystal and common pebbles'. Since he was a Muslim and outsider, his statement caused irritation and even anger though it is essentially the same as Āryabhaṭa's. A similar statement, even more colourful is due to Johannes Keppler, scientist and mystic:

No one should regard it as incredible that out of the nonsense and godlessness of astrology,
not a useful thought or insight,
out of dirty slime, not something edible for a snail, mussel, oyster or eel,
out of a big heap spun by caterpillars not a spider,
and finally out of a stinking pile of excrement, by an industrious chicken
not something, a good grain, even a pearl or gold pellet, can be extracted and found.

It looks as if Keppler knew, or would have loved to know, that the lotus is born from mud (*paṇkaja*). If his verdict applies to the history of science, should we expect the bulky Brāhmaṇas to be excluded? They are not and it is time for us to look for gold pellets.

The Rigvedic Aitareya Brāhmaṇa (AB) is the earliest source that is explicit about the Sarasvatī river 'ending in the desert'. As we have seen at the beginning of Part I, the Rigveda called it Sarasvatī after a river their ancestors or predecessors had encountered earlier: the *Harax'aitî*. Both names mean 'provided with ponds'. and refer to two rivers that ended in the desert. The AB knew this because it was familiar with Sind which the Rigveda was not. The same information is found in other Brāhmaṇas, such as the Jaiminīya and the Pañcaviṃśa of the Sāmaveda, which add details on rituals performed on the very spot where the river disappeared in the sand.

On a different level, the AB provides valuable pearls in its description of some of the details of Vedic pronunciation. These include a first discussion of the concept of *upāṃśu* and reflections of phonetics and phonology that pertain not only to Vedic recitation, but to the emerging uses of the living language of spoken Sanskrit. They led to the *Prātiśākhya* treatises of the Vedic science of language, to Pāṇini's Sanskrit grammar and to modern linguistics as will be sketched later in Chapter **14**.

Other valid insights are hidden in the muddy contexts of the Aitareya Āraṇyaka (AA). We shall see in that same Chapter, that Śākalya separated the words of the Rigveda Saṃhitā from each other in his Padapāṭha. The AA was familiar with earlier terminologies that refer to these varieties. The AA also discussed nominal compounds such as the expression *pada-pāṭha*, 'recitations of words', itself; and the various relationships between its two members. The AA chronicles mythological views according to which the prior part of such compounds refers to earth, the later part to the heavens, and their Saṃhitā combination to the wind. Others argued that Saṃhitā is the space between heaven and earth. Whatever one may think of the speculations, they presuppose precise knowledge of *sandhi* or 'euphonic combination', syntax and the properties of nominal compounds.

The Kauṣītaki Brāhmaṇa of the Rigveda, commenting on the *puroruc* 'prior light' recital that precedes the recitation of a Rigvedic hymn, provides a bit of slime on which we almost slipped in Chapter 7 (*pages* 132–3). It is not contradictory but slimy because it is tantamount to saying: it may be A because of X, or perhaps B, or maybe C.

I conclude that there is much in the Vedic tradition that we do not know or understand. The same holds for the Brāhmaṇas and other Vedic prose, but with one difference: they did not want us to know. That makes trying to know more difficult, but still enables us to draw two conclusions that apply to both Vedic poetry and prose: (1) the composers might have known more than we do; and (2) there is no reason to believe that the smartest among us are smarter than the smartest among them.

TEN

~

UPANIṢADS

Generalities

The Vedic or Classical Upaniṣads are sometimes called Vedānta or 'End (*anta*) of the Veda'. The term occurs first after the end of the Vedic period, in the Muṇḍaka Upaniṣad (fourth to third centuries BCE?), when the Upaniṣads were looked upon as a separate group and it was felt that the ritualistic Veda had reached its 'end', the English word that is not only etymologically related to Sanskrit *anta* but has its same double connotation: the final portion of a thing, and also its goal, ultimate aim or destination. Not only aficionados of the Upaniṣads stress the latter meanings, they are the only ones that are acceptable because the composers of the Upaniṣads did not adopt a historical perspective. But the term Vedānta has an entirely different meaning also. It refers to a group of Indic philosophies that look at the Upaniṣads as their source of inspiration, not necessarily the only one. One of the earliest of these is the philosophy of Bhāskara who lived around 800 CE. Many of his works have been lost and he left no school. More or less contemporary with him is Śaṅkara, also a follower of the Upaniṣads, to whose theories Bhāskara made vitriolic references. But Śaṅkara eclipsed him and became the most famous philosopher of India. His Vedānta is called A-dvaita Vedānta because its position is 'non-dual'. Another Vedānta is the Viśiṣṭādvaita Vedānta of Rāmānujā (twelfth century CE) who defends a 'qualified non-dualism', yet another is the Dvaita Vedānta of Madhvācārya (thirteenth century CE) who accepts dualism. And there are others.

I recommend that the reader make a distinction between these later philosophies, all of whom invoke the Upaniṣads, and the Upaniṣads themselves; and take care not to interpret the latter solely or too strictly in terms of them. All such interpretations are anachronistic.

The term *upa-ni-ṣad* is derived from *sad-*, *ni* and *upa* which mean 'sit,' 'down' and 'close' (as in *upāṃśu: pages* 123–4), respectively. Most modern scholars have interpreted its changing meanings as referring to mystical hidden connections. But these were already a favoured topic of the Brāhmaṇas and Āraṇyakas, referred to by the Sanskrit term *bandhu*, which was widely used. I accept the traditional interpretation: 'sitting close (to the teacher)' and therefore: secret (*rahasya*). It is a one-to-one relationship. There are several reasons for this interpretation. The Upaniṣads are full of stories of students looking for teachers. Sitting is venerable, auspicious even, a topic on which I shall expatiate in Chapter **13**. Secrecy is the last remnant of the originally secret oral traditions of families and clans. There is one paradox: the Upaniṣads became the most famous part of the Vedas. Does it mean that if one keeps something secret, it will eventually become public? Given the obsession with exposing secrets (or scandals), the answer must be, yes.

The Upaniṣads are an open-ended class. There are more than a hundred of them. That includes the Saṃnyāsa Upaniṣads, a large group of so-called Minor Upaniṣads and the Allah Upaniṣad. If that Upaniṣad had been regarded as secret and had been canonized like the Classical Upaniṣads, it might not have been forgotten and could be invoked by Indians and Pakistanis, Muslims and Hindus, who are eager to improve relations.

We shall be confined to the Vedic or Classical Upaniṣads, a group of twelve or thirteen which are attached to Vedic schools as depicted on Table I.

The earliest are perhaps the Sāmaveda Upanisads which fit in the context of Chapter 6 for they are connected with chant and especially with OM. Their chronological layers continue to be discussed, but the most well known of them remains the Chāndogya Upaniṣad which may be assigned to the seventh or sixth century BCE and was composed in the Kuru-Pañcāla region. About equally old is the Bṛhad-Āraṇyaka Upaniṣad, the final sections of the Śatapatha Brāhmaṇa, largely composed much further east in Videha.

The two are similar in some respects; but the differences are remarkable in that they may have something to do with Buddhism, both with regard to contents and in terms of geography. The CU, with its emphasis on chanting, is more *positive* than the BĀU which emphasizes the *via negativa*, the negative path that culminates in the famous declaration *neti neti*, 'it is not this, it is not that.' That emphasis is a characteristic of Buddhism as we shall see in Chapter 16. It describes how the Buddha, born at the Himalayan foothills, close to the modern border between India and Nepal, made his way southward, crossing Videha until he reached the kingdom of Magadha with which we have been familiar since the map of Figure 2 where it is indicated by **Mg**. There is a historical gap of almost two centuries, but that large region of Videha is also where parts of the BĀU were composed. Is that negative path a characteristic of the eastern extremities of Vedic India? That thesis would be supported by geography and history for it would require a leap across at least one century during which the Taittirīya, Aitareya and Kauṣītaki Upaniṣads were composed. These five Upaniṣads, including CU (Chandogya Upaniṣad) and BĀU (Bṛhad-Āraṇyaka Upanisad) are almost certainly pre-Buddhist.

A striking feature of the early Upaniṣads is the tradition of public debates that took place at the court of a king. It is a step in the direction of what is nowadays called the public domain. Wandering sages, philosophers, women, naked ascetics, monks and others attended. Serious attention was paid to logical argumentation and who were the winners and losers. This feature earned the Upaniṣads the Greek or English label 'philosophy'.

The majority of these works, composed orally in classical Sanskrit, represent the perspective of Brāhmaṇas or brahmans, as we may now call them, on the one hand; and kings, princes or chieftains, referred to as *kṣatriya*, on the other. Such *kṣatriya–brāhmaṇa* alliances, often assigned to an earlier period, may have started only by this time. It is not merely a political alliance between knowledge and power: it signals the emergence of rulers who became famous as intellectual leaders. It does not imply, of course, that a caste system of three or four existed. *Jāti* and *varṇa* keep their Vedic sense.

The Upaniṣadic renaissance is part of a deeper and wider ferment in culture and society. Its significance has been overrated, but there is no doubt that it presents one of the basic cognitive and intellectual junctures in human history, and in that sense a culmination of the Vedic period. Apart from their language, the great contributions of that period have little that is 'Aryan' or 'Indo-Aryan' about them. Though presented as such in our Vedic sources, they are not confined to brahmins and kṣatriyas. We have to look behind and beyond them to find out more about other participants and contributors and strengthen what we find with supplementary information from other sources, e.g., the contemporary Jaina and the later Buddhist.

I shall illustrate the procedure with the help of the claim I made that participants in the public included 'wandering sages, philosophers, women, naked ascetics, monks and others'. The Upaniṣads refer mostly to the king and many brahmans as the active and creative participants in the debates. 'Brahmans' may be members of a class or, simply, learned men. Women participants are mentioned by name but there is no mention of 'naked ascetics and monks'. Why did I include them? Because they were a common feature of the period. They included the adherents of earlier religions or sects such as the Jaina and Ājīvika, as well as the later Buddhists, the only ones who did not go about naked. All these non-Vedic groups refer to brahmans, are familiar with their doctrines and adapt, adopt or criticize them. The non-Vedic groups are not explicitly mentioned in the Upaniṣads, because they were not Vedic which the Upaniṣads were.

All these facts are likelihoods, as empirical facts are bound to be, but we can gain strong confirmation of them by looking at *names*. About 300 words that occur in the Rigveda are not Indo-Aryan or Indo-European and come from elsewhere (Chapter **1**). Chapter **6** on Sāmaveda described how Rigvedic verse were set to melodies that belonged to an indigenous lineage that had long been settled and had its own language or languages. A closer look at the forest songs showed that some of the names in them are non-Indo-European and some have the structure of the reconstructed BMAC language as we have seen.

The Upaniṣadic descriptions of debates are similarly replete with names of sages that are non-Indo-European. Most important—because they refer to a more distant past—are names that occur in lineages at the end of some Upaniṣadic chapters. My impression of about sixty-five names at the end of the fourth chapter of the BĀU, starting with Pautimāṣya and ending with Brahman, is that almost half are non-Indo-European. Many look Indo-European but may not be. They may be Sanskritizations of non-Indo-European words like the term for brick in the BMAC language that became *iṣṭakā*, also discussed in Chapter **1**. There is enough material for a book that could make a valuable contribution provided it is written by a linguist who knows Vedic, Indo-European and is familiar with the general characteristics of other language families in Asia.

Other than language, there are social indications in the dialogues and debates of the Upaniṣads that demonstrate that their authors belonged to an open society in which people from different backgrounds came together. The crossing of boundaries started modestly. 'Different backgrounds' is perhaps an insufficient description of an important inclusion: that of women. I shall give two positive and one negative illustration, but the most important is the first because it points to the past: some of the lineages to which I just referred show that parts of the transmission were matrilineal (e.g., BĀU 6.5.1–3).

The other positive illustration does not apply to women in general but comes from Yājñavalkya who taught his greatest secret to his wife as we have seen at the outset of this book. He said to her: 'The two of us are like two halves of a block' (BĀU 1.4.3). But he meted out a different treatment to another woman, Gārgī, a descendant of Garga who composed a poem in the Rigveda, and was a great debater. She was called 'Vācaknavī', which means eloquent as well as loquacious and is also used for men. Gārgī asked Yājñavalkya a long series of questions starting with: 'Since this world is woven back and forth on water, on what, then, is water woven back and forth?' He answered 'air' whereupon Gārgī asked the same question with regard to the intermediate region—and so on it went with sun, moon, etc. Finally, Yājñavalkya says: 'Don't ask too many questions!' Gārgī fell silent, but after a few more exchanges, turned to the audience: 'Distinguished brahmins! You should consider yourself lucky if you escape from this man by merely paying him your respects. None of you will ever defeat him in a debate!'

The crossing of boundaries started modestly, as I mentioned, and the same applies to Vedas, Vedic schools and differences of age as at least one example illustrates.

Once king Janaka wished to perform a large ritual. He corralled a thousand cows. To the horns of each cow, ten pieces of gold were tied. Brahmans from Kuru and Pañcāla flocked to his court and he addressed them: 'Let the most learned man among you drive away these cows!' No one moved. So Yājñavalkya, a White Yajurvedin, called his pupil: 'Sāmaśravas! Son, drive these cows away!' He did, the Brahmins were furious and murmured: 'How dare he claim to be the most learned!' Sāmaśravas, 'Song Fame', was obviously a strapping young Sāmavedin.

The crossing of the brahman class line is illustrated by the story of Satyakāma,'Truth Loving' Jābāla. It is referred to several times in the CU and the BĀU and was obviously popular. 'S.J.,' as I shall call him, told his mother he wanted to become a Vedic student and asked for his lineage. His mother said:

> Son, I don't know what your lineage is. I was young when I had you. I was a maid then and had a lot of relationships. It is now impossible for me to say what your lineage is. But my name is Jabālā and your name is Satyakāma. So you should simply say that you are Satyakāma Jābāla.

S.J. went to a famous teacher and asked to be accepted as his student. The guru asked him for his lineage and S.J. repeated, word for word, what his mother had told him, adding at the end: 'So I am Satyakāma Jābāla, Sir.' The teacher said: 'Who but a brahman could speak like that!'

and accepted him. Why did he do it? Because *satyakāma* means 'lover of truth'. By accepting S.J., the teacher added fuel to two beliefs that imply each other: the belief that he accepted a brahman pupil and the belief of all brahmans that all brahmans always speak the truth—that is why they are wise men, not on account of birth.

It is clear that at the time of the Upaniṣads, the term 'brahman' was still a flexible term. It had neither genetic content, nor did it occupy a fixed place in a rigid system of classes let alone caste. It continued to be so in later times, not within the subcontinent, where the caste system hardened, but in different societies elsewhere. The brahmans of Southeast Asia had strong ties with the rulers, but were brahmans in a very loose sense.

The *Upaniṣads* as 'sitting down close' (*page* 160) of pupil and teacher were sometimes the outcome of a public debate where a famous thinker had been asked questions and dispensed answers. If the questioner was not satisfied with the answer, such a dialogue ensued.

Karma, Rebirth and Life after Death

The most celebrated Upaniṣadic speaker and philosopher was Yājñavalkya. The debate, recorded or imagined by the composer of the BĀU, took an unexpected turn when he was asked by Ārthabhāga what happens when a man dies. He took a number of steps and his first question was: Where does the breath of a dead person go? Yājñavalkya gave the kind of down-to-earth answer that is typical of him: 'His breaths do not depart of him. They accumulate within his body, causing it to swell and become bloated.' Many further questions follow, but they are not rebuffed as we shall see. Ārthabhāga asks where go speech, mind, hearing, body, self, hair, blood and semen when a man dies. Yājñavalkya provides answers to all those questions, but Ārthabhāga persists and asks: what happens to the person himself? Yājñavalkya replies: 'My friend, we cannot talk about this in public. Take my hand, Ārthabhāga; let's discuss this in private.' So they leave, and talk about it. What did Yājñavalkya and Ārthabhāga talk about? They talked about:

> Nothing but action (*karma*). And what did they praise?—they praised nothing but action. Yājñavalkya told him: 'A man turns into something good by good action (*puṇya karma*) and into something bad by bad action (*pāpa karma*).' Thereupon Ārthabhāga fell silent.

This famous passage touches not so much on secrecy as on the distinction between public and private. Unlike my earlier characterizations of the Upaniṣads, it is a step away from the public domain. The common translation 'in private' corresponds to *na sajana* in the original. It means literally 'not with people'. Vedic has *sa-jana* which simply means 'with people' or 'public'. Later Sanskrit has *vi-jana* which means 'without people' or 'private'. The Upaniṣadic words are correctly translated as 'in private'.

Why should these apparently innocent phrases not be

discussed in public? The question has been much discussed. Here are two samples, one classical and one modern.

Toward the close of the eighth century CE, the time of the great Pallava and early Chola temples and sculptures of South India, an explanation was given by Śaṅkara, the famous philosopher of the Advaita Vedānta. According to him, breath, speech, mind, blood, semen, etc., are rational topics of discussion. We may not agree with his subdivisions and explanations, but we accept that they are apt topics for a public debate. It could take place at a student society of a medical school. But the topic of Ārthabhāga's question is different, says Śaṅkara:

> Different schools have imagined or construed (the Sanskrit is: *parikalpitāni*) different answers, e.g., nature (the opinion of the Mīmāṃsā school, Śaṅkara's rival), chance (the materialists), time (astrologers), action (followers of the Vedas), gods (believers in gods), consciousness-only or emptiness (two Buddhist schools). When there are so many basic differences, determining the truth cannot simply be achieved by defeating the opponent (*jalpanyāya*).

Śaṅkara explains Yājñavalkya's insistence on privacy by arguing that it is concerned with a different kind of topic and therefore the usual methods cannot be applied. What then did they really talk about? Śaṅkara says: 'Having agreed on time, action and gods, they praised only good action which is enjoined by the tradition. Since bad is the opposite of good, it follows that the opposite holds for bad.' Śaṅkara's explanation, that these are matters of choice and not of logic, confirms that he was a Vedāntin or follower of the Vedic tradition. It is a flaw in a philosopher, magnified when attributed to an ancient sage, because the Vedānta is closer to a religion than to a philosophy; but that is not the point. It is a rational explanation for Yājñavalkya's insistence on privacy.

The only modern author, who has addressed the question, has offered a different but equally rational explanation: a famous anthropologist and original thinker, Gananath Obeyesekhere. In his book *Imagining Karma*, he has shown that among the world's eschatologies, *rebirth* is the default option. It occurs among Buddhists, Greeks, moderns and in small indigenous societies of West Africa, Melanesia and North America. But Obeyesekhere has another item on his agenda. He is concerned with showing that the Buddhist concept of rebirth is ethical because it employs the same terms, good action (*puṇya karma*) and bad action (*pāpa karma*), which he interprets as referring to 'religious merit' and 'sin', respectively. He attributes Yājñavalkya's desire for privacy to the fact, that knowledge of karma and rebirth was new to the Vedic tradition. That is far from obvious, but a discussion of this problem has not so far been undertaken. It shows that Vedic studies are still replete with unexplored treasures.

Traces of rebirth are found not only in the Rigveda, but are connected with a general belief expressed in many Indo-European sources, and elsewhere, that departed ancestors return as birds. In the Rigveda, these birds may take up a human body in the same family from which they departed before they became birds. The Brāhmaṇas take a different line: man is born first from parents, then through ritual, and a third time through the fire of cremation. In all these cases, ascension to the place of the ancestors is regarded as temporary which implies that rebirth is an option.

In the Sāmaveda, return to earth from the next world may be effected by chanting *stuti*s. The Tāṇḍya Mahābrāhmaṇa explains: 'Just as one, having climbed up to the top of a big tree, would get down by taking hold of branch after branch, so he gets down onto this earth by means of this arrangement of *stuti*s, in order that he may get a firm support' (translation Yasuke Ikari).

Quotations from the Sāmaveda may support Obeyesekhere's idea, that rebirth is not Vedic, if it is true, as I have argued, that the Sāmavedic chants belonged to an indigenous lineage. But the Rigveda itself and other Vedic sources have other relevant things to say.

Funeral mantras from the Rigveda allude to meetings with the ancestors through an entity called *iṣṭāpūrta*, the reward of the correct performance of ritual and good deeds: 'Unite with the ancestors, with death, with your *iṣṭāpūrta* in the highest heaven. Leaving behind all imperfections, come home again; merge with a (new) glorious body' (RV 10.14.8). Elsewhere, Agni is asked to treat the body, that has been burnt at the cremation, gently: 'Set him free to go back to the ancestors, Agni, when he freely wanders having been offered to you with the funeral meal. Dressed for a new life, he descends again to those who stayed behind. Let him merge with a new body, O Knower of Men!' (RV 10.16.5).

Apart from mantras, it is funeral rites that provide the most telling evidence. Yasuke Ikari had already drawn attention to one such rite that suggests that the grandfather is reborn as his great-grandson. Similar cases occur in a variety of cultures Obeyesekhere has discussed. The largest number of references to *iṣṭāpūrta* from a great variety of Vedic sources is provided by P.V. Kane in Vol. II, Part II of his *History of Dharmaśāstra*. We will need renewed study of Vedic funeral rites, neglected since Caland's pioneering monograph of 1896, reprinted in 1967. Many are still performed in corners of the subcontinent, in Gokarna, for example.

The two Rigvedic verses I have quoted belong to the late tenth circle—composed, say, around 1,100 BCE. Similar verse from the Atharvaveda may belong to a slightly later period. The lateness of the two verses may support Obeyesekhere.

I have kept for last the most widespread Vedic idea about karma as rebirth which requires less discussion because it is so well known. It operates with a cyclical concept of time and two paths, the path of the ancestors (*pitṛyāna*) and that of the gods (*devayāna*). Those who take the former, associated with the moon, return to earth. Those who take the latter, associated with the sun, do not return but go to the world of the gods.

I have gone far enough to show, that Gananath Obeyesekhere's book has opened up new vistas of which the end is not even in sight.

Karma, Jñāna and Bhakti

The Upaniṣads are not all like the famous dialogue between Yājñavalkya and Ārthabhāga. They continue from the Brāhmaṇas and Āraṇyakas and contain, therefore, the usual mixture of pearls and dung. A striking specimen of the latter is crisply formulated by the CU (1.3.3):

> The interval between exhalation and inhalation is suspended breath. Suspended breath is language.

I am not familiar with any theory of language that is more succinct than this. Armand Minard, the greatest expert of the Śatapatha Brāhmaṇa since Eggeling, paid it a kind of compliment which I translate from the French:

> If this passage assimilates phonation and suspended breath, it is not a sign of ignorance but an esotericism that moves within a circle of thought that is closed to vulgar knowledge even if it is scientific.

Minard does not give an example of a scientific insight from within that esoteric circle of thought, but the explanation lies undoubtedly in Sāmavedic chants and other similar recitations that have to be sung without taking breath. This is not easy as may be gathered from the transcriptions I have given in Chapter 6 which do not mark where breath is taken. I measured the length of the initial 'o' of several chants: the average is 18 seconds. During such an interval of suspended breath, I would have plenty of time to do some talking—more than enough to serve as a foundation for a succinct theory of language.

Fortunately, large sections of the Upaniṣads are pervaded by a current of fresh air that is different from anything found in earlier Vedic. The only exceptions, which sometimes surpass them, are the speculative poems of the late Rigveda. They were composed further west a few centuries before the earliest Upaniṣads.

If I were forced to generalize about the differences between the immediately preceding Brāhmaṇas and the Upaniṣads, I would say that *karma* or 'ritual' is to the Brāhmaṇas what *jñāna* or 'knowledge' is to the Upaniṣads. It does not contradict Yājñavalkya's praise of *karma* as moral activity so let me try to be a little bit more precise.

The term *karma* means many things. It always refers to some kind of activity but in the Brāhmaṇas it refers primarily to ritual activity. The Upaniṣads teach that humans are bound by ritual and freed by knowledge. The embarrassment with regard to mantras and ritual that we encountered in the previous chapter, gives way in the Upaniṣads to a radical denunciation of ritual and an impassioned plea for pure knowledge that confirms their *Vedic* nature and would be an adornment to any institute of higher learning.

My simplistic explanation of the distinction between Brāhmaṇas and Upaniṣads in terms of *karma* and *jñāna* is inspired by the Bhagavad Gītā (BG), which was itself inspired by the Upaniṣads. It is called an Upaniṣad in some of its colophons. BG belongs to the epic and is later than the Śvetāśvatara, one of the latest classical Upaniṣads. It would, therefore, be an anachronistic explanation. We have always treated anachronistic explanations with caution, but what exactly is wrong with them?

An anachronistic interpretation is often misleading because it neglects history. Anachronistic interpretations impose modern concepts on ancient ones that have nothing to do with them. To say of the chariot, on which the Aśvins travelled through space, that it was an airplane is a good example. It is based on errors of history, omissions and confusions. Constructing an airplane is based upon a technology that derives from the science of aerodynamics, a discipline that could develop only after Newton had created dynamics. He in turn could not have done so if he had not studied Euclidian geometry and his successors could not have made this effective unless the Arabs had introduced algebra to Europe.

Using the BG to interpret the difference between Brāhmaṇas and Upaniṣads is not as bad because composers of the Upaniṣads would at least understand it—though *bhakti*, to which I return, would be unfamiliar to earlier ones. So let us tread carefully and try to avoid pitfalls.

The BG is helpful because it puts *karma* and *jñāna* in the context of life and death with which everyone is familiar. Arjuna asks Shri Krishna whether he should fight or not. Yes, says Krishna, you must act, that means kill, but you should abandon the fruits of action (*karma-phala-tyāga*). The term *tyāga*, 'abandonment' reminds us of Vedic ritual where the patron says after each oblation: 'this is for Agni, not for me' (and similarly for other gods). It is a simple rite and the patron does not give up the fruits, but merely the ownership of the substance of his oblation. Outside ritual, abandonment of attachment to the fruits of action is difficult as Arjuna is about to discover. Shri Krishna helps him by placing his dilemma in a wider perspective. There are, he says, three 'ways': *karmayoga*, *jñānayoga* and *bhaktiyoga*.

About *karma* and *jñāna*, the Gītā says many different things. Discipline of action (*karma-yoga*) is better than renunciation of action (5.2). But knowledge is better than ritual (4.33), a statement that summarizes the message of the Upaniṣads and their reaction to the Brāhmaṇas and Āraṇyakas. The BG is not a philosophical treatise attempting consistency. It is a devotional work. But it is clear in the long run that it prefers to *karma* and *jñāna*, *bhakti* or 'loving devotion' which does not occur in the Vedas. *Bhakti* makes its first appearance in Upaniṣads such as the Śvetāśvatara and Muṇḍaka, probably composed during the last few centuries BCE. The Śvetāśvatara refers to the grace of god. It is a god who is 'higher than *Brahman*' and known as 'the Lord'. It also refers to 'one Rudra who has not tolerated a second' (recall that, in Chapter 8, Kautsa noted that this Vedic statement contradicts another). These theistic tendencies came to the fore in later Indic sects or religions and have always been predominant in the monotheistic religions of western Asia. The Rigveda contains nothing like it. It is hardly the same thing when the Bharadvājas, composers of the sixth circle say to Agni: 'You are our dear guest!'

The Gītā's juxtaposition of ritual and knowledge pays no attention to difficulties that philosophers have raised. The two paths are not easily compatible and *karma-phala-tyāga* is not the same as *jñāna*. Early Indic philosophies tried to find and analyse a similar synthesis which they called: *karma-jñāna-samuccaya*. It is a good point of departure for beginning students of Indian philosophy. Śaṅkara tried to solve the difficulty by declaring that *karma* and *jñāna* are intended for different classes of persons.

To illustrate the Upaniṣadic critique of ritual at its best we should not look at early Upaniṣads like the CU or BĀU, which display sparkling new ideas but conform elsewhere to the ritualism of the Brāhmaṇas and Āraṇyakas. Such Upaniṣads do not even go as far as a poet in the last circle of the Rigveda:

> You will not find him who has created
> Some obstacle is in your way.
> Enveloped by mists and stammering
> Taking life, the reciters wander.

Later Upaniṣads are more radical, e.g., the Muṇḍaka (with parallels in the Kaṭha and Maitri):

> Unsteady boats are these ritual forms, eighteen in number, in which the inferior karma is said to reside. The fools who delight in this ritual as the highest good go again and again through the cycle of old age and death. Abiding in the midst of ignorance, wise in their own estimate, fancying themselves to be learned but really obtuse, these fools go around in a circle like blind men led by the blind.

The Muṇḍaka is not only radical, it uses a more vernacular form of Sanskrit. That shows that it was popular, not that it was influenced by Jainism or Buddhism, traditions that were first expressed through the medium of a Middle-Indic language. All are critical of ritual, but the Upaniṣadic critique paves the way for *jñāna* and specifies what *jñāna* is knowledge *of*. *Jñāna* is *brahma-jñāna*, 'knowledge of the absolute,' the somewhat opaque but convenient English translation of a principle that holds the universe together. Other Upaniṣadic passages declare that that *brahman* is identical with our self (*ātman*) and that knowledge is its realization. The universe is one and we are part of it in our inner selves. The question is: how? Light is thrown on this question by a recent discovery.

'In That Way You Are'

We have encountered several meanings of brahman. It means sublime 'language' in the early Rigveda and the brahman priest is an officiant attached to the Atharvaveda. In the Upaniṣads, brahman is something entirely different. It cannot be easily defined and its frequent translation as 'absolute' does not contradict the fact that it must sometimes be translated as 'language'. The word *ātman* is even more intractable. Etymologically related to an Indo-European word for 'breath' (German *Athem*, Dutch *adem*), it is used in Vedic and Sanskrit as a reflexive pronoun for all three genders and persons, as in English: 'he did it himself', 'they went out by themselves', 'the book itself says so'. In English, one cannot say 'the self' just as one cannot say 'the we.' 'The I' is only used by philosophers (psychologists prefer 'the ego'). 'The self' and 'the Self' occur only in English writings on Indian philosophy.

A simple way of formulating the basic identity taught by the Upaniṣads is: 'I am Brahman' (*aham brahmāsmi*). That insight can only be obtained from a teacher and its oral transmission goes from person to person, not from an individual to a group. It is not obtained by listening to a lecture, let alone reading. It is not really *transmitted* because it arises in the pupil from within. It dawns upon him when he realizes its truth; and *realize* is the proper word because he realizes himself for which he does not need any evidence from outside. The teacher may have prompted it by a silent mantra or a snap of the finger.

The identity of ātman and brahman is expressed by similes, e.g., light. King Janaka asks Yājñavalkya what its source is. He answers: 'The sun, your Majesty, is the source of light. It is by the light of the sun that a persons sits down, goes about, does his work and returns.' Not satisfied, the king asks what happens when the sun sets. Yājñavalkya replaces sun by moon and repeats the same phrases. When sun and moon have set, the answer is fire, followed by voice in case the fire has gone out. When voice has stopped, 'The self is then his own source of light' followed by the same refrain. But unlike the knowledge of light, the knowledge of self has no specifics. It seems to answer our first question at the beginning of this book about what Yājñavalkya might have had in mind. But if there is no awareness of specifics, what does Yājñavalkya say?

Perhaps another teacher in another Upaniṣad gives the answer. Uddālaka Āruṇi instructs Śvetaketu in the CU (6.8–16). He tells him nine stories, each ending with the famous *Tattvamasi*. But its meaning has been misunderstood for two-and-a-half millennia—another example (after what I wrote about the Atharvaveda and Obeyesekhere's thesis) of a major new discovery in the field of Vedic studies. The customary translation of *Tattvamasi* is 'Thou Art That.' But in 1986, Joel Brereton pointed out that this interpretation is not in accordance with the rules of Vedic syntax which require that the neuter pronoun *tat* ('that') cannot refer to the masculine *tvam*, 'you' or 'Thou'. In Vedic, if you want to say 'You are that,' you must say: *sa tvam asi*. Since the only other relevant meanings of *tat* are 'in that way', 'therefore', or some such translation, *Tattvamasi Śvetaketu* must mean: 'In that way are you, Śvetaketu!'

Now the context. Uddālaka Āruṇi tries to explain a certain 'minuteness' (*aṇiman*). He returns to it nine times, each time starting with a different preliminary. One starts on the previous evening, when he asks his son to put some salt in a container of water and come back the next day. Next morning, he asks him to find the salt in the water but the son cannot find it.

'Now, take a sip from this corner,' says the father. 'How does it taste?'

'Salty.'

The father tells him to take a sip from the centre and

from another corner, and the son gives the same answers. Then follows the famous statement in its context which is made nine times: 'That which is this finest minuteness, that the whole world has as its self. That is the truth. That is the self. *Tat tvam asi.*'

I have followed Brereton's translation, replacing his 'finest essence' for *aṇiman* by the more literal: 'minuteness.' I thereby avoid the term 'essence', which in English means perfume but also substance, the equivalent of Sanskrit *dravya*, a loaded term in Indian as well as European philosophies, from Plato who exalted it to Heidegger and the existentialists who denounced it in discussions, none of them minute.

Could *Tat* refer to *aṇiman*? It cannot because that word has the masculine gender also. We are left with 'Therefore you are.' No one has challenged Brereton's interpretation, as far as I know. I can think of only one way one could do it. It is far-fetched but not out of the question because some of the great Upanisadic sages were great eccentrics. Uddālaka Āruṇi might have wanted to impress his son by making not only a Great Statement (*mahākāvya*) but also an Outrageous Statement, one that rages beyond humdrum grammar. Its meaning would not be clear, like *aham brahmāsmi,* 'I am *brahman*,' but ungrammaticality is not unprecedented. The statement of abandon by the patron: *agnaye idaṃ na mama*, 'this is for Agni, not for me,' is ungrammatical as we have seen in Chapter 7.

Having seen what Uddālaka Āruṇi said, what did Yājñavalkya have in mind? I am not sure. Things are different from what they seem to. It shows that more work is needed even on the famous great statements (*mahāvākya*) of the Upaniṣads.

Dhyāna, Meditation and the End of the Veda

Whether or not we are brahman and whether or not the ethical dimensions of the *karma* doctrine are Upaniṣadic, the karma doctrine is related to something else that is Indic and goes beyond it: techniques of concentration or meditation (*dhyāna*, *abhidhyāna*). They are Vedic because they occur in the early Upaniṣads, but they are found elsewhere, for example in Jainism and Buddhism, where they are referred to by different terms and are often specific meditations on the cycle of rebirth. They spread through Buddhism over large parts of Asia first and of the world now. There is no general agreement about what meditation is and what it is not, but in some senses it is monotheistic and probably universal. It is not something to be discussed in the present context. What is the Vedic context?

The kinds of meditation that concern us are connected with almost all the topics we have treated in the previous chapters and the present. Vedic meditation is the product of a long process of *interiorization*. It started when a fire ritual, the Agnihotra, was interiorized by performing it through breathing. Other rituals came to be performed mentally. In the Soma ritual, there is a 'mental (*manasā*) cup'. Mental performances of Vedic rituals enabled the grammarian Patañjali to declare that ritual is without end like language.

Meditation is related to the mental chariots and wheels of the beginning of Chapter 2 and to the Rathakāra, but ritual when interiorized, chant when inaudible, recitation when ineffable and breathing itself, all turned into forms of meditation in later Vedic where they are looked upon as *karma*, that is: an activity. Why? Because they have a beginning and an end. They are not knowledge which is instantaneous, beyond time. But what sounds as recitation or meditation may be knowledge, e.g., of *pūrṇam*, 'fullness'. We return to such exceptions in Chapter **14**.

The Sāmavedic CU begins with speculations about the *udgītha* chant which culminates in OM. OM unites Rig and Sāman as man and woman unite and satisfy each other's desires. OM unites A, U and M. Its foundation is 'the most natural order of sound production: an opening of the mouth followed by its closure' (Roman Jakobson).

Elsewhere the CU meditation (*dhyāna*) is one of a long chain of realities, each greater than the preceding one. The Praśna Upaniṣad declares that meditation on the sound A leads to a speedy return to earth; AU jointly together leads to the lunar world, but only AUM leads to the world of brahman (*brahmaloka*)—a variation on the traditional doctrine of the paths of the ancestors and that of the gods. The section ends with a corrupt verse or versified speculation:

With Rig stanzas this world;
With Yajus formulas, the mid-regions;
With Sāman chants, the poets' proclaimed place.
By the support of OM alone does a man attain

that which is serene, beyond old age
and death, free from fear, the supreme.

There is no mention of knowledge in these rambling verses. The Chāndogya is close to the Sāmaveda, especially at the beginning where chanting takes precedence over meditation or knowledge. In later sections, the CU and the BĀU draw from 'the common stock of Upaniṣadic lore' (as Patrick Olivelle put it) and concentrate on knowledge. In Buddhism, meditation had a great future, but it was topped by wisdom which corresponds to the Upaniṣadic knowledge (Chapter 16, *page* 315). In the middle and later Upaniṣads, knowledge is gradually replaced by epic and religious notions such as salvation and bhakti. The search for salvation signals the Vedānta or end of the Veda.

Another signal of the approaching end is the breakdown of the notion of Vedic school or *śākhā*. I have quoted freely from the CU, the BĀU and other Upaniṣads which belong to different schools. I did not jump around to such an extent in earlier chapters. The breakdown of the schools is not mentioned explicitly in the Upaniṣads, as far as I know, but it is found in other developments during the same period. In grammar, the position of the earlier *Prātiśakhyā* ('one for each *śākhā*') treatises is eclipsed by Pāṇini's grammar which is applicable to all, that is, to the Sanskrit language as a whole (Chapter 14). There is an echo in the Vedānta or Brahma Sūtra which states that meditation belongs to all schools and is not *pratīvedam*, 'one for each Veda'.

The Two Main Contributions of the Upaniṣads

If I were asked to point at the greatest contributions of the Upaniṣads and the Vedānta, I would mention two. The first is public discussions and rational dialogues without restraints (e.g., 'political correctness'). Rational discussions never existed between the two Jaina sects, who did not talk to each other, but survived in Indian philosophy, in the Buddhist Councils, in the Council of Lhasa that allegedly took place between Indian and Chinese Buddhists, and among Tibetans, though no longer in Tibet itself. In India, they continued to exist in religious contexts, at least until half a century ago in Kanchipuram, when I looked up at the leaders of the two main Viśiṣṭādvaita schools or sects, arguing with each other, high above me on elephant back and surrounded by throngs of followers. The name of one was Prativādam Bhayaṃkaram, 'Terrible Refutation'. Logic and religion combined in one fantastic spectacle. What a lesson for the twenty-first century!

The second great contribution of the Upaniṣads goes deeper into the recesses of human thought. It is insight in the nature of knowledge as a guide to what is reality as distinct from the appearances. This kind of insight is different from the literally superficial knowledge to which Behaviourism or Phenomenology aspire, and altogether different from what is believed by many people who have not given the matter much thought. It lies at the heart of modern science, whether it is theoretical physics or genetics, which is a search for features of reality that are hidden. The general theory of relativity, quantum theory or the theory of DNA, all deal, or dealt in their original form, with 'things' that lie behind and beyond the appearances. They are not enumerations of facts; they are not *saṃkhyā* or 'enumeration', they are *theories*. A simple example comes from the theory of heat: what appears to us as heat, viz. the appearances, is due to the movement of particles, viz. the underlying reality. The faster the particles move, the hotter it feels to us. The phenomena or appearances are studied in another science: thermodynamics. Though it deals with appearances, it is not superficial: it led to the discovery of entirely new concepts such as *entropy*.

Many philosophers, worldwide, have made the distinction between reality and appearance. The Upaniṣads do so throughout. The Muṇḍaka distinguished explicitly between a lower and a higher knowledge. The Advaita Vedānta thrives on it. The Platonic tradition is its European counterpart, but with an important difference to which I return in a moment. Other philosophers have felt uneasy about something that appeared to them to be metaphysical. But it is not meta-physical: like all theoretical science, it is meta-phenomenological. It seeks true knowledge behind the phenomena.

Even brilliant thinkers have been deceived. Young Bertrand Russell took on the bastion of Hegelian thought in the form it was defended by a British Hegelian, F.H. Bradley, whose chief work was entitled *Appearance and Reality*. Russell had a good time with it. Bradley wrote before Einstein, but not before Maxwell's *Theory of Electromagnetics*, Marx, Freud or Darwin, all pointing at realities behind the appearances. Russell, primarily a logician and mathematician, did not realize at the time, that those discoveries were about concealed realities. That was discovered by the Upaniṣads as it was by Plato. Modern civilization would not exist without it.

The Upaniṣadic insight is deep and speculative but we should not be blind to its limitations. It tells us that the world as it appears is not real, but does not explain how it comes about; Śaṅkara declared that it could not be done. Science demonstrates that it can be done though it is not final. That, of course, is obvious to everyone who gives it some thought; though there are scientists who do not seem to understand it themselves.

That the theories of theoretical physics are theories does not mean that anything goes: they are highly confirmed. According to Roger Penrose, Newton's theory of gravity is accurate to one part in 10^7 and Einstein's General Relativity to one part in 10^{14}. In the Upaniṣad, *jñāna* is not so confirmed. Vedic sciences were improved upon by later scientists. Later Indic thought stressed the opposite: regress all the way down from the *Satyayūga*. Perhaps it can apply somewhere, I am unsure about ethics and/or moral or immoral behaviour, but if there is progress anywhere it is in knowledge. The history of science has demonstrated it. It does not imply that Keppler or Einstein deserve more respect than Yājñavalkya or Śākalya but millennia have intervened. If my book has succeeded in showing that it makes a difference because history does, I shall be pleased.

That book has come to its own Vedānta, but not to its end: it has reached the end of the long development that led to the canonization of the compositions that are listed and related to each other in Table I. Though there is much I have ignored or neglected, we have reached the end of the Veda. What remains to be done?

We must look at the forest behind the trees. With so much material on our hands that has not yet been explained, we have to turn to a more analytical form of exposition and try to find out whether it may assist our understanding.

PART III

Analysing the Vedas

How to Discover

We have studied origins and backgrounds in Part I and focused on the Vedas in Part II. The reader should by now be familiar with the subject matter of this book. Part I answered the old questions about Indo-European, Indo-Aryan and other contributions to Indic civilization. Discovering the Vedas depends on the answer to a second and more important question that has never been asked: what have the Vedas contributed to Indic intellectual history? It is clear that the Upaniṣads influenced the philosophies of the Vedānta; and that mantras and rituals are the chief channels through which Vedic contributions entered what came to be known as Hinduism. The second question is concerned with deeper analytical issues. We must do what sage Uddālaka Āruṇi told his son Śvetaketu ('White Flame') to do in the Chāndogya Upaniṣad (CU 6.12):

'Bring a banyan fruit.'
'Here it is, sir.'
'Cut it up.'

'I've cut it up, sir.'
'What do you see there?'
'These quite tiny seeds, sir.'
'Now, take one of them and cut it up.'
'I've cut one up, sir.'
'What do you see there? '
. . .

The reader will see in Chapter **15** *what Śvetaketu saw inside the tiny seed. We have to look deeper in a similar spirit and take off cover after cover as 'discovering' implies. It is like peeling an onion, with the difference, that we will never know whether the last cover we peeled off was the final one.*

The intimate connections between mantras and rituals will be examined in Chapters **11** *and* **12**. *Chapter* **13** *provides another link to the geography of Part I. It shows that the movement of the composers from west to east coincided with a development in the ritual proceedings themselves: they started 'facing east' and ended, on the Agnicayana altar, to face all directions. The Vedic contribution to Indic intellectual history lies in that move towards universality.*

ELEVEN

~

MANTRAS

The Meaninglessness of Mantras

Mantras are not mysterious statements with deep meanings. They have no meaning because they are not statements and they are not statements because they are not language. Language is a human faculty which is concerned with *meaning* in its primary sense. In natural language, the domain of meaning is part of an intricate system. We shall take a closer look at this system in the next section, but it may be illustrated first by three expressions of language, each belonging to a different category:

1. *banana* which is a word, a noun in fact, that has a meaning to which I shall refer as 'banana'.
2. *eating bananas* which is a phrase also has a meaning.
3. *Hiroshi likes bananas* which is a sentence also has a meaning.

What is systematic about these expressions is that indefinitely many, but not *any* other expressions may be substituted for any of their constituent words which would again lead to a similar category, that is a word, phrase or sentence:

In (1), any other word of the dictionary may be substituted for *banana* and the result will still be a word, by definition.

In (2), any noun that refers to an edible thing may be substituted for *banana*, but not *rivers* or *hesitations*; and similarly, a large number of verbal phrases may be substituted for *eating*, e.g., *liking, anticipating, throwing* but not *formulating* or *proposing*.

In (3), *Hiroshi* may be replaced by almost any name or expressions such as *the national hero of Finland*. But if we replace it by *King Janaka* we must replace *likes* by *liked*. Otherwise, the same conditions as were applicable to *eating bananas* in (2) apply to *likes bananas*. Note that all true or false sentences must be meaningful, but a meaningful sentence such as (3) need not be true, e.g., *Adolf Hitler loved Jews*.

The meaning of 'last Sunday's sunset' is unlike the meanings of examples (1) to (3). It is not shared by the members of a community who share a language. It is much more restricted. It may have a meaning for *me* but only when it refers to a particular Sunday that I experienced. Perhaps I share some of it with others who witnessed the same sunset. But it is not part of their language. If you look up the dictionary under 'Sunday' you will not find my meaning there.

The same holds for the expression: 'meaning of a mantra'. A mantra may have power or may perform a particular function. It has to be pronounced on a particular occasion. It may consist of the words of a language—Vedic Sanskrit, for example—but the meaning of the mantra is not the meaning of those words and *none* of the systematization of the expressions (1) through (3) applies to mantras unless it is by chance. There are a few exceptions to this general statement, e.g., mantras that belong to a special class such as *agnaye idaṃ na mama, prajāpataye idaṃ na mama*—of Chapter 7—not to mention the simple reason that the meaning of all the words that make up the mantra, or that of the entire sentence, if it is a sentence, need not be known to the users of the mantra.

Some of what applies to mantras applies to ritual. We shall return to ritual in the next chapter, but it is obvious that it is even further removed from language than mantras are. Ritual is a physical activity of the body but not only of the mouth and ears. It may accompany mantras as well as language but it is different from both.

If it is true that mantras and ritual have no meaning in the only intelligible sense, and are not language, are they not powerful and important? They are indeed as powerful and important as many other entities, say elephants or mice. Outside mythology, no one would even think of trying to explain an elephant by language. Perhaps an elephant, or elephants, or something about them may be explained with the help of biology, the theory of biological evolution, genetics, DNA or something else. Explanations of mantras and ritual that start from language, are similarly barking up the wrong tree. We must begin to accept, or regain the feeling that some readers who picked up this book may have had at the outset, that there is something to discover because we do not yet understand. It has nothing to do with familiarity. I am familiar with cars but I do not know how they are put together and have only the vaguest of notions about their origins in the history of human technology. Familiarity breeds not only contempt but a vague reaction like: yes, it is a mantra. If we wish to understand properly we must start with a sense of puzzlement, a sense of mystery even. Such a person feels lost. The reader who understands mantras and ritual already must stop here and go to Part IV.

Those of us who are puzzled and mystified may be pleased that the same embarrassment existed in Vedic India. As we have seen from Kautsa's thesis (*pages* 141–45), the Vedic tradition began to be questioned by its own followers. Kautsa focused on one particular feature: if mantras are regarded as language, they are meaningless. Part of the reason, and only a small part, lies in a particular historical development. The early portions of the Rigveda were jealously guarded by families who spoke a language, accompanied their rites and invoked their divinities in a language that was not at first understood by others who heard it spoken or used. It did not prevent these others from regarding Vedic mantras as powerful. Some were familiar with Sāmavedic chants that were similarly meaningless.

It is useful to remember that the historical development I sketched contributed to the unintelligibility of mantras, but more important to understand is that this is only a small part of the reason. Meaninglessness belongs to the nature of mantras. It is a feature of mantras as such. Kautsa's arguments showed this clearly and the core of the argument is that mantras are not language. They lack the systematic nature that was illustrated by examples (1) to (3) above, but we need to know more about the system itself. Kautsa did because he was a linguist and I assume that most of my readers are not. More is now known about language than Kautsa knew and there are stronger and more decisive reasons that support his thesis.

Language, Syntax and Recursiveness

When I use the term 'language', what I have in mind is languages such as English or Sanskrit, modern or classical, world languages or tribal languages. Languages change and evolve over time. They are born and they die. They belong to or originate in a specific community though they may be adopted by others and become widespread. But language is a system in which everything hangs together, *où tout se tient* as de Saussure put it.

The scientific study of language or linguistics distinguishes three domains: Phonology, Syntax and Semantics. Phonology deals with the sounds of language. It is typically concerned with such differences as Śākalya studied when he made his distinction between Saṃhitā and Padapāṭha in Chapter 4. It is dependent on structures of the mouth and the inner and outer ear, which restrict the sounds of human language and distinguish it from the chirping of birds or the mowing of cows which are also systems of sound that are used for communication but are not language.

Syntax deals with the structure of sentences. It distinguishes statements from questions or commands, actives from passives, future and past tenses, singular and plural and many other modes and categories. It may or may not be restricted by word order.

Semantics deals with meaning, that is, the world to which language refers, which it denotes or connotes, addresses, hears, sees, smells, remembers, listens to, imagines or depicts. Language does this by means of words but not only words. Semantics is closely connected with syntax because we understand not only words but also sentences. Which is primary—word meaning or sentence meaning—is a favourite topic of discussion among Indian linguists and philosophers of language. Words are, obviously, more manageable than sentences. They constitute a finite set and can be listed in a dictionary or encyclopaedia, in alphabetical or another order. Sentences are infinite in number.

How can sentences be infinite in number and how can infinite numbers of things be learned or interiorated? First, we have to know what infinity means. It means indefinitely large. An example is the set of integers: 1, 2, 3, 4, 5, ... It is infinitely large not because we arrive, at a certain moment, at an integer written with a special symbol that stands for 'infinite'. It means: whenever '1', belongs to it, the next number '2' also belongs to it; and if '2' belongs to it, '3' does too. The set of integers is infinite because for each of its members, the next member is also a member and there is no end to that . . . . As it happens, '2' is the same as '1 + 1,' '3' is the same as '2 + 1', etc. We are able to express it neatly with the help of a little algebra: the set of integers has infinitely many members, because for any number n, it also has the next number: $n + 1$. That process can be repeated as often as we like and the number of natural numbers is therefore indefinitely large. There is no upper limit.

Returning to language we have seen that the number of words is finite but the number of sentences is infinitely large. This is due to a property of syntax called *recursiveness*. It means that also in language a structure may be repeated indefinitely often without there being an upper limit. An example from English is '*He said A*', where '*A*' is a sentence.

That structure is repeated in *He said that he said A*; and once more in *He said that he said that he said A*. And so on. The reader may object that such sentences do not actually occur in English. It is true, but some English sentences cannot be analysed without presupposing that such structures underlie them, e.g., *Betty told me that Kumar, when asked about his opinion, immediately said that he had said A already.* When such sentences get longer they become increasingly unintelligible, but their underlying recursive structure remains the same. In other cases, the intelligibility or unintelligibility continues unabated, as in teacher's lineages (*guruparamparā*) such as: 'Pautimāṣya from Gaupavana, Gaupavana from Kauśika, Kauśika from Kauṇḍinya, Kauṇḍinya from Śaṇḍilya, Śaṇḍilya from Kauśika and Gautama, Gautama from Āgniveśya' etc. in the Bṛhad-Āraṇyaka Upaniṣad.

Do we actually find very long sentences in natural languages? I am not a writer so I cannot construct a good example but the reader who is familiar with any of the following may look at Sanskrit compounds, a page of the Kādambarī, Navya-Nyāya, Proust or Thomas Mann. Take the longest compound or sentence you can find. Assume that the longest sentence you can find occurs in Proust. Call it P. I can *always* construct a longer one. Here it is: 'Proust wrote *P*.' This can be repeated ad libitum, and there is no upper bound.

How can things that are infinite in number be learned? By learning general principles that generate infinity. Recursiveness is one of these. It may be represented by an inverted tree. I shall start with a finite example, a simple syntactic structure that occurs in natural languages, perhaps in all languages (an empirical matter): the distinction between subject and predicate. It is *not* recursive.

Take the example: 'Yājñavalkya taught Maitreyī' or 'Y taught M'. In English syntax, 'Y' is the subject and 'taught M' is the predicate. The predicate, therefore, consists of two parts: a verb and an object. Not all sentences in all languages have that simple structure. But a surprisingly large number can be reduced to such structures, using an astonishing proliferation of rules. So let us put those rules aside and concentrate on the basic structure of the sentence which is a *hierarchical* structure because it consists of two levels: subject and predicate, and, within predicate, verb and object:

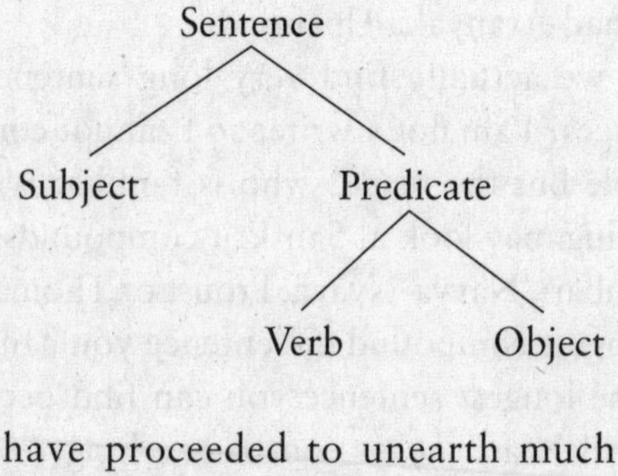

Linguists have proceeded to unearth much more abstract structures; but for our purposes it is enough, and we are going to generalize in other directions. The above structure shows a relation between some syntactic categories, which can also be expressed by simply stating: a sentence *consists* of a subject and a predicate; and: a predicate *consists* of a verb and an object. It does not necessarily have anything to do with word order, though the order of the figure is that of the example 'Y taught M'. What the linguist does, he *generates* the sentence. It may be done by adding substitution rules that refer to a dictionary together with a list of names and that may be expressed by dots, as follows:

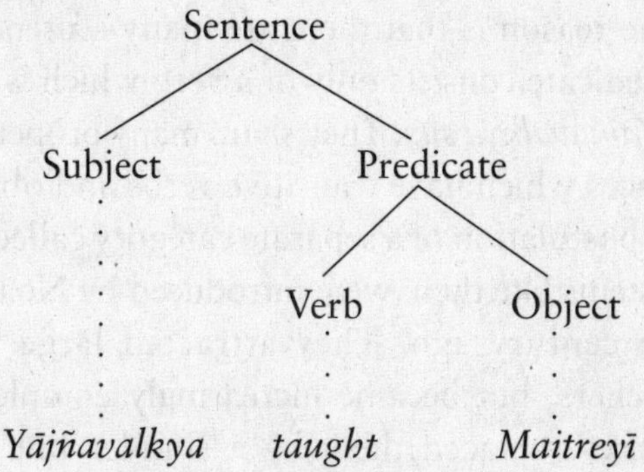

This picture shows that a sentence, the *linear* structure *Yājñavalkya taught Maitreyī*, has an underlying two-dimensional *non-linear* structure (perhaps other systems use more dimensions, but I don't know them). That non-linear structure, or some structures like it, have been referred to as deep structure. It has a mysterious ring about it, but teaches us that the analysis of sentences shows that there are underlying, invisible structures that have to be postulated in order to explain the sentences that are produced and that we can hear.

How do we know that the above structure is the correct one? By analysing thousands of sentences. It makes no sense, for example, to analyse as follows:

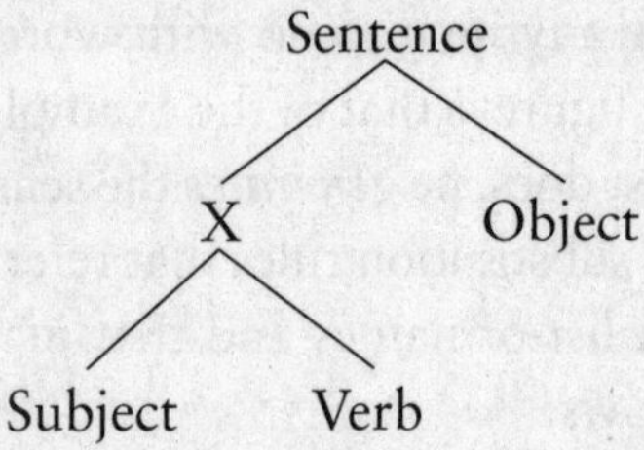

One reason is that there are many sentences in which the predicate consists only of a verb which is intransitive, e.g., *Yājñavalkya sits*. They share many properties with the sentences which have transitive verbs and objects leading to the postulation of a separate category called 'Predicate'.

Systems like these were introduced by Noam Chomsky half a century ago. They attracted large numbers of researchers, but became increasingly complex. In 1995, Chomsky replaced them by a simpler but much more abstract system called *The Minimalist Program*. Since then, developments in linguistics have become even more explosive.

Our problems are different. We are interested in infinite recursive structures. Take the sentence: 'He said *A*'. I shall not analyse it into Subject ('He') and Predicate ('said A') but cut it up differently, illustrating thereby what we call *quoting*. Quoting is recursive, we can continue to do it: 'He said, "He said *A*".' I can go on but let me introduce a little variation: 'A retorted, according to B, that C had said *X*.' It is still abstract and stilted, so 'We might think of the Professor who claimed that Proust had written *Vanity Fair*'. That is better although Proust himself is miles ahead: 'And so I could not help reciting to myself, when I saw them, not indeed the lines of Racine that had come into my head at the Princesses de Guermantes's while M. de Vaugoubert stood watching young embassy secretaries greet M. de Charlus, but other lines of Racine . . .' and on it goes without losing the attention of the attentive reader or syntactician.

Let me be a little more systematic and distinguish *right-recursive* and *left-recursive*. An English example of the first is: 'Remarkable is the rapidity of the motion of the wing of the hummingbird.' The noun phrase to which something is added is always on the right:

> the rapidity of the hummingbird,
> the rapidity of the wing of the hummingbird,
> the rapidity of the motion of the wing of the hummingbird, etc.(?)

We are lucky in that English possesses a similar structure which goes the other way and is therefore called *left-recursive* because the noun phrase is always on the left:

> the hummingbird's rapidity
> the hummingbird's wing's rapidity
> the hummingbird's wing's motion's rapidity, etc. (?)

Psychologists are interested in these recursions. I have taken the last six phrases from an article by George Miller on psycholinguistics that is almost half a century old. It illustrates the distinction Chomsky introduced between *competence* and *performance*. The rules of grammar depict a speaker's competence. The six phrases are examples of performance.

But I have put a (?) at the end of some of them. How far can the reader go? Asking Harvard undergraduates, Miller arrived at the conclusion that the third and sixth illustrate their limit.

The reader will now have an inkling of what mantras and Vedic rites can be like. Our next question is different: how can these different structures be learnt?

Through the interplay of empirical information and innate knowledge. Learning a language takes place for a only a small part by explicit instruction of a mother, father or teacher. It is mainly picked up by babies, from a very early age, by being immersed in a language community in which people, including playmates, visitors, salesmen, brothers, sisters, fathers, mothers, teachers or anyone or anything within hearing of the child, including the TV, uses the language. This picking up of language occurs within a few years and is similar to the way scientists learn about the world. They construe a succession of theories, each the result of earlier theories and new data. Children are quick to change their theories when they make a wrong generalization, for example, in English: from *trees*, *dogs* and *books* to **mans* and **womans* (the asterisk denotes ungrammaticality) until they notice or are told that they should say *men* and *women*.

Many 'deep structures' are innate. The deeper they are, the more abstract they look to us. What is not innate is the association of fragments of speech with events, occurrences or objects in the outside world. Those are picked up by the child by not only listening but by seeing and using other mental capacities such as association, generalization, combinations of various kinds and, of course, memory.

Mantras are similar in some respects. They incorporate recursive structures. They may be long and there are many of them. In Tantrism it is said that seventy million of them exist in superior worlds. But mantras are not learnt in the way language is picked up as we shall see at the end of this chapter.

Steps Beyond Kautsa

Kautsa gave four reasons for the meaninglessness of mantras. (1) The sound of mantras may not be changed unlike in language where sounds may change provided meaning remains the same. (2) The order of elements in mantras may not be changed, unlike in Sanskrit where word order is to a large extent free. (3) If mantras were meaningful, it would have to be conceded that they are often contradictory or inconsistent with each other. That is not uncommon in language, where it is common for speakers to say different things, but it becomes an embarrassment when dealing with canon formation, i.e. the establishment of a source of authority. (4) There is a tradition to transmit the sounds of mantras but not their meanings, unlike the connection between sounds and meanings in language that is sometimes taught but generally picked up by children. It is the last reason with which I have been chiefly concerned in the previous section and to which we shall return most often.

Before we do so we must note that there are other reasons which Kautsa might have mentioned. A reason (5) to which we have referred already in Chapter 8 is that mantras are repeated incessantly. It may be expressed by a simple recursive rule of the type we have studied in the previous section. In English, we may say: *Please, please, please pass me the salt* if we have already asked before and are repeating our request. It sounds a little odd, and if we were to repeat *please* four times it would definitely be looked upon as eccentric. Mantras, on the other hand, are happily repeated. It holds not only for mantras like OM, which are repeated many times and during long periods without intermission, but for mantras couched in language such as the Gāyatrī mantra which an 'orthodox' brahman repeats every day. *Orthodox* ('of right opinion') is not the appropriate term here because such repetitions involve ritual where *orthoprax* ('of right action') is the correct appellation as we shall continue to observe.

If Kautsa's perspective had not been confined to Vedic India and he had been able to look beyond its borders and to the future, he would have come up with at least two other reasons in support of his thesis: mantras remain invariant in history (6) and in geography (7). They are different from language in these respects. Languages change over time and change across language boundaries where they are translated. Mantras do not. Though often kept secret and guarded jealously, some Vedic mantras were inherited by Buddhists and Tantrics. Often referred to as *dhāraṇī*, they travelled from India to South-east Asia, crossed the Himalayas from Kashmir into Central Asia, China, Korea, Japan and Tibet, and finally reached the Euro-Americas. The emperor of China accepted them in exchange for tea, silk, porcelain and lacquers and in California they fetched high prices. During these travels, the mantras did not change. That mantras are untranslatable, like proper names, was recognized by Chinese pilgrims such as Hiuan-tsang (Xuanzang) who were translators themselves.

When a mantra is introduced into a new linguistic environment, its forms may be affected to some extent. Though OM remains the same in Tibet or Japan, SVĀHĀ is adapted to the phonetic structure of Japanese where it became SOWAKA. Within India itself, mantras couched in Vedic such as the Gāyatrī were preserved without change, but the language of the reciters changed from Vedic to other Indic languages. Maintaining the original forms of a ritual language is advocated in a similar spirit with respect to Latin in the Catholic Mass and Arabic in the Qur'ān. Reasons (6) and (7) illustrate again that what counts for mantras is not *meaning*, let alone social contexts, but *form*. Emphasis on form is a basic feature of ancient Indian civilization and accounts for much of its emphasis on explicit statements, its scientific creativity and many of its other strengths.

Pragmatics, Speech Acts and Bird Song

If mantras are not language, for the analysis of which specialized disciplines such as linguistics, philology or literary criticism have been developed, where do we find more adequate concepts and categories to study them successfully? Can we learn something from logic or philosophy?

A popular approach to the study of mantras has been *pragmatics*. I am not referring to the pragmatism of William

James, John Dewey or other philosophers, but to a discipline that is closely related to logic and that deals with so-called indexicals. Bertrand Russell called them 'egocentric particulars'. These expressions of language do not refer to the outside world but to the speaker in his or her immediate context or situation. Examples are: 'I', 'you', 'here', 'now' or 'to-morrow'. What is the difference between these and other expressions of language? If the reader and I say 'tree', both of us refer to the same thing. If we both say 'I', the reader refers to the reader and I refer to myself. If we say 'you', the reader refers to me and I refer to the reader. In both cases, we use the same words but do not refer to the same things.

Within the domain of pragmatics, a productive subcategory of indexicals or egocentric particulars is that of 'speech acts'. These were introduced by J.L. Austin, the Oxford 'ordinary language' philosopher, refined by his former assistant Paul Grice and by John Searle, both at Berkeley, along with others. Many students of mantras have argued that mantras are speech acts. What are speech acts?

Speech acts are language utterances by which an act is performed. They depend on context and on the speaker, and are therefore indexicals. The only language from which empirical evidence for the existence of such a separate category has been studied on a large scale is modern English. Speech acts have uncommon properties. They depend on the qualification of the agent who utters them. If a priest or minister addresses two people with the words: 'I unite you in marriage,' he has not merely said something. He has performed an act by which the two are now married to each other. If a non-qualified person such as myself addresses two people with the same words, it has no effect. It is an utterance of speech, but not a speech act. The people addressed may also have to meet special requirements. They may be required to be two in number and, in many places, of different sex or gender.

Most of the utterances of language are not speech acts. If I say 'it is raining', it may be true or untrue depending on time and place, but its meaning is the same and I have not performed an act. If I say 'I promise to see you tomorrow', the meaning varies with the referents of the indexicals ('I' and 'tomorrow') and it may or may not be an act, depending on my character. If I am a reliable person who keeps his promises, I have bound myself to someone else and staked my reputation. In that case, it is an act and, therefore, a speech act.

Some scholars have widened the domain of speech acts beyond Austin so as to encompass *all* utterances of language. It illustrates one of the great strategies of empty scholarship. If *all* objects of an inquiry are labelled with a new name, nothing has changed and no new insight has been obtained. A new name may carry a whiff of suggestion; but if the name already denotes members of a particular class, the suggestion is confusing. Calling an utterance an act is such a misleading suggestion. For we would still have to distinguish between acts that merely speak and acts that 'really' act. If I kill a person with an axe it is an act and not an utterance.

I conclude that mantras are neither language nor speech acts. Their powers are different and distant from the concepts and categories that are used in logic, philosophy and the human sciences. That is in accordance with a simple fact that we have not so far taken into account: mantras are not confined to humans. That has never raised an eyebrow in Indic civilization, and other civilizations like it, which do not regard humans as basically different from other animals. The Upaniṣads accept it as a matter of course that needs no further discussion. The Chāndogya tells us about dogs that are gathered around a white dog and said to him: 'Please, Sir, find us some food by singing!' They sat down together and made the sound *huṃ*. Then they sang: 'OM! Let us eat! OM! Let us drink!'

If the human sciences cannot make sense of mantras—just as they throw no light on elephants or mice—it stands to reason that we should widen our net and study them in the context of the animal kingdom. It is a productive approach with plenty of empirical support. Animals chirp, grunt, bark, moo, bellow, roar, mew, cry, twitter and twit. Many of these sounds belong to structured systems and some of them have been studied in detail and depth. I shall confine myself in our context to one of the richest, most varied and impressive animal sound systems: bird song. It has not been studied by humans as long and deeply as human language, but there exists an extensive literature about it. The study of bird song has not led to unanimous conclusions with regard to its meaning or semantics, but its *syntactic* study, though in its infancy, has been fruitful and the results are uncontroversial.

The syntactic study of bird song was initiated by a composer and musicologist, François Bernard Mâche, who discarded the traditional use by ornithologists of spectrograms. Spectrograms show continuity. Mâche used musical and other symbolic notations that show that bird song consists of discrete, digital units. The units of bird song may be referred to by notes, letters or approximated by transcriptions into the English alphabet such as *chyup*, *chup-chup-zee*, or *churrr*. As we have seen in Chapter 6, musical notations are helpful in the study of the Sāmaveda, where no one would even think of using spectrograms. Their use has been common since the Renaissance when the Jesuit polymath Athanasius Kircher studied a bit of Sāmaveda.

The Sāmaveda illustrates clearly that not only language but also stobhas, a type of mantras, possess a syntax that consists of discrete units that are combined with each other and may be converted into other structures by syntactic rules. Such rules transform one sequence—*agna āyahi vītaye*—into another: *o gnā i / ā yā hi vā i / tā yā i tā yā i /*. Some were formulated in the *Puṣpasūtra*, a late work that belongs to the Kauthuma school of the Sāmaveda. The syntax of stobhas is extremely complex as I have illustrated elsewhere (Staal 1989, 1993, Chapter 19).

The syntactic structures of language, mantras and bird songs are generally different but sometimes overlap. Mantras are in some respects closer to bird song than to language. It is difficult to evaluate the significance of such a fact because the comparative study of these three distinct domains has remained virtually unexplored and would need to be embarked upon before we know where mantras belong, if anywhere. In the present section, I shall briefly discuss two examples from the domain of mantras, leaving a third for the following section which deals with ritual. Example 1 illustrates a feature that is shared by mantras and bird song but is absent from language. Example 2 illustrates a feature that is found in all three domains. Example 3 illustrates again a feature that ritual possesses and mantras in its wake, but that is absent from language.

Example 1 is the simplest and we have met with it already: mantras and bird songs both repeat the same sounds indefinitely: A A A A . . . . The recursive rule is: **A > AA**. Language does not have such a rule because utterances like *please, please, please* soon have to stop as we have seen.

Example 2 exhibits a more basic structure of which the repetitions of Example 1 may be regarded as the simplest and least interesting case. I am referring to the *recursiveness* that is a property of the syntax of human language and that we have already met in the section on language (*pages* 196–203).

Linguists have claimed that recursiveness is a basic characteristic of human language and is not found anywhere else. Mantras and bird song provide two counter-examples to this claim. Let us begin with mantras with which we are already familiar. The clearest examples come again from the Sāmaveda. Sequences such as *bhu bhā bhi bha bhe bha bha bhī bhā bha bha bhi bha bha bhā bha* (above *page* 109) are created by replacing the syllables of the underlying song by syllables that retain their vowel but substitute for their initial consonant or consonants *bh*-. It is a process that can be continued indefinitely with respect to the number of syllables or sentences, as in: *it is a bhobhess bhat bhan bhe bhonbhibued inbhebhibhibhebhy*, etc., but this is not a procedure we find in a natural language.

We need to spend a little more time on the case of bird song which may be unfamiliar to some readers. A well-studied case is that of the Black-capped Chick-a-dee tit. Its songs consist of discrete or digital units which I shall represent by capital letters. Four units, *A*, *B*, *C*, *D*, are repeated indefinitely but with certain constraints: *A* may be followed by *D*, and in that sequence, *AD*, both elements may be repeated indefinitely. The same holds for *BCD*, where *C* may be repeated indefinitely. We may find, for example, *AAAADDD* or *BCCCD*. But we never find *DCA*. There are several underlying rules which we can state more precisely when we take more details into account.

The same holds for language and mantras. In language, a *different* beginning may be followed by an *identical* end. For example, *Maya was eager to go to the concert* and *all her disciples were eager to go to the concert*. Conversely, the beginnings may be the same and the ends different: *Maya was eager to go to the dinner* and *Maya was eager to go to the concert*. What we do not find is the opposite one , i.e. **dinner Maya was eager to go to the*. A borderline case may depend on emphasis in context: *She detested cocktails but to the dinner Maya was eager to go*.

The same holds for mantras but in a different manner. It may lead to confusions or mistakes as T.P. Mahadevan and I encountered during the Morning Litany of a Soma ritual performed in 2003. The difficulty is due to the fact that 356 mantras from all over the Rigveda are recited but in a different order from the one in which they had been studied first and continue to be recited on other occasions.

What happened is that RV 5.79.1, the 218th mantra in the sequence, begins with *mahe no adya bodhaya*. Another mantra in the Rigveda, 7.75.2, begins with *mahe no adya* but then continues: *suvitāya bodhi*. It is very confusing not only because *bodh-* occurs in both mantras, but also because RV 7.75.2 does not occur in the Morning Litany at all though each of the poems 7.73, 7.74, 7.77, 7.78, 7.79, 7.80 and 7.81 are recited there, almost as if a trap was planned. The reciter of the Litany fell into it but not the young assistant, sitting at his side.

The lapse implies that 'mindless' recitations of colossal amounts of mantras are not a mindless matter. It contributes, moreover, to the 'picking up' of mantras by youngsters during performances of Vedic rituals, which though similar to the picking up of language, occurs much more rarely.

But that is not the end of the story for the error that was made is different in structure from replacing *Maya was eager to go to the dinner* by *Maya was eager to go to the concert*. In order to explain this we have to look deeper which we shall do at the end of the next section on the Gāyatrī mantra. We should keep in mind that, whatever the similarities between mantras and bird song, we do not descend from birds. What does that imply? That the causes for the similarities in structure lie deeper. About mantras we still know little. As for recursiveness, there are different kinds and natural language, birds, mantras and ritual reveal instructive similarities and differences.

We can say one thing about the power of mantras. It

pertains to those who possess them. Mantras strengthen memory and breath. The remaining questions about mantras are about the activity they accompany: do they strengthen it in some sense or other? Can they replace it as the mental or *mānasa* cup replaces a cup made of clay? We raised such questions in Chapter 8 in connection with the Atharvavedic mantras that accompany surgery. I have *ad hoc* ramblings but no general answer. But that is not very different from the results the study of bird song had reached about a decade ago when Catchpole and Slater (1995) described the state of the art: the diversity is so great, that it 'defies explanation' and we are left 'to puzzle over the resulting richness and variety that evolution has created'.

The Gāyatrī Mantra

The Gāyatrī mantra is called after its metre (*page* 89): it consists of three verses of eight syllables which are long '—' or short '^' as in the following scheme:

— ^ ^ — ^ — ^ —
— — — ^ ^ — ^ ^
^ — — — ^ — ^ —

How close mantras are to ritual is shown by the teaching of the Gāyatrī mantra which takes place during the initiation ritual of *upanayana*. Similar in formation to *upaniṣad* ('sitting near'), *upanayana* means 'taking near'. 'Near' may again be to the teacher, here called *ācārya*, or to the stage of studenthood after which the student is called a *brahmacārin*. There are many ceremonies after which the teacher takes the boy's hand and makes him look at the sun. After numerous other exchanges, variously described in various manuals, student and teacher sit north of a fire, the student facing east, that is, looking at the teacher, and the teacher facing west. The teacher then makes him repeat the first verse:

tat savitur vareṇyaṃ.

He then makes him similarly repeat the second:

bhargo devasya dhīmahi

and the third:

dhiyo yo naḥ pracodayāt.

Finally he makes him repeat all three:

tat savitur vareṇyaṃ
bhargo devasya dhīmahi
dhiyo yo naḥ pracodayāt.

The boy is then given a staff, a grass girdle and several instructions, e.g., he should remain standing during the rest of the day. During the years of study that follow, he will be taught to learn by heart the Vedic school to which he belongs. He should not sleep by day and put a fire-stick on the fire in the morning and the evening. He should continue to recite the mantra every day at sunrise and sunset, at least ten and not more than a thousand times, depending again on his Vedic school.

Though the mantra has come to stand for the essence of the Veda, its recital at sunrise and sunset connects it with the sun. Savitā is the sun or rather, to distinguish him from Sūrya, the driving force behind the sun. The *brahmacārin* may sense that much though there is no rule that he should be told. The teacher may happen to be a scholar, traditional or modern, by inclination, but it is not part of his ritual task. He does not interpret or explain. The teaching is *orthoprax*, not *orthodox*. Kautsa had already drawn attention to the fact that there is a tradition for mantras to be learnt by heart, but no corresponding tradition to teach and thereby preserve their meaning.

It is difficult to say why the Gāyatrī mantra became so famous. It comes from an early poem of the Rigveda that invokes various deities. P.V. Kane refers to its 'grand simplicity' but that might be apparent to a learned scholar only. To a modern reader, the entire effort may make little sense apart from being a training of memory and an exercise in discipline. A modern or postmodern scholar may add that a sense of 'identity' is installed here. Yes, the *brahmacārin* is initiated into his Vedic school. It is his 'second birth' after he was born already in the general and non-Vedic sense, becoming a human and not a fish. I wonder whether humans in traditional societies think about 'identity'. A modern and trendy concept. The Gāyatrī mantra as I have described is conveyed to a student at the time of his *upanayana* or initiation into the Brahman community. With the hardening of the caste system in post-Vedic times, ritual discussions proliferated about the question whether the three classes of 'twice-born' castes, *brāhmaṇas, kṣatriyas* and *vaiśyas* should all be initiated with the same mantra or with different mantras. If the latter, mantras are differentiated from each other by their metres: *triṣṭubh* (four verses of eleven syllables) and *jagatī* (four verses of twelve syllables). The system remained the same and preserved the same formal character.

Kautsa's observation that there is a tradition for mantras to be learnt by heart, but no corresponding tradition to teach and thereby preserve their meaning, is full of significance and deep implications. To understand it better we must take a closer look at that tradition.

Transmitting the Gāyatrī mantra requires an elaborate ritual setting. For the student, it is an act of intense concentration, whether or not he is puzzled by its significance. It is very different from picking up a language, almost unconsciously, by hearing what other people, including fathers, mothers, other family members, teachers, playmates, visitors, salesmen or anyone within hearing of the student say and do when they use their language. This picking up of language occurs within a few years and is based upon knowledge and capacities drawn from an innate component or components of the mind.

Some of these features apply, or apply in a more or less similar fashion, to mantras. Youngsters who sit around when teachers are reciting or priests perform rituals pick up something. But they have to be explicitly taught a great deal more, unlike the babies or small children who acquire mastery over the partly innate faculty of language that humans possess. Unless it is a particular song—like a password—a youngster is never taught a sequence of words like the *brahmacārin* who learns to recite: *tat savitur vareṇyaṃ bhargo devasya dhīmahi dhiyo yo naḥ pracodayāt*. He has to repeat that sequence at sunrise and sunset, and on other specified occasions, throughout most of his life. No sentence of a maternal language needs to be repeated like that.

Picking up language includes another feature that is different from recitation: infinitely many other forms are picked up as well. After picking up: 'Give me a piece of bread,' the child may substitute another word in order to obtain another effect: 'Give me a cookie.' Note that the child may never have heard that same sentence before. I am not a child psychologist, so must confine myself to simplistic constructions, but there are others known from history which are not simple and make the same point. The British historian T.B. Macaulay was regarded as a retarded child until he opened his mouth for the first time when he was almost ten years old. During a party, a lady slipped and poured a pot of tea over the poor dumb child who then opened his mouth and said: 'Don't worry Madam, the pain has much abated.' Can we do anything like that with the Gāyatrī mantra? Can we substitute a single word, keeping the same structure, for example, and produce another mantra:

> * *tat śivasya vareṇyaṃ bhargo devasya dhīmahi dhiyo yo naḥ pracodayāt*

or more daringly:

* *tat savitur vareṇyaṃ bhargo śivasya dhīmahi dhiyo yo naḥ pracodayāt*

or worst of all but still keeping the structure:

* *tat savitur vareṇyaṃ bhargo devasya śivasya dhiyo yo naḥ pracodayāt*?

(asterisks indicate here that the following expression is not a mantra).

Why did I say, in the last case, 'worst of all'? Because I know the language and therefore the syntax which the reciter or the reader need not. Even so, the reader will have noticed that I substituted the name of a god (Śiva) with an ending (*śivasya*) in the first two cases for forms of the names of another god (*savitur*) or for the word god itself (*devasya*). In the third case, I replaced a different kind of word, in fact, a verbal form (*dhīmahi*) by *śivasya*. None of these things can be done with mantras though they all illustrate what a child learns when it learns a language; but the last case illustrates a thing children who learn a language never do. They may say *mans* when they should say *men*, but they would not continue to say *cookie* when they mean *go out*.

We cannot take a mantra and add it recursively to another, or another to it, or something else similar to the manner in which it is done in learning a natural language. There is only one recursive rule that can be used in the realm of mantras and that of *stobhas* in the Sāmaveda: repetition. But did we not see, in the Morning Litany, that mantras were recited in the same manner in which *Maya was eager to go to the dinner* was replaced by *Maya was eager to go to the concert* (earlier in this chapter)?

We did, but if we look more closely the two situations are totally different. The two sentences about Maya differ *syntactically* as well as semantically: the objects of Maya's eagerness are syntactic objects, *dinner* and *concert*, and they occur in a specific place in the structure of the sentence. The common part of the two mantras, *mahe no adya*, has no syntactic status at all. They are merely the first three words of a series of words. They have no internal structure and can only be depicted by an expression of the unstructured form:

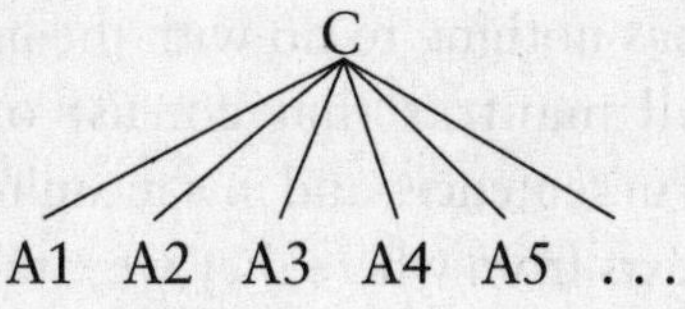

Mantras are memorized from left to right and if two mantras happen to begin with the same two sequences, like **A1 A2 A3**, mistakes like the ones that were made during the 2003 Soma ritual are likely to occur. It does not imply that mantras do not have a structure—we have seen that they do—but it is totally different from the syntactic stucture of a natural language and learning that structure is a totally different process also.

Not only their structure, also their function is entirely

different. And last but not least, apparent words or what look like words in mantras cannot be replaced by others, one of the most striking characteristics of natural language which accounts for its extraordinary creativity and is largely responsible for distinguishing the human animal from other animal species.

It is a good thing that there is a tradition for mantras to be learnt by heart for otherwise there would be no Vedas. My conclusion, that the system of mantras is unlike the system of language, does not affect and has nothing to do with their value. But we should know what they are and what they are not, and what we have learnt in this chapter is that Vedic mantras, whether we are referring to obviously meaningless syllables such as the stobhas, or to mantras that consist of words, are learnt in a manner that is differerent from the manner in which a natural language is learnt.

All of this has nothing to do with the undoubted fact, that almost all mantras that consist of words were originally used in sentences and in a meaningful fashion in the Vedic contexts from where they were taken. They may be bits and pieces of these original sentences, or entire sentences like the Gāyatrī mantra. As we are coming to the end of the present chapter, the reader may be curious to know *what* the meaning of that mantra is, even if it is only distantly related to our topic. By 'meaning' I mean: the meaning of the language of the verse of the Rigveda from where it is taken which is RV 3.62.10. Its meaning is: 'May we receive this excellent splendour of the god Savitā, which should inspire our thoughts!' It may be understood by the reciter, all or in part, depending on his knowledge of the language; perhaps he is a student of Sanskrit or on his way to becoming one. But understanding its language is nowhere required and has nothing to do with the ritual functions of that mantra. That is the full significance of Kautsa's fifth thesis: 'There is a tradition for mantras to be learnt by heart, but no corresponding tradition to teach and thereby preserve their meaning.'

TWELVE

~

RITUAL

Mantra and Kalpa

Much of what we found in the preceding chapter is formulated briefly, but clearly, in a post-Vedic work of uncertain date, the *Ṛgvidhāna*: 'The mantras attain the (desired) result by the correct method (*vidhi*) in the *brāhmaṇa*; they give success, when they are employed in the right ritual manner (*vidhivat*)' (translated by J. Gonda).

At the end of the previous chapter we have studied the upanayana initiation during which the Gāyatrī mantra is taught to a young student. I have argued that the way it is learned is totally different from the manner in which children learn or rather pick up their native natural language. But just as mantras derive their effectiveness from ritual, and not from language, no Vedic rite should be performed without mantras. In ritual, mantras are also treated differently from the sentences of a language. In the utterance of the latter, shouting, whispering or silence are options that individuals may use on whatever occasions they wish. If I cannot be heard, I may decide to raise my voice. If I wish to inspire confidentiality, I may whisper. But in ritual contexts, the occasions are fixed. When offerings are made, the accompanying mantra ends with *vauṣaṭ*! 'May (Agni) lead the offerings to the gods!' The priest should shout the second syllable ṢAṬ! at the top of his voice. In a larger number of contexts, mantras are recited mentally (*manasā*), more specifically *upāṃśu*, 'articulated but inaudible' (*pages* 124–5), which is distinguished from the ritual being performed *tūṣṇīm*, 'in silence'.

Unlike mantras, ritual consists of acts. I can do no more than give a rough idea of a syntactic study of Vedic ritual. We cannot even envisage instituting a large-scale syntactic comparison between mantras, ritual, language, bird song, other animal sound systems and rituals not to mention music and dance. Such a research programme lies in the future. If it is ever done, the study of Vedic mantras and ritual will be an integral part of it.

A common Indic term for ritual is *karman,* derived from the root *kṛ-* which means 'to do'. I have used it before and shall use it again, but it means so many other things that it is best avoided. Its vagueness may be an asset when describing references in the Rigveda that are too fragmentary to help us reconstruct specific rituals. In the Yajurveda, where many rituals are known in precise detail from Sūtra texts and performances, I shall use the term *kalpa*, which means both ritual practice and the science of ritual as we have seen. It is derived from a root *kḷp-* which means 'prepare' or 'arrange'. Its derivative *vikalpa* or 'alternative' denotes practices and rituals of other schools such as Baudhāyana or Āpastamba—not rival schools since they do not contradict but co-exist and are compatible with each other, as are the different lineages themselves.

The Exclusion of Śrauta from Anthropology in English

We have mainly looked at Śrauta rituals (*pages* 124–6) which are described in the Śrauta Sūtras. The other important component of *kalpa* are the Gṛhya or 'domestic' rites which include birth, initiation, marriage, funeral ceremonies and other life-cycle ceremonies. They were not included in Table 1 (*pages* 80–1) but incorporate the *upanayana* ceremony of which we needed an approximate idea because it provided the ritual background and context for the Gāyatrī mantra. One reason for the exclusion of life-cycle ceremonies from the present account of Vedic ritual is that these types of ceremony occur worldwide. Though their forms vary greatly, their social functions and significance are well understood since Arnold van Gennep whose ideas were developed by a group of British, American, and other anthropologists that include Victor Turner, Mary Douglas, Clifford Geertz and others. Life-cycle ceremonies may be explained in terms of boundaries that are crossed. I shall confine myself to the Śrauta rituals not only because they are, in Vedic India, more basic, but also because they cannot be explained with the help of the conceptual machinery of these anthropologists. It is here that the theories of ritual of many scholars of religion and of social scientists, especially in the English-speaking world, break down. The other reasons for not including the domestic rituals here is that the only remarkable features they possess beyond 'liminality' are influenced by or modelled on Śrauta rites.

Claude Lévi-Strauss could have made a great contribution were it not for the fact that he, perhaps wisely, excluded Indic materials almost entirely from the data on which his work was based. There is one apparent exception: in the 1950s, Lévi-Strauss did fieldwork in East Pakistan, among Buddhists of the Chittagong area. Unlike Obeyesekhere, whose work exudes lifelong familiarity with Sri Lankan Buddhism, Lévi-Strauss gave the Burmese surface a good scratch: he interpreted their 'Buddhism' as if it were a kind of Protestantism, neglecting the Mahāyāna which is or was part of Buddhism both in Sri Lanka and Myanmar. We shall return to these distinctions in Part V.

Lévi-Strauss could have made a contribution to the understanding of Śrauta rites because he had the basic background. He knew that appearance and reality are not the same thing. He attributed that insight, common to Plato and the Upaniṣads (Chapter 10), to his knowledge of geology and his familiarity with Marx. But he was also inspired by the distinctive features that the linguist Roman Jakobson had introduced in phonology. It might have opened new vistas and may still do so, if a modern student combines these insights with the study of Śrauta ritual.

One reason for the failure of modern anthropologists and other social scientists in the English-speaking world to come to terms with Śrauta rites is that they failed to see that the authors of the ritual Sūtras also had theories as they did themselves. That failure is surprising since the road was paved in 1899 by two French scientists: Henry Hubert and Marcel Mauss.

According to Mauss, Hubert did most of the work. It is unlikely because the cooperation between these two in a number of publications was remarkably close. Marcel Mauss was the greater scientist. He was the son-in-law of Emile Durkheim, the leader of French sociology until his death in 1917 when Mauss took over. In France, sociology is a serious and important subject which includes the study of civilization, the history of religions and much else. Sociological journals such as *L'Année Sociologique* are read not only by university professors but discussed by intellectuals. One of Mauss's most famous books that he published under his own name was 'An Essay on the Gift'. What enhances his importance to Vedic studies is that he had studied with the brilliant Sanskritist Sylvain Lévi who taught him a course on Vedic ritual in which he was the only student. The work that was published by Hubert and Mauss in 1899 incorporates these studies. Its first part, an 'Essay on the Nature and Function of Ritual,' is chiefly based upon Vedic and Jewish rites but provides what is perhaps the most serious sociological and anthropological study of ritual. Does it provide us with meanings?

It does not but the reader may wonder whether contemporary performances, more within the purview of anthropologists, may not provide those very meanings that have eluded us so far. T.P. Mahadevan and I have studied such performances and, not surprisingly, found that meanings are assigned to these performances and some of their elements or features. However, they reflect belief systems with which the rituals have nothing to do. That does not only apply to anachronistic interpretations of Vedic ritual in terms of 'Hinduism', but also to Vedic myths such as we have touched upon in Part II. In other words, rituals are like mantras: they tend to remain the same but interpretations change. That includes Vedic myths that are not invoked by the Śrauta Sūtras, but by Brāhmaṇas and modern scholars. Even in Vedic times, experts agree that Vedic ritual had little to do with Vedic mythology. According to Renou: 'Vedic religion is first and foremost a liturgy, and only secondarily a mythological or speculative system; we must therefore investigate it as a liturgy.' R.N. Dandekar wrote in a similar vein: 'The Rigvedic mythology can be shown to have hardly any relation to the 'solemn' (i.e. *śrauta*) ritual.'

Sometimes interpretations change rituals. This seems to apply especially to more recent or contemporary performances. When it was no longer believed that the ritual patron and the sacrificial animals would attain heaven, and when not only the Jainas but society in general condemned the ritual killing, or any killing of animals, goats were replaced by substitutes in South Indian Vedic ritual as we described in AGNI, our account of the 1975 performance of an Agnicayana. Robert Sharf has studied a more radical development in the Japanese Shingon ritual, which is related to the Vedic (ladles of the same shape are used, for example) and where theologians have for many centuries discussed and added to traditional rituals. Semantic content clearly mattered. Do the Japanese like adding—Indic syllabaries to Kanji characters without choosing like the Koreans—to some extent? I like Sharf's emphasis on powerful and mysterious forces. I doubt psychology or sociology, as I know them, will assist, but it is obvious that these discussions have not come to an end.

Self-Embedding and Other Animals

One difficulty for ritual theory that Hubert and Mauss did not confront is that rituals form a hierarchy and rites at the top of it may last a thousand years or more. To state such a fact, we need recursiveness for statements cannot be infinitely long. Recursiveness is needed to explain language as we have seen. But recursiveness occurs in ritual also and there is a link between grammar and ritual theory. The grammarian Patañjali, author of the *Great Commentary* on Pāṇini's grammar, was the first to arrive at that important insight. He wrote that neither rites, nor forms of language can be enumerated because no such enumeration would reach the end. Ritual and language can only be described and explained by treatises that provide *rules*. Such rules are called *sūtra* and that is what the Śrauta Sūtras and Pāṇini's grammar are therefore called.

We have studied *left-recursive* and *right-recursive* rules. Ritual exhibits another feature of recursiveness that ritual possesses and mantras in its wake, but that is rare in language: *self-embedding*. Fortunately for us, it may be constructed by combining simple *left-* and *right-recursive* sentences from English (the latter exhibits the same syntactic forms as we looked at before). The following examples are increasingly stilted, but have been constructed in accordance with the rules of English grammar:

(1) left-recursiveness:
The roof of the building which may be represented as BA;
The chimney of the roof of the building or CBA;
The colour of the chimney of the roof of the building or DCBA.

(2) right-recursiveness:
The building's roof or AB;
The building's roof's chimney or ABC;
The building's roof's chimney's colour or ABCD.

(3) *self-embedding*:
The roof the building has or BAB;
The chimney the roof the building has has or CBABC which is, in fact, C(BAB)C;
The colour the chimney the roof the building has has has or DCBABCD which is, in fact, D(C(BAB)C)D.

All three examples are artificial but (1) and (2) are possible and may become more natural if we introduce variations (as in: *the colour of the chimney that sits on the roof of the building)*. All but the first of (3) are simply unintelligible. We can have billions of have-nots, but English cannot combine two *haves* together.

In Vedic ritual, (3) is very common. Here is a simplified example of D(C(BAB)C)D:

D: constructing the enclosure
C: entering the enclosure
B: preparing the fire
A: making an offering
B: covering the fire
C: leaving the enclosure
D: destroying the enclosure.

Note that the last sequence corresponds to the first, the pre-final to the second, etc. It is a very common practice when performing an activity. We enter the room, open the cupboard, take out the cigar box, unlock and open it, take out the diamonds, close and lock the box again, close the cupboard and leave the room. We have, in this structure, taken one step more: EDCBABCDE or E(D(C(BAB)C)D)E. It does not occur in language unless it depicts an ongoing activity and someone expresses it with the help of concatenation as I just did. Self-embedding exists in mantras because Vedic rites are performed with mantras which mirror their ritual structure. It is obvious that these structures come from the domain of activities and not from language.

I have called these well-known structures of Vedic ritual 'self-embedding'. That was in 1989, the year in which the same term was used to refer to the same structure by the American Sanskritist C.Z. Minkowski. Both worked independently and did not even know each other. Others have also independently found these structures and called them by diverse names: nesting, frame structures, ring composition and sleeping dogs which curl up. Similar expressions have been used with reference to mantras: rings within rings, omphalos structure, etc. In both domains, attention has been paid to the preponderance of a centre, even if it is empty.

Some philologists and even innocent readers may wonder: do such concepts occur in the texts? 'Center,' 'nest' and 'sleeping dogs' do, others do not, but asking that question is barking up the wrong tree. Oral compositions and texts both have to be understood. Understanding may emerge when we try to *analyse* what we study, which is what we have been trying to. It is not only necessary, but also the salt without which food has no taste.

The advantage of the term 'self-embedding' goes a step further. It embeds the work of Vedicists in the much more developed theories of contemporary linguistics which themselves occupy a tiny corner in the theory of recursive functions in logic, mathematics and computer science. Recursive procedures are ultimately inspired by the sequence of natural numbers 1, 2, 3, ... Indic recursivity is connected, therefore, with the fact that India, unlike ancient Greece, was not afraid of very large numbers or infinity.

Is there any need to return from syntax to semantics once again? The meaninglessness of ritual is rather obvious in the case of Vedic ritual because it is a domain of activity which has nothing to do with language. It can also be established with the help of Kautsa's criteria. It is easy to see that six of the seven reasons that Kautsa gave or could have given for the meaninglessness of mantras (*pages* 141, 203) apply again. Vedic rituals have not changed much over time, their forms or structures have changed ever so slightly, their meaning is not taught. Shapes of wooden ladles that were used to pour oblations into the fire in Vedic times were taken over by Buddhists and Tantrics and can be found even now in the Shingon fire rituals of Japan. I leave it to the reader to check on the other reasons. The only reason which does not apply is Kautsa's criterion number 3. It does not show that ritual is meaningless, but throws much light on it as we have already seen. Rites do not contradict each other because, like mantras, they cannot be: they are activities not statements. This explains part of their soothing nature and popularity. Rituals do not create conflict. They are mutually compatible and ritualists are naturally tolerant. The Śrauta Sūtra of Baudhāyana regularly uses expressions of the form: 'Baudhāyana says that one should prefer 'P'; Śāliki says that one should not; Aupamanyava says . . . .' These are the *vikalpa* 'alternatives' we met with before.

The comparison between mantras and bird song is relatively new, but the insight that rituals are performed by non-human animals is as old as the Vedas. When Vedic stanzas declare that the layers of grass on which offerings are made constitute a nest, it is not a poetic simile but an obvious fact not requiring further comment. More relevant to the study of religion, though steadfastly ignored by many of its numerous experts who preserve a monotheistic outlook, is the fact that animal rituals have been studied for over half a century by ethnologists and almost equally long by historians of religion. I have the impression that we already know more about animal rituals than about Vedic ritual though it has been studied in India for thousands of years. Since there are many more animal species that engage in ritual than the few species of humans, we should expect much greater ritual variety among animals than in our own species.

Animal rituals go back at least as far as insects. There are large families of ritual structures that humans share with other animals. Most of them seem to be related to domestic rituals. Foremost among them are mating and territorial rites. The former ranges from courtship dances to marriage ceremonies; the latter from hopping around a favourite spot to military parades. Both are combined in preparing a nest or entering a new home. Whether animals have recursive Śrauta rituals I do not know, but a simple a priori argument suggests that they do not. There is only one uncontroversial fact that sets humans apart from the other animal species: language. Since the *theory* of ritual is expressed through language, the Śrauta rituals, in which theory and practice pervade each other, may be not only the most typical, but the only exclusively human ritual.

How the Priests Work Together

Vedic ritual is a cooperative activity between priests on behalf of the patron or *yajamāna*, who is almost always accompanied by his wife. He will remunerate the priests at the end for their work by giving them a *dakṣiṇā* or ritual gift. This is how Vedic rituals in general are often characterized, and illustrated by descriptions of the more spectacular occasions, such as the Royal Consecration or the famous *aśvamedha* or horse sacrifice. But when we witness the more commonly and frequently performed

Śrauta rituals, and study their history, another and different picture emerges.

Since the Yajurvedins started re-organizing the ritual, they increasingly emphasized the role and the tasks of priests. They assigned four priests to each of the four Vedas. All sixteen, and in addition an optional Sadasya, who is in charge of the Sadas, are needed to officiate in the Soma and all larger Śrauta rituals that are based upon, or related to them.

There is a simple form of Vedic ritual in which only four priests take part. An offering of rice and barley cakes is made by the Adhvaryu of the Yajurveda with the assistance of three others: the Hotā of the Rigveda, the Agnīdh who is responsible for one exclamation and the Brahman who is silent and supervises the rites without participating. There are three episodes, each consisting of two elements and it is from such elementary episodes that larger units are constructed with the help of recursion:

EPISODE I.
Element 1. Adhvaryu commands Hotā to address the deity, e.g., Agni, by saying: 'Address Agni!'
Element 2. Hotā addresses Agni by reciting mantras from the Rigveda.

EPISODE II.
Element 3. Adhvaryu exclaims to Agnīdh: 'Make him hear!'
Element 4. Agnīdh shouts at the top of his voice: 'So be it! May he hear!'

EPISODE III.
Element 5. Adhvaryu commands Hotā: 'Say the offering verse for Agni!'
Element 6. Hotā begins by murmuring 'Earth! Air! We who are saying the offering verse . . .', raises his voice, recites the Rigvedic verse and ends with an exclamation: 'May (Agni) lead (the offerings to the gods)!' At the last syllable, which Hotā shouts at the top of his voice: *vau ṢAṬ!* (*pages* 222–3), Adhvaryu makes the offering by throwing or pouring it into the fire. At the same time, the patron pronounces his 'renunciation' (*tyāga*): 'This is for Agni, not for me!'

A slightly more complex ritual may be constructed from this basic rite by adding another element that is substituted in the proper place—the first step of a process that, when extended further, may be described in recursive terms. In the animal sacrifice, an animal offering is substituted for the offering of rice or barley cakes and one more priest is needed: the Maitrāvaruṇa of the Rigveda. His insertion into the ritual proceedings is effected by extending Episode I with one element, as follows:

Element 1. Adhvaryu commands Maitrāvaruṇa to command Hotā to address the deity.
Element 1'. Maitrāvaruṇa commands Hotā to address the deity.

The reader will have noted two things. In this simple ritual, the patron or *yajamāna* performs only one rite: he renounces his ownership of the rice and barley cakes which he is offering to Agni. In the larger rituals, his tasks are more complex, but they are still negligible in comparison with all the chanting, recitation and ritual activities in which the sixteen priests engage. It may be compared to the building of a house: it is done by the architect with the help of numerous specialists who build the foundation, lay bricks, build walls and a roof, install the pipes and other mechanisms and contraptions through which water, electricity, etc., flow. There must be an owner also, who may or may not plan to live in the house but who has paid for everything. Just as building the house is done by the architect with his specialist assistants, performing the ritual is done by the priests.

Performing a ritual may be compared to making music. The conductor leads, the orchestra plays, and someone pays or makes money or is especially honoured on the occasion of the performance. Śrauta rituals are similar, the art of ritual is perfected by the performing priests, and the patron plays an essential but subordinate role. That tendency must have been present from the beginning and reaches its logical conclusion at the end of the Vedic period when so-called *sattra* rituals were performed by only priests, or priests who were all *yajamānas*, which comes to the same thing. In post-Vedic times, that pattern prevailed and in the end, the patron performs his tasks as if he were one of the priests.That is why Patañjali, when he compared the infinity of language to that of ritual, mentioned that it pertains to expressions that are never used 'just like protracted *sattras*'.

The second thing that the reader will have noted is that I used the term 'sacrifice' to refer to the animal sacrifice. I could have used that loaded term once before when I referred to the atypical so-called 'Hymn of Puruṣa' where a primordial male is dismembered and killed (*pages* 59, 65). I did not because the term 'sacrifice,' which many scholars use to refer to what I call 'ritual,' comes with the ballast of a millennial tradition which is not Indic: the monotheistic tradition which started with Abraham's willingness to sacrifice his son to his god, went on from there to the idea that god sent his son as a sacrifice to liberate humanity, and has presently reached the stage where the ultimate form of sacrifice is mass-suicide. Those ideas are not found in Vedic ritual and I believe that the term 'sacrifice' should be used in our context only in the very prescribed sense in which I have used it here, namely, to refer to a ritual in which an animal is killed.

Human Sacrifice

Most Śrauta rituals require the sacrifice of goats. In the Puruṣa poem, the animal is human and it raises the question: did human sacrifice exist in India? We might start with the noun *medha* which refers in the Rigveda to the juice of meat or the marrow and later to any animal sacrifice. The term *puruṣamedha*, coined like *aśvamedha* or horse sacrifice, is mentioned in the Yajur- and Atharva Brāhmaṇas. The Śatapatha Brāhmaṇa is quite explicit on it and how could it not? There is nothing with which the Brāhmaṇas do *not* deal, as we have seen. In 1882, the learned translator of these texts, Julius Eggeling, had some worthwhile things to say on them.

The first is that the *puruṣamedha* is always treated as a symbolic, not an actual performance. That is not due to the fact that Professor Eggeling would be scandalized by this because he isn't, not even by their 'flimsy symbolism' which he compared to the 'speculative vapourings of the Gnostics'. He takes up the *puruṣamedha* first in a footnote where he crosses daggers with his old teacher, the famous Albrecht Weber, one of the great Vedic scholars of the nineteenth century, brother of the still more famous sociologist Max Weber. Albrecht had written that the would-be victims 'may possibly at one time have been intended to be all of them slaughtered.' Julius retorts, as a good pupil should his teacher, that that supposition 'can hardly have been meant seriously. One might as well suppose that, at the *aśvamedha*, all the "evil-doers" who, according to Kātyāyana, are to bathe in the river, "were meant to be drowned".'

According to Eggeling, the 'human sacrifice' was a theoretical scheme intended to complete the system.

Another argument, perhaps more straightforward is: if the ritual system included human sacrifice, it would lead to cannibalism, since the patron and his priests eat the omentum of the animal that is slaughtered, whether it is a goat (the common option) or a horse. No patron would want to be responsible for cannibalism and no participant would consent to engage in it either.

The two Eggeling arguments I have just sketched have an ethical ring about them. Perhaps the Vedas had no ethics. This is more or less Obeyesekhere's thesis (*pages* 170ff). Eggeling's third argument has no such ring and is based upon straightforward philology and textual analysis. The only two Sūtras that describe the *puruṣamedha*, of the Śāṅkhāyana and Vaitāna schools, are in all details copies or adaptations of descriptions of the *aśvamedha* which had no existence in and by itself. I believe that is the best of Eggeling's arguments but one must know something about the *aśvamedha* which I have not so far mentioned.

Performances of the horse-sacrifice have been popular because it is a royal ritual, meant to expand the king's territory. It is mentioned in inscriptions, mostly read by scholars, but was popular in the Mahābhārata. Its popularity survives in Varanasi, where the central and most famous ghāt is called *daśāśvamedha*, not because there was a 'Ten Horse Sacrifice' (as Diana Eck writes), but because there were supposed to have been ten performances of the *aśvamedha* that ended there.

A special reason for the popularity of the *aśvamedha* is that it is not a ritual only for a king. It is a king whose queen has to lie next to the horse, covered by some kind of garment, a symbolic act since the horse is dead.

A final word about the terms 'ritual' and 'sacrifice'. I have proposed to distinguish them from each other by using 'ritual' for the general category and reserving 'sacrifice' for a ritual in which an animal is ritually killed. I am not the first who made a distinction between the two terms. Albrecht

Weber, whom I just mentioned, took the general meaning of Hotā to be 'sacrificer', not just 'priest'. The verbal root from which Hotā is derived means either 'sacrifice' or 'invoke'. According to Renou, the name of the Hotā priest must be connected with sacrifice, not invocation. J.C. Heesterman, from whom I learned a great deal about Vedic ritual, used 'ritual' in earlier publications, notably in his 'Essays on Indian Ritual, Kingship and Society' that are widely known as *The Inner Conflict of Tradition*. Later he published *The Broken World of Sacrifice* with the subtitle 'An Essay in Ancient Indian Ritual'. The Introduction of that book begins with the lapidary statement: 'Sacrifice seems to be out of fashion. In anthropology, where once it was an important theme, it seems to have fallen in disuse, if not disrepute.' Heesterman maintains the distinction and his book describes ritualism as the total subjection of sacrifice to the rule of ritual.

Despite a massive amount of solid data, ever increasing in number, and an ever-expanding discussion that has engaged many top-class minds, my present chapter remains open-ended. I have tried to give an idea of some of the conceptual problems that bedevil the understanding of mantras and ritual, but we have not reached the core, let alone the end. The powers of mantras and ritual seem to be beyond the grasp of the human and social sciences and have not been explained by contemporary scholars or scientists. The same holds for meditation which is closely related to recitation and chant; and for bird song as we have already seen.

I conclude that we may with equanimity and for the time being, pay no serious attention to the ponderous ruminations and platitudes of some of our contemporaries. I prefer Yājñavalkya's explanation of mantras, which may also apply to rituals: their power comes from the sun. He may also have accepted the Chāndogya claim that the sun, in its circular movements, makes the sound OM. Though I live in the country, I have been unable to hear it, but since most of the energy available on our planet comes from the sun in any case, Yājñavalkya's explanation, while insufficiently precise, lacking in intelligible detail and certainly incomplete, is basically correct.

THIRTEEN

~

SECRETS OF THE SADAS

Soma Sequences

All the larger Soma rituals are characterized by sequences of rites which I have called 'Soma Sequences'. Each consist of a Sāmaveda chant (*stuti*), a Rigveda recitation (*śastra*), Soma offerings and Soma drinking by the ritual patron and some of his priests. The Soma offerings are made out in the open, on the offering altar at the eastern end of the ritual arena. The other three rites take place behind the walls of the Sadas. Its position is shown in Figure 16. But it is only now that we will get an inkling of the significance of the Adhvaryu's statement, which is issued at the beginning of each sequence: 'You are the bed for coupling Rik and Sāman for the sake of procreation!' Procreation of what?

Each of the four parts of a Soma sequence consists of several elements.

A. The first part consists of four elements: 1) the Adhvaryu's statement above; 2) a joint recitation by two Yajurveda priests that ends with 'OM! Chant!'; 3) the *stuti* itself; 4) a joint recitation by Adhvaryu and patron called 'Chant Milking.'

B. The second part consists again of four elements but

the first consists of two sub-elements that flow into each other: 1A) the *puroruc* or 'prior light' on which we almost slipped and 1B) which is the *śastra*; 2) a piece by the Rigveda reciter called 'Recital Strength'. 3) 'Recitation Milking' which corresponds to 'Chant Milking' followed by a special piece by the ritual patron:

> The ritual has been, has been produced,
> It is born, it has grown,
> It has become king of the gods.
> May it turn us into kings,
> May we be masters of wealth!

C. The third part is the Soma offering. It has the recursive ritual structure studied in Chapter **12** and ends with the exclamation *vauṣaṭ*, 'may (Agni) lead (the offerings to the gods)!'.

D. The fourth and final part is the culmination of the Soma sequence. It consists again of four elements: 1. Each priest who is about to drink addresses the Adhvaryu: 'Adhvaryu, invite me.' 2. The Adhvaryu replies: 'You are invited'! 3. Then comes Soma drinking. It is called Soma 'partaking', that is, 'drinking' or 'eating' (*bhakṣaṇa*), and consists of sipping accompanied by Rigveda recitals. 4. The Adhvaryu recites a long piece from the Rigveda called 'Long Drink'.

The structure of this ritual construction may be expressed by an inverted tree:

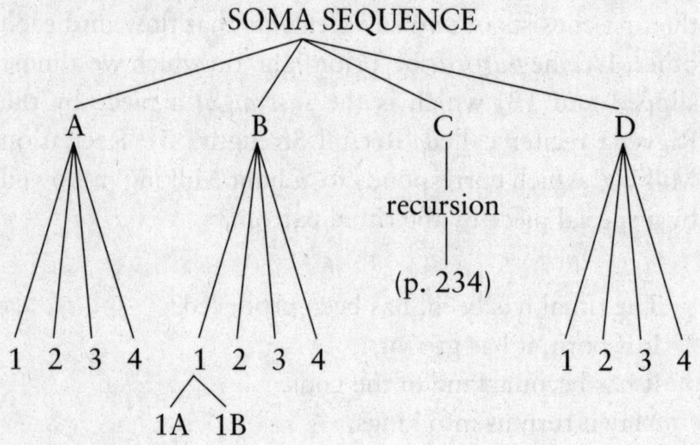

We have here a careful construction in which everyone protects himself from all sides, that is: from other parties and possible rivals. This holds especially for the Yajurveda Adhvaryu and his colleagues. They see to it that they are involved everywhere and in control, if possible. The patron is also involved to the maximal extent and repeatedly joined by the Adhvaryu. All in all, it is a powerful demonstration of the strength of ritual along Yajurveda lines.

Offerings are given to the gods in the open. They involve again a good amount of Rigveda recitation and Sāmaveda chant. But the full weight of ritualism resides in the Sadas; and it provides an answer to the question: Procreation of what?

The Sadas is the locus of SV *stutis* and RV *śastras* for the sake of procreation and preservation of the oral tradition under supervision of the Yajurveda.

Sitting inside, the Sadas provides a link between ritual and the Upaniṣads and points, therefore, to the future. The early Upaniṣads continued to elucidate and interpret ritual. The Bṛhad-Āraṇyaka is an Āraṇyaka, as its name says, a continuation of the Śatapatha Brāhmaṇa. The chief message of the Upaniṣads became to reject ritual and replace it by knowledge, but the connection between Sadas and Upaniṣad is obvious to all speakers of Sanskrit since the verbal root *sad-* of Upaniṣad is the same as the *sad-* of the *sadas*. It refers to a place to sit. Sitting was obviously important and that is not because chairs had not yet been invented. Sitting on the ground connects with the earth. So does sleeping on the ground which is sleeping with mother earth. The king does more than sleeping with her: he is her husband. The sitting Buddha makes a vow by touching the earth in a similar spirit and with a well-known gesture. Later meditators continue to sit. Zen made a cult of it. It is connected with breathing and may have something to do with erect spines. It also points to a *sedentary* civilization for *sed* equals *sad* which equals *sit*.

Moving South and East

Part I emphasized links of Vedic civilization with Central Asia and the Near East. Part II showed how that civilization moved south-east, adapted itself on the subcontinent to a new environment, interacted with other cultures and began to settle down. Ritual, history and geography illustrate how those settlements moved further east. Figure 16 shows how the Ritual Arena for the Soma ceremonies corresponds to the historical map of Central Asia including Vedic India. The officiating priests are not aware of those correspondences and they remain unexpressed by the large majority of our sources.

The three arrows on the historical map, two earlier and one slightly later, depict the movements of Indo-Aryan. They originate from the Central Asian homeland, around the BMAC (**3** and **6** on the Frontspiece), where speakers of Indo-Aryan or Proto-Indo-Aryan made offerings on a flat piece of soil on which a fire had been installed. It survives in the Ancient Hut on the left or west of the Ritual Arena where the flat piece of soil has been replaced by small altars as in Figure 15. The fire embers were carried in a pot to wherever the family pitched its tent. It corresponds to the carrying of fire to the new home of the ritual patron as mentioned in Chapter 7. The western part of the Ancient Hut was reserved for the patron's wife and the remaining space was used for domestic or quasi-domestic rites, and functioned as a kitchen for the preparation of food or offerings to the gods. Because of its domestic character, the Ancient Hut is surrounded by walls, like the Sadas but for different reasons: the protection and privacy of the wife.

To the east of the Ancient Hut a new enclosure is constructed. Its first structure is the Sadas which points to Pirak, where the earliest excavated Vedic altars come from. Their extraordinary shapes are similar to those of the altars in front of which the Rigvedins recite their *śastras* (Figure

20). To the east of the Sadas is the enclosure where the Soma is prepared and kept. It is connected with Mount Mūjavat in the Pamirs, near the source of the Oxus, where the best Soma came from. At the eastern end, the bird-shaped offering altar represents the Kuru area where, around 1,000 BCE, the Yajurveda and the other Vedas were composed and the ritual piling of the Agnicayana took place for the first time.

Moving east within the ritual enclosure does not *mean* moving east from the Indus to the Ganges Valleys, but the correspondence with the outside world need not surprise us: facing east, which is ritually auspicious, is also the direction of the rising sun, and the same holds for the clockwise circumambulations that are common in many rituals of the northern hemisphere.

The basic movements are defined by all the ritual sūtras and most authoritatively by the Śrauta Sūtra of Baudhāyana. It declares at the outset of the list of metarules with which it begins: 'Facing east (*prāṅmukham*), turning to the right (*pradakṣiṇam*), invested with the sacred thread, he performs the divine rites.' 'He,' the subject of *karoti karmāṇi* ('he performs the rites') is the default officiant: the Adhvaryu priest of the Yajurveda, the Veda to which Baudhāyana belongs. The Adhvaryu is the organizer and manager of the ritual, whose historical task was the incorporation of Rigvedic recitations and Sāmavedic chants, specifically the *śastras* and *stutis*. The notion of default occurs in the Śrauta Sūtras as we shall see in Chapter **14** (*page* 264). But we have not explained why the Adhvaryu hid these important contributions behind walls.

Never Seeing Eye To Eye

One might simplify Vedic ritual by describing it as a cooperative effort of priests from three Vedas: the Rigvedins recite, the Sāmavedins chant and the Yajurvedins perform rites. Some Rigvedins may be descendants through the male line of composers of the Rigveda. The Sāmavedins took their verse and set them to music, following melodies their ancestors had sung on the words of another language. There were rivalries between the two groups and our ritual sources show that the Sāmavedins were often discriminated against.

The Yajurvedins were in charge of everything concerned with ritual, including the Sadas. We have seen how Sāyaṇa described it in Chapter 7: it displays the beauties of Rigveda and Sāmaveda on its walls like exquisite murals. The Yajurvedins made use of the rivalries between the two earlier Vedas and sought control over the two older priestly groups. They made those who recite Rigveda sit in a row on the eastern side, facing the auspicious east. They put those who chant Sāmaveda on the western side, facing all directions but the east, singing towards the north, west and south. The most important Sāmaveda priest is the Udgātā. His name means: 'singing to the north'. Rig- and Sāmavedins could have sat quite differently—we shall return to that possibility—but the Yajurvedins made them sit with their backs to each other, literally never seeing eye to eye.

'Never seeing eye to eye' is an accurate description as we can see on Figure 17 where arrows depict the opposite directions the officiants face in the Sadas when they go through their sequences.

In Figure 18, we are looking east into the Sadas. In front, the three Sāmavedins are singing in their three directions. They mark the progressions of their chant on a piece of cloth with sticks. The bald Udgātā sits on the right with folded hands, singing to the north. Those who recite the Rigveda face east and the viewer therefore sees their backs. They are not reciting now, they are waiting for stage directions from the Sāmavedins. There are many rounds and calculating from the sticks, I would say it will take at least another thirty minutes.

What is kept hidden here behind walls? I believe it is the manipulations of the Yajurvedins, who were newcomers and upstarts. The other two may have been rivals, but they had already cooperated with each other. Without them, there would be nothing. Then the Yajurvedins took charge, introduced structure and established their power, following the principle of divide and rule. It fixed and empowered the Oral Tradition with the Yajurveda in control.

Facing All Directions

Baudhāyana described the ancient paradigm: 'Facing east (*prāṅmukham*), turning to the right (*pradakṣiṇam*), invested with the sacred thread, he performs the divine rites.' In the course of the development of the Śrauta ritual, between say 1100 and 900 BCE, a paradigm change took place. 'Facing east' was replaced by 'facing all directions' (*sarvatomukham*). It is explicitly specified for the *Agnicayana* altar where, on each layer, the bricks are arranged and consecrated in specific directions. What applies to the directions of bricks applies to the directions of the officiants themselves. Baudhāyana repeats it five times in his Śrauta Sūtra formulations, at the beginning of each of the five layers and with the help of two statements which I shall put between single quotes. They quote metarules (*page* 262) (between double quotes) as is their wont. First he says: 'Metarules like "he deposits them toward the east, he deposits them toward the west" denote the series of bricks when there are groups.' Then he continues: 'Metarules like "he deposits it toward the east, he deposits it toward the west" indicate that the agent who does the depositing faces in that direction.' He mentions east and west explicitly but it is obvious throughout that it applies to all the four directions.

The new paradigm explains two things, one about the Yajurvedins, the other about the Sāmavedins. The Yajurvedins, who took over the organization of the ritual during Kuru times, had to accommodate two rival parties and thereby created the edifice first of three, then of four Vedas, sealed their canonization and tried to safeguard the supremacy of the Vedas and of themselves for all times.

The case of the Sāmavedins is special as we have seen. The words of the original, indigenous Sāmaveda chants are lost; but we know something about them because of some of their names and the names of some of the altars with which they were associated. They are non-Indo-European: some have a recognizably BMAC structure and a few are

Dravidian. The words of the Rigveda often do not fit and the melodies seem to reflect another language.

What do we know about the development of ritual during those periods? We possess a fragmentary knowledge of Rigvedic rites and know nothing or next to nothing about the rites of the ancestors of the Sāmavedins. The development of Vedic Śrauta ritual started with their halting cooperation and was subsequently organized, systematized and brought to completion by the Yajurvedins during the Kuru period. Reciters and chanters were familiar with other ritualists and ritual constructions, representatives of more distant or eccentric groups (some from the BMAC), but it is cooperation with each other that they primarily sought. At the stage of development depicted in the original or proto-Sadas, that cooperative effort was in its infancy. Later it became more universal as signalled by the paradigm change to 'all directions'.

During the mature Kuru period, Rig- and Sāmavedins had lived in the same surroundings and society for some time. First they were rivals who could not and did not want to understand or communicate with each other, let alone enquire or learn about each others myths and speculations or teach their own. It goes a long way to explain, that Vedic Śrauta ritual has nothing to do with Rigvedic mythology. It is a characteristic of all ritual, its mantra counterpart occurs in Kautsa and there are exceptions in more modern developments (e.g., in contemporary performances in Kerala) and in the Shingon ritual of Japan. Even so and on the whole, it is characteristic of Vedic ritual, and apparently of Indic rituals in general, that they continue to live a life of their own. They have to be performed in the correct manner as we have seen in Chapter 12 and that is all there is to it.

Such a situation is common in music, dance or science and shows where ritual belongs. Musicians are able to cooperate closely without being able to converse, understand or read the same language. It applies to singers, orchestras or chamber music—Caland likened the ritual ensemble of the four Vedas to a string quartet—especially when there are last minute substitutes, visiting performers or alien maestros. Scientists are also able to cooperate closely without knowing each other's natural language. What they need to understand is artificial languages such as the language of algebra (to which we return in a wider context in Chapter 15). Rituals, mantras and equations are like dance of which Isadora Duncan said: 'If I could tell you what it meant, there would be no point in dancing it.'

Epilogue

Towards the end of the Vedic period, rivals appeared on the horizon: Buddhism was one to which we return in Part V; literacy another. In the long run, Buddhism did not stay in India. Books bound in India continue to fall apart but the Vedic Oral Tradition is still there.

As for the Sadas, it would have been easy for Rig- and Sāmavedins to face each other. One solution would be to face all directions. Another, for each party to continue facing its preferential directions but face each other by sitting in a circle. It is a common practice in the round-table conferences of contemporary politics and looks like the most transparent solution, but it has another drawback: it is a display of insularity because the participants hide behind their backs something even more important—the wide open universe. Thus they resemble two-dimensional beings crawling within a circle.

Proceeding to the third dimension, imagine we were inhabiting the inside surface of our globe. On that interface we would be equally close to, or distant from each other as on the outside of the surface, the soles of our feet almost the same size. Inside there would be a small sun with the Himalayas tapering to insignificance. After some time, no one would notice the difference.

PART IV

WHAT CAN WE LEARN FROM THE VEDAS?

Analysis and Discovery

Part IV combines two topics that appear to be different. The first is concerned with the Vedic Sciences, a well-defined set. The second examines a small number of insights that I call 'Vedic Insights'. The latter may be related to the Vedic Sciences but, like numerous other disciplines, they do not conform to the scheme that distinguishes between 'exact', 'human', 'life' and 'social' sciences.

Whereas the Vedic Sciences are often outdated and superseded by later developments, the Vedic Insights seem to show that there are things that the composers of the Vedas knew but we do not. It supports what we do know: many topics are beyond our present understanding of the universe and all that it contains.

FOURTEEN

~

SŪTRA: VEDIC SCIENCES

The Concept of Science and its Ancient History

Science is universal, but the concept of science varies in different cultures. English *science* is different from French *science*, German *Wissenschaft,* Japanese *gaku,* Russian *nauka*, etc. English *science* refers to what it regards as the 'exact' sciences, viz., mathematics, physics and other so-called 'natural sciences'. The French and the other quoted terms include human, life, social and other sciences. They are all exact in that they strive for explicitness and avoid contradictions. The definition I adopt is the widest I could find within these constraints: science is the search for systematic, exact and highly confirmed knowledge of the universe which includes, of course, ourselves. Thus defined, science is similar to *veda*. However, it recognizes more clearly and explicitly the duality of facts and logic.

The history of science is not a random enumeration of sciences that are found throughout history or at different times. Structure and development are inherent in it. Einstein understood more than Newton and Newton more than Aristotle. Medieval Indic mathematicians understood more than their Vedic predecessors and Srinivasa Ramanujan understood more than both. The history of science exhibits not only a gradual widening of knowledge but also a deepening of insight. It is on this history that technology and much else depend. None of this implies that progress is always made. There is no dearth of dead ends; mistaken assumptions have reigned for centuries before they were abandoned and there must be much that is irretrievably lost. We should not therefore regard ancient sciences as more or less clumsy attempts to express modern scientific ideas. But even worse is to think that each science reflects a particular culture. Vedic mathematics is mathematics before it is Vedic. Modern science is not 'Western'—a term that should be avoided anyway, just as much as 'Eastern', 'Occidental' or 'Oriental'. 'Modern' science is modern in that it represents the most recent phase, for modern is a relative term; what is modern today may not be modern tomorrow. Science is universal in precisely that sense, and is universal by its very nature.

What does it mean: 'Science is universal by nature'? Imagine we want to transform a rectangle into a square with the same area. There are many ways to do it, but Greek and Vedic geometers devised the same method in a similar ritual context. It would seem likely that one influenced the other but as it happens, the particular solution they arrived at originated in ancient Mesopotamia. In other cases, solutions may have been arrived at independently. All we know is that there were opportunities for Greek, Vedic and Chinese mathematicians, astrologers or astronomers and other scientists to meet their colleagues in Iran, Alexandria or Central Asia. If they could find a solution to a problem, it did not matter where it came from. It does not even require a common language. And there were no governments or pharmaceutical companies trying to prevent it.

If we study the history of ancient and medieval science, we must reckon with two major insights that have been evolved by historians of science over the last half a century, roughly speaking from Otto Neugebauer and Joseph Needham to David Pingree (*pages* 284–5, *note*). These insights are based upon the textual and historical study of source materials in the classical languages of science that include Arabic, Old-Babylonian, Chinese, Greek, Latin and Sanskrit. The first insight is based upon empirical results, that is, facts; the second upon epistemological analysis, that is, upon a reflection of how we are able to know facts.

The first insight is that ancient and medieval science can only be adequately understood if the Eurasian continent is treated as an undivided unit. It is depicted in Figure 19, which portrays some historical relationships between Eurasian sciences. It shows first of all that Mesopotamian science is earlier than Indian and Chinese. It influenced both in the areas of astronomy and mathematics. Furthermore, it implies that Indic science does not stand alone and cannot be studied by isolating it artificially from the remainder of the Eurasian continent. That is not an obvious fact: it has been established by empirical study. There may be links between that large unit and scientific developments in Africa, but not, for example, with Meso-American cultures which grew in total isolation until the sixteenth century.

The second insight was formulated with special force and clarity by Joseph Needham, whose monumental work is not only about China, but abounds in information on Indic, Near Eastern and European sciences: 'to write the history of science we have to take modern science as our yardstick—that is the only thing we can do—but modern science will change, and the end is not yet.'

The Traditional List and the Concept of Sūtra

The Vedic sciences are not objects that moderns are at liberty to make up. Much is known about them and what we know is in accordance with a traditional classification of sciences that belong to the late Vedic period. This was anticipated by a more adventurous or generous list in the early Chāndogya Upaniṣad (7.1.1–4). It uses the term *vidyā* which is closely related to *veda*, both meaning 'knowledge'. The Chāndogya passage starts with sage Nārada asking Sanatkumāra, 'Eternal Youth,' to teach him what he knows. Sanatkumāra returns the question: 'Tell me first what you know. Then I'll tell you what more there is to know.' Nārada gives a long reply in which he refers to the four Vedas, the corpus of histories and ancient tales, ancestral rites, mathematics, soothsaying, the art of locating treasures, and the sciences of ritual, spirits, government, heavenly bodies and serpent beings. 'All that, sir, I have studied.' Eternal Youth responds wisely: 'All that is nothing but names.'

A later and more realistic Vedic classification refers to seven sciences as *vedāṅga,* 'limbs of the Veda'. The word 'science' is an apt interpretation of *aṅga*, 'limb', provided we interpret 'science' not in the idiosyncratic English manner.

I have counted the Vedic sciences as seven though the first two are combined. Their names with rough translations into English are: ritual (*kalpa*) to which geometry (*śulba)* is attached; phonology/phonetics (*śikṣā*); etymology (*nirukta*); grammar (*vyākaraṇa*); prosody (*chanda*s) and astronomy/astrology (*jyotiṣā*). All were orally conceived and transmitted.

Two features of this list deserve notice. The first is that the science of ritual stands in front which is in accordance with the findings of our Chapters **7**, **9** and **12**. It is also consistent with our chronology because *kalpa* is the subject of the Śrauta Sūtras, which overlap in time with late Brāhmaṇas and early Āraṇyakas and Upaniṣads, all earlier than the traditional Vedic limbs. We have seen that the Śrauta Sūtras consist of detailed descriptions and provide a theoretical and analytical account which justifies their inclusion among the 'limbs of the Veda' and in this chapter. The second special feature of the list is that four of the sciences deal with language. That is strikingly different from the entire Euro-American development in which these sciences, despite the fact that language is the chief characteristic of our species, have always played a relatively minor role. As for philology, an ancient and venerable discipline, it is not a science of language but is concerned with texts.

The science of ritual is the first in which the notion of *sūtra* or 'rule' comes to the fore. I have used that term often but not explained it so far. Literally, it means 'thread' and belongs to a family of related terms and concepts that originated in the domain of textile manufacture. Many of these terms are applied to scientific works: *grantha*, 'knot', *tantra*, 'loom' or 'warp', *nibandha*, 'tying', *prabandha*, 'band' or 'tie', etc. *Sūtra* or 'rule' suggests a scientific work in which objects are woven together in the manner in which strands are sewn/woven/turned together into a thread. Rules contrast with 'enumeration' (*saṃkhyā*) because they are analytic and tend towards generalization and universalization. In the introduction to his Great Commentary *(Mahābhāṣya)* on Pāṇini's grammar, the grammarian Patañjali explained that the expressions of language cannot be enumerated because they are infinite in number. Unlike an analytical science that makes use of rules, an enumeration would never reach the end. Patañjali concluded that a treatise of rules and exceptions must be composed instead. Pāṇini's grammar is that treatise. It is Vedic in spirit because *brahman* and *vāc* were both regarded as infinite. But it is not Vedic in extent because it described and analysed the spoken language of Pāṇini's time.

A common definition of *sūtra* of later date is that it 'consists of a few syllables, not leading to doubt, containing the essence of a topic, fully explicit, without embellishment and faultless.' The term I have translated as 'embellishment' is none other than the Sāmavedic stobha. The concept of sūtra was soon deepened and widened. Deeper insights into language led to the concepts of meta-language and of *paribhāṣā* or 'metarule'. Metarules are rules about rules (*page* 250). Like other technical concepts of the science of language, their roots lie in the science of ritual. An example is 'The rule "he deposits Brick A" comes before "he recites mantra B for brick A".'

The Science of Ritual

Following the order of the 'limbs of the Veda,' we begin with the science of ritual. It deals with many more scientific concepts than the notion of ritual evokes in a modern mind. There is nothing in modern science that corresponds to such a discipline unless it is directly inspired by it, like Hubert and Mauss. It is a science because it provides systematic and highly confirmed knowledge of ritual structures such as self-embedding and other forms of recursiveness mentioned or alluded to in Chapters **11** and **12**. Other civilizations have been interested in the study of ritual—the Confucian and Taoist in China and the Orthodox and Catholic during the European middle ages—but it is unlikely that they attained the high level of technical and theoretical sophistication that we find in the Śrauta Sūtras because they lacked the close interaction between ritual and grammar that characterizes Vedic science. Some technical concepts of the Vedic science of ritual anticipate linguistics, modern logic and computer science.

Since we have come across illustrations from the Vedic science of ritual in earlier chapters, I shall illustrate it in the present section with another notion which exemplifies at the same time the concept of metarule: the notion of *default*. Its practice is clear: what I type on my keyboard appears in *roman* on my screen because that is the default option; it appears in *italics* when I push additional keys or move the mouse accordingly. Its theoretical status is clear: it is a meta-concept.

In the domain of *śrauta*, the road that led to these discoveries was paved by practical abbreviations in the formulation of rules. They have to be studied with the same care as formulas in a textbook of mathematics. For example: 'whichever among the divinities have secondary names, for them (mantras are recited) in low voice or softly; as for the others, loudly, provided there is an explicit statement.' Similarly: 'when there is no special statement, the usual one about the sacrificial fees prevails.' In this last statement, 'the usual one' refers to the default option.

Metarules for default are illustrated by all the Śrauta Sūtras and are explained in simple terms by Āpastamba. It singles out default options for oblations, priests and implements such as ladles. It begins with specifying the default oblation as clarified butter. It means that the oblation is clarified butter if nothing else is stated. The default priest is the Adhvaryu. It means that he has to perform the job at hand if no one else is specified. The default implement is the *juhū* ladle. There are degrees of default: when the *juhū* is already used, and no other implement is specified, the oblation has to be made with the help of the *śruva*. The notion of default is common among the grammarians and the notion of multiple default occurs in Pāṇini's theory of syntactic relations or *kāraka* which is preceded by the metarule: '(the following rules apply) when it [i.e., the *kāraka*] is not (already) expressed.'

Metarules about default are formulated in the sūtra style which is terse and brief, as laid down in the definition. The rules of Āpastamba are exemplary and I shall list them as they appear in Sanskrit to illustrate that brevity. The first rule is long, but part of it is implicit in the next three: *juhotīti codyamāne sarpirājyam pratīyāt*, 'if offering is stated, clarified butter is implied'; *adhvaryuṃ kartāram* 'Adhvaryu (is) the agent'; *juhūṃ pātram* '*juhū* the ladle'; *vyāpṛtāyāṃ śruveṇa*, 'if already employed, the *śruva*'.

The science of ritual was the first to display the kind of brevity of expression about which a later grammarian wrote: 'grammarians rejoice over the saving of half a syllable as over the birth of a son.' But brevity is not sought for its own sake. It expresses the most general solution to a particular problem as Paul Kiparsky has explained.

Geometry

Vedic geometry is attached to ritual because it is concerned with the measurement and construction of ritual enclosures (such as the ritual arena of Figure 15) and of altars (Figures 21–22). Our knowledge is based to a small extent upon the living tradition, but more complete information survives in the Śulba Sūtras. The most important are Baudhāyana, Āpastamba and Mānava, which are attached to Śrauta Sūtras of the Black Yajurveda, and Kātyāyana which is attached to the White. The term *śulba* means rope. Ropes and pegs are used for measurements, to mark a straight line or circle and construct a square, rectangle, trapezium or straight line parallel or orthogonal to another.

A common problem in Vedic and Greek geometry was the construction of a square equal in area to a given rectangle. It was applied to the construction of altars. The

Vedic geometric tradition seems to preserve earlier forms. Eight of them are squares which consist of sun-fired bricks that are themselves squares and rectangles or oblongs. Six are assigned to priests and situated in or near the Sadas. They include the altars of the Rigvedins in Figure 20. All are identified with the ritual patron: they are *his* altars. That means: they are functions of or relative to his size. The patron's size is measured from the tips of his fingers, raised above his head, to the ground.

The uncommon patterns that these altars display are not only described in the Śulba Sūtras, but supported by archaeology, for similar patterns of slightly larger square altars have been excavated by Jarrige and other French archaeologists at Pirak at the foot of the Bolan Pass (Frontispiece, 8). The dates lie roughly between 1500 and 1200 BCE when Vedic Indians had already settled there. Eight of these altars are depicted in Figure 20.

They are arranged in increasing complexity in order to present a reconstruction of Proto-Geometric evolution. The similarity between altars from the Sadas and the excavated variety is striking. The reader is invited to identify which is which as a kind of exercise. (The answer is given at the end of the Geometry section on *page* 272.)

The development illustrates how altars known from the later Vedas are situated within the period of those that were excavated at Pirak—a result that is in accordance with our present understanding of the sequence of development and the absolute chronology. There is one exception: Number 8. It fits nicely in the sequence but comes from Greece where

I found it near the famous temple of Poseidon in Delphi. I inserted it for good measure, but the two experts on Greek architecture I consulted, say that the altar is a late construction and has nothing to do with my Vedic altars. I don't dare to doubt them.

Next in complexity is the domestic fire altar of the Soma ritual, a square consisting of five layers of bricks that are fired in a kiln. It replaces the small square at the eastern end of the Ancient Hut in Figure 16 (referred to on page 122). The origin of the Vedic word for brick, *iṣṭakā*, is non-Indo-European though it is Sanskritized in appearance: it comes from the lost language of the BMAC ('Bactrian-Margiana Archaeological Complex') of Central Asia (6, on the Map). Each of the five layers consists of 21 = 3 x 7 such bricks. Each brick is rectangular and the lengths of its sides stand in the proportion of 7 to 3 so that each layer is square. The total number of bricks is 5 x 3 x 7 = 105. The configuration of bricks in the first, third and fifth layer faces one direction, that of the second and fourth the other direction that is perpendicular to it. See Figure 21.

The configuration of the thousand bricks in the offering altar of the Agnicayana ritual is much more complex. There are five layers of 200 bricks each, and the altar has the shape of a bird. The bricks are not only square or rectangular. Some are triangles of various sizes and shapes. Numerous rules have to be followed when the bricks are 'piled', for everything must fit. It signals the beginning of geometry proper and can be dated with some measure of probability because some of the mantras, with which the bricks are consecrated, occur in the earliest Yajurveda Saṃhita, the

Maitrāyaṇī, about 1,000 BCE. Figure 22 depicts the configuration of bricks in the first layer.

The bricks may be deposited in any order, but the numbers in the Figure indicate the order in which they are consecrated with mantras.

Vedic geometry developed from the construction of these and other complex altar shapes. All are given numerous interpretations in the Brāhmaṇas and Āraṇyakas, enumerated in lists and competing with other lists that show, by their mutual inconsistencies, that they are purely arbitrary—food for mythologists or psychologists of the Jungian variety, perhaps. But most of these shapes are also found in ancient Greek geometry which adds three-dimensional varieties such as the cube. India and Greece seem to be related, the Indic being the earlier because it was less developed. But the relationships may be more complex since Greece and India both derived mathematical knowledge from the Old-Babylonians who had developed it a millennium or more before.

The Old-Babylonians were also conversant with the so-called Pythagorean triples, e.g., 5, 12 and 13 with the property that $5^2 + 12^2 = 13^2$ (in our modern notation). The Śulba Sūtras contain the earliest extant verbal expression of the closely related theorem that is still often referred to as the Theorem of Pythagoras but that was independently discovered by Vedic Indians, Greeks and Chinese. The theorem is expressed in identical terms by Baudhāyana and Āpastamba: 'the diagonal rope of an oblong produces both what the flank and the horizontal ropes produce separately.' Put differently, the sum of the areas of the two squares constructed on the flank and the horizontal equals the area of the square constructed on the diagonal.

The figure that was in the minds of Baudhāyana and Āpastamba and that they must have pegged with ropes in sand or on the ground, is illustrated in Figure 23. It has been preserved in manuscripts of later date. The numbers that have been added reflect the 'Pythagorean' triangles I mentioned just now. These and other such triplets were undoubtedly known to Baudhāyana and Āpastamba but they did not write them down. The words that I have added could not have been written by them either since they were not familiar with the art of writing.

The Theorem of Baudhāyana (as it is now often called in India) was not proven in the Śulba Sūtras as they have come down to us. Perhaps a proof was added by the teacher and remained part of an oral tradition. A diagram of later date suggests that a proof was known to Bhāskara I in the first half of the seventh century CE.

Chinese mathematicians discovered that theorem during the Han Period (202 BCE–220 CE). A proof was given in algorithmic form by Liu Hui in 263 CE. It corresponds to the sketch in Appendix I (*page* 349) where it is explained.

Pythagoras, who was born about 570 BCE on the island of Samos, may or may not have discovered the theorem named after him. It was probably a discovery of the Pythagoraean school which was active in the sixth and fifth centuries BCE in ancient Greece and Italy. It became a theorem between then and around 300 BCE when Euclid included it in his

Elements together with a proof. This could be around the same time as Āpastamba or a little later and certainly later than Baudhāyana. Before we discuss the implications of this, the reader may like to take a look at the proof that Euclid gave in his *Elements* and that is not algorithmic or algebraic but purely geometrical. It is given, in Heath's translation, in Appendix II. It is quite complicated, for two reasons. First, Euclid treats the general case, where the sides of the rectangle may have any length. That is unlike the Chinese case where the only rectangles that are considered have sides where the 'horizontal rope' and the 'flank' consists of units with lengths of 3 and 4, respectively. The other reason for complexity is that Greek and Vedic used geometry but not algebra. Algebra is much easier than geometry—for us. Newton and Descartes still regarded algebra as a barbaric art but they were getting out of date. Leibniz had already seen that algebraic notations were the way of the future.

The similarities between Greek and Vedic geometry go far beyond the identity of the two theorems we have discussed. Greek and Indic geometries are historically related but how can their relationship be explained? Certainly not by the fact that Greek and Vedic are Indo-European languages, for why did all those other IE speakers or their ancestors—Iranians, Tocharians, Slavs, Celts or Germans—not produce geometry? Another possibility is the Babylonians whose importance for the early history of Asian science I have mentioned several times. They developed mathematics and astronomy/astrology long before Greeks and Indians and influenced them both. At first, I speculated that Babylonian influence on Vedic geometry was unlikely because the Vedic/

Greek variety was connected with altars and the Babylonian seemed to be inspired by celestial bodies. I concluded that both Greeks and Indians must have picked up the elements of geometry from the inhabitants of the BMAC who constructed large fortresses from square and rectangular bricks; and whose word for brick was adopted by the Indians. The idea is supported by the geography depicted on the Map: the speakers of Hittite and Mitanni, to whom arrow 9 points, lived in, or close to, what is now called Turkey or Asia Minor, a large chunk of land where Greek was spoken on the coastal regions and many Greek mathematicians originated. If speakers of Indo-Aryan passed through BMAC territory and picked up geometry it would have linguistic implications. The BMAC word for kiln-fired brick, *iṣṭakā*, would have been taken to India by Indo-Aryan speakers instead of being brought there by BMAC visitors or immigrants. The word occurs in the Yajurveda. It points to the Kuru period and region, an area where various cultures met.

I then met Jens Høyrup who knows mathematics and its history, Old-Babylonian and a great deal more. He explained that sections of Euclid's *Elements* consist of 'cut-and-paste' results, long known from Babylonian sources. It seems likely, that *Śulba* geometry was in several respects influenced by the Babylonians. That Babylonian influence reached the Yajurveda is clear from the 'mysterious sixty' in the second recitation of the patron or Yajamāna: 'May these bricks, o Agni, be milch cows for me' (Chapter 7, *page* 131). The number 'sixty' is prominent in the Rigveda itself.

[Answers to Which Is Which (Figure 20): #1 comes from Pirak; #2–#5 are Sadas altars; #6, #7 and #9 come again from Pirak.]

Numbers and Infinity

We have so far looked at 'Vedic geometry', but is there no other mathematics in the Vedas? Though the term is used in several senses, there certainly is no trace of algebra. What about those very large numbers that we have come across (in Chapter 7) and what about the concept of infinity which is almost omnipresent in some form or other? I offer two observations, one speculative which takes us to a distant past, another factual which takes us to more recent times.

Starting from integers, we must make a distinction between *ordinals*, which are integers ordered in a series such as 1, 2, 3, . . ., (as discussed in Chapter **11**) and *cardinals*, which refer to the number of elements in a set. The identity of cardinals may be known without knowing how many there are. For example, there may be many sheep in my corral and also many coins in the bag of a prospective buyer. If I let the sheep pass one by one through a gate and take out a coin whenever a sheep passes, I may discover that there are as many sheep as there are coins without knowing what is the number of either. Let us say that two sets which contain the same number of elements or members are *equivalent*. The discovery I just made is that the set of sheep and that of coins are equivalent. The set of my hands and that of my feet are equivalent also and so are the numbers of feet of elephants and dogs. The next step is to define a cardinal number as *a set of equivalent sets*. The number '2', for example, is the set of all pairs—hands, feet, eyes, ears, etc. It does not imply that I know that '2' comes after '1' and before '3' in the series of ordinals. Of course, I do know such things about 1, 2 and 3, but if there had been 164 sheep in my corral and 164 coins in the bag, I could have found out their equivalence without knowing that the number is 164. Other cardinals may be defined in the same way.

Does this ring a bell? The reader wil recall the nonsensical equivalences of the Brāhmaṇas of Chapter 7 on which even scholars who spent part of their life translating them have heaped invectives. Renou writes with greater dispassion and probably thinking of *bandhu*: 'the hidden connections that they try to establish cannot be accepted; it is too visibly the product of the priestly mind.' The reader will recall one of these litanies: 'He offers with an oblation ladled up four times, cattle have four feet; thus he wins cattle; the quarters are four; thus he finds support in the quarters.' Barring 'sympathetic magic'—a common phrase but hardly an explanation—what is their significance? Do these foursomes of oblations, feet and quarters refer to a set of equivalent sets? Taken together, do they define the number '4'? Could that take us back to much more distant times, when our ancestors discovered cardinal numbers or did that happen later? These questions take us beyond the Vedas.

My second observation is about the infinite. It is referred to by several terms throughout the Vedas and is related to the very large numbers of the Yajurveda, etc., that verge on it. The infinite was loved throughout Indic civilization, but abhorred by the ancient Greeks, from Pythagoras onward. It was ultimately very productive in science and led, in the fourteenth century CE, to infinite power series of **pi** and the trigonometric functions that Indic mathematicians discovered three centuries before Newton and Leibniz, long after the Vedas.

Long before that, the infinite is also found in a poem about *pūrṇam*, 'fullness' that occurs or has been inserted in some Upaniṣads. Those who composed it understood the mathematical sense of infinity, i.e. something like the following.

Look at the interval between the integers '0' and '1.' Think of it as a small line segment: /——————————/. There are infinitely many points on that segment. Infinitely many of those points, but not all of them, may be represented by *fractions* of the form '*m*/*n*'. This may be shown by cutting the segment into small segments of various sizes. To make it easier, I shall cut it in segments of equal size. We start by cutting the segment in four: /——/——/——/——/ with cuts at '1/4', '1/2' and '3/4'. Continue cutting each of those intervals in half, i.e.: '1/8', '1/4', '3/8', '1/2' '5/8', '3/4' and '7/8'. This may continue indefinitely. Now return to the interval between '0' and '1' once again and cut it in two pieces, anywhere. The argument we have gone through just now applies to each of the two pieces. It follows that even if we take an infinity away from the segment, an infinity remains:

pūrṇam adaḥ pūrṇam idam pūrṇāt pūrṇam udacyate/
pūrṇasya pūrṇam ādāya pūrṇam evāvaśiṣyate//

'Fullness is there, fullness is here, fullness from fullness proceeds,
When fullness is taken from fullness, fullness remains.'

'Vedic Mathematics'

A few paragraphs should be added about the book *Vedic Mathematics* by Bharati Krishna Tirtha Maharaja (1884–1960), former Śaṇkarācārya of the Govardhana Maṭha at Puri and published long after his death. (A Śaṇkarācārya is pontiff of one of the four or five traditional schools of the Advaita Vedānta, founded by the original Śaṅkara according to tradition.) A Hindi edition of *Vedic Mathematics*, called *Vaidika Gaṇitā*, and a revised English edition, published in Delhi in 1992, were reprinted many times in the following years. There are also active web-sites and a *Vedic Mathematics Newsletter*.

Vedic Mathematics is neither mathematics nor Vedic. It is not *mathematics* unless simple and sometimes fast ways of multiplying, dividing and factorizing numbers, together with other tricks that are playfully explained and appeal to children and unschooled adults, are glorified by that label. It is not *Vedic* unless we follow His Holiness who wrote in his *Preface* that it is 'in the fitness of things' that the Vedas include Ayurveda (the science of life or medicine), Dhanurveda (archery), Gandharva Veda (the science and art of music) and Sthāpatya Veda (which deals with architecture, engineering, etc.); and goes on to explain that his book is based upon an appendix of the Atharvaveda that no one had heard of or seen.

What we have seen is that *Vedic Mathematics* consisted very largely of geometry, in many respects similar to the ancient Greek variety and often going back to Babylonia. In Europe, it lasted until Newton whose *Principia* is still modelled after Euclid. In India, geometry was replaced by trigonometry and algebra almost a millennium before Newton. I did mention the remarkable progress that followed and led to the discovery of infinite power series. *Vedic Mathematics* is not a work of progress. It portrays regress, unadulterated regress.

Some say that introducing *Vedic Mathematics* into the curriculum was a deliberate effort to keep people ignorant and the masses of India backward. If modern India wishes not only to cooperate but also compete with China—and why should she not?—it would be good to give wide publicity to the international conference '*Strings 2006*' that took place in the Great Hall of the People in Beijing. Stephen Hawking and 800 theoretical physicists and mathematicians from all over the world were there, discussed the state of the art with each other and addressed an audience not of uneducated dreamers or fanatics, but of 6,000 Chinese graduate students.

The Prātiśākhyas and the Padapāṭha

The classification of sciences as 'limbs of the Veda' with which we began includes four sciences of language. I shall try to simplify, reconstruct their salient features differently and treat them in three sections. The first examines the Prātiśākhyas and the Padapāṭha with which we are already familiar from Chapter 4.

The Prātiśākhyas are attached to each of the Vedic schools (*śākhā*) as their name indicates. It will be helpful, therefore, to caste another glance at Table 1 on *pages* 80–1. The most important is the Rik-Prātiśākhya. The Yajurveda, has one for the Taittirīya and another for the White Yajurveda. The Atharvaveda has two and the Sāmaveda possesses a number of compositions that deal with the many features of its ritual chants. Scholars have long discussed whether the early Prātiśākhyas pre-date the famous grammarian Pāṇini and if so, which of them. The fact is that their linguistic content is basically pre-Pāṇinian though the present form in which we know them has been influenced by Pāṇini's grammar which in due course eclipsed them all because it went beyond the śākhās and described the spoken language of his time and place. This remark is relevant to the development of linguistic systems and to the chronological sequence of scientists and their works. There were Bloomfieldians left, chronologically speaking, after Chomsky's first revolution, which does not contradict the fact that Chomskian linguistics was, among other things, a reaction against Bloomfield and, therefore, best understood and described as a new chapter in the history of linguistics.

The Prātiśākhyas deal mostly with what are nowadays called phonetics and phonology but their focus is on empirical completeness, not theoretical development. That explains their being formulated for each of the four Vedas separately, and being complete for each of those compositions. They often deal with *sandhi* or 'euphonic combination', the distinctive feature of the continuous speech of the *saṃhitā* which contrasts with the word-for-word analysis of the Padapāṭha as illustrated for the Rigveda in Chapter 4, which also gives an idea of some of its complexities. For *sandhi* is not a simple matter in Sanskrit. It occurs in other languages, but often on a smaller scale. It applies to the distinction in English between two forms of the indefinite article: '*an apple*' before a vowel, but '*a banana*' before a consonant. Important in our context has been the word *upa-ni-ṣad* where the dental *s* of *sad* 'to sit' turned into the retroflex *ṣ* of *ṣad* because of the preceding *i* so that *upa-ni-sad* became *upa-ni-ṣad*.

The Padapāṭha follows the sequence of verse and hymns in the Vedic corpus, that is, it marks the boundaries of words, stems, prefixes, suffixes, roots, etc., each time they occur. It does not make generalizations and the same holds for the Prātiśākhyas. They contain, therefore, much repetition but, at the same time, the result is an extremely extensive inventory and compilation of linguistic facts. These cannot be called 'grammar' or 'linguistics' because they do not deal with the infinity of a living language. On the contrary, they are concerned for each of the Vedas with a finite corpus of a large size. Within that corpus they sought and achieved completeness of description. Surya Kanta called the Rik-Prātiśākhyas '*entirely* free from all oversights'. W.D. Whitney noted on a section of the Taittirīya Prātiśākhyas, that he could not discover any case of a retroflex nasal in the Taittirīya Saṃhitā from a dental nasal in the Taittirīya Padapāṭha 'that was not duly provided for'. This completeness provides a magnificent demonstration of Patañjali's remark that enumerations, which may be complete for a finite corpus, cannot be used to characterize the expressions of a living language because they are infinite in number and therefore require a grammar that consists of rules.

The rules of the Prātiśākhyas are often concise. The rule that *t* becomes *l* when *l* follows is expressed as: *takāro le lam*. This metarule states: 'a change (in the *object*-language: i.e., of *t*) is expressed as an Accusative (*dvitīya* in the Sanskrit metalanguage: i.e., *lam*) when *l* follows which is a Locative (*saptamī*), i.e., *le*)'. Other rules are longer because they apply to a number of cases, e.g., the definition of *savarṇa* or 'homorganic' as 'having the same place, producing organ and effort of articulation in the mouth.' Here, 'place' refers to throat, palate, teeth, etc. 'Producing organ' means tip of the tongue, rolling back the tip of the tongue, tip of the teeth, middle of the jaw, etc. 'Effort of articulation' refers to closed, semi-closed, open, etc. The close attention that is paid here to movements and processes within the mouth is in tune with the close attention paid to breath (*prāṇa*) throughout the Vedas.

All these discoveries are closely related to the oral tradition. They originated not *in spite of* the absence of writing but *because* of it.

The Sound Pattern of Language

The second Vedic science of language as I have reconstructed it led to a major empirical discovery with profound implications for the methodology of linguistics. It was made by Vedic reciters who were engaged in composing Prātiśākhyas and constructing Padapāṭhas or were already familiar with them; and arrived at in stages during roughly the same period. Because the reciters did not think of changes in the Vedic language—what we interpret as such, for example, in the distinction between early, middle and late Vedic (Chapter 4)—they would interpret them as characteristics of different regions (which was often the case). They emphasized, therefore, what we would call synchronic linguistics, not diachronic philology. All the time they used purely empirical methods: they did not prescribe but describe. They went further than most modern linguists. They did not imagine that language starts from the larynx. They knew that its deeper source lies in the intention, that is, the mind or heart of the speaker. In so doing, they anticipated by more than two millennia the spirit of synchronic linguistics, initiated in Europe by de Saussure; and of psycholinguistics which began to develop in the twentieth century.

After reaching a sufficiently high level of sophistication, the reciters made the major discovery of which the likely beginnings are depicted in Figure 24. It illustrates how the sounds of a language are produced by constricting the vocal tract at a particular point along its stationary portion. If we move from the larynx or throat to the lips, we pronounce *ka, ca, ṭa, ta, pa* (the short *a*'s are added for the sake of pronunciation). Each syllable exists unvoiced or voiced, provided with more or less breath, which may be made to pass through the nasal cavity. Thus we produce, in the case of *ka*, the sequence *ka*, *kha*, *ga, gha, ṅa*; and similarly for the other four consonantal syllables. The two directions are combined in the two-dimensional square or *varga* that is depicted here. In order to complete the picture, a few more consonantal syllables have to be added along with semi-vowels and vowels.

The Vedic system of the sounds of language exhibits and embodies what is nowadays called phonetics, but is close to phonology, which studies features of those same sounds as parts of a system. The system exhibits universal properties of language. I do not imply that it is the same for all languages. Retroflexes (*mūrdhanya*), which have been put in a box, are common in Indic languages but do not occur in all languages. Whatever they are, the sounds of human speech may be accommodated in some such scheme.

As far as I know, the Vedic discovery of the sound pattern of language was made only once in human history. Modern linguistics uses distinctive features, but they would not exist if the sound pattern of language had not been discovered two-and-a-half millennia earlier.

The sound pattern of language was of great historical importance because it underlies many of the scripts of South, South-east and East Asia including Balinese, Bengali, Burmese, Devanagari, Grantha, Gujarati, Gupta, Gurmukhi, Japanese, Kannada, Khmer, Khotanese, Korean, Lao, Malayalam, Nepali, Oriya, Pallava, Sinhala, Tamil, Telugu, Thai and Tibetan. None of these were alphabets; all were syllabaries. This presents us with a paradox, because a strictly oral tradition influenced countless writing systems.

The discovery of the sound pattern of language was oral in two senses: it was concerned with the mouth as the place where language becomes audible and took place in an oral culture before the invention or introduction of writing. Neither was understood in western Asia or Europe and both are still beyond the grasp of most moderns who are not Indians. The most recent work on *The World's Writing Systems*, a tome of almost a thousand pages, regards the Vedic syllabary as a kind of alphabet. The *Oxford English Dictionary* writes that a syllabary 'serves the purpose of an alphabet.' This is not so, and these verdicts are simply cultural constructs, based upon alphabets that arose in western Asia. These alphabets continue to cause problems of spelling and pronunciation in languages such as English, whether it is someone's first or *n*-th language. Unlike ABC's, to which there is no rhyme or reason, the Vedic syllabary is rational and practical like Indian numerals. Other Asians adopted and adapted it for those reasons.

Notations and Artificial Languages

The third Vedic science of language as I have reconstructed it may be looked upon as a methodology but its significance is wider. The Prātiśākhyas introduced, along with rules and metarules, the beginnings of the metalinguistic study of language. To see what that means we should start with some simple facts about rules. Many rules of language are of the form 'A > B'. This may be read as 'A becomes B' or 'B is substituted for A.' 'A > B' is a modern artificial notation. The Prātiśākhyas did not use variables such as 'A' and 'B' or expressions such as '+' and '>', but other artificial notations.

Their rules made metalinguistic use of the case endings of the object language, that is, Vedic. Thus two expressions, distinguished in English as 'becoming' and 'substitution,' correspond to a single artificial expression:

A + Nominative ending, B + Accusative ending.

In order to apply this metarule or *paribhāṣā*, we have to treat the element 'A' as if it were a Sanskrit word of the object language and attach the Nominative ending to it. Similarly for 'B' and the Accusative ending. We met with an example on *page* 279: *takāro le lam*. The beginning of the Padapāṭha of Chapter 4 alluded to a case that is a little more interesting: two rules operate on three elements in order to explain (in modern notation):

ā + *uru* + *aprāḥ* > *orvaprāḥ*.

The two rules are (again in modern notation):

ā + *uru* > *oru* and:
oru + *aprāḥ* > *orvaprāḥ*.

The question is in which order should they be applied.

I mentioned this case only in order to illustrate the level of sophistication we meet with in the Prātiśākhyas. They introduced other technicalities and artificial expressions. They did not combine into a full-fledged artificial language such as was created by Pāṇini for his grammar of the spoken language. His orientation was different but he stood on the shoulders of the Prātiśākhyas, other Vedic sciences of language and other early grammars.

There is more to Vedic linguistics but it is a technical topic and one should know some Vedic or Sanskrit to make it palatable. As it stands, our topics illustrate that Vedic linguistics led not only to the foundation of the science of language, but to the concept and formation of an artificial language. It shows in passing that artificial languages are not only found in sciences such as mathematics or physics and in modern civilization, but exist across sciences and civilizations.

Astronomy and Astrology

The reader need not raise eyebrows about the combination of astrology with astronomy during the Vedic period. It is and has been common all over the world for a long time. The combination occurs in pre-modern and even in early-modern science. Kepler, Tycho Brahe and Newton were all interested in astrology though Newton's real passion was alchemy. I shall be brief on the entire subject and rely on Michio Yano and the late David Pingree who died on 11 November 2005, when I was struggling with a first version of the present section.[1]

[1]The only footnote in this book should be dedicated to David Pingree, in recent times the greatest scholar of the ancient sciences of Asia and the Middle East, especially mathematics and astronomy. In roughly forty-three books and 240 articles he used and edited Akkadian, Arabic, Greek, Latin, Persian and Sanskrit sources. His students came from

I can do no better than begin by quoting and endorsing the opening phrases of a chapter published by Pingree in 2001:

> This is a topic that has elicited for over a century many fanciful and implausible interpretations on the alleged astronomical meaning of the Vedic texts. In this chapter I have tried to avoid such fantasies and to restrict discussion to the overt meanings of passages where the authors of the Vedas clearly are referring to astronomical phenomena or are describing some aspect of astronomical theory.

The Rigvedic contribution to astronomy does not appear to have been very remarkable. It did not distinguish the five planets (*graha* in later texts) from the fixed stars. The Vedic term *jyotiṣā*, which comes from *jyotiḥ*, 'light (in the sky)' or 'luminary', is not very distinctive either. That lack of distinction is not altogether surprising. It reflects semi-nomadic

all over the world and many are now teaching these subjects, especially in the USA and Japan. The day before he died, Pingree was informed by the current Provost Robert Zimmer of Brown University in an e-mail that they were contemplating closing down his program that was founded in 1974 by Otto Neugebauer (*page* 259). If that happens, Brown will be remembered for a wanton act of destruction longer than anything else it may have achieved. In such cases, the President of the University is accountable, just as whoever is the chief of armed forces is accountable for what his army does. As for the history of Indian science, 2005 was a bad year. Professor K.V. Sharma died on 14 January at Chennai. He wrote and edited more than 100 books and 400 articles, a worthy counterpart to Pingree.

origins. Astronomy flourishes in sedentary civilizations which are able to concentrate on the skies from a fixed point and during prolonged periods of time. The Vedic astronomy/astrology may have been conceived in basic outline before the Vedic Indians were settled. It explains that later Indic astronomy was very different.

The main purpose of the *jyotiṣā* was the preparation of a calendar in order to fix the dates when rituals have to be performed. The calendar that was arrived at divided the year into 366 days. An adjustment was needed—adding one day about every sixty-four months—in order to preserve the relation between ritual dates and lunar phases. The term *nakṣatra* in *jyotiṣā* was restricted to twenty-seven or twenty-eight groups of stars that were regarded as lunar stations along the ecliptic. In the system of twenty-eight, the distance between the *nakṣatra*s is irregular. The two systems are also found in Chinese and Islamic astronomy—the former probably an independent development and the latter influenced by the Indic.

Solar and lunar eclipses were famously attributed to a demon who pierced the sun and the moon with darkness. Later called Rahu, then *graha*, literally 'seizer', he came to refer to any of the five planets. The demon myth was ridiculed by the astronomer Lalla who wrote in the eighth or ninth century CE: 'if you are of the opinion that an artful demon causes eclipses by swallowing, then how is it that an eclipse can be determined by calculation?'

Late Vedic texts were not only inspired by Mesopotamian mythology and omens but influenced by Babylonian astronomy. The transmission was facilitated by the establishment of the Achaemenid Empire, which included in the sixth century BCE the Gandhara area on the upper Indus, now part of northern Pakistan. Mathematical astronomy came also from the Near East but that was in the second century CE, more than half a millennium after the Vedic period. It is then that astronomy began to flourish and the five schools called *siddhānta* were established. One of these, the Paitāmaha ('ancestral') school continued the *vedāṇga* tradition, but it disappeared after having been rejected by Varāhamihira (ca. 550 CE), a 'Zoroastrian/Maga Brahman' allegedly descended from Iranian Magi, who wrote about the five schools: 'the Pauliśa is accurate, that pronounced by Romaka ('Roman') is close to it, the Sūrya is more accurate and the remaining two have gone astray.' Should it be held against Vedic astronomers that they were largely wrong? It is not an uncommon occurrence in the history of science as Āryabhaṭa, al-Bīrūnī and Keppler explained to us in Chapter 9.

FIFTEEN

~

VEDIC INSIGHTS

Towards Universality

It is often maintained that progress is a Western notion. But the term 'Western' is as misleading as 'Eastern' or 'Oriental'. I discovered this in California when I noted that Japan was not in the east but in the west. All such terms are subjective: they throw no light on the locality of the user and provide no information about the locality of the place to which they refer. Unlike 'Western,' *progress* says something about what happens or does not happen in the world. The Vedas do not mention progress, but did not regard themselves as 'eternal' or 'of non-human origin' (*apauruṣeya*), ideas that originated in the post-Vedic philosophy of the Mīmāṃsā. They depict their human composers, tell us stories about their eventful lives and describe developments that take place around them. It is I who is asking: did they make progress within that long Vedic period which lasted from ca.1700 to 450 BCE?

The Rigveda starts from the smallest social unit, the family. It exhibits everything that is clannish: tightly-knit links, atavistic beliefs, close and exclusive attachments to the tribe, to local poets and leaders. All seek wealth, success, long lives and sons. In the later Rigveda there emerge great speculative poems. They are almost contemporary with the earliest Upaniṣads which, though secret by definition, became most widely known. In that development, the Sāmaveda remained mysterious and the Yajurveda played a conservative role. But the breakdown of the schools and the emergence of the classical Upaniṣads depict the movement of a civilization towards universality.

That universality is incompatible with a narrowing religious outlook. That is one of the reasons I have stressed from the beginning that the Vedas are not a religion. They are a civilization.

A narrowing religious outlook and intolerance are two sides of the same coin. Examples abound. At the time of writing, Pope Benedict XVI declared: 'Catholic faith obliges us to hold that souls are immediately created by God.' It is implied that soul means: human soul, i.e. humans have souls, but animals do not. Composers of the Vedas also had wide-ranging opinions. But they never doubted that there is a gradual transition from animal to human. It is in accordance with the mounting evidence from evolutionary biology. Those who close their eyes to that evidence live in a dream.

The phrase 'narrowing religious outlook' comes from Jawaharlal Nehru. He may or may not have been thinking of Rigvedic poetry when he wrote about the Upaniṣads: 'We cannot go back to that old pantheistic outlook, and yet perhaps we may still sense the mystery of nature, listen to her song of life and beauty, and draw vitality from her.' Nehru's lament was perhaps in part an expression of the longing of a great statesman for his native Kashmir. He then went further: 'We have to get rid of that narrowing religious outlook, that obsession with the supernatural and metaphysical speculations, that loosening of the mind's discipline in religious ceremonial and mystical emotionalism, which comes in the way of our understanding ourselves and the world.' That description applies to post-Vedic Upaniṣads and religions when the meaning of *veda* as knowledge was simply forgotten.

The notion of intolerance is not applicable to mantras or ritual. Stobhas such as *īḍā* and *ilā* belong to different schools, but that has nothing to do with dichotomies such as true/false or right/wrong. Even Baudhāyana holds the left palm up and the right palm down on a bundle of grass during the *nihnava* ceremony, because he is a Taittirīyaka Yajurvedin, whereas a Kauṣītaki Rigvedin does it the other way round during the same ceremony. The actual differences are as minuscule and insignificant as the differences between religious sects; but reciters of mantras, chanters of songs or ritualists do not kill each other.

The simple and simplistic observations that I have offered in this section on the Vedic way toward universality are not idle observations on a topic that belongs to a distant past. They take us right to the present. Dreams of paradise are no longer harmless; they have turned into violence. Looking in all directions, we must unite, save life and protect our poor Gaia in so far as it can still be done. Vedic nomads destroyed many forests but the Vedas are on our side.

The Powers of Language

We have seen that the greatest contributions of the Indian sciences were in the understanding of language. To grasp their origins, we have to go back further than the Prātiśākhyas, the Padapāṭha and the Sound Pattern of Language to the Rigveda where the earliest meaning of *bráhman* was 'sublime language'. It is connected with one god, Bṛhaspati, and two goddesses, Vāc and Sarasvatī, barely touched upon in my account so far. I have not neglected the sounds of language or linguistics, but never tried to derive a general conclusion from all that is said with respect to these topics in the Veda.

'Speech' is the traditional translation and interpretation of *bráhman* as well as *vāc*. The correct translation is *language*. In modern usage, the two are clearly distinguished. Speech is what we say; it is a manifestation of language which is an innate faculty of the mind. In Indian studies it is often said and written that 'speech' is regarded as a transcendental power in the Vedas and Vedānta, Mīmāṃsā, Sāṃkhya-Yoga, the philosophy of grammar and Kashmir Śaivism; but as conventional and arbitrary in the Cārvāka and in early Buddhism. The Vedas, however, do not call *vāc* 'transcendental' (*paramārtha*). They regard it as the direct manifestation of thought or mind (*manas*). That applies, to language but not to speech which is often mindless. We have already come across important uses of *manasā*, 'with' or 'in the mind.' The Vedic Indians imported chariots into the subcontinent *manasā* (Chapter 2). Sanskrit *manas* is etymologically related to English *mind*. That does not prove much, but helps to clear the jungle and 'mind' is relatively clear in modern usage.

The Rigveda devotes two hymns to *vāc*. One is 'a paean of self-praise' as Wendy Doniger calls it. The other, RV 10.71, begins with the verse:

> Bṛhaspati! When they (the first poets and seers) set in motion the first beginning of language (*vāc*), setting up names, what had been hidden in them as their best and purest good became manifest through love.
>
> Where the sages fashioned language with their thought (*vāc manasā*), filtering it like parched grain through a sieve, friends recognized their friendships. Their beauty was marked on the language.

We should make a correction in the first verse, not an emendation but a reminder. Language does not consist of names. It is an old error, found across the globe. The ancient Chinese, Greeks and Hebrews accepted it as did the Vedas as we see here—though not without serious qualification. Perhaps the phrase 'setting up names' (*nāmadheyaṃ dadhānāḥ*) escaped from the heart of the poet involuntarily, like a seed that falls from a blossom and is carried through the wind until it settles down somewhere.

Why does language not consist of names and why is 'naming' not the first step of language? Because names are only a subclass of words and words are only a small part of language which consists of sentences, syntax, semantics, grammar and is linked with thought—*vāc manasā*—as the second verse says. All these things were known throughout the Vedic period and brought to perfection by the Sanskrit grammarians and all the Indic linguists that followed—touched upon in Chapters **11**, **12** and **14**.

In the second verse, the phrase 'filtering it like parched grain through a sieve' evokes the filtering of the Soma beverage.

The Rigveda links language not only to 'thought' but also to 'vision' (*dhī*), a word from which comes *dhyāna*, 'meditation' in one of its later meanings. Like *vāc manasā*, 'language from thought', *manasā dhī*, 'vision from thought', is a common expression. Elsewhere the inspiration of the poets is expressed by *vip*, related to English 'vibration', which evokes the shaman who trembles under the influence of his or her vision. Since language originates from thought, vision, love, the heart and the self, its understanding is difficult, says the Rigveda; therefore: 'he who studies understands, not the one who sleeps.'

Fascination with *vāc* did not stop with the Rigveda for its powers are great. In the Chāndogya Upaniṣad, Uddālaka discusses cause and effect, like when clay is transformed into a pot. He says: 'the effect is *vāc-ārambhanam*' which means: 'it originates from language.' This is not correct in the case of the pot, which is different from clay also in shape, as later Indic philosophers observed; but it is true in other cases, for example in *speech acts*, where the appropriate authority who pronounces the words: 'I unite you in marriage' has not merely said something. He has caused two people to be married to each other as we have seen in Chapter **11**.

The powers of language enable us not only to communicate with each other, but to talk about the world and express our feelings and ideas. Our languages divide us but enable us at the same time to go into great detail about an infinite number of topics. In that respect human language is more powerful than the systems of communication used by non-human animals though the transitions—very controversial for the time being—are likely to be gradual. It is a large topic upon which we have touched in Chapters 11 and 12.

The powers of language are a favourite topic of philosophers but only those who have a specialized knowledge of the topic seem to have been able to arrive at valuable insights. According to Bhartṛhari (fifth century CE), a philosopher as well as a linguist, there is no knowledge without language. Earlier he made a different observation: language is no guarantee of truth, it is an imagined construction of being, 'a mismatch for reality' as Saroja Bhate expressed it. It follows that reality cannot be understood by using ordinary language. Bhartṛhari sought clarification in a Vedic scheme of four levels of language that had a great future in Indic speculation. I shall discuss it in the next section, but one thing is clear. Seers come at the top, what humans speak comes at the bottom.

I am sure that similar ideas have been expressed by poets, thinkers, mystics and writers in other civilizations. What distinguishes the development that started in the Vedas from others is its close association with the sciences of language. It has empirical foundations. I am familiar with two more recent scientists whose insights were not only similarly profound, but equally well informed about language. One is Wilhelm von Humboldt (1767–1835), whose numerous works include three volumes on the language of Java. Especially famous and influential, and often obscure, is its 300-page *Introduction* entitled 'The Diversity of Human Language-Structure and its Influence on the Mental Development of Mankind'. The other is Roman Jakobson (1896–1982), who was equally prolific and combined not only a professorship at the Massachusetts Institute of Technology (MIT) with one at Harvard University, but linguistics, literature, poetics, semantics and Slavic studies—all topics on which he expressed himself not only forcefully but with great clarity. The insights of these two giants display the same breadth and depth as the Vedic and it is clear that the latter will play an increasingly important role in any future science and philosophy of language.

The Limitations of Language

We return from having sat, briefly, at the feet of three gurus: Bhartṛhari, Wilhelm von Humboldt and Roman Jakobson. The third expressed himself most clearly, but only Bhartṛhari seems to have had an understanding of what the present section is about. This is because he was inspired by the Rigveda. It was there that he found awareness of the limitations of language and of what language may *not* be able to express. It is a necessary component of the richness of language studies that I tried to call up from afar in previous sections.

Poets and thinkers of the Rigveda regarded language as an expression of their greatest good. But it has limitations which are described in an apparent riddle (RV 1.164). It is a long poem, consisting of fifty-two verses. The one that concerns us here is verse 10. It puts language, *vāc*, at the top of the universe where it 'knows all, but does not move all.' 'Knowing all' is expressed by the compound *viśva-vid*. The 'moving' is part of another, more difficult compound:

viśvaminvām. The *viśva* is easy or is it *viśvam*? How do we analyse the compound, that is: where does the *m* go? The Padapāṭha understood it: the *m* goes with the second part. Sāyaṇa follows and interprets the rare verb *minv-* as 'being busy', not too different from the 'moving' of most modern translators. A similar expression occurs in the Atharvaveda.

Verse 10 suggests that many speakers of language do not know what they are talking about. Probably true, but we would hope that it means more than that. We have to wait for verse 45 which finally explains:

> Language is divided into four parts
> Which the inspired brahmans know.
> Three parts are hidden in secret; they do not circulate.
> The fourth part of language is what humans speak.

Here is the foursome to which Bhartṛhari referred. It is not immediately perspicuous because it seems to be a riddle; but Vedic 'riddles' or 'puzzles' are not mysterious. They have a key, and once it is found, everything falls in place.

A simple example of a straightforward solution to such a puzzle is the first verse of the same poem: Rigveda 1.164.1. It says: 'Of this beloved Hotṛ priest, grown grey, the middle brother is hungry. The third brother carries clarified butter on his back. Here I saw the lord of the people with his seven sons.' The solution is: the ritual arena (Figure 15). The three brothers are the three altars. The middle one is hungry because few oblations are made on it. The third one is the offering altar on which oblations of clarified butter are made. At the same time, it indicates the place where the patron will move with his fire and settle down with what is hoped for: a large family.

The lowest of the four parts of language in Rigveda 1.164.45 is the simplest. The more mysterious higher levels shine forth clearly, provided we understand the uses of some of the many technical or semi-technical terms and concepts that we have met in earlier chapters. These are not later than 1.164 which maybe assigned to the tenth century BCE

One of these terms is *anirukta* which I translated as 'ineffable' for lack of a better term. It properly refers to the unintelligible ritual chants of the Sāmaveda (Chapter **6**). The famous composer of 1.164, Dīrghatamas, 'Seeing Far into Darkness', must have known that the Sāmavedins set verse of the Rigveda to their own melodies and expressed some phrases in a different language which consisted of *stobha* 'embellishments'. The term *anirukta* is used in similar contexts, including language as *bráhman*. Another term is *anirvacanīya*, 'which cannot be expressed,' said of the world and also used in Advaita Vedānta.

Though we may take our cue from the Sāmaveda embellishments, the broad category of mantras illustrates the deficiencies of ordinary speech in a different manner. For if it were the case that natural language could do what mantras do, their would be no need for them. I have not been able to state precisely what mantras can and cannot do (Chapter **11**). They are syntactically similar to bird song which, according to some experts, 'defies explanation'. We know about mantras even less than about bird song or human language. All are unknown like the depths of the ocean as it appeared to Albert Einstein standing on the beach, trying to see far into the darkness.

Mantras, like sāmans, must belong to the higher levels of the hierarchy of Rigveda 1.164.45. They have been discussed in chapters 6, 7, and 11, especially *page* 204, some are *upāṃśu*, 'articulated (within the mouth) but inaudible', sometimes, less technically, rendered as 'indistinct'. As for rites, some are performed without mantras, that is *tūṣṇīm*, 'in silence'. Examples are not needed but I shall make some space for them here for the reader to ponder:

Before the reader exclaims: 'I know all that mystical stuff!' let me explain why it is significant in our context. It is undeniable that mystics all over the world have used similar expressions. But there is an important difference between worldwide expressions of mystic intuitions and the Vedic tradition. The latter couches these limitations of language in a language that is itself precise and scientific—a metalanguage, in fact—because it rides the waves of well-developed scientific disciplines such as the sciences of ritual and language. They put the equally inaudible and unintelligible mutterings of mystics in other parts of the world in the dim light where they belong.

I conclude that our ordinary, natural language is unable to express all that is true about the universe. But now we have also arrived at an explanation for the miraculous appearance and development of artificial languages in India at a much earlier date than anywhere else. Such insights were already available in the Rigveda. Higher levels than the ordinary fourth that humans speak incorporated not only mantras, but left vacant spaces large enough to be filled by artifical expressions and other forms of language.

If we look at Europe, we are struck by the firmly entrenched resistance to strange and artificial symbols. It was first directed at the Indic numerals which were introduced by Fibonacci and, immediately, presented problems of assimilation. Should they be written within texts or in separate boxes outside them? One solution was to simply outlaw them, which occurred as late as the seventeenth century CE in Sweden. The 'barbarous' algebra of the Arabs had already been rejected by Descartes, Newton and others. Only Leibniz understood it. Resistance to artificial languages survives in the third millennium in the minds of 'ordinary language' philosophers who believe that they can and should be translated into natural language which is one thing they cannot be.

Scientists know that progress in science does not depend on natural language but proceeds from equations. It holds for the artificial expressions of Pāṇini's metalanguage of linguistics, for Newton's apparently simple formula $f = ma$ which was due to Euler—the original having been in Latin, for Maxwell's differential equations, for $E = mc^2$ and all the equations of theoretical physics together with the less formidable ones used in numerous other disciplines, from econometrics to DNA genetics. The Ultimate Theory, the theory of everything if there will be one, will be 'a finite set of marks on paper' as Freeman Dyson put it.

I am not claiming that these marks occur on some of the three levels of language that are hidden according to the Rigveda. The composers of the Vedas had no idea about these matters but they were not held back by a behaviouristic or phenomenologic, 'scientistic' outlook and left ample space for a great variety of other languages to develop.

What can we learn from it? That our language, the characteristic of our species, is mysterious and has profound limitations of which we know little. Our understanding of the world and of ourselves necessarily suffers from these limitations. There is hope if we are willing to let languages expand.

Conclusions

anupāsitavṛddhānāṃ vidyā nātiprasīdati

'Science does not smile on those who neglect the ancients.'

Bhartṛhari

Vedic sciences and insights paved the way for the sciences of ritual and language. Both took account of the relevant facts and exhibited theoretical sophistication which included the uses of an artificial language. It is not easy to judge the merits of their insights. What we can say is that contemporary scientists working on language and the cognitive sciences have amassed vast amounts of information and reached deep insights of which their Vedic colleagues could have had no inkling. Did some of their insights go beyond present understandings? Can their ideas on *upāṃśu*, *aniruktagāna*, *tūṣṇīm*, breathing, mantras and the rest be understood and explained by other types of modern scientists—physiologists, neurologists and others as yet unborn?

The Vedic perspective on language took account of levels about which we seem to know little. Mantras, in particular, spanning the divide between ritual and language, have hardly been studied in a scientific spirit. Nothing is known about, say, mantras and aphasia. Our distant predecessors had a different perspective and were familiar with different facts about the human mind. Their knowledge may be as valuable as that of our successors in the future.

Due respect to the ancients should, of course, be based upon rational standards and stay away from politics. Governments have expressed opinions and made decisions they are not competent to make. In India, they have declared that 'whatever is very ancient in India, that precisely is most modern for the world.' In the USA, they have claimed that 'intelligent design' is another form of science. Such declarations show that these dignitaries are not familiar with the sciences and insights their institutions are supposed to embody. It demonstrates that *elementary* education, in important parts of even the 'developed' world, has sunk to dangerously low levels. If that continues, it will not affect the past but the future of sciences and insights, and, therefore, the future of the species, the environment and life on earth.

PART V

THE VEDAS AND BUDDHISM

After the Vedas

The book is complete in a manner of speaking but how can we end it and do justice to the topic unless we place it in a wider perspective? Several worthy endings may be considered. A natural end might consist in the story of what happened to the Vedas after the Vedas—the 'Destiny of the Veda in India' as Louis Renou called it in a memorable study. Renou's 'Destiny' was supplemented with an article on inscriptions, but it could be further improved and should be updated. Its orientation is exclusively textual. It does not mention, for example, the Vedic revivals of the dynasties of the Gupta (fourth–fifth century CE*), Chola (ninth–eleventh century* CE*) and Vijayanagar (fourteenth–fifteenth century* CE*)*

Much is now known about the arrival of Vedism in South India. T.P. Mahadevan distinguishes two waves. The first is represent by pūrvaśikhā brahmans with their fronted top-knots. They are well established in the Tamil country by the Sangam period, thus plausibly departing from the core areas of Vedic culture by circa 100 BCE*. The second* *are aparaśikhā brahmans with their top-knots towards the back of their heads, making a ponytail. They arrived during the Pallava and Chola periods, from the fifth century* CE. *These periods are of special interest because they carried traces of Vedic to South-east Asia, a large topic that includes the wanderings of brahmans and so-called brahmans and is only beginning to be explored in depth.*

Even if Renou's work had dealt with earlier revivals, it could not have mentioned more recent ones, especially in Kerala. These and other contemporary developments have been studied by Harold F. Arnold, C.G. Kashikar, David M. Knipe, T.P. Mahadevan, Asko Parpola, V. Raghavan, Frederik Smith, Michael Witzel and myself.

I have looked for another appropriate challenge and found it in Buddhism, an immense and immensely specialized area outside my field of expertise, like many others that I have touched, but altogether fitting. Buddhism is in some respects closer to the Vedas than some of the later developments in Indic thought and religion. Before its spread beyond the borders, it was part of the same civilization.

SIXTEEN

~

BUDDHISM

Why Buddhism?

Kāśyapa or Mahākāśyapa, whose first name was Pippali, was born in Magadha around the fifth century BCE. His name comes from *kaśyapa* which means 'tortoise' and is a non-Indo-European word. His father, Kapila, was a rich brahman, perhaps a descendant of a Vedic family of Indic origins. *Kapila* is a Vedic colour term referring to a brownish hue, perhaps derived from *kapi* or 'monkey'. His mother's name was Sumanādevī. He married Bhadrā Kāpilānī, a girl from Śākala but the marriage was not consummated. Both decided to retire from the world and went their own ways as was not uncommon during those Upaniṣadic times at the end of the Veda. They left their names which provide us with some information, but a great deal more is known about Kāśyapa.

Just as Kāśyapa or Kaśyapa is an old Vedic name, *pippala* refers to the fig tree after which the Paippalāda school of the Atharvaveda was named. Was Kāśyapa a follower of that school, which originated further west but certainly existed in Magadha by that time? It would not contradict the fact that his fiancée came from Sialkot in the Punjab—another couple of hundred miles even further to the west. Prominent people had long been settled by that time but were travelling widely and mostly on foot.

Kāśyapa's path crossed that of the Buddha, recently enlightened and already surrounded by throngs of followers. The Buddha led him aside, gave him three pieces of advice and admitted him to the Sangha or order. They exchanged robes. Eight days later, the Buddha declared that Kāśyapa was the first who followed 'the ascetic rules'—thirteen as mentioned in the Pali texts of the Theravāda or 'Doctrine of the Elders', and twelve in the traditions of the Mahāyāna, the 'Great Vehicle', sometimes preserved in Sanskrit, but often lost in India and better preserved in Chinese and other languages. Fragments of such texts are sometimes preserved in pots, found until very recently in Pakistan and Afghanistan.

The Theravāda is sometimes called Hīnayāna, the 'Abandoned Vehicle', a pejorative attributed to followers of the Mahāyāna. The Theravāda went from India to Sri Lanka and spread over South-east Asia. The Mahāyāna went to Central Asia, China, Korea, Japan, Tibet and Mongolia. The story of Kāśyapa's conversion is preserved in both traditions which differ in many respects but are equally valid for our knowledge of Buddhism.

Traditions agree that Mahākāśyapa, now 'the Great Turtle', outlived the Buddha and was an important figure in early Buddhism. How do we distinguish traditions from facts? The early development of Buddhism was undoubtedly oral, but it did not use techniques for its preservation like the Vedic. We must pick carefully among the many traditions, even if they agree, until we reach the dated inscriptions of Emperor Aśoka who lived some centuries later—from 268 to 233 BCE. The 'picking' can only be done by experts. They would reject the tradition that Kāśyapa composed the *Abhidharma Piṭaka*, the important third of the three baskets *piṭaka* . They should be distinguished from the three jewels (*ratna*): Buddha, Dhama and Sangha treasures, neither Buddha nor Sangha occur in the Vedas. But the word *dharma* is common from the Rigveda onward. Referring to rituals performed for the gods who were performing rituals themselves, the late hymn to Puruṣa (*page* 59) exclaims: 'Those were the First Dharmas!' (*tāni dharmāṇi prathamāny āsan*). Of course, the word *dharma* did not mean the same. Words change their meanings.

It is generally accepted that Mahākāśyapa presided over the first Buddhist Council which sought to settle what the Buddha had taught and about which we have much information. He was then said to be the seniormost of the monks alive and questioned others about what they remembered of Buddha's words. It is through brahmans like him that the Vedas could have influenced Buddhism. Or did Buddhism influence the Vedas? That depends, in the first place, on history and chronology. But are we not rushing ahead before addressing a weightier question: are we not comparing incompatible entities? Is not Buddhism a 'religion' founded by a historical person while I have repeatedly stated and demonstrated that the Vedas are not a religion, in that or any of the many accepted meanings of the term? These seem to be questions we have to answer before we can even begin. As a matter of fact, we cannot; but will pursue them in the following pages.

Let us return once more to Kāśyapa. When he felt that his end was near, the earth engulfed and concealed him until the end of times when Maitreya, the future Buddha, appeared and received from his hands the Buddha's robe.

It is not easy to determine whether the Vedas influenced Buddhism, but there is plenty of evidence in the texts of the Pali canon that their authors—Buddhist monks—were well informed even about details of Vedic mantras and ritual. Words of mantras such as the Gāyatrī, are quoted in Pali transliteration. It is known that the mantra consists of three lines of eight syllables as we have seen in Chapter **11**. Details of Śrauta and other rituals are referred to, including the *aśvamedha* horse sacrifice and the human sacrifice (see chapter **12**). It is typical monkish knowledge, not intended for Buddhist laymen who are not conversant with these details. How did Buddhist monks acquire such knowledge? It is obvious that it comes from brahman converts such as Kāśyapa.

I shall end this brief discussion with an apparent case of Buddhist influence on an early Upaniṣad. The relevant passage occurs in the early Chāndogya Upaniṣad and I have quoted it already at the outset of Part III but without including its conclusion. I shall repeat it here, beginning with sage Uddālaka Āruṇi instructing his son Śvetaketu and now adding the conclusion:

'Bring a banyan fruit.'
'Here it is, sir.'
'Cut it up.'
'I've cut it up, sir.'
'What do you see there?'
'These quite tiny seeds, sir.'

'Now, take one of them and cut it up.'
'I've cut one up, sir.'
'What do you see there?'
'Nothing, sir.'

The question that arises here is: does 'nothing' refer to the doctrine of emptiness (*śūnyatā*), a celebrated Buddhist teaching that seems to state the exact opposite of what we read about the fullness of brahman in some Upaniṣads and throughout the Vedānta or 'end of the Veda'?

The context provides the answer. Chāndogya Upaniṣad 6.8–16 consists of nine short sections in which Uddālaka Āruṇi instructs his son Śvetaketu. Each section gives a different answer and ends with the same phrase: 'That which is this finest minuteness, that the whole world has as its self. That is the truth. That is the self. In that way you are (*tat tvam asi*)'.

It is difficult to tell whether the 'nothing' of 6.12, the fifth of these nine sections, displays a whiff of Buddhist influence or emerged from Uddālaka's brain or somewhere else, but it is obvious that he did not treat that nothing as anything special.

History, Geography and an Inkling of Nirvāṇa

Questions concerning the early relations between Buddhism and the Vedas are highly controversial and can only be answered by taking a closer look at history and geography.

We also have to widen the perspective. Jainism is

demonstrably older than Buddhism and did certainly exist at the time of the Upaniṣads. Jainism is generally ascribed to Mahāvīra, an older contemporary of the Buddha, but Jaina sources mention many precursors of which one, Pārśva, is historical, pushing the date back to the ninth century BCE—the time of the Yajurveda. For the Buddha's death or *nirvāṇa* (a term that means 'enlightenment' or 'extinction', literally 'blowing out', and does not occur in the early Upaniṣads), we have two chronologies, the long and the short. The long one assigns it to around 486 BCE. The short one assigns it to around 368 BCE. There is no controversy about his place of birth, which is Kapilāvastu, a place below the lower foothills of the Himalayas, located close to the modern border between India and Nepal. From there the Buddha made his way southwards and reached the kingdom of Magadha with which we have been familiar since the map of Figure 2 where it is indicated by **Mg.** It is south-east of the Ganges near Pāṭaliputra, modern Patna. The later portions of the Rigvedic Aitareya Brāhmaṇa were familiar with this area and tell us that the Vedic sage Viśvāmitra adopted Magadha tribes that were living there. During this period, major clearance of jungle areas took place, facilitated by the increased use of iron tools. It led to an expanse of rice cultivation with a surplus in production which allowed lavish spending on large rituals such as those performed by King Janaka, a figure known to the composers of the Bṛhad-Āraṇyaka Upaniṣad and in Buddhist sources which does not prove much since both refer to the past often.

It is clear that the middle and later Upaniṣads were familiar with ideas and doctrines that are similar to those of Jainism and Buddhism. At the time of writing (late 2006), a controversy was raging on the Indology web-site about the relationships between early Buddhism and the earliest Upaniṣads, the Bṛhad-Āraṇyaka and the Chāndogya, to which I shall refer as BĀU and CU, respectively. It was initiated by Jan Houben of Leiden who asked whether the BĀU was written (?) in Buddha's time. A flood of reactions followed. Those who were primarily familiar with one side argued, predictably, for that side. No one paid attention to geography though all of them knew, presumably, that the Buddha Śākyamuni, 'Sage of the Śākyas', was born at Kapilāvastu, near the present border between Nepal and India. I mention two of these reactions by way of illustration.

Matthew Kapstein, a Sanskritist who has done much work on Tibetan Buddhist texts, claimed that the 'final redaction' of the CU was composed 'post-Buddha'. He hardly explained 'final redaction', but let us assume that he refers to the composition left behind by the final editors of the CU and BĀU who drew from 'a common stock of Upaniṣadic lore', as Olivelle put it. There are, however, other facts that must be taken into account, e.g., that BĀU is the final portion of the Śatapatha Brāhmaṇa which was composed, in the recension that is relevant in our context, in Kośala, close to the birthplace of the Buddha, and belongs to ca. 800–700 BCE.

Kapstein does not seem to have taken into account that the CU was composed much further west, probably in Pañcāla, and deals very largely with typically Sāmavedic topics such as the syllable OM which refers to the *udgītha*. Nor does he seem to know that Masato Fujii has shown that the Jaiminīya-Upaniṣad-Brāhmaṇa, a similar Sāmaveda Upaniṣad, is earlier than the CU.

My second illustration comes from Toshifumi Goto who is familiar with both sides. He has drawn attention to unexpected similarities between Yājñavalkya's characterization of the *ātman* in the BĀU and four kinds of suffering in Buddhism. The BĀU uses four terms to qualify the self: *ajara* 'unaging', *amara* 'undying', *amṛta* 'immortal' and *abhaya* 'fearless'. They occur together and generally in this order. What happens when we remove the negative prefixes '*a*—', that is, the negations from these terms, and change the order? We begin by replacing *ajara* by *jara* 'aging'. Goto then replaces *abhaya* by *vyādhi* 'sickness' because it is a common and concrete example of something we fear in our daily life. Next comes *amara* which does not occur in Vedic. Goto replaces it by *maraṇam* 'death.' Finally, we replace *amṛta* by *jāti* 'birth', which refers primarily to the second birth, that of initiation. We are left with a description of old age, sickness, death and the enlightened monk and recall the tradition of the young prince Siddhārtha witnessing those four when he had left his home and before he became a Buddha. He then preached the Four Noble Truths which are again reminiscent of the foursome at least in part and which I list here as translated by Lamotte: (1) everything is suffering; (2) the origin of suffering is desire; (3) there exists a Nirvāṇa, an end to suffering; (4) a path, defined by the Buddha, leads to Nirvāṇa.

Goto shows that BĀU and early Buddhism are both operating with similar concepts.

Whether the correspondence is perfect or not, it is an

ingenious exercise of an excellent philologist which draws attention to deep similarities that had never been brought to the surface. Goto wisely abstained from any conclusion about priorities.

How can we establish priorities when the paths are so slippery? Discussions about the particular use of an isolated term, the rice-and-ghee of the philologist's menu, are practically useless when we do not even know which language the Buddha spoke. Terms that seem special to us may have come into common usage without us knowing anything about it because the texts are silent. Chronological discussions about priorities cannot be solved by concentrating on these compositions in isolation from wider historical developments and geographical backgrounds. It is important that the BĀU is the final portion of the Śatapatha Brāhmaṇa and that after the BĀU there must have been enough time for composing other pre-Buddhist Upaniṣads.

That we have to pay attention to a wide perspective is the important conclusion that follows from the work of Michael Witzel. He took account of *all* Vedic compositions and placed them in a sequence that reflects such a perspective. I have followed Witzel often, as mentioned in the Preface. His comments on details are, of course, open to the scrutiny of other specialists, but the extended chronology that he made accessible by placing *all* Vedic compositions in a credible sequence, enabled him to provide us with a perspective that is not only wider but also deeper than the common perspective (or lack of perspective). It established, for example, that both the Sāmaveda and the Black Yajurveda originated in Kuru times, that is, ca. 1,000 BCE, and that the Śatapatha belongs to ca. 800–700 BCE, as I mentioned a moment ago. That is well before Buddhism though we cannot say exactly how long.

Apart from chronology, *general* matters of content also play a role. If we compare CU and BĀU we cannot fail to notice that the former is more positive than the latter in the following sense. It is closer to Rig- and Sāmaveda than the BĀU which combines Yajurvedic ritualism with the Upaniṣadic emphasis on renunciation. BĀU characterizes the *ātman* as *neti neti*, 'neither this nor that'. Buddhism is similarly negative when compared to the earlier Vedas, especially the Rigveda.

The Rigveda consists of poetry and it likes puzzles. That spirit survives in the joy that composers of early Upaniṣads experienced in long sequences of questions and answers and public debates. The Buddha did not approve of such debates and was not interested in the pursuit of knowledge for its own sake. This is epitomized in the story of the man who was struck by a poisonous arrow and asked many questions about who had shot it, what wood the arrow was made of and what its poison contained. The Buddha said: that man would die before he got his answers. In the Upaniṣads, Yājñavalkya presented a variation when he told Gārgī: 'Don't ask too many questions!', as we have seen in Chapter **10**.

We should return to the Four Noble Truths. All such enumerations, famous as they are, do not sound like insights of the Buddha. They are school examples, formulated for mass consumption, possibly by the master himself later in life or by his pupils. Buddha's insight was Nirvāṇa, the culmination of a path that was subdivided by teachers into steps: morality (ethics), meditation or *samādhi* (variously translated), and wisdom (*prajñā*). Note that *prajñā* contains the same verbal root *jñā*—as does *jñāna* or 'knowledge', a synonym of Vedic *veda* and *vidyā*.

The term *prājña* 'wise'—with different position of the long ā—occurs in the BĀU: 'Like a man in the embrace of his beloved knows of nothing outside, nothing inside, that person in the embrace of the wise *ātman* (*prājñena ātmanā*) knows of nothing outside, nothing inside.' This speaks for itself and need not refer to anything else, but if we want to, it could be interpretated as a reaction against the tedium of Brāhmaṇas and Āraṇyakas of which it announces the end. It illustrates at the same time an embrace that we do not find in early Buddhist texts,

The Buddhist *prajñā* is not a gnosis of vague and imprecise content. It is a clear vision, as Lamotte emphasizes: 'embracing the Noble Truths and penetrating in depth the general characteristics of things—impermanence, suffering and the impersonality of phenomena—as well as the peace of Nirvāṇa'.

Clear to Lamotte, no doubt, but Indic philosophies introduced a little more clarity as we have seen at the end of Chapter 10, which referred to the ritual philosophy of the Mīmāṃsā, closely related to the Śrauta Sūtras, and its distinction between activities that have a beginning and an end and those that do not (p. 183). It is relevant here.

The Mīmāṃsā philosophy consists of two parts: the first or Pūrva Mīmāṃsā deals with Vedic injunctions which pertain to what is to be accomplished (*sādhya*). That applies to ritual and meditation. The Pūrva Mīmāṃsā is also a philosophy of language (more specifically: of the sentence) and therefore sensitive to linguistic distinctions. The second Mīmāṃsā is the higher or superior Uttara Mīmāṃsā of the Upaniṣads and the Vedānta which coined the pejorative Pūrva Mīmāṃsā just as did the Mahāyāna with respect to what it called Hīnayāna, the Abandoned Vehicle. The aim of the Vedānta is knowledge which is instantaneous and beyond time. It corresponds to the vision of *prajñā* mentioned by Lamotte. It is 'accomplished' (*siddha*), not 'to be accomplished' (*sādhya*) like ritual or meditation. This is an accurate observation with a tinge of ordinary language argumentation supporting it. Knowledge is not a process; *acquiring* knowledge is a process. I do not say: 'I have the acquisition of knowledge' but: 'I have knowledge.' This holds not only of English. The same applies to the Buddhist concept of wisdom.

Language has serious limitations as we have seen in Chapter 15. No wonder that meditation and wisdom go beyond language. Since there is no special language, apart from mantras, should we be silent in spite of the loquacity of some masters? Recall that the Japanese Zen comes from the Chinese Ch'an which comes from the Sanskrit *dhyāna*. It requires silence and sitting and has a beginning and an end. Zen Masters may render further assistance.

History and geography are concerned with one more topic: the spread of Buddhism over large parts of Asia. Proselytization is absent from the Vedas and Buddhism resembles, in that respect, religions like Christianity and Islam. Even so, the Vedas and Buddhism both moved, albeit in opposite directions. The relevant information was gathered in Part I and is depicted by the Frontispiece at which the reader is invited to take another look. It shows to what extent the movements of Vedic Indo-Aryans and those of Buddhist monks mirror each other. I shall not repeat what I wrote there but we may derive a further conclusion: the tracks numbered **2**, **4**, **5**, **6**, 7 depict not only continuous movements and exchanges between people, ideas, rites and goods which show the artificiality of labels such as 'Vedic' or 'Buddhist', they also explain that, in due course, Buddhism returned to where some features of the Veda came from.

About the Vedas and Buddhism

Are we getting immersed in details, history and geography, and losing the forest for the trees? I have three general quotes to keep the reader on our track of discovery, two from modern scholars, one from Indian philosophy and a small Indic diversion to widen the perspective before we take a plunge into deeper waters.

The Rigveda went further than deriving pleasure from poetry and poetics. It presents us with a positive outlook on life that is not absent from the Sāmaveda, becomes more turbid in the Yajurveda and returns in the Upaniṣads. I am not preaching a return to the Vedic life or adoption of the Buddhist path. I am looking for light they may throw on each other and what we can learn from this. Here a quote about the spirit of the Rigveda from Wendy Doniger in her chapter on 'Realia' is useful. It does more than that label suggests and was written, I am sure, without the author giving Buddhism a thought:

> The *Rig Veda* is a sacred book, but it is a very worldly sacred book. Nowhere can we find the tiniest suspicion of a wish to renounce the material world in favour of some spiritual quest; religion is the handmaiden of worldly life. The gods are invoked to give the worshipper the things he wants—health, wealth, long life and progeny. That is not to say that there is anything superficial about Vedic religious concerns, but merely that these meditations stem from a life-affirming, joyous celebration of human existence.

Buddha did not display so positive a spirit. Neither did he seek support from the Vedas by invoking them for legitimation, whether innovatively or out of context as did the Purāṇas and other later perspectives on India's past. Does it imply that we are now ready, after fifteen chapters on the Vedas, to plunge into Buddhism without further ado? We must first ask what kind of thing Buddhism is. Are we comparing incompatibles? In partial response to that question, I shall quote Etienne Lamotte, a Catholic priest, and generally regarded as the greatest Buddhist scholar of the twentieth century. He never made comparisons but had some affinity with the topic:

> Adhesion to the Buddhist faith does not require that the adept rejects his ancestral beliefs or denounces

the religious practices that are current in his *milieu*. Through one of those compromises of which India has given so many examples, everyone is free to worship apart from the Three Treasures (Buddha, Dharma and Sangha, p. 307), the deities of his region, caste or choice and perform the appropriate rites. Throughout history one meets with famous Buddhists who continue their worship of spirits, Nāga and Suparṇa, Yakṣa, Vajrapāṇi, Women and Fairies. Householders, benefactors of the Sangha, remain loyal to the gods of their class: Kuvera, spirit of riches; Hāritī, the fairy with the children; the tutelary Couple, etc. The higher castes continue their demand for the great Vedic and Brahmanic deities: Indra, Brahmā, Māra, etc. The advent of Buddhism has never produced a 'twilight of the gods'. Śākyamuni does not oppose the pagan gods of Hinduism. He recognizes that 'the deities, honoured and worshipped by man, will in turn honour and worship him.' He does not condemn pagan rites: he disapproves of sacrifice in which living beings are killed; he recommends peaceful offerings devoid of cruelty; certain practices based upon pure superstition, ritual baths, etc., are practically without value. What is important is to put everything in its place: gifts to pious monks are better than the cults of the gods; taking refuge in the Three Treasures is better than giving gifts; the highest achievement of sacrifice is to enter the order.

The Cārvāka materialist school had no compunction with regard to the Vedas but most of its works are lost. The Advaita philosopher Śrī Harṣa, who lived in the twelfth century CE, wrote an epic poem about Nala's adventures which Phyllis Granoff, the leading expert on his philosophic work, called 'lusty'. Here is how Śrī Harṣa presents Cārvāka, tucked away by Surendranath Dasgupta in an appendix to the first and hidden at the end of the third volume of his monumental *History of Indian Philosophy*:

> The scriptural view that the performance of sacrifices produces wonderful results is directly contradicted by experience, and is as false as the Purāṇic story of the floating of stones. It is only those who are devoid of wisdom and capacity for work who earn a livelihood by the Vedic sacrifices, or the carrying of three sticks, or the besmearing of the forehead with ashes. There is no certainty of the purity of castes, for, considering the irrepressible sex-emotions of men and women, it is impossible to say that any particular lineage has been kept pure throughout its history in the many families on its maternal and paternal sides. Men are not particular in keeping themselves pure, and the reason they are so keen to keep the women in the harem is nothing but jealousy; it is unjustifiable to think that unbridled sex-indulgence brings any sin or that sins bring suffering and virtues happiness in another birth; for who knows what will happen in the other birth when in this life we often see that sinful men prosper and virtuous people suffer?

Early Buddhism was very ascetic but adopted a Middle Way. Buddha rejected the extremes he had tried himself under the guidance of Yoga masters before he reached enlightenment. Buddhism was, accordingly, faulted by adherents of more severe traditions. Rarely fair or balanced, they may be amusing as is the following quote from a Jaina source, translated from the German translation by Hermann Oldenberg in his monograph *Buddha: His Life, His Doctrine and His Order*:

> Resting on a soft bed during the night,
> Followed by a good drink in the morning.
> Eating before noon, drinking in the evening,
> Sucking sweets before dozing off—
> Finally reaching Supreme Enlightenment:
> Thus goes the fancy of the Śākyamuni.

Entering the Order, Women and Sexualities

Buddhism consists of three parts: Buddha, Dharma and Sangha. We have touched upon the former two but it is the Sangha or Order that exhibits the most important differences between Buddhism and the Vedas. Institutionalization like that of the Buddhist Sangha existed already in Jainism. But Jainism remained isolated and conservative and never seems to have posed a challenge to Vedic Indians. The Rigveda describes wandering sages, but they do not seem to belong to sectarian groups and the Vedic nomads were wandering anyway.

We have read what the Buddha taught: 'the highest achievement of sacrifice is to enter the order.' Leaving society to enter the Order and become a monk is subject to numerous monastic rules and engaged in a plethora of additional rites, and is concerned, like the Vedas, with ritual *orthopraxy* or 'correct practice.' Buddhism insisted, in addition, on *orthodoxy* or 'correct opinion,' in the first place for monks and for laymen to a limited extent. The Mahāyāna challenged the distinction between monks and laymen. Other monks chose isolation after ordination and retired to the forest. They are still found in Myanmar and Thailand.

The Buddha's teachings address all living beings but the large majority of Buddhist monks were converted from the three higher classes which, at the end of the Vedic period, were beginning to be defined. One innovation was that birth could be followed by a second birth, the initiation of *upanayana* that culminated in the Gāyatrī mantra as we have seen in Chapter **11**. Entering the Sangha is also a second birth and becoming a monk was marked by the *upasampadā* ritual, in many respects similar to *upanayana* and certainly inspired by it.

What about women? They were subservient to fathers, husbands and sons, ties they could break if they entered the order. The *upasampadā* could have been adapted as the *upanayana* had been. Just as Vedic women could wear 'the upper garment in the manner of the sacred thread', nuns could have adapted the monk's robe to their needs. But that is not what happened.

Tradition has it that the Buddha allowed only men to become monks, but that his favourite pupil, Ānanda, pleaded for the admission of women. The Buddha told him that, if he were to permit it, the Sangha would last five hundred years instead of a thousand. Even so, he consented and admitted women as nuns, provided they would be kept separate from the monks. His prediction turned out to have been wrong—Buddhism has lasted for two-and-a-half millennia, though women have again been excluded from ordination in Theravāda countries.

In Buddhism, eligibility does not depend on class or caste. Handbooks of monastic discipline exclude only one category of humans from entering the order. They are *paṇḍaka*s, often translated as 'eunuch' but, in fact, transvestites and/or passive homosexuals. One of the stories about them describes a *paṇḍaka*, just admitted to the order, who went up to a group of young monks and asked them to make love to him. They said: 'Away with you, *paṇḍaka*, we don't want you!' Thereupon, he approached a group of older monks who gave the same answer. Finally, turning to the elephant keepers, he was satisfied.

The reason for the exclusion of *paṇḍaka*s has nothing to do with the murky reasonings that have recently re-emerged from the Vatican, Evangelicals and others with regard to gays. It is practical. It is not easy to decide whether the *paṇḍaka*s must be regarded as male or female and the difficulty arises where they should be housed: in monasteries or nunnaries newly to be established? Also, would laymen provide the funds?

Homosexuality thrives in monasteries as it does in armies. Not much is known about it in the Buddhist monasteries of India; more is known about China and a great deal about

Japan, where monks were running after novices and pages as well as women. Does it reflect intrinsic differences in sexual mores between India, China and Japan? I believe it reflects different periods of history, different sources and other differences that I have not yet been able to ferret out.

Ahiṃsā and the Public Domain

In spite of the special cases that have just been described, the Buddhist teaching or Dharma is open to everyone: it is *public*—like the Upaniṣads became eventually. The Aṅguttara Nikāya, an early Buddhist Pali text, declares: 'Three things are hidden and not public: the wife, the mantras of Brahmans and erroneous views. Three things shine in public and are not hidden: the moon, the sun and the dharma.' This is a magnificent piece of public relations though it did not prevent the eventual disappearance of Buddhism from India after ca. 1,000 CE.

Performances of large Vedic rituals were generally hidden but they became public in India after the 1975 performance of the Agnicayana that has been described in the Preface. At that time a discussion arose about the sacrifice of goats which belongs in the present chapter. Vedic Indians were not vegetarians. Non-violence or *Ahiṃsā* was prescribed by Jainas and by Buddhists. It has become widespread among brahmins and in modern India, especially since Gandhi overthrew British colonial rule by strictly non-violent means. Many Nambudiri brahmins opposed the sacrifice of goats accordingly; or were unhappy about it. In 1975, I was visited by a delegation of Jaina monks who described the implications of violence to living beings. All I could do is explain that our personal feelings were irrelevant and that it was our task to record whatever would happen. Earlier, in the area of Udipi, where many Jainas live, Vedic brahmans had used figurines of animals. After much discussion, the Nambudiris decided to replace goats by packages of rice flour, put in banana leaves in the manner this is done for the ancestors at other rites.

In 2003, it was explicitly recognized that Vedic ritual was becoming public when a successful performance of a Soma ritual by Nambudiri brahmans took place in Trichur, Kerala. It was successful also in financial terms, partly because a Dakṣiṇāmūrti shrine, erected at the edge of the ritual arena, attracted donations from large numbers of visitors, increasing rapidly day after day. The event was attended by T.P. Mahadevan and myself and what we witnessed did strike us as a turning point in the tradition. So far, ritual eligibility for the performance of Vedic ritual had not, or not yet changed. I know one Nambudiri girl who recites Rigveda, but the Trichur performance represents a new Śrauta model in the sense that its *patron* changed: it was the public at large.

The first who characterized it as such was the Udgātā priest of the 2003 performance who mentioned it to T.P. Mahadevan in private conversation. He said that it was a *parasya*, that is 'public' performance. The ritual may be on its way towards the 'public domain', but its roots are firmly planted in Indian history and Sanskrit semantics. The term *para-*, in the sense of 'public', has a venerable history in

Kerala astronomy and mathematics. The *Parahita* system of astronomical computation was introduced in Kerala in 683 CE. A Malayalam commentary explained its name as 'being accessible to all people'. But the discussion started with Buddhism and its clear demarcation between what is hidden and what is public. Buddhism wavered about women, but it conquered the world by being accessible to everyone.

Eschatology and Karmic Arithmetic

We are now ready to return to the thesis of Gananath Obeyesekhere, discussed in Chapter **10**: in matters of life and death around the world, rebirth is the default option. I showed in that context that rebirth does occur in the Vedas but did not comment on Gananath's other thesis: the Buddhist concept of rebirth is ethical unlike the Vedic varieties. I believe that is only partly true. Vedic ideas about rebirth display features that are ethical such as notions of merit and demerit. They refer to 'ritual' and 'good' acts at the same time because they are not clearly distinguished from each other. The same is true of Buddhism as we shall now see.

Buddhism's great step was—I quote Lamotte—'to place action in the mind'. It is explicit in the 'Four Noble Truths' which mention desire and clearer in Mahāyāna texts ascribed to the Bodhisattva layman Vimalakīrti: 'pure mind is the root of good acts; divided mind is the root of bad acts.' This is close to Yājñavalkya's statement in the BĀU with mind being added as had *manasā* from the beginning (Chapter 2).

Desire is also mentioned in the BĀU and in a different context. Death desires: 'Would that a second body be born for me' (BĀU 1.2.5). Later in the Upaniṣad, Prajāpati teaches 'DA' which means *dāmyata*, 'self-control', *datta*, 'charity' and *dayadhvam*, 'compassion' (BĀU 5.2.1–3), all ethical notions.

If the Vedas are familiar with the ethical interpretation of good and bad actions, the question remains why did Yājñavalkya not want to discuss it in public. I believe that there is another explanation besides those given by Śaṇkara and Obeyesekhere for Yājñavalkya's reticence. That explanation applies to Buddhism as well as Vedic and later Indic religions and I shall characterize it as 'Karmic Arithmetic' or 'tit-for-tat'. It is eminently possible that Yājñavalkya regarded it as simplistic and unethical and thought it was therefore, better not to declare openly that: 'a man turns into something good by good action (*puṇya karma*) and into something bad by bad action (*pāpa karma*).'

Figures 25 and 26 show some pictorially striking illustrations of 'Karmic Arithmetic' or 'tit-for-tat' from later Buddhism. I show them for the same reason as the later Indic representations of spoke-wheeled chariots in Chapter 2: we lack pictures in Vedic studies but we have them in later Indic art.

The illustrations that follow are realistic, of high artistic quality, and come from the greatest monument of Buddhism, if not of classical Indic civilization: the Borobudur of Central Java which was built around 800 CE. They occur on the so-called 'hidden base' of the monument, called after the fact that it needs to be covered most of the time by large blocks of stone in order to prevent the entire construction from sliding down the hill. By carefully removing the blocks from each portion whilst keeping all others in place, Dutch, Indonesian and French Sanskritists, Sinologists and archaeologists have been able to show that the hidden reliefs correspond to descriptions preserved in Chinese translations of largely lost versions of a Sanskrit Mahāyāna Buddhist text, the *Karmavibhaṅga* or 'The Divisions of Karma', one of several texts known by that name. This discovery inspired Jan Fontein, art historian, archaeologist and museum director with a good knowledge of Sanskrit and Chinese, to write an illustrated account of the reliefs and the corresponding phrases in Chinese that explain them in precise detail. They show that there is nothing 'ethical' about the Buddhist doctrine of karma as it is expressed there because it works in the purely literal and automatic fashion of 'tit-for-tat'.

One relief (Figure 25) shows on the right a wealthy couple seated on the gallery of their house. The husband points his finger at some people that are obviously regarded as ugly. They are ridiculed by two others, standing behind them. The latter are as fashionably dressed as the couple and belong to the same family. On the left, the next relief portrays the same couple as they are reborn themselves equally ugly: the wife has hanging breasts and a child on her back, the husband has fallen on the ground. They are now in turn ridiculed by others who will be ridiculed themselves in their next birth, etc.

Another frieze (Figure 26) shows a similarly prosperous couple, smugly seated on their verandah, grinning at low-class street musicians who are begging in their garden.

Unfortunately, we have no relief to show what happened to them in the next life but the text is clear and we can easily guess.

Why have I spent time on Tit-for-Tat? Because there is nothing ethical about it: it is entirely mechanistic, like Descartes's idea of the life of animals. And yet, it seems to be widespread not only in Buddhism but all over the world. Whether the Buddha himself taught any such interpretation of the doctrine may be deemed unlikely. It seems certain that he accepted the idea that desires and intentions determine one's future destiny in a general manner. I don't know whether he thought that merit and demerit can be quantified exactly. That idea is not found in the Upaniṣads either. They rather expatiate on the opposite: all desires are extinguished but fulfilled in the absolute which is a true *nirvāṇa* though the term is not used. The Muṇḍaka Upaniṣad expresses the synthesis or identity that is the end-point of the Vedic perspective as follows: 'When one's desires are fulfilled, and one's self is made perfect, all desires disappear in this very world.' The theistic Upaniṣads introduce gods. The Śvetāśvatara declares that the Lord is free from desires. I have not treated these later Upaniṣads in Chapter 10 because they go beyond the end or final period of the Vedas.

Buddhist hells are a related matter and are not Vedic. The Vedas refer to Yama, god of the underworld and ruler of the spirits of the dead. The Rigveda does not tell us much about him. He builds a house for the dead and his arrival there is announced by a pigeon. A word for hell, *naraka*, occurs for the first time in the Taittirīya Āraṇyaka but we are spared the gruesome tortures that became a favourite topic in popular Buddhist religion, all over Asia, with Yama reappearing as the infernal judge. In China, he assumes the features of a magistrate with mandarin cap and gown. It is in the description of pain that the similarities between Buddhism and the monotheistic religions in other parts of the world become painfully manifest.

Conceptual Problems

We may now turn to the more exalted level of philosophy in the Vedas and Buddhism. Both seem to accept an absolute. That applies in the Vedas primarily to the Upaniṣads and in Buddhism especially to some philosophies. The common perception is that the Upaniṣadic *brahman* is positive. It is described as 'fullness', *pūrṇam*, as we have seen. The corresponding Buddhist negative is expressed as 'emptiness' (*śūnyatā*). It plays an important role in Buddhism unlike the 'nothing' of the CU, furthest away from Buddhism in time and space, where no special attention is paid to it. The BĀU accepts an absolute to which it refers as *neti neti* as we have seen. It seems to exhibit the distinction made in some European philosophies between metaphysics or ontology, which deals with what there is (e.g., an absolute), and epistemology, the theory of knowledge, which asks how we can know or describe it, e.g., 'in the negative', as by *neti neti*. The distinction is obsolete because it cannot be expressed in Chinese and is, therefore, not universal, as A.C. Graham has shown.

There are conceptual or logical problems with absolutes

and fullness and emptiness in particular. It is not mere sophistry like the argument that starts from the true premise that a half-empty glass is also half-full; and concludes, after mutiplying by two, that empty is the same as full. The most serious difficulty that affects all absolutes is that they are all alike. An absolute is defined by having no attributes that distinguish it from anything else. It is *anirvacanīya*, nothing can be asserted of it. But if 'emptiness' or 'nothing' is different from 'fullness' or 'everything', one of them must be different from the other in at least one respect which provides it with an attribute so that it is not an absolute. I conclude that absolutes are not only all alike, they are all identical. It is similar to an apparent paradox inherent in Spinoza's belief in 'God or Nature'. It was accepted by religious people, who were happy that nature was god, and by Marxists, who were happy that god was nature. But it does not support either because Spinoza's identity is a symmetrical relation: $a = b$ is the same as $b = a$.

Kamaleswar Bhattacharya has looked into similar problems in the context of the allegedly Buddhist statement that the self does not exist. He quotes Buddhist texts that declare unambiguously that it does exist. Bhattacharya admits that in some early Buddhist sources the self was 'negated'. But these refer to the aggregate of the *skandha*s, 'aggregates' or 'sheaths', such as feeling or volition, that are *erroneously* identified with the self.

These problems are of interest because they are alluded to in one of the very few passages in the Buddhist canon that are believed to have been uttered by the Buddha himself—not exactly, to be precise, since he spoke in a

Middle Indo-Aryan dialect or Prakrit that was subsequently translated into Pali and only then committed to writing in Sri Lanka in the first century BCE. The early Buddhist traditions were orally transmitted, like the Vedas, but without the special Vedic techniques and precautions of the Oral Tradition that belong to Late-Vedic (see Chapter 4). Hence the enduring uncertainties about what the Buddha said.

With these provisos, the Buddha is reported to have declared at the second sermon in Benares with reference to each *skandha*: 'This is not mine, I am not this, this is not myself.' Even a person without Pali can understand how the words express what they seek to express—when carefully looked at: *n'etam mama* 'this is not mine'—*n'eso 'ham asmi* 'I am not this'—*na m'eso atta* 'this is not myself.' It is almost Sanskrit (note that Pali *atta* corresponds to Sanskrit *ātman*), later adapted by Buddhist philosophers because it enabled them to discuss with other Indic philosophers. These expressions are as famous as the Upaniṣadic *tattvamasi*. But the Buddha does not say that the self does not exist. It is only the 'imagined *ātman*' of the *skandha*s that does not exist. This is one reason that I quoted Yajñāvalkya, at the outset of this book, explaining to his wife that there is no awareness of specifics after death.

Early Buddhist texts mention *brahmans*. This may refer to learned men or to the class or caste. Often, no value judgements are attached. Some of the first converts were themselves brahmans by birth—Mahākaśyapa, as we have seen—and respected for that reason. Other 'brahmans' were criticized, especially because of their fondness of rituals—the same commodity that in due course invaded

Buddhism itself. Harsher expressions are used in post-canonical Buddhist writings. One text says that brahmans are 'prattling liars' (*asatpralāpa*). Another, proffering a philosophic variant of Kautsa, that what the Vedas say is constantly changing, which belies any claims about their immutability. In later times, Buddhist philosophers and the philosophers of the Mīmāṃsā refuted each other with avalanches of argument. Śaṅkara, to whom I referred as an Upaniṣadic philosopher, had his go at Buddhism when commenting on the Brahmasūtra's sūtra: *anusmṛteś ca*, 'and on account of memory'. It is a cryptic refutation as a sūtra is expected to be, but the context is clear: the empirical fact that we have memory refutes the Buddhist notion of 'momentariness', i.e. the doctrine that nothing is permanent and that reality consists of a series of unconnected moments.

Śaṅkara's argument is a good example of 'ordinary language philosophy', but also a good argument. He starts with two statements that refer to memory. One says: 'I remember what I saw yesterday' and the other: 'I remember what you saw yesterday.' The first is a statement about memory. The second is not: it is a statement about what you saw. I may know about it, but I cannot remember it. Only I can remember what I saw. Since I remember what I saw, there is continuity of the 'I' and no series of unconnected moments.

Dharma and Cakra

Buddhism made use of Vedic terms and concepts not only because it was part of the current language. It also inherited and made judicious use of the spoked wheel (*cakra*) of early Indo-Aryans and Indo-Europeans. It accounts for the name of the Buddha's first exposition of his doctrine as *Dharma-cakra-pravartana*, 'the setting into motion of the wheel of Dharma'. *Pravartana* is derived from *vartana* which comes from the verbal root *vṛt*—and was used around 1380 BCE in Kikkuli's Mitanni treatise to refer to the 'turns' that horses are taught to take in the course of their domestication as we have noted in Chapter **1**. The wheel of the Buddhist Dharma, was set into motion by the Buddha in the Deer Park at Sarnath, outside Benares. It is depicted in Theravāda and Mahāyāna Buddhist art, beginning with Sanchi and throughout the Buddhist world. It has even been adopted by the Bonpos of Tibet but they turn it in the other direction.

Dharma-cakra-pravartana was another fortunate choice of Buddhists who were concerned about public relations. The entire expression consists of ideas and words with venerable Vedic antecedents and prefigurations. The eleventh verse of the puzzle-poem 1.164 in Chapter **15** sums up the Vedic evidence for the theory of *dharmacakra*. It deserves to be quoted in full:

> The wheel of time with its twelve spokes
> Turns around and around the sky and never ages.
> Here, O Agni, the sons stand in pairs,
> Seven hundred and twenty.

The first thing we notice is that a word for *time* takes the place of *dharma*. The original is *ṛta*, often interpreted as a principle that governs the Vedic universe. 'Setting into motion,' *pravartanam*, is expressed by a rare Vedic form of the same verbal root *vṛ-*, the *intensive* which is a strong expression and uses a reduplication: *varvarti*. It was explained by the medieval commentator Sāyaṇa as *punaḥ punar vartate* 'turns again and again'. Seven hundred and twenty is two times 360 and obviously refers to the days and nights of a year of twelve months. The Vedic calendar according to Vedic astronomy was more precise: it comprised 366 days, adding one day about every sixty-four months in order to preserve the relation between ritual dates and lunar phases (*page* 286).

In the Vedic instance, *dharma* is 'time', but it is not a single thing: there are many *dharmas*. This is expressed towards the end of the hymn by other famous lines which the reader will understand by looking at the original and a literal translation: *yajñena yajñam ayajanta devāḥ / tāni dharmāṇi prathamāny asan*, 'the gods ritualized ritual with ritual / those were the first *dharmas*.' Here the dharmas are generally translated as ordinances or principles. There are several different ones and not a single *dharma* as in the Buddhist case (if we exclude the *dharmas* or 'constituents' that occur in some Buddhist philosophies).

The cakra occurs in Vedic not only as a wheel but also as a weapon. Rigveda 2.11.20 says of Indra: *avartayat sūryo na cakram*, 'he hurled forth his *cakra* like the sun.' The *avartayat* of 'hurled forth' is again derived from the verbal root *vṛ-* of *pravartana*. In English, such a *cakra* is called a discus. It has a disk-like shape and refers to the disk of primordial resplendence which is the sun. Vishnu generally holds the weapon in his right upper hand, but in some early images it is on his left. In the art of Kashmir, Vishnu wears a turban which sometimes resembles those of early Kushan Bodhisattvas, and the right hand seems to be in *abhaya mudrā*, the gesture of fearlessness which is an artistic and iconographic borrowing from Buddhism.

A Sāmavedic Brāhmaṇa, the Pañcaviṃśa, described a *sattra* ritual which has a complex structure and is defined in terms of a large number of *stutis*: 'By means of this *sattra*, Prajāpati came to set in motion the whole universe.' All these compositions are pre-Buddhist. That does not hold for all of the Mahābhārata, which refers in similar terms to the Naimiṣa forest where 'according to the laws of an earlier creation, the wheel of *dharma* was set in motion.' The bards may have been familiar with or inspired by Vedic or Buddhist antecedents or both.

Jainism and Buddhism contributed not only to the end of the Vedas or Vedānta, but evolved new ideas. Foremost among them are the decline of dharma through four ages (*yuga*) and the endlessness of *kalpa*, a term that in later Vedic meant 'possible', 'practible' or 'ritual'. Romila Thapar has quoted colourful illustrations. One Buddhist text imagines an enormous mountain, brushed with a silk scarf every hundred years: when it is eroded, a *kalpa* has passed. An Ājīvika construct starts from a huge river, 117,649 times (that is, seven to the sixth power) the size of the Ganges. If every hundred years a grain of sand is removed from the river bed, that will be one *sara*. One *mahākalpa* equals 300,000 of these and 8,400,000 are needed to complete the transmigration of a soul. These calculations are based on the large numbers of Vedic mathematics. Thapar calls them 'a fantasy on ciphers'.

Monks must have used these large numbers to spread fear and kindle the desire for Nirvāṇa. In due course, it spread beyond Buddhism to the Purāṇas, which looked not at Buddhism but sought legitimation in the Vedas whose authority they did not question though they did not know their contents. The only hope for the future became Kalkin, the tenth *avatāra* of Vishnu and a counterpart to the Maitreya Buddha.

The Vedic revival of the Gupta period (320–500 CE; *pages* 119, 303) affected mostly the upper classes, now castes. It also marked a revival of Buddhism and those monks who wrote Sanskrit treatises were converts from the same classes. Like Buddhism, the Guptas spread from Magadha, mirroring Vedic movements of the past, first to former Kurukṣetra and the Western Gangetic plain and later over large parts of the subcontinent, excluding only the south. The Gupta revivals included arts and sciences incorporating Vedic studies, sometimes under Buddhist patronage.

The First University and Buddhist Logic

After the Vedas, Sanskrit became the language of learning with Prakrit or Prakrits as close seconds in Buddhist circles. Many traditions remained oral but after Aśoka (268–231 BCE), writing began to be used. With the development of cities, some became known for their Sanskrit learning. Most famous were Kāśī, Varāṇasī or Benares in the north and Kānchīpuram in the south. Buddha's first sermon, the *Dharma-cakra-pravartana* of the previous section, took place at Sarnath, just outside Benares. Kānchī became a centre of Buddhist learning later. During my last visit to its numerous temples, I came upon a large image of the Buddha kept in the garden of the police station.

Sanskrit learning was transmitted by pandits in their own houses and sometimes at the courts of chieftains or kings. The Vedas were transmitted not only within families but through *Vedapāṭhaśālas*. Medicine prospered in close association with clinics and hospitals which were patronized by emperors like Aśoka. Libraries were attached to many centres of learning and especially to Buddhist monasteries.

The first large universities in the modern sense were organized by Buddhist monks and financed by Buddhist laymen. Buddhist learning was increasingly expressed through Sanskrit, a classical language that possessed greater precision than any modern language. The Theravāda, which was studied in Valabhi in the west, may still have paid attention to Prakrits, but the earliest and most famous university was Nālanda in the east. The medium of instruction was Sanskrit which had been adopted by all Mahāyāna schools and philosophies in order to be able to interact with others. Many courses were taught by Buddhist monks, carefully selected for their learning. The basic curriculum consisted of Sanskrit grammar and logic. Specialists were attracted from elsewhere for mathematics, non-Buddhist philosophies, medicine, astronomy, fine arts, politics and the art of war.

Students came to Nālanda from all over Asia and were free to study what they wanted provided they passed an entrance examination. The working day for teachers and students was eight hours, indicated by a water clock. At the end of the year, academic degrees were granted according to the students' qualifications. Most students wisely limited their studies to a few disciplines. Some were familiar with more but only the most famous of a series of rectors or chancellors, Śīlabhadra, was claimed to have understood all topics. Philosophy and the logic of perception and inference were especially popular among young scholars.

The University of Nālanda is the first university in the history of mankind. Reportedly founded in 427 CE, at the end of the Gupta period, it was located near Pāṭaliputra or Patna, the same region where Śākalya and Yājñavalkya had excelled many centuries earlier, a few hundred miles south-east of the birthplace of the Buddha. How are we so well informed about these matters?

Our information is due to Chinese pilgrims who came to India to study not only Buddhist subjects but scientific topics, especially medicine. Chinese as well as Indians, and not only Buddhists, looked upon Buddha as Bhaiṣajya Guru, the Great Healer. Chinese scholars and scientists, soon joined by Koreans, Japanese, Tibetans and others, studied Sanskrit for the same reason Europeans were to study Arabic later: it gave them access to new developments in the sciences.

The most important Chinese visitor was Xuanzang (Hiuan-tsang: 602–64 CE) who was in Nālanda between 629 and 646 CE. We know much about him because of his student and biographer Hui Li. Both left detailed information on Sanskrit and Sanskrit grammatical works, not known from any other source. After mastering Sanskrit, Xuanzang spent five years studying the philosophy of the Yoga system under the tutelage of Śīlabhadra. When he had become famous as a scholar himself, Xuanzang started teaching courses and made many friends with whose help he collected manuscripts that were copied for him on the spot. On the way back to China, he lost one horse-load of them when crossing the Indus. He had a list which he sent back to India, requesting replacements.

The next important visitor from China was I-tsing (634–713) who spent some fifteen years at Nālanda. His description of the curriculum is very detailed. He mentions the names of the Sanskrit works that were taught, beginning with Pāṇini and Patañjali and adding known and unknown works by Bhartṛhari and others. In the mean time, Nālanda had begun to decline. It came to an end when the buildings were destroyed by Muslim invaders.

The most recent information about Nālanda comes from two sources. The first is Amartya Sen's book *The Argumentative Indian*. It contains a picture of Xuanzang's caravan loaded of boxes with books carried on the backs of horses. Xuanzang found India very hot and when, in the end, he wanted to return to China, his Indian friends and colleagues argued that he should stay. Sen quotes in full what they said:

> India is the land of Buddha's birth, and though he has left the world, there are many traces of him . . . . Why then do you wish to leave having come so far?

> Moreover, China is a country of barbarians who despise the religions and the doctrine. That is why the Buddha was not born there. The mind of the people is narrow, and their coarseness profound, hence neither saints nor sages go there. The climate is cold and the country rugged—you must think again.

Xuanzang replied with two counter-arguments. Without questioning the first premise, he disputed the inference by invoking Buddhist universalism: 'It is true that the Buddha established his doctrine here so that it might be diffused to all lands. Who would wish to enjoy it alone, and to forget those who are not yet enlightened?' He thereupon disputed the second premise because it was not in accordance with the facts:

> Besides, in my country the magistrates are clothed with dignity and the laws are everywhere respected. The emperor is virtuous and the subjects are loyal, parents are loving and sons obedient, humanity and justice are highly esteemed and old men and sages are held in honor. How then can you say that Buddha did not go to my country because of its insignificance?

Recently there seem to have been attempts to revive Nālanda. My only information is a letter of December 2006 in the *International Herald Tribune* by Jeffrey Garten, a professor at the Yale School of Management. It refers to a forthcoming meeting in the Philippines, where senior officials from India, Singapore, Japan, etc., are scheduled to discuss what to do with $500 million that still have to be raised (!), to build the university and develop the roads and other infrastructures. Garten is right that 'a bolder vision is in order.' His thoughts are about training future leaders and move in the direction of religious dialogue, but he displays his ignorance of Asia's universities when he writes that they have 'a long way to go to be in the top tier', by which he means Harvard, Yale or Columbia. Nor does he seem to be familiar with what has happened in India during several decades and is happening in India, China and the US right now.

In India, the Tata Institute of Fundamental Research in Mumbai and several national institutes of advanced studies, some of them founded or inspired by Jawaharlal Nehru, have flourished for many decades. I am not referring to the Indian schools that produce 184,000 engineering graduates annually (as against 71,000 in the US in 2003). I am writing about small institutions where top scientists do creative work on basic science.

Relevant facts about American universities are that many of the best graduate students in the sciences have been Asians because American students 'are no longer hungry or ambitious', as Paul Kennedy put it, adding about the Asians that 'most of them will be teaching and working in India and China.' It sheds much light on Nālanda: students kept going there as long as it was the best centre of learning they could find. But there was competition, not only in India. The institution of public examinations in China, Korea and Japan pre-dated Nālanda. It was the foundation for the reforms that Chinese pilgrims made in Chinese Buddhism after their return from India. This led to the formation of translation centres in Central Asia where Sanskrit was translated into Chinese. Central Asia was and remained a meeting point of Indian and Chinese sciences throughout the millennia.

Neither Amartya Sen nor Jeffrey Garten mentions logic which was as basic at Nālanda as the study of Sanskrit. Xuanzang displayed his mastery when discussing the relative merits of India and China. How do we know these facts? It's the logic, stupid!

Buddhist scholars made important contributions to Indian logic. Before Patañjali used logical techniques in linguistics, around 150 BCE, Kauṭilya had written a work 'for the edification of princes' in which he introduced *ānvīkṣikī* or 'investigation'. Centuries later, an author of the *Nyāyasūtra*, now known as 'the Ancient School of Indian Logic,' declared that, *nyāya* is the same as *ānvīkṣikī*.

Buddhist logicians criticized the ancient school and initiated the 'Medieval School of Indian Logic' which was in due course replaced by the 'Modern School of Indian Logic' or *Navya-Nyāya* which criticized both predecessors. Buddhist Logic does not include the work of the famous Nāgārjuna who tried to demonstrate the absurdity of all intellectual notions and the logical impossibility of all experience like a medieval Derrida. The greatest Buddhist logician was Dignāga who lived around the time of the probable foundation of Nālanda and introduced what we would nowadays call *formal* logic. He constructed the eightfold *Hetucakra* or 'Wheel of Reasons'. It puts together all possible combinations of reasons and conclusions in a table of eight of which two corresponded to the Old Nyāya. This work is lost in the original Sanskrit but was translated into Chinese and became known as *Hetuvidyā*, the 'Science of Logic'.

I participated in a conference on *Hetuvidyā* which took place in Hangzhou near Shanghai in 2006. Earlier, I had attended a 'masterclass' convened by Sheldon Pollock on 'Comparative Intellectual Histories in Early Modern Asia' at the University of Leiden, The Netherlands. The Hangzhou conference and Leiden masterclass throw light on the study of Buddhist logic within the wider perspective of Indology and Buddhology which, because of ever increasing degrees of specialization, have greatly diverged from each other. Leiden and Hangzhou also diverged but they mirrored and complemented each other, like the routes of Vedic and Buddhist on the frontispiece. The Leiden participants who knew Sanskrit did not know that, in between the Old and the New Nyāya, there had been a medieval Nyāya which was Buddhist. Some participants at Hangzhou, who knew Sanskrit, Tibetan and Chinese, assumed that *Hetuvidyā* was Indian logic and there was no other logic in India.

A third international meeting, after Leiden and Hangzhou, took place in the Great Hall of the People in Beijing and was called *Strings 2006*. I referred to it already (*page* 276) and need only add, that the statement of the official from Chinese Academy of Sciences predicted the transfer of academic eminence from the US and Europe to India and China, no one knows how soon. The rest of Asia would follow suit once it was discovered that business administration or management are not enough and that there is no technology, economics or a future without basic sciences which include subjects such as physics, logic and Vedic studies.

Nālanda was a great university that was more than a debating club or dialogue between religions. It was based upon the logical study of facts and a further step in the tradition and evolution of the Vedas and Upaniṣads towards universal knowledge. *Viśvatomukham*, 'looking in all directions', is the starting point of *viśvavidyālaya*, 'university', storehouse of knowledge, *vidyā* or *veda*, hence its inclusion at the end of our discovery of the Vedas.

Final Conclusions

The Vedas are not all of a piece and it would be unreasonable to expect a single final conclusion about them. What I can do is make a few remarks about Buddhism and the Vedas and try to place them in a wider perspective.

Vedic civilization does not offer us a founder, order or doctrine. Buddhism provides the Buddha and the Sangha, but if we look at its many schools and ramifications, it is clear that it does not offer a single doctrine either. There are many similarities in ideas propounded by the Vedas and doctrines taught by Buddhist schools at different points during their long careers.

The term *nirvāṇa* does not occur in the early Upaniṣads but is not uncommon in later Sanskrit, as a near synonym of *mokṣa* in some of its meanings. Lamotte's formula is clear enough: 'Nirvāṇa is a clear and precise vision, embracing the Noble Truths and penetrating in depth the general characteristics of things—impermanence, suffering and the impersonality of phenomena—as well as the peace of Nirvāṇa'. Any comprehensive knowledge about the universe including ourselves will have to 'penetrate in depth the general characteristics of things' and enlighten us about the human condition.

The University of Kyoto is a great university for many reasons. Not only is it one of the best centres globally for Sanskrit studies, but it has a weekly seminar with a tradition of inviting visiting scholars to give a lecture. The faculty sit around a large table and there are many extra chairs for graduate students. The seminar starts at 2 o'clock and after the talk, which may last for an hour or more, people do not leave but stay on, not to drink tea (though they do drink tea) but to ask questions and discuss until the end of the afternoon.

I was fortunate to give such a lecture and the discussion became wide-ranging. A distinguished scholar of Buddhism, himself a Buddhist, raised the question: Would the Buddha have known what a modern physicist knows? A silence fell and people looked at me because I had given the lecture (which had nothing to do with Buddhism). But the chair intervened—perhaps it was five o'clock—and said we had had a fine discussion. I do not blame him.

What could I have said? I was ready to say: No, he could not have known. One reason is related to the talk I had just given: the level of mathematical knowledge during Buddha's time would not enable anyone to formulate what is now known in physics because it can only be done in an artificial language, and the first that might have been suitable, the language of algebra, was not known then and there. Could there have been a clear vision of what holds the universe together and what, if any, might be our place in that world?

Should one delve into the matter, starting with the universe, and check out whether any of the large numbers divined by seers and sages of the Vedas, authors of Jaina and Buddhist works, bards of the Epics and theologians penning Purāṇas, are the ones we seek? Even if they were thinking of cows, there is no need. With so many large numbers to choose from, lots will correspond to those that physics and cosmology need now or later. According to recent estimates, perhaps already outdated, the age of the universe is only 10^9 or 20^9 years. The characteristic size of particles is about 10^{-15} of a meter and the radius of the observable universe about 10^{27} meters. Even if we add 15 and 27 as an exponent of 10, it is only a fraction of what India has come up with. Contrast the story of creation in the Jewish Ancient Testament, accepted by Christians and repeated in the Qur'ān: it took six days. Heaven was a garden, the Garden of Eden or 'Adn, believed to be located in Mesopotamia.

In our corner of the universe, we still have not resolved problems of impermanence, suffering, the impersonality of phenomena and least of all peace. As for knowledge, we have little. Physicists tell us that 2 per cent of the universe is now known. About life we know less, and about the development and history of our own species much less. Perhaps we have not been selected for such tasks, our priorities are wrong, or both. But even monotheists have not failed to note—provided they were learned like Pascal—that 'our intelligence occupies in the order of intelligible things the same rank as our body in the vastness of nature.'

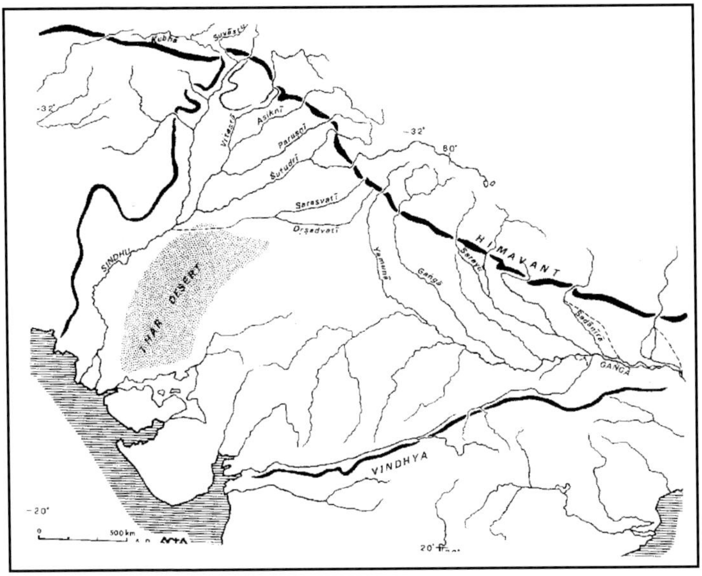

Figure 1. Geography of the Vedas: Rivers

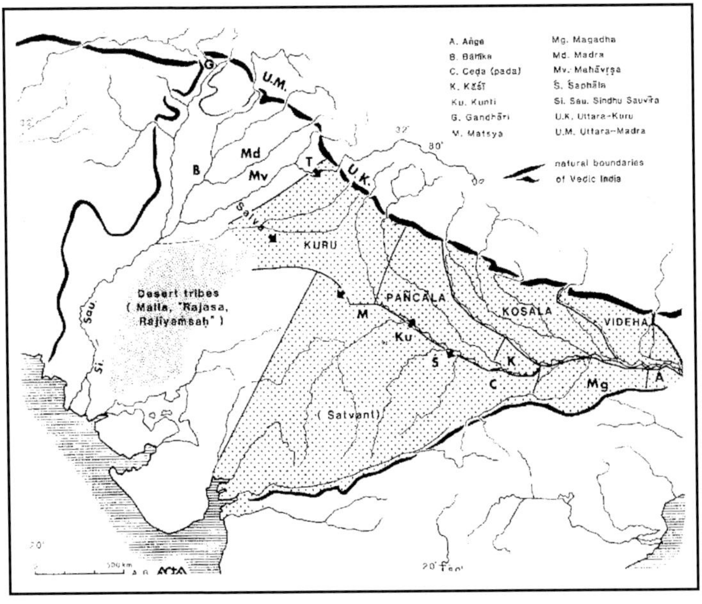

Figure 2. The Rigveda and the Other Three Vedas: Tribes

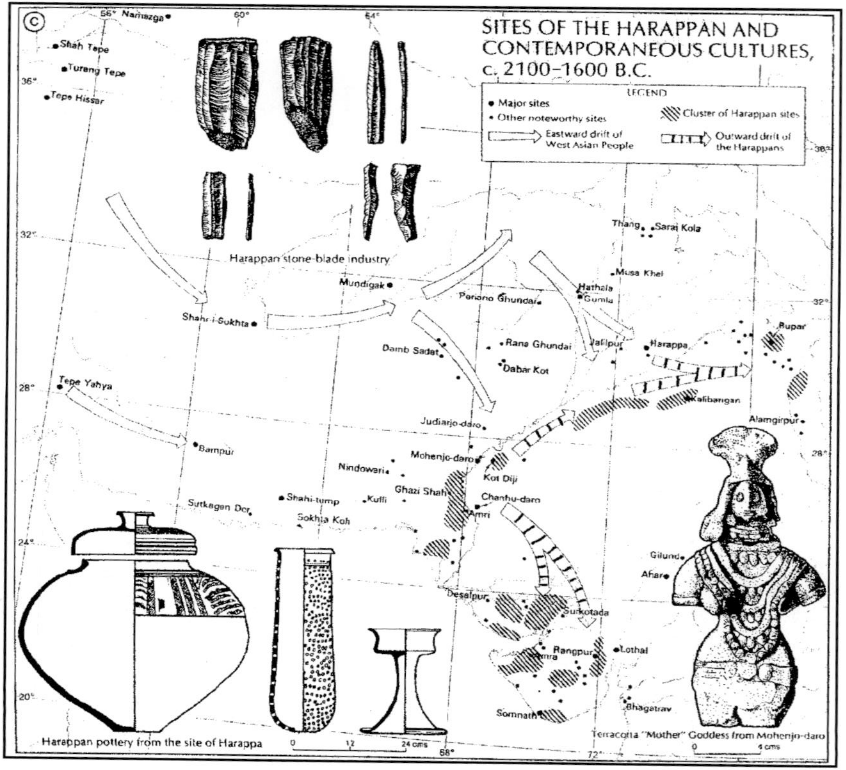

Figure 3. The Indus Civilization between 2100 and 1600 BCE

Figure 4. Two Pages of Kikkuli's Treatise

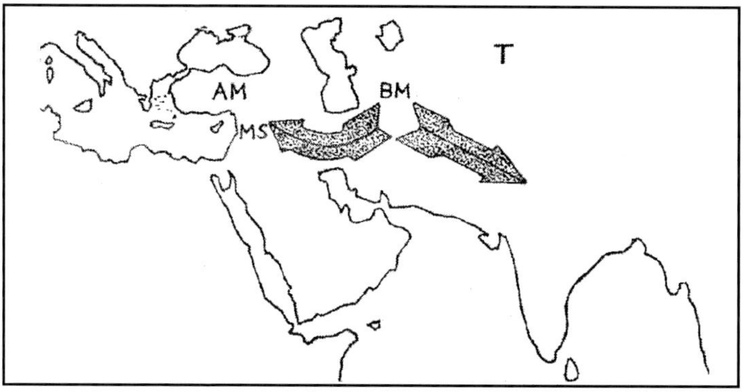

Figure 5. Indo-Aryan, the Language of the Vedas
(AM: Asia Minor– MS: Mitanni Syria–T: Tocharian BM: BMAC)

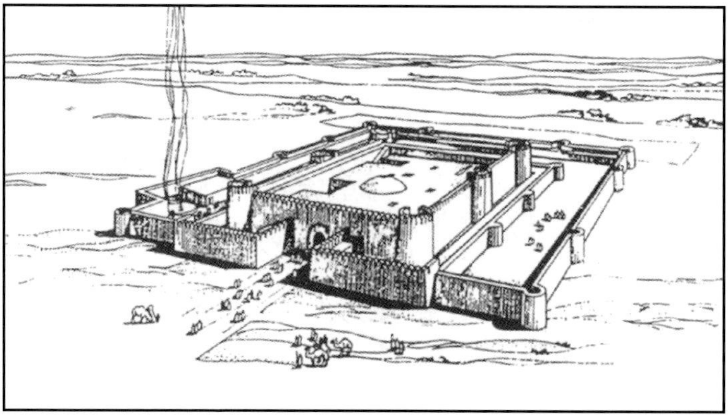

Figure 6. Togolok-21, BMAC, reconstructed by
Viktor Sarianidi

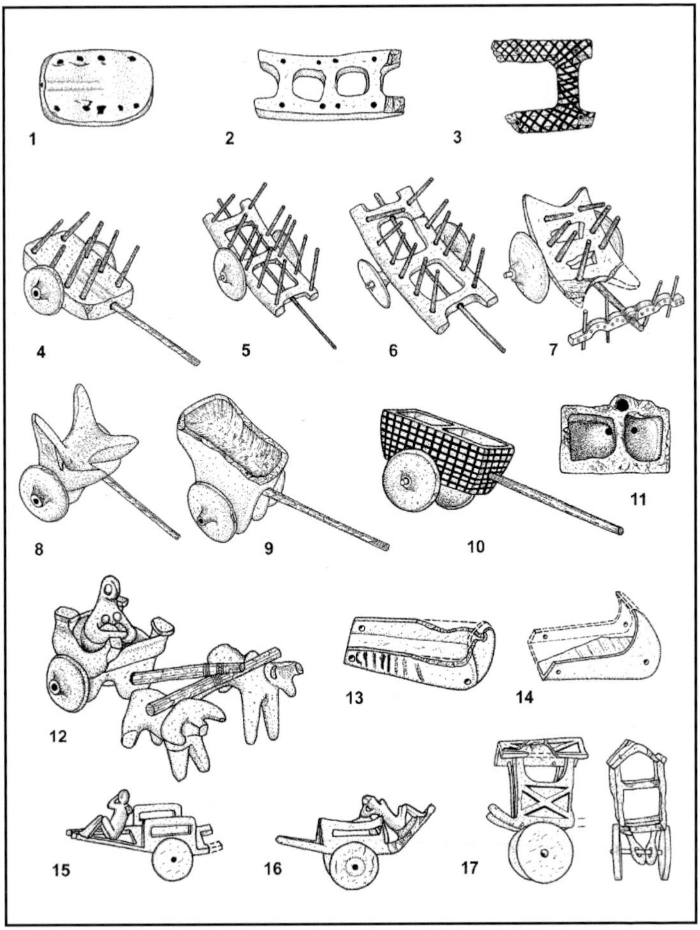

Figure 7. Carts from Harappa (2100-1600 BCE)

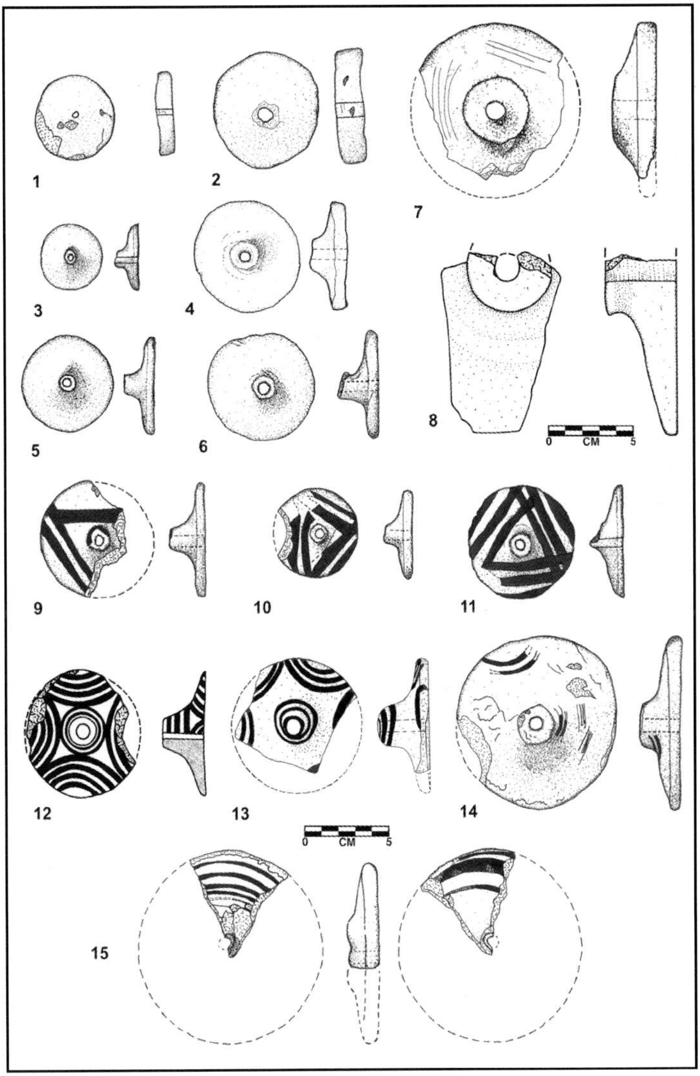

Figure 8. Wheels from Harappa (2600-1900 BCE)

Figure 9. Panel from Sanchi with Spoked Wheels

Figure 10. Rock Paintings from Mirzapur

Figure 11. Spoked Wheel from the Sun Temple at Konarak

Figure 12. Procession Cart
with Solid Wheels from a Temple
at Kumbakonam

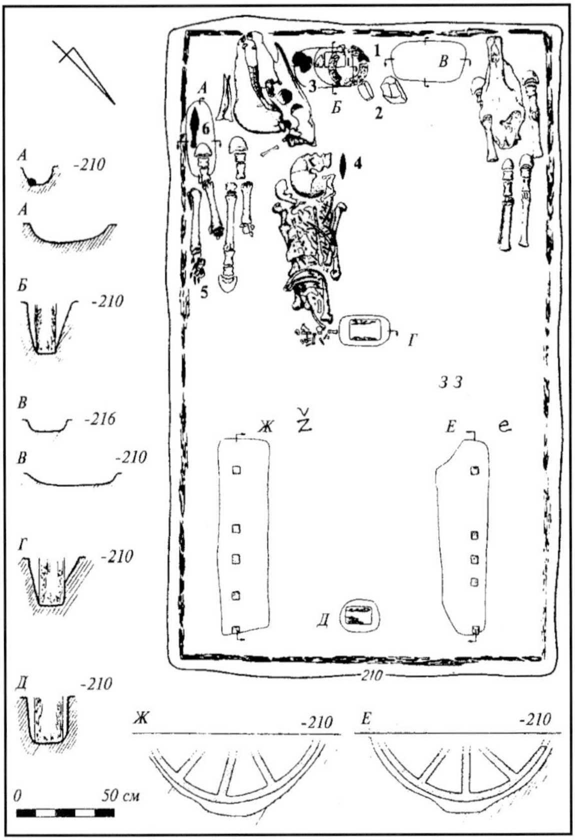

Figure 13. Sintashta Graves
(between 2200 and 1800 BCE)

Figure 14. Ceiling Panel of Sage Vidyāraṇya

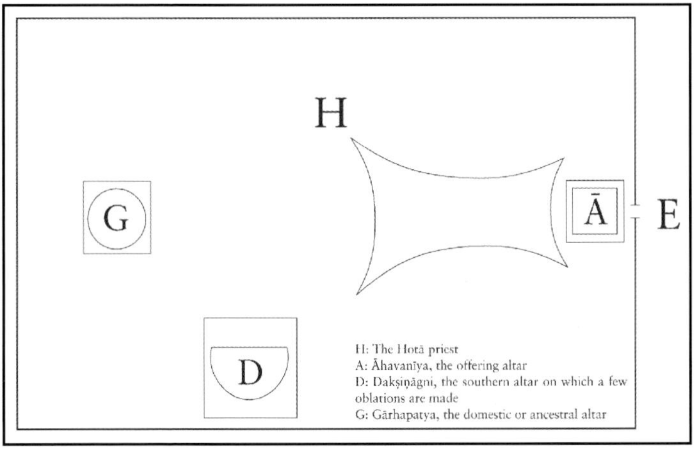

Figure 15. Ritual Arena for the Soma Ceremonies

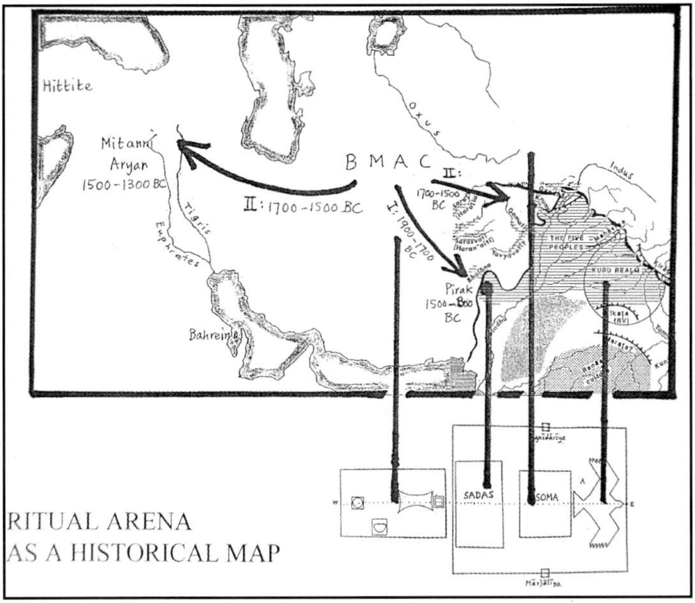

Figure 16. The Ritual Arena as a Historical Map

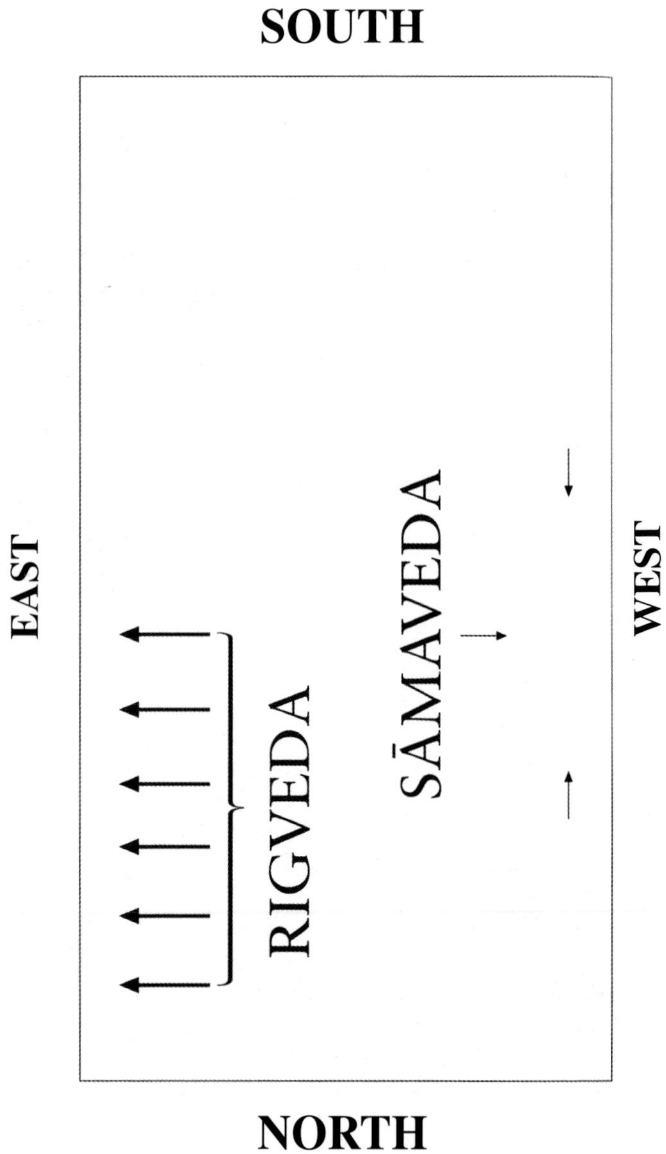

Figure 17. Facing Opposite Directions in the Sadas

Figure 18. Looking East into the Sadas

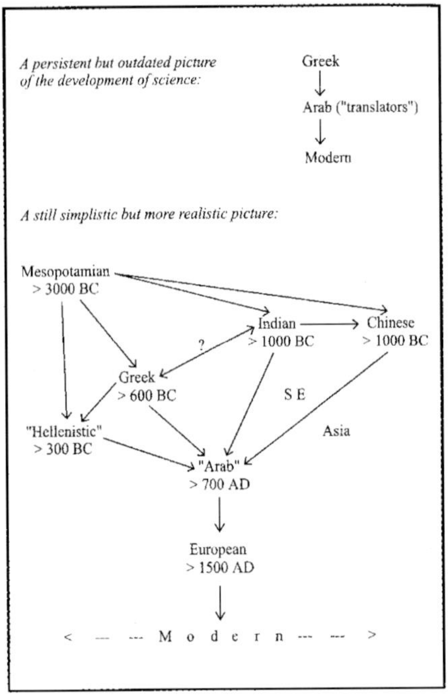

Figure 19. The History of Ancient and Medieval Science

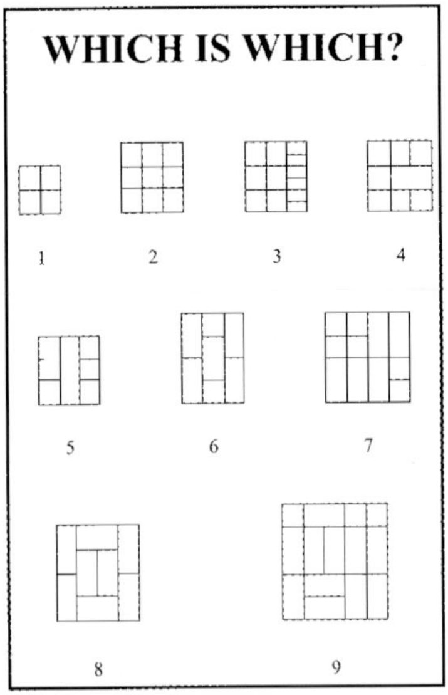

Figure 20. Squares and Oblongs in Proto-geometry

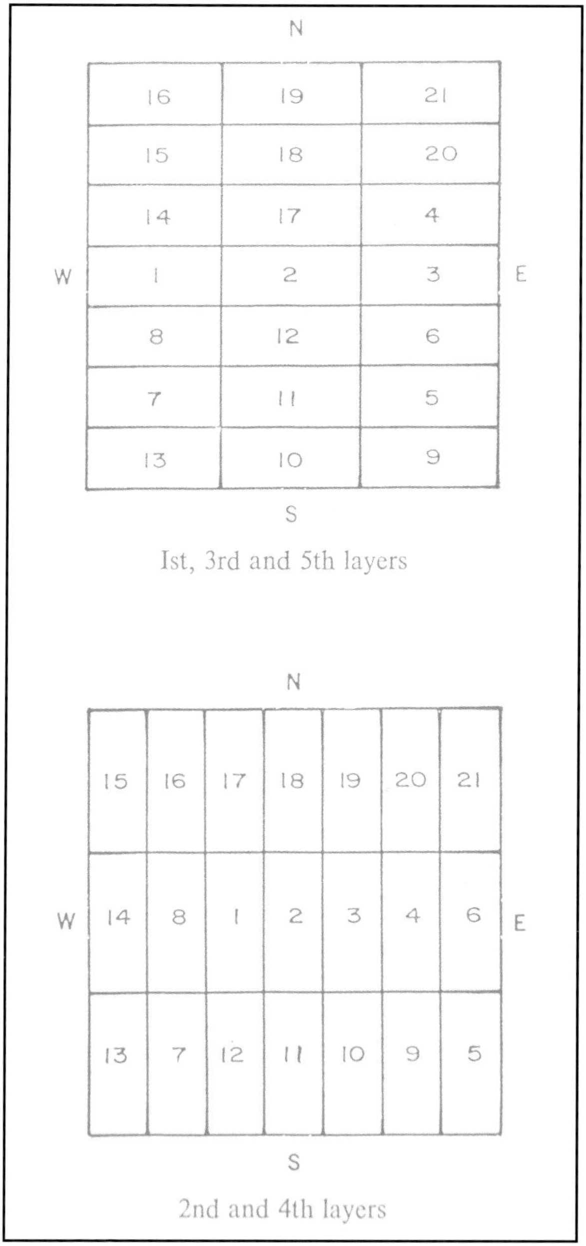

Figure 21. The New Domestic Altar

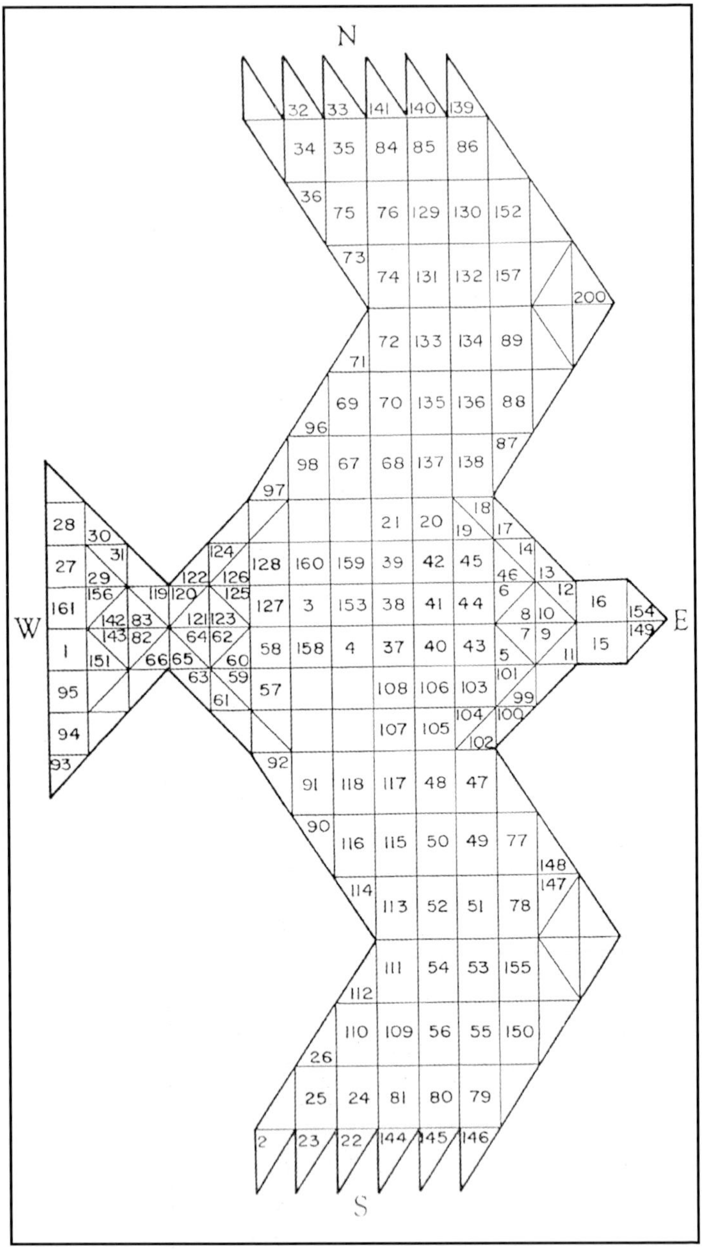

Figure 22. First Layer of the Piling of Agni

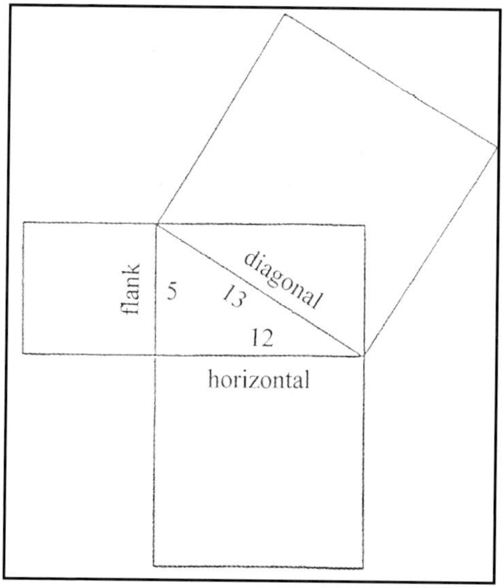

Figure 23. The Theorem of Baudhāyana

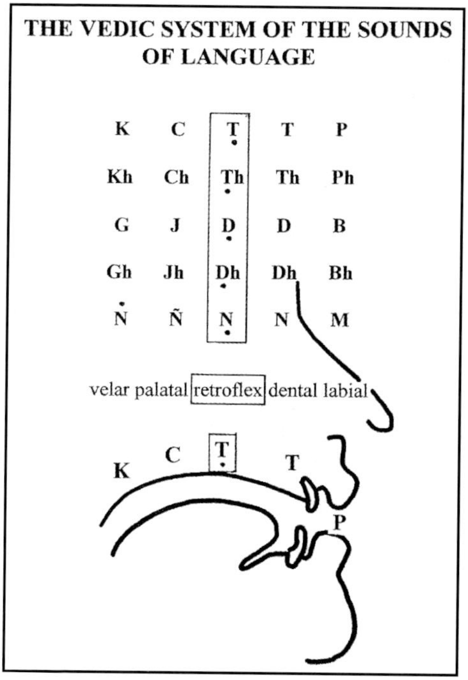

Figure 24. The Sound Pattern of Language

Figure 25. Karmic Arithmetic or Tit-for-tat I:
Ridiculing Ugly People

Figure 26. Karmic Arithmetic or Tit-for-tat II:
Despising Low-class Musicians

APPENDIX I

~

LIU HUI'S PROOF OF THE THEOREM OF BAUDHĀYANA

Liu Hui lived in the third century CE. His proof was given in algorithmic form and corresponds to the figure below. It starts with a rectangle of 3 by 4 (HIGD). The diagonal (HG) is 5. Draw a square on this diagonal (GHEF). By this 'piling up of rectangles' (as the Chinese put it), visible inspection shows that the theorem holds: 3-4-5 is not only a 'Pythagorean triple' of numbers but a 'Pythagoraean triangle' in geometry: the square on 3 is AMIH, on 4 is MBFL and on 5 is GHEF. The reader may be able to *see* this but for moderns the algebraic notation $a^2 + b^2 = c^2$ is not only much easier, but it is generally applicable: to other triples of integers, to rational, real numbers, etc. But algebra did not exist in 263 CE.

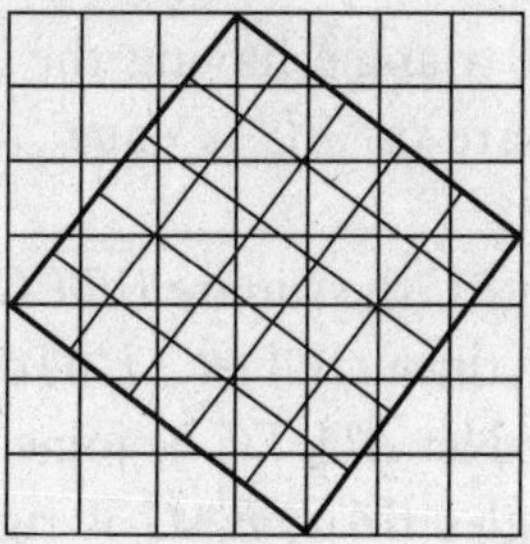

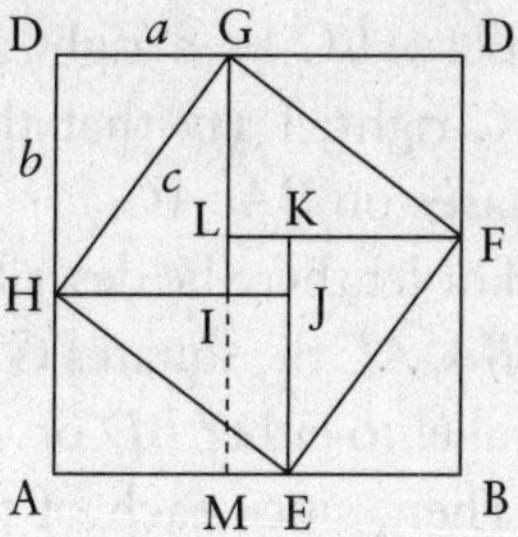

APPENDIX II

EUCLID'S PROOF OF THE THEOREM OF BAUDHĀYANA

Euclid was probably taught geometry in Athens by Plato's pupils. He taught himself in Alexandria (Al-Iskandarīya) where he started his own school. What follows is his proof as translated from the *Elements* by Thomas L. Heath. It may be understood by looking at the figure but is fully explicit and remains difficult. I have omitted references to axioms or earlier theorems.

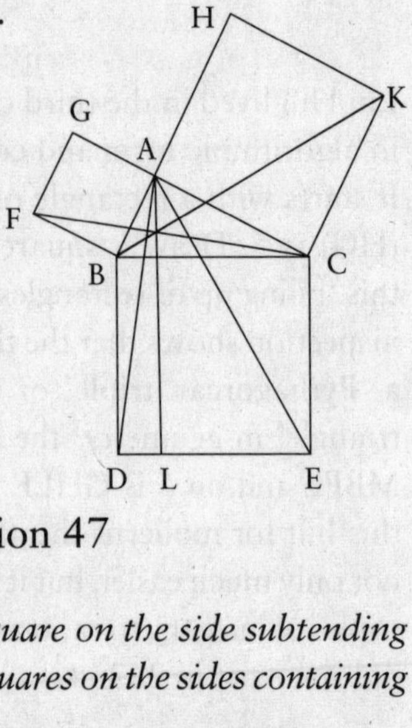

Proposition 47

In right-angled triangles the square on the side subtending the right angle is equal to the squares on the sides containing the right angle.

Let *ABC* be a right-angled triangle having the angle *BAC* right; I say that the square on *BC* is equal to the squares on *BA, AC.*

For let there be described on *BC* the square *BDEC*, and on *BA, AC* the squares *GB, HC*; through *A* let *AL* be drawn parallel to either *BD* or *CE*, and let *AD, FC* be joined.

Then, since each of the angles *BAC, BAG* is right, it

follows that with a straight line *BA*, and at the point *A* on it, the two straight lines *AC, AG* not lying on the same side make the adjacent angles equal to two right angles; therefore *CA* is in a straight line with *AG*.

For the same reason *BA* is also in a straight line with *AH*.

And, since the angle *DBC* is equal to the angle *FBA*: for each is right: let the angle *ABC* be added to each; therefore the whole angle *DBA* is equal to the whole angle *FBC*.

And, since *DB* is equal to *BC*, and *FB* to *BA*, the two sides *AB, BD* are equal to the two sides *FB, BC* respectively, and the angle *ABD* is equal to the angle *FBC*; therefore the base *AD* is equal to the base *FC*, and the triangle *ABD* is equal to the triangle *FBC*.

Now the parallelogram *BL* is double of the triangle *ABD*, for they have the same base *BD* and are in the same parallels *BD, AL*.

And the square *GB* is double of the triangle *FBC*, for they again have the same base *FB* and are in the same parallels *FB, GC*.

[But the doubles of equals are equal to one another.]

Therefore the parallelogram *BL* is also equal to the square *GB*.

Similarly, if *AE, BK* be joined, the parallelogram *CL* can also be proved equal to the square *HC*; therefore the whole square *BDEC* is equal to the two squares *GB, HC*.

And the square *BDEC* is described on *BC*, and the squares *GB, HC* on *BA, AC*.

Therefore the square on the side *BC* is equal to the squares on the sides *BA, AC*.

Therefore etc. Q.E.D.

READINGS

This brief section is written for readers who are looking for basic expositions and reliable, unabridged translations of the Vedas with explanatory notes. Full titles and publishing information are given in the following Bibliography and here I have only listed books that are relatively easily obtainable, often in Indian reprints. The German classics have been reprinted but are unaffordable and often specialized.

The inaccessibility of the Vedas has become a glaring scandal, especially in the English-speaking world and that, astonishingly, includes India. If I had to recommend a single general book about the Vedas in English, I would fall back on Louis Renou's *Religions of Ancient India* which is certainly outdated. Fortunately, there is access, but only in India, to three of the Vedas without having to pass through the written word.

For the Rigveda, there is no reliable translation into English. The two English translations by Griffith and Wilson are nineteenth-century fantasies and best discarded. For those who read German, Geldner remains the best guide. But see the Preface, p. xxix for good news.

For the Sāmaveda, good chanters may be found through *Vedapāṭhaśāla*s although reciters of Rig- and Yajurvedas are more common. Sāmaveda recordings are available in various formats but generally bereft of good explanations.

For the Yajurveda we have two reliable translations that are old: Keith for the *Taittirīya Saṃhitā* of the Black Yajurveda and Eggeling for the *Śatapatha Brāhmaṇa* of the White Yajurveda. There are rare possibilities, in India, of witnessing authentic performances of Vedic ritual which is as important for the understanding of the Yajurveda as is listening to chants for that of the Sāmaveda.

The Atharvaveda has remained what it has always been: fairly inaccessible. (Whitney is outdated.)

The Upaniṣads have been translated often, and often badly. The best recent translation into English is that of Patrick Olivelle.

Those who wish to get an idea of more specialized studies should consult Dandekar's *Vedic Bibliography*, in several volumes from 1964. Witzel has started a series of 'Opera Minora' attached to the *Harvard Oriental Series*. Two volumes contain the *Proceedings* of Vedic workshops. The results of a more recent meeting found their way to Egbert Forsten in Groningen. It is a beautiful production, strictly unaffordable not only for people but also for libraries.

Specialist articles continue to appear in 'Orientalist' journals, too many to list. If I had to select five outside India, they would be: *Indo-Iranian Journal, Journal Asiatique, Journal of the American Oriental Society* (affordable), *Wiener Zeitschrift für die Kunde des Morgenlandes* and *Zeitschrift der deutschen morgenländischen Gesellschaft.*

~

SOURCE NOTES

These notes provide background information, references and some entertainment for the interested reader and scholars. They furthermore seek to relate the Vedas to other civilizations, including the modern. I have not included references to my own publications as listed in the Bibliography since their titles speak for themselves. The notes follow the chapters and pages of the book and are attached to the beginning words or key terms of the sentence which they elucidate. To distinguish notes from pages, the symbol # is used to refer to notes.

PREFACE

xvii. 'It is analytic and attempts to shed light . . . absurd statements circulate:' Rigveda 1.164.44 puts *iṅgayanti* in context on *pp*. 295–7.

xix. 'Kurt Gödel and Alfred Tarski': Feferman and Feferman 2004.

xxii. 'W. H. Auden': Auden 1948.

xxv. 'Robert Gardner': Gardner 1992.

xxv–xxvi. 'The chief result was AGNI, *The Vedic Ritual of the Fire Altar*': The long title of *AGNI,* included in the Bibliography, will be abbreviated into 'Staal, CV and Itti Ravi 1983.'

xxvii. 'Other boxes contained other primary sources . . . and secondary sources that had become classics in their own right': Wilhelm Caland': especially Caland and Henry 1906–07. 'Louis Renou' especially Renou 1953 and 1955–69.

xxxiii. 'I have not been shy': Staal 1998 and http://philosophy.berkeley.edu/staal.—Schwab 1950 has been explicit on the classical backgrounds of Oriental studies and has been freely copied, with acknowledgment, by Said, Edward. 1979. *Orientalism*. New York: Vintage Books—a book that rightly objected to the term but did not attest much familiarity with the subject.

xxxv–xxvii. The apparent complexity of diacritics is due to the arbitrary order of the letters of the ABC. It becomes easy when the sound pattern of language as discovered by Indian grammarians is understood: pp. 279–281 with Figure 24.

CHAPTER 1

***Page* 3.** 'Yājñavalkya, a Vedic sage, taught his wife Maitreyī': Bṛhad-Āraṇyaka Upaniṣad (BĀU) 2.4.12, 4.5.15 as translated by Olivelle, Patrick. 1996, 1998.

Upaniṣads. Translated from the Original Sanskrit. Oxford: Oxford University Press, 30, 71. I shall make frequent use of this excellent book and refer to it simply as 'Olivelle.'—I have added 'of specifics' for clarity (shown by the context).—'Yājñavalkya was a native of Kosala' and 'the eastern fringe of the Vedic area': Witzel 1997: 313–15.—Witzel, Michael. 2003. 'Yājñavalkya as ritualist and philosopher, and his personal language,' in Adhami, S. (ed.), *Paitimāna. Essays in Iranian, Indo-European, and Indian Studies in Honor of Hanns-Peter Schmidt.* Vols I–II. Casta Mesa CA: Mazda Publishers, 2003, pp. 103–143, goes much deeper into the different personalities of Yājñavalkya, his ideas, style and personal language. #91.

8. Figures 1 and 2: Witzel 1989, Maps 100, 114. Figure 3: Schwartzberg 1978: Plate II.3(c).—'Schwartzberg devotes two sentences to them': Schwartzberg, p. 158.

9. 'What these symbols are and what they are not': Farmer and Witzel 2000: 4; Farmer, Sproat and Witzel 2004.

10. 'Romila Thapar summarizes: "They could have been"': Thapar 2002: 84.

11–13. 'Mitanni Vedic': *Rad und Wagen.* Kikkuli: Raulwing and Meyer 2004 provides the most recent and extensive information.

14. 'Much more careful recent investigations': Carvalho-Silva c.s. 2006; Sengupta c.s. 2006.

16. 'In due course, Vasiṣṭha became the domestic priest who was the victor in the War of the Ten Kings': Dandekar 1997: 45, Witzel 1997: 263.

17. 'Light horse chariots with spoked wheels replaced traditional carts . . . pulled by oxen': *Rad und Wagen* 2004, especially Kenoyer, Jonathan Mark. 2006. 'Cultures and Societies of the Indus Tradition' in *India: Historical Beginnings and the Concept of the Aryan.* Delhi: National Book Trust, pp. 41–97; Levine etc. 2003. Anthony 1995, 1998 is not only earlier but more general and speculative.—'It happened in most of these places . . . in China slightly later': Lubotsky 1998 and Mair 2003, both extremely informative.—'What about actual numbers of people?': Thapar 2002: 53.

20. 'Their relatedness was discovered by Sir William Jones': quoted or referred to in many histories of India and other general sources. The original address was delivered in 1786 to the Royal Asiatic Society of Bengal. Contrary views, now less common, are discussed with respect to a telling case: Hock 1999. More independent and original views on Jones' views on history, politics, poetics, aesthetics, and other topics: Mukherjee, S.N. 2002. *Citizen Historian: Explorations in Historiography.* Kolkata: Subarnarekha.

22–4. 'The BMAC or "Bactrian-Margiana Archaeological Complex"': Hiebert, F.T. and C.C. Lamberg-Karlovski. 1992. 'Central Asia and the Indo-Iranian Borderlands,' *Iran*: 1–15; Sergent 1997: 151–79 (informative but to be read with some caution); Mair 1998 (especially Hiebert), Lubotsky 2001, Staal 1999: 120–1 with further references, 2000; Witzel 1999a with summary on p. 390; 1999b: 16–8, 2000. Speculative but by the original excavator: Sarianidi,

Victor. 1998. *Margiana and Protozoroastrism*. Athens: Kapon Editions. BMAC in a wider context: Jarrige 1985.

23. 'About 300 words that occur in the Rigveda . . . come from elsewhere': Kuiper 1991 and quotes in previous note.—'Many come from Muṇḍa . . . or Proto-Munda. It accounts for words starting with *ka-, ku-, ki-*': Witzel 1999b: 10.—

24. 'Madhav Deshpande has shown how such contacts': Deshpande 1999.

25–8. 'The Tarim Mummies': Mair 1998 I-II.

26. 'There are many arguments to show that Tocharian': section on linguistics in Mair I, 1998: 307–534, especially Hemp; Lubotsky 1998, 2001; Parpola 1998; Pinnault 1998, 2002.

27. 'Samarkand . . . a city with which Xuanzang or Hiuan-Tsang . . . fell in love': most recently Sen 2005, Chapter 8 which refers to the main sources.

28. 'Along the southern branch, a series of finds . . . leads to Khotan': Stein, M. Aurel. 1907, 1975. *Ancient Khotan. Detailed Report on Archaeological Explorations in Chinese Turkestan.* Oxford: Clarendon and New York: Hacker Art Books. 'The conclusion at which we are arriving . . . about the Soma, a rare hallucinogenic plant': Wasson: 1968: 23 etc., including pp. 93–147 by Wendy Doniger O'Flaherty, 'The Post-Vedic History of the Soma Plant.'—'The best Soma comes from Mount Mūjavat': Witzel 1999a: 344–5, 363 and several other publications from 1980 ('Early Eastern Iran and the Atharvaveda,' *Persica*, 16–7, 104).

29. 'It implies that speakers of Indo-Aryan . . . passed through the Pamirs': Curzon, George N. 1896. *The Pamirs and the Source of the Oxus*. London: The Royal Geographical Society. By the later Viceroy who walked there in his younger years; still very useful. 'The effects of ingesting those plants were slight': Flattery and Schwartz 1989: 35.

30. 'This explains that horses . . . crossed the Bolan Pass and reached Pirak and Kachi': Jarrige 1985, 1979.

CHAPTER 2

32. 'Oral traditions provide us with information on localities and civilization . . .': Falk 1981 on ruins.

33. 'Figure 7 provides us with small models of toy carts': Kenoyer in *Rad und Wagen*. Mackay, R. and R.E.M. Wheeler. 1938. *Further Excavations at Mohenjo Daro*. Delhi: The Archaeological Survey of India. Chariots in the Near East: Richter 2004.

35. 'The Rigveda derives from the terminology of chariots and spokes': RV 1.164.11 which will be quoted on *pp*. 334–5.

37. 'Connections have been sought . . . but these pots do not provide pictorial representations . . . as on Greek vases': Williams, Dyfri. 1985. *Greek Vases*. British Museum: British Museum Press, e.g., Figure 12 which depicts a 'Chariot Approaching Archer' from about 1350–1300 BCE and is not unlike Figure 10 in this book.

38. 'The one with lion capitals from Sarnath' and 'It comes from the gateways of the Sanchi Stupa': illustrations are common. 'Figure 10 illustrates such an occasion . . . from Morhana Pahar in Mirzapur': Sparreboom 1985: 84 after Allchin. B. 1958. 'Morhana-Pahar: A Rediscovery'. *Man* 58: 153–5.

39–40. 'Sintashta': Genning, V.F., G.B. Zdanovich and V.V. Genning. 1992. *Sintashta. Archaeological Sites of Aryan Tribes of the Ural-Kazakh Steppes* (in Russian). Chelyabinsk: Yuzhno-Ural'sko knizhnoe izdatel'stvo; Witzel 2000: 283–6.

40. 'It comes from Krivoe-Ozero which is north of Odessa': Carpelan c.s. 2001 with dates on page 129.

41. 'In the east, they easily went from Mongolia into China': Mair 2003; Lubotsky 1998.

44. 'These tracks seem to have been used throughout history . . .': Klimburg-Salter, Deborah E. (ed.), 1985. *The Silk Route and the Diamond Path. Esoteric Buddhist Art on the Trans-Himalayan Trade Routes*. Los Angeles: UCLA Art Council; Staal 1986. 'In the Realm of the Buddha', *Natural History* 95: 34–45; Staal 2004. *Drie Bergen en Zeven Rivieren*. Amsterdam: J.M. Meulenhoff (Chapter 10). Khotan: # 27.

45. 'The only people who did it, as far as I know, are Sir Francis Younghusband and his Balti guides': French 1994 (excellent and often amusing).—'From there one might go straight south and cross the Indus . . .': Klimburg, Maximilian. 1985. 'The Western Trans-Himalayan Crossroads' in Klimburg-Salter, p. 34.

47. 'I shall mention two of these languages and cultures here . . . Kafiri . . . and . . . Kalasha': Witzel 2004a: 604–15.—'Asko Parpola found about 340 camp-sites . . .': Parpola in Carpelan-Parpola 2001. Grierson, who initiated the Linguistic Survey of India at the beginning of the nineteenth century, regarded Kafiri as a branch of Dardic. Since Independence, the *Census of India* made great strides forwards but in 1969, a world-wide survey of *Current Trends in Linguistics*, declared in its fifth volume by mouth of Braj Kachru (Sebeok 1969: 286), that the final status of the Dardic family was still undecided. However, the Census report of 1961 had made it clear that 'the Kafir and Kowar groups of speakers have their main concentration outside the Indian territory' (Sebeok 1969: 287, *note* 23). The future of Kalasha is much more endangered. At the time of writing this note (August 2007), a journalist quotes a Kalasha woman: 'The Taliban are motivated by George Bush's war on terror. The boys go through a form of military training. It is brainwashing and when they finish they believe they are defending their own culture' (source withheld).

48. 'Bolan may reflect the name of the Vedic tribe *Bhalāna*': it has the typical BMAC structure of 'trisyllabic words with long middle syllable': Lubotsky 2001, p. 305. *Ha* turning into *o* is equally common.—'After crossing the Bolan Pass . . . one reaches Pirak': #29.—'In the same neighbourhood lies Mehrgarh': Jarrige, J.F. and M. Le Chevallier. 1979; 'Excavations and Mehrgarh, Baluchistan. Their Significance in the Context of the Indo-Pakistan Borderlands' in Taddei, M. Naples: 463–535.

49. 'The use of "Aryan" is a more serious matter . . .': On the Iranian see Bailey, H.W. 1959. 'Iranian arya and daha,' *Transactions of the Philological Society*: 71–115. Burrow, T. 1973. *The Sanskrit Language*. London: Faber and Faber, p. 390, provides quotations on *ārya* as applied to the language of the Indo-Aryans from Śāṇkhāyana Āraṇyaka 8.9 and Aitareya Āraṇyaka 3.2.5. 'Madhav Deshpande has shown . . .': Deshpande 1999. On 'Hindu' see Stall 2008c.

CHAPTER 3

54. 'It begins to be visible in late Vedic works and in the Post-Vedic *Dharma Sūtras* . . . and . . . in the law book of Manu': Olivelle 1999 and 2004 are the most recent and reliable translations into English. For Dharma in Indic civilization from the Vedas onward: Olivelle, Patrick. (ed.), 2004, Special Issue of the *Journal of Indian Philosophy* 32/5–6: 421–870. #335. 'Nor is there evidence for 'free Aryans and subjugated indigenous people': Kulke and Rothermund 1998: 34, 39.

56. 'Promote the *bráhman* . . .': RV 8.35, quoted and translated in a similar context in Gonda 1963a: 120.

57. 'Vedic society is much more complex than the simplistic triads that Dumézil suggest . . . the critique of John Brough': Dumézil 1958 and Brough 1959.

59. 'I am referring to the 'Hymn to Puruṣa' (RV 10.90)': during the Fourth International Vedic Workshop which I attended at the University of Texas, Austin (*Preface,* xxix), Stanley Insler told me that according to Paul Mus, RV 10.90 was the latest addition to the Rigveda; but his ideas were never published.

60. 'The Taittirīya Saṃhitā of the Black Yajurveda mentions *kṣatṛ*': Kane, Pandurang Vaman. 1930–1962. *History of Dharmaśāstra (Ancient and Mediaeval Religious and Civil Law)*. Vols. I–V in seven parts. Poona: Bhandarkar Oriental Research Institute, Vol. II, Part I, p. 41.

62. 'Three stages of this process may be distinguished': Rau 1997. 'Rathakāra': a more detailed study, *Rathakāra Manasā*, is forthcoming in the Proceedings of the Fourth International Vedic Workshop at the University of Texas, Austin (see *Preface* above *page* xxx). Earlier on Rathakāra: Minkowski 1989a.

63. 'The term *rathakāra*, which becomes prominent later . . .': Kane. 1941. *History of Dharmaśāstra*. II, 1, p. 21.

67. 'Wilhelm Rau tells us that during the *Brāhmaṇa* period, the *rathakāra* owned palatial residences': Rau 1957:112. 'Hertha Krick makes the same mistakes as Kane': 1982. *Das Ritual der Feuergründung* (Agnyādheya). Wien: Verlag der österreichischen Akademie der Wissenschaften: 44.

68. 'According to Manu's post-Vedic book of laws, women are eligible to perform rites but without reciting the accompanying mantras': Manu 9.18, which seems to go further in Olivelle's translation: 'No rite is performed for women with the recitation of mantras.'

CHAPTER 4

69. 'Yājñavalkya is said to have received his mantras directly from the Sun': a theme of the Chāndogya Upaniṣad with respect to OM; below, *pp*. 127–8.

71. 'The Bharata chieftains are portrayed as practitioners of a multilateral policy': Witzel 1997b: 262–4. The names of Bharatas, Kurus, Pañcālas and others are recited during performances of Vedic ritual: below, *p*. 75. *Bharat* did not only become the name of India but spread with Vedic fire rites over large parts of Asia as the name of one of the fires: Strickmann, Michel. 1983. 'Homa in East Asia' in Staal, CV and Itti Ravi 1983, II: 418–55 records various forms: *Pitara* in Japan (which has nothing to do with 'fathers'), *Baratha* in Tibet, etc.:

72. 'In the case of the Kurus, this region was the dictrict of Meerut . . .': Witzel 1997: 267. 'Leading historians of India are not in full agreement about what kind of structure': Stein 1998: 59–61; Kulke and Rothermund 1998: 49–50; Thapar 20: 138.

74. 'Each school (*śākhā*) goes back to . . . a particular area': Witzel 1997: 304.—'The Yajurveda invokes Soma as a guide against hostilities': Caland and Henry 1906–07, Vol. I, p. 110, *note* 106.6.

77. 'The Padapāṭha was the work of a great scholar and scientist': insightful studies include Jha, V. N. 1973, Deshpande 2002.

78. 'Nor did he know that his Padapāṭha was creating a paradigm': Raghavan 1957, Deshpande 2002 studies further variations (*vikṛti*)—'The Apotheosis of Schools': Renou 1947.

82. 'It is the linchpin of the system, the *ratha*-derived metaphor used by Romila Thapar': above *p*. 72.

82. 'The Four Vedas' was originally inspired by the Table 'Tableau des écoles védiques' in Renou, Louis et Jean Filliozat. 1947. *L'inde classique. Manuel des etudes indiennes*. I:310–11. Paris: Payot; adapted in Staal, CV and Itti Ravi, 1983, I: 36 and further adapted here.

84. 'They include the youngsters that will be the ritual experts of to-morrow': Mahadevan and Staal 2003, 2005.

85. 'I can do no better than end with a quote': Octavio Paz 1995: 91.

CHAPTER 5

87. 'Other Vedic compositions . . . about which Renou wrote: 'One cannot grasp': Renou 1953: 34.

90. 'The anthology by Wendy Doniger remains the most accessible': Doniger 1981. On Wendy herself: Doniger 1998.—'The reader who wants more and knows German': Geldner (1951, 1957) and #352.—'Renou has also translated most of the hymns in French': Renou (1955–69).—'No one can find anything without the concordance': Rau (1969). Now see also: Brereton and Jamison (above, *Preface:* xxix).

91. 'The most important Vedic gods . . .': no mention is made of the Ādityas: Brereton 1981. Gonda 1960, Vol. I provides general accounts of Vedic deities.

92. 'The poem is on the theme of unification': RV 10.191.

96. 'Dāsa and Dasyu, terms used of enemies . . .' and 'Śambara has been interpreted as an Austro-Asiatic name . . .': speculations are numerous, e.g., Parpola, Asko. 1997. 'The Dāsas and the Coming of the Aryans' in: Witzel, (ed.): 193–202.—'SOMA': Thompson 2003.

98. 'The best Soma comes from Mount Mūjavat:' #28. 'Doniger enumerates more than 140 theories': Doniger O'Flaherty 1968.—'Wasson introduced a fresh and new approach': Wasson 1968.

99. 'Wasson's work was reviewed by . . . the leading Vedicists of the day': Bailey's evaluations have changed over time and are published in several inaccessible places starting with Bailey, H. W. 1974. 'The Range of Colour ZAR in Khotan Saka Texts'. *Mémorial: Jean de Mensace*. Louvain: Fondation Culturelle Iranienne: 369–374.—'Daniel Ingalls of Harvard': Daniel H.H. 1971. 'Remarks on Mr. Wasson's *Soma*.' *Journal of the American Oriental Society* 91:188–91. —'F.B.J. Kuiper of Leiden': 1970. 'Review of *Soma. Divine Mushroom of Immortality*'. *Indo-Iranian Journal* 12: 279–85. 'John Brough of London': Brough 1971.

100. 'The next major contribution': Flattery and Schwartz 1989. 'No unanimous conclusion': Falk 1989.

101. 'There is no myth, no past, no need for harmony': Ingalls' review (#99), p. 191.—'A Speculative Poem': Brereton 1999.

103. 'Tatiana Elizarenkova has quoted them': Elizarenkova 1997.

104. 'Of course, a good rationalist respects the facts and a good empiricist respects logic': Wujastyk, D., 1998. 'Science and Vedic Studies', *Journal of Indian Philosophy* 26/4: 335–45:343: 'If Vedic study and research is to be successful, it must proceed on trustworthy lines, asking important historical questions, and always taking care to remain watchful, original, rigorous and objectively testable.' # 275.

CHAPTER 6

107. 'The Sāmaveda takes all its words from (the Rigveda)': Renou 1952 on those that do not so derive.—'The Sāmaveda or Veda of Melodies or Chants . . . set to music': van der Hoogt 1929; Faddegon, Barend. 1951. *Studies in the Sāmaveda*, Part I, Amsterdam: North-Holland Publishing Company, is solid and often entertaining.—'The reason is not that two melodies are mentioned in the Rigveda by name': RV 10.181.1–2 mention Rathantara and Bṛhat.

108–09. 'Much more systematic study is needed': we return to *stobhas* or *stutis* on *pp.* 209 and 242–44; Staal. 1989. 'Vedic Mantras' in Alper, Harvey P. *Understanding Mantras.* Albany: State University of New York (SUNY) Press: *pp.* 48–95.

110. 'Gentlemen! Join us in chant to him!': RV 9.11.1: *upāsmai gāyatā nara*'. . .

116. 'Paz contrasted India with the New World': #85.—'All we can say is that those were golden times': Thapar 1996's judgement is not flattering: #347.—'Charles Malamoud related *araṇya* to *ari*': we shall return to these matters at the end of this book (*pp.* 347 ff.).

CHAPTER 7

118. 'Sāyaṇa, a scholar of a deep and wide-ranging knowledge': Renou 1947: 9 quotes Sāyaṇa's words from his commentary on the Taittirīya Saṃhitā: *bhittisthānīyo yajurvedaś citrasthānīyāv itarau.*—'Stephen Lindquist is right that we should sometimes': Stephen Lindquist 'On Shattered Heads and Daft Robbers: Rethinking Śākalya in BĀU 3', forthcoming, in Proceedings of the Fourth International Vedic Workshop at the University of Texas, Austin (see *Preface,* xxx).

119. 'He (Harold Bailey) once made a passing suggestion': 1984. 'Vedic *kṣumpa*—and connected data.' Joshi, S.D. (ed.), *Amṛtadhārā: Prof. R.N. Dandekar Felicitation Volume.* Delhi: 17–20.

120. 'Revere Memory!': CU 7.13.1 (*smaram upāssva*).

121. 'He looks like a great sage rather than an insignificant ascetic': different versions as described by T.M.P. Mahadevan 1957 from whose frontispiece Figure 14 has been reconstructed.—'The Ritual Arena': looks like a house: Renou 1939.

122. 'The central position of the Sadas is clear from Figure 16': the south-eastern quarter of the map is adapted from Witzel 1989: 242.

123. 'They mutter brief formulas referred to as *yajus*': Renou 1937, Brereton 2004 and Bhagwat 2004.

126. 'One of the most highly developed and famous *Śrauta* rituals': Staal, CV and Itti Ravi, 1983, I–II.

127. 'The following are taken from the Taittirīya Saṃhitā, based upon Keith's translation': Keith, A. B. 1914. *The Veda of the Black Yajus School entitled Taittiriya Sanhita.* I-II. Cambridge, Massachusetts: Harvard University Press: II, 289–99

130. 'The Rigveda tells us about Apālā, a young woman': Hanns-Peter Schmidt. 1987, 1–29.—'The majority were with women, but he . . . became the wife of "Bull Horse Man"': the passage is recited during the Soma rituals and the Agnicayana ('Subrahmaṇyā Chant': Staal, CV and Itti Ravi 1983, I: 369, Plate 61) and has been discussed by Faddegon, Barend. 1951. *Sudies on the*

Sāmaveda I. Amsterdam: North-Holland Publishing Company: 23–24. After referring to its 'ritual use and crude popular contents, Faddegon discusses the birth of music, touching on Schopenhauer and Nietzsche.

131–2. 'May These Bricks, O Agni, be milch cows for me . . .': Staal, CV and Itti Ravi 1983, I: 508, Plate 80, 511.

132. 'The *yajus* recitation has a technical name: *puroruc*': Gonda, Jan. 1981. *The Praügaśastra*. Amsterdam: North-Holland Publishing Company. P. 63. E.R. Sreekrishna Sarma, 'The Kauṣītaki Brāhmaṇa on the Atirātra', in Staal, CV and Itti Ravi 1983, II: 679.

CHAPTER 8

136. 'The composer-priests were Āṅgirasas and Bhārgavas': clans of priests and composers of circles of the Rigveda discussed by Witzel 1997b: 262, 292. H.W. Bailey related the word Āṅgirasas to English *angel*.

137. 'These were spectacular finds . . .': Bhattacharyya, Durgamohan. 1957. 'A Palm-Leaf Manuscript of the Paippalāda Saṃhitā: Announcement of a Rare Find'. *Our Heritage* 5:81–86. 1970. Paippalāda Saṃhitā *of the Atharvaveda. Volume Two. Edited from Original Manuscripts with Critical Notes.* Calcutta: Sanskrit College. Bhattacharyya, Dipak. 1997. *The* Paippalāda Saṃhitā *of the Atharvaveda. Edited from Original Manuscripts with Critical Notes.* Calcutta: Sanskrit College. *Volume Two. Edited from Original Manuscripts with Critical Notes.* Calcutta: Sanskrit College.

138. 'Dhātar, the arranger, is a creator . . . similar to the *demiurge* of the ancient Greeks': Plato, *Timaios*, describes how the *demiurge* fashions the world, putting everything together like an architect, not like a creator *ex nihilo*, 'out of nothing.'

141. 'The principal composers of the Atharvaveda were closely related to chanters of *sāmans* . . .': Stanley Insler in lectures, apparently unpublished, but see Insler 1998a. 'An early treatise on phonetics and phonology': Deshpande 1997 and 2002.—'The second Kautsa was a grammarian-cum-ritualist and keenly aware of the difference between language and mantras': there is urgent need for a book on Kautsa, the earliest rationalist thinker of India. The sources should be put together, in the original and translation, from Yāska's *Nirukta*, one of the Vedāṅgas (Vedic sciences, p. 261) and from Jaimini's commentary on the *Pūrva-Mīmāṃsā-Sūtra*. Yāska probably belongs to the fifth century BCE like Pāṇini, but the priority remains open: Cardona, George. 1976. *Pāṇini: A Survey of Research*. The Hague: Mouton (Indian reprint, 1980: Delhi: Motilal Banarsidas), p. 273. Jaimini must be later than the third century BCE: second century according to Nakamura, Hajime. 1983. *A History of Early Vedānta Philosophy*. Delhi: Motilal Banarsidas, English translation, p. 400. Some of the relevant materials have been discussed in Oertel, Hanns. 1930. *Zur indischen Apologetik*. Stuttgart: 1930.

141. 'His thesis was that, unlike language . . . "mantras are without meaning"': On Kautsa's thesis in general see the first section of Chapter **11**, 'The Meaninglessness of Mantras,' *pages* 191–4 which runs parallel to the meaninglessness of ritual in Chapter **12** and corresponds to the gap between Vedic ritual (as described in the Śrauta Sūtras) and mythology (as described by the Brāhmaṇas): earliest and clearest statement by Tsuji, Naoshiro. 1952. *On the Relation between Brāhmaṇas and Śrautasūtras*. Tokyo: The Toyo Bunko, in Japanese with English Summary, p. **187:** 'Brāhmaṇa-writers pursued an object different from that of Sūtrakāras. The former endeavoured to interpret the meaning of mantras and to explain the origin and mysterious significance of ritual proceedings, and in doing so they happened to give, often rather briefly or vaguely, prescriptions as to this or that action of a rite which they presupposed to be well known to the initiated. The Sūtrakāras, on the contrary, aimed at a systematic description of each Vedic ritual in its natural sequence.' Echoed by Renou 1953: 29 and Dandekar 1982:77 (related to Dandekar 1997:43), already quoted in the text p. 227.

142. 'The second Kautsa was a revolutionary but . . . gave reasons for his views': Thite, G. U. 2004. 'Vicissitudes of Vedic Ritual', in Griffiths and Houben, (eds.), 2004: 558–9 argued that 'What Kautsa seems to have meant is that not the mantras but rather their meaning is meaningless.' Since it corresponds in time to the third or Sāmavedic period in the history of Vedic ritual, 'which seems to be the decadent period,' these rituals are impossible to perform, therefore fictitious and probably also of Sāmavedic origin. I refer to these ideas because we shall relate the meaninglessness of mantras, the meaninglessness of ritual and the Sāmaveda to each other in Chapters **11** and **12**—without implying any decadence except in #250.

144. 'Since the *Śrauta* ritual of the Yajurveda is performed for its own sake . . . the more philosophic Upaniṣadic or Buddhist emphasis on knowledge (*jñāna*) or wisdom (*prajñā*) . . .': p. 315 with note.

CHAPTER 9

147. 'The civilization of the Brāhmaṇas and Āraṇyakas or 'Forest Books' . . . illustrates at the same time that *forest* continued to be contrasted with *village*': Malamoud 1976 treats forests and villages, Sprokhoff 1981 and Rau 1997 villages.

148. 'He (Agni) could not cross the Sadānīrā': Śatapatha Brāhmaṇa 1.4.1.14.

149. 'We have seen that the term *Brāhmaṇa* is used in several senses . . . one of them: a Vedic composition in prose': Rau 1957, 1970 and 1976 examine the society that is depicted in these Brāhmaṇas. Since at least 1962, more than a hundred scholarly studies have been devoted to the society of the Brāhmaṇas and related topics, especially ritual, by Klaus Mylius. They are listed in Göhler, Lars (ed.), 2005. *Indische Kultur im Kontext: Rituale, Texte und Ideen aud Indien unde der Welt. Festschrift Professor Klays Mylius,* Wiesbaden: Otto Harrassowitz:

457–473. Mylius was the most well-known Vedic and Sanskrit scholar in what was formerly known as the German Democratic Republic. It explains some Marxist phrases, easily abstracted, and would fit in the wider historical perspective of India at the time of the Brāhmaṇas as studied by Basu 1969, outdated in parts.—'That is what brahmins always remained, in India as elsewhere': Skilling, Peter. 2007. 'King, Sangha, and Brahmans: Ideology, Ritual and Power in Pre-Modern Siam' in Harris, Ian, (ed.), 2007. *Buddhism, Power and Political Order*. London and New York: Routledge: 182–215, is much more detailed and specific.

153. '*Parokṣakāmā hi devā*': Śatapatha Brāhmaṇa 6.1.1.2 and elsewhere.

154. 'We can speak here of esotericism or the keeping of secret doctrines': # 173.

153. 'This was clearly explained by Āryabhaṭa': Clark, W.E. 1930. *The Āryabhaṭīya of Āryabhaṭa*. Chicago: The University of Chicago IV: 49.—'Al-Bīrūnī, equally great as a scientist and also a student of Indic civilization': Sachau, E. 1888, 1910, etc. *Alberuni's India*. I-II. London. I: 25.

154. 'A similar statement, even more colorful, is due to Johannes Keppler': it is the first of three mottos from the *Archive for History of Exact Sciences*. Staal. 2000. '*Vyākaraṇa* and *śulva* in the light of Newton's Lesson' in Tsuchida, Ryutaro and Albrecht Wezler (eds.), *Harānandalaharī. Volume in Honour of Professor Minoru Hara on his Seventieth Birthday*. Reinbek: Dr. Inge Wezler: Verlag für Orientalistische Fachpublikationen: 349–74, puts it in more context.—'The Rigvedic Aitareya Brāhmaṇa (AB) is the earliest source that is explicit about the Sarasvatī river 'ending in the desert': Arthur Berriedale Keith. 1920, 1971. Rigveda Brāhmaṇas: The Aitareya and Kauṣītaki Brāhmaṇas, Translated from the Original Sanskrit. Cambridge, Mass.: Harvard Oriental Series and Delhi: Motilal Banarsidas: 148, tells the somewhat confusing story: 'The seers performed a sacrificial season on the Sarasvatī; they drove away Kavaṣa Ailūṣa from the Soma, "The child of a slave woman, a cheat, no Brahman; how has he been consecrated in our midst?" They sent him out to the desert, (saying) "There let thirst slay him; let him drink not the water of the Sarasvatī." He sent away to the wilderness, afflicted by thirst, saw the "child of the waters" hymn (RV 5.75.9). "Forth among the gods let there be speeding for the Brahman." Thereby he went to the dear abode of the water; him the waters welled out after; all around him Sarasvatī hastened.'—'The same information is found in other Brāhmaṇas': Caland, W. 1931. *Pañcaviṃśa Brāhmaṇa: the Brāhmaṇa of Twenty-Five Chapters*. Calcutta: Asiatic Society of Bengal: 25.10.1, p. 634, is more concise: 'They (the participants of the sattra) undertake the consecration at the place (*i.e.,* to the south of the place) where the (river) Sarasvatī is lost (in the sand of the desert).'

157. 'Other valid insights are hidden in the muddy contexts of the Aitareya Āraṇyaka': Deshpande 1997a. Introduction, Chapters. 4 and 5.

CHAPTER 10

159. 'The term occurs first at the end of the Vedic period': 'The ascetics who have firmly determined their goal through a full knowledge of the Vedānta, have their being purified by the discipline of renunciation' (Muṇḍaka Upaniṣad 3.2.6, tr. Olivelle).—'One of the earliest of these is the philosophy of Bhāskara': Ingalls, Daniel H.H. 1967. 'Bhāskara the Vedāntin,' *Philosophy East and West. A Journal of Oriental and Comparative Thought*: 61–7 says it is replete with 'vitriolic references' against Śaṅkara.—'His Vedānta is called A-dvaita Vedānta because its position is "non-dual"': the term *advaita* was coined by Yājñavalkya: Witzel 2003 in #3.

160. 'The Upaniṣads are an open-ended class . . . That includes': Saṃnyāsa Upaniṣads: Olivelle 1992 and 1914. *Thirty Minor Upaniṣads translated by K. Narayanasvami Aiyar.* Madras: Vasanta Press, Adyar.

161. 'That emphasis is a characteristic of Buddhism as we shall see': *pp.* 309, 316, 330.

162. 'This feature earned the Upaniṣads the Greek or English label "philosophy"': I am not referring to the Greek word 'philosophy' which means 'love of wisdom', but to the Greek tradition of public debates that took place in Plato's academy and is generally initiated by Socrates: #168.—'The majority of these works . . . represent the perspective of the Brāhmaṇas': Renou 1953a.

163. 'Though presented as such in our Vedic sources, they are not confined': Bronkhorst, Johannes. 1999. 'Is there an Inner Conflict of Tradition?' in Bronkhorst and Deshpande, p. 42.

165. 'She was called Vācaknavī, which means eloquent as well as loquacious': BĀU 3.5 and 3.8.—'Finally, Yājñavalkya says': we know that Yājñavalkya easily lost his temper and was especially rude to Śākalya (whose version we do not have) to whom he exploded: 'What an imbecile you are to think that it (viz., the heart) could be founded anywhere other than ourselves' (BĀU 3.9.25). A little later in the same Upaniṣad and about another topic, he exclaims: 'If you will not tell me about such-and-such a spirit, your head will shatter apart.' BĀU 3.9 26 continues: 'Śākalya did not know him and his head did, indeed, shatter apart.' It is a traditional theme; other links are discussed in Insler 1998b.

166. 'Sāmaśravas', Song Fame, 'was obviously a strapping young Sāmavedin': BĀU 3.1.2. There may be elements of regional rivalry here: Olivelle: xxxix, 308.—'So you should simply say that you are Satyakāma ('truth loving') Jābāla': CU 4.4–9; BĀU 4.1.6, 6.3.11.

167. 'The debate, recorded or imagined by the composer . . . when he was asked by Ārthabhāga': BĀU 3.2.

168. 'Take my hand, Ārthabhāga; let's discuss this in private': at the beginning of Plato's dialogue *Phaedrus*, Socrates' pupil of that name asks Socrates where he wants to sit. Socrates says (229a): 'Turn this way; let us follow the Ilissus (a small stream) and sit down at a quiet spot'. Socrates asks Phaedrus to lead the way and Phaedrus points to a shady area with gentle breezes and 'grass on which we may either sit or lie down' (found and translated with the help of J.M. Hemelrijk; *p.* 160; # 161, 166).

169. 'Different schools have imagined or construed (Sanskrit *parikalpitāni*)': Āpte, Mahādeva Cimaṇājī, (ed.), 1953. BĀU with Śaṅkara's commentary and Ānandagiri's gloss. Ānandāśrama Sanskrit Series: 412.

170. 'The only modern author who has addressed the question': Obeyesekhere 2002. Gananath Obeyesekhere is a brilliant anthropologist who combines impeccable scholarship with a wide range of theoretical perspectives. Author of a series of thought-provoking contributions, his chief work remains: 1984. *The Cult of the Goddess Pattini*. Chicago and London: The University of Chicago Press.

171. 'In the Sāmaveda, return to earth from the next world': Ikari 1989. Such an arrangement of *stutis* is depicted by Figure 18. For *viṣṭuti*: Staal, CV and Itti Ravi 1983, I: 627, 641, 652, 682, *Illustrations* 48–51 and #249.

172. 'The largest number of references to *iṣṭāpūrta* from a great variety of Vedic sources': Kane (note 58) Vol.II, Part II. 1941, 853–4. Caland 1897, 1967.

173. 'If this passage assimilates phonation and suspended breath': Minard, Armand 1956, II: 181, *note* 450a, last sentence. Minard refers to technical terms used in the Chāndogya Upaniṣad (2.22.3–5) but he prefers esotericisms: #153. Later in the same volume, II: 317, *note* 864c, he attacks Renou's declaration that there is nothing 'voluntarily esoteric' in India, 'even in the Tantras', lists a large number of statements by Renou to the contrary and happily settles on the phrase about 'esoteric language, the supreme goal (*fin suprème*) of the Vedas.'

176. 'It is a god who is "Higher than *Brahman*" and known as "the Lord"': *Śvetāśvatara* 3.7, throughout Chapter 4 and occasionally elsewhere.—'It also refers to "One Rudra who has not tolerated a second" "*Śvetāśvatara* 3.2."'—'These theistic tendencies came to the fore': Hopkins 1966: 12 quotes Bhāgavata Purāṇa IV.29.47: 'When Bhagavān, self-created, favours a person, that person lies aside thought that is thoroughly dependent on the world and on the Vedas.' In theism, authority of the Vedas is not denied provided it does not conflict with *bhakti*; but *bhakti* is not Vedic.—'It is hardly the same when the Bharadvājas . . . say to Agni': 'You are our dear guest!': RV: 6.2.7: *asi priyo no atithiḥ*.

176–7. 'The Gītā's juxtaposition of ritual and knowledge pays no attention': long Sanskrit compounds express the problem clearly provided the parts are separated and they are read (in these examples) from right to left: *karma-phala-tyāga* as 'abandon (*tyāga*) of the fruit (*phala*) of activity (*karma*)' and *karma-jñāna-samuccaya* as 'synthesis (*sam-uc-caya*) of knowledge (*jñāna*) and activity (*karma*).

177. 'You will not find him who has created . . .': RV 10.82.7. 'Unsteady boats are these ritual forms . . .': Muṇḍaka 1.2.7–8; also Kaṭha 2.5, Maitri 7.9 and Psalms 12.9.

178. 'The Muṇḍaka is not only radical, it uses a more vernacular form': Salomon 1981.

179. 'A simple way of formulating the basic identity . . . "I am Brahman"': BĀU 1.4.10.—He answers, 'The sun, your Majesty, is the source of light': BĀU 4.3.1–6.

180. 'But in 1986, Joel Brereton pointed out that this interpretation': Brereton 1986.

182. 'Vedic meditation is the product of a long process of *interiorization*. It started when a fire ritual, the Agnihotra, was interiorized by performing it though breathing': Bodewitz, H.W. 1973. *Jaiminīya Brāhmaṇa I, 1–65. Translation and Commentary with a Study: Agnihotra and Prāṇāgnihotra*. Leiden: E. J. Brill. Bakker 1989 concentrates on breathing (*prāṇa*) as a natural philosophy of the wind in several Upaniṣads and related sources.—'In the Soma ritual, there is a "mental (*manasā*) cup"': these are cups for the Soma juice used in the Soma ritual but they are made of mind (*manas*). For *dhī* ('vision') leading to *dhyāna* ('meditation'): #293 and Bronkhorst 1999 #163.

183. 'The Sāmavedic CU begins with speculations about the *udgītha* chant': Olivelle 1996 translates 'High Chant . . . the central element of a Sāman' (actually, the second: above Chapter 7, *p*. 110). 'OM unites Rig and Sāman as man and woman unite': *p*. 242 with note: 'You are the bed (*upastaraṇam asi*) . . .'—'Its foundation is "the most natural order of sound production: an opening of the mouth"': Jakobson, Roman. 1962. 'Why "Mama" and "Papa"?' *Selected Writings I*. The Hague: Mouton, 538–45: p. 541. Roman Jakobson, one of the great scholars of the twentieth century, author of over 650 books and articles on linguistics, phonology, literary criticism, Slavic studies, poetics and semiotics, was not thinking of OM when he wrote: 'the most natural order . . .'. Jakobson held a joint appointment at Harvard and was Institute Professor at the Massachusetts Institute of Technology (MIT). When Harvard was about to appoint Nabokov as a Professor of Russian Literature, he put a stop to it by saying: 'You don't appoint an elephant as a Professor of Zoology.'—Are these matters relevant to the Vedas? See #281, #294–5.

183–4. 'With Rig stanzas this world; With Yajus formulas . . .': Praśna Upaniṣad 5.5.7.

184. 'In later sections, the CA and the BĀU draw from "the common stock of Upaniṣadic lore"': Olivelle 1996, *Introduction*, xxxvi and elsewhere.—'There is an echo in the Vedānta or Brahma Sūtra which states . . . not *prativedam*, "one for each Veda"': Vedānta Sūtra 3.3.55.

185. 'The second great contribution of the Upaniṣads . . . is insight in the nature of knowledge': Dumont, Louis. 1959. 'Le renoncement dans les religions d'Inde' (Renunciation in the Religions of India), *Archives de Sociologie des Religions* 7: 45–69: 'what is striking (about that contribution) is its intellectualism.' (p. 58). Dumont has been badly translated, often misunderstood and it is not often that a sociologist comments with insight on the significance of the Upaniṣads. Hence I translate: 'These ideas appeared before the caste system properly speaking had come into existence, they are a precocious product of that extraordinary post-Vedic and pre-Hindu development which ranges from the earliest Upaniṣads to the Bhagavad Gīta, of that golden age of speculation when, discovery after discovery, all the important currents of Indian thought made their appearance.' Dumont's reflections were preceded by fieldwork in two areas, resulting in a small ethnography on the Tarask, a magical animal of the Tarascon of Southern France; and a large volume on a subcaste of South India: 1957. *Une sous-caste de l'Inde du sud. Organisation sociale et religion des Pramalai Kallar*. Dumont's most famous work, 1966. *Homo Hierarchicus. Essai sur le système des castes*. Paris: Gallimard, deals with Hinduism, but refers in similar terms to the Vedas and Upaniṣads, (e.g., p. 236).

186. 'The Muṇḍaka distinguished explicitly between a lower and a higher knowledge': Muṇḍaka Up. 1.1.4.—'The Advaita Vedānta thrives on it': the two levels go by various names, e.g., *vyavahāra*, 'ordinary communication,' and *paramārtha*, 'ultimate knowledge.'—'The Platonic tradition is its European counterpart': Murti 1963 explains the similarities between the Indian philosophy of language and the Platonic theory of ideas.—On Murti himself: Coward and Sivaraman 1977.

187. 'It tells us that the world as it appears is not real . . . Śaṅkara declared . . .': Bhattacharyya 2001 on the ineffable *anirvacanīya*.—'According to Roger Penrose, Newton's theory of gravity . . .': Penrose, Roger. 1997, etc. *The Large, the Small and the Human Mind.* Cambridge: Cambridge University Press: p. 26.—'Later Indic thought stressed the opposite: regress all the way down . . .': *p.* 345 and #347.

CHAPTER 11

193. 'If it is true that mantras and ritual have no meaning . . .': even Alper, Harvey. P. 1989. *Understanding Mantras*. Albany: State University of New York (SUNY) Press, an impressive collection of articles and the most authoritative bibliography until that date, does not arrive at a clear conclusion of what mantras are. He does pay reasoned attention to a variety of views and opinions.

195. 'Language is a system in which everything hangs together': De Saussure, Ferdinand. 1915, etc. *Cours de Linguistique Générale*. Publié par Charles Bally et Albert Sechehaye. Paris: Payot. I have not found the phrase *où tout se tient* in this book but it expresses his basic insight which is tantamount to saying that language is a *synchronistic* system—a reaction against the *diachronistic* philology of his predecessors. Pāṇini also presents a *synchronistic* system but for different and erroneous reasons: he believed that Sanskrit did not change—a belief that de Saussure did not share. Beliefs however do not matter: what counts in science are the results, not what scientists say or believe about it. ('Newton's Lesson': Staal. 1993, 94. *Concepts of Science in Europe and Asia,* Chapter 1. Leiden: International Institute for Asian Studies.)—It would not be surprising for *tout se tient* to apply to language if it applied to the universe. Evidence is mounting; but it has not been demonstrated.

197. 'Pautimāṣya from Gaupavana, Gaupavana from Kauśika, Kauśika from Kauṇḍinya, . . .': BĀU 2.6.1.

200. 'Chomsky replaced them by a simpler but much more abstract system': Chomsky, Noam. 1995. *The Minimalist Program.* Cambridge and London: The M.I.T. Press.

200–203. 'Our problems are different. We are interested in infinite recursive structures': the theory behind what can and cannot be solved by computing machines. Recursion theory spans the period between Gödel, Church and Turing. Expertly and intelligibly discussed in Feferman and Feferman 2004, who take their reader by the hand, beginning with the 'Unity of Science' in Vienna before WWII up to the date of publication of their book, and full of telling details (on pp. 145–6, they depict Church as a solid American citizen, just as stubborn as Tarski who was an immigrant from Poland).—Here is an example of what infinite recursive structures are about: recursiveness leads to infinity but infinity need not be based upon recursiveness. Readers who are not used to logic, recursion theory or computer science, but familiar with numerals, will be in a position to appreciate the difference between *recursive infinite* and *non-recursive infinite* numerals. 1/3 or 0,33333 . . . is a *recursive infinite* numeral because the '0' is followed by infinitely many '3's. But **pi** or 3,141592920 . . . is a *non-recursive infinite* numeral: there are infinitely many numerals after the '3' but there is no pattern: they do not repeat. We shall see (p. 273 and #) that Vedic mantras and ritual incorporate recursive structures, and that the Vedas loved the infinite which was abhorred by the ancient Greeks. See Stall, forthcoming and b.

200. 'That is better although Proust himself is miles ahead': Proust, Marcel. 1981. *Remembrance of Things Past*, Vol. II: *The Guermantes Way.* Translated by C.K. Scott Moncrieff and Terence Kilmartin, New York: Random House, p. 802. There are other masters of the long sentence. The *Kādambarī* and Thomas Mann come to mind. German and Sanskrit have other means at their disposal that the French language lacks: nominal composition. English can do it to some extent by simply putting words together as in *car engine.* The eighth century critic Daṇḍin comments on Sanskrit: 'the frequent use of compounds gives power to its prose, it is its life force' (*oja'samāsabhūyastvam etad gadasya jīvitam*): Hock, Hans Heinrich and Pandharipande, Rajeshwari (1978), 'Sanskrit in the Pre-Islamic Sociolinguistic Context of South Asia.' *International Journal of the Sociology of Language* 16.11–25: 22.

201. 'Psychologists are interested in these recursions.': Miller, George. 1964. 'The Psycholinguists,' *Encounter*, 23 (July): 29–37 discusses three cases of recursiveness: *right-recursive, left-recursiveness* and *self-embedding*. The text does not mention the third which is exemplified by: 'the rapidity that the hummingbird has (is remarkable)'. It is common and easy for every speaker of English. Few can manage the next step: 'the rapidity that the motion that the hummingbird has has'. Everyone has trouble with: 'the rapidity that the motion that the wing that the hummingbird has has has'. We return to self-embedding in ritual in the next chapter: p. 228 with note.

202. 'This picking up of language . . . is similar to the way scientists learn about the world': Gopnik, Alison (1999), 'Small Wonders,' *The New York Review of Books*, May 6: 41–5.—In Tantrism it is said that 70 million of them exist in superior worlds ('higher levels of the hierarchy of RV 1.164.45': p. 296 below): Brunner, Héléne. 1986. 'Les membres de Śiva', *Asiatische Studien/Études Asiatiques*, 40:91 and *note* 9.

203–6. Kautsa: *pp.* 144*ff*.

204. 'It holds not only for mantras like OM, . . . but for mantras such as the Gāyatrī mantra': last section of this chapter, *p.* 213*ff*.

205. 'That mantras are untranslatable, like proper names, was recognized by Chinese pilgrims such as Xuanzang or Hiuan-Tsang': # 27.—'Though often kept secret and guarded jealously, some Vedic mantras were inherited by Buddhists and Tantrics': Tantric mantras play an important role in several of the essays published in Goudriaan, Teun, (ed.), 1992. *Ritual and Speculation in Early Tantrism. Studies in Honor of André Padoux*. Albany: State University of New York and White, David Gordon (ed.), 2000. *Tantra in Practice*. Princeton: Princeton University Press. In Buddhism, the Mantrayāṇa is called after them. Tantrism is not unique to India, Buddhism or Hinduism: Strickmann, Michel, (ed.), 1981–83. *Tantric and Taoist Studies in Honour of R.A. Stein.*—I-III, Bruxelles: Institut Belge des Hautes Études Chinoises.

205. 'Maintaining the original forms of a ritual language is advocated in a similar spirit': Jucker 2006 for the Catholic Mass which is also recursive in structure as the author shows.—'Arabic in the Qur'ān': Qur'ān 12.1, 20.112, etc. 'this is an *Arabic* Qur'ān.' The Qur'ān, therefore, may not be translated into another language.

206. 'Bertrand Russell called them "egocentric particulars"': Russell, Bertrand. 1940. *An Inquiry into Meaning and Truth*. London: George Allen and Unwin, Chapter VII and elsewhere.

206. 'Many students of mantras have argued that mantras are speech acts': McDermott, A. C. S.. 1975. 'Toward a Pragmatics of Mantra Recitation', *The Journal of Indian Philosophy* 3, 3: 238–98; Wade T. Wheelock and John Taber in Alper 1989: #193. More recently, the study of pragmatics in language has developed in various new directions. In 1993, the *Journal of Historical Pragmatics* devoted a special issue to ritual language behaviour. Gabriela Nik. Ilieva ('The Ṛgvedic Hymn as a Ritual Speech Event. About some grammatical-rhetorical features of 10.39 from a pragmatic perspective': pp. 171–94) discusses many of the complexities that a pragmatic study of a single hymn entails and that involve speaker- and hearer-oriented terms of address, plots, ellipses and ideological background. I do not know whether 'ritual speech event' as a technical term adds to conceptual clarity. What is important in the present context is to distinguish between a particular Ṛgvedic verse and a *mantra*. The former may *become* a mantra but is not or not yet a mantra. The two basic principles or meta-rules of the Śrauta Sūtras (below, *pp.* 263–5) that govern the relation between mantras and acts in Vedic ritual are: *ekamantrāṇi karmāṇi*, 'each act is accompanied by one mantra' and *mantrāntaiḥ karmādīn saṃnipatayet*, 'one should let the beginning of the acts coincide with the end of the mantras' (Āpastamba Śrauta Sūtra 24.1.38). There are of course exceptions, but these two principles are, on the whole, sufficient for our purpose.

208. 'The Chāndogya tells us about dogs that are gathered': CU 1.12.5.—'The syntactic study of bird song was initiated by a composer and musicologist': Mâche 1983 inspired Staal. 1985. 'Mantras and Bird Songs,' *Journal of the American Oriental Society* 105: 549–58.

209. 'The syntactic structures of language, mantras and bird song': note *syntactic,* not *semantic*. The distinction is not always made when the press reports on 'talking' birds like the famous African Grey Parrot 'Alex' who passed away on 6 September 2007. Such birds, when trained by humans, do not only repeat, but construct new patterns that are syntactically more complex. Whether they understand and, if so what, is controversial.

212. 'As for recursiveness, there are different kinds and natural language, birds, mantras and ritual': #198–201.

213. 'Similar in formation to *upaniṣad* ('sitting near')': *p.* 160.

214. 'The boy is then given a staff, a grass girdle and several instructions': Kane. 1941. Vol.II, Part I, Chapter VII: 268–415 for a full description.

215. 'P.V. Kane refers to its "Grand simplicity"': Kane (publication details #60), II. I, p. 303.

CHAPTER 12

222. 'Much of what we found in the preceding chapter . . . *Ṛgvidhāna*: "The mantras attain the desired result"': Gonda, J. 1951. *The Ṛgvidhāna*, Utrecht: Oosthoek, 1.

223. 'Unlike mantras, ritual consists of acts. I can do no more than give a rough idea': 'The Syntactic study of Vedic ritual': the chapter on 'Ritual Structure' in Staal, CV and Itti Ravi 1983, II: 127–35, was perhaps the first sketch of that idea but it was very incomplete. Forerunners in anthropology, sociology and religious studies include Hubert and Mauss 1899 (pp. 224–5); and in the sister discipline of linguistics, the Sanskrit grammarians and Chomsky, Noam 1957. *Syntactic Structures*. The Hague: Mouton, which inspired major advances in linguistics and led to new disciplines such as the cognitive sciences. In a wider context, emphasis on syntax characterizes mathematics and modern logic.—On Vedic ritual the scientific literature is immense, starting as it does with the Vedic treatises, the commentaries of Sāyaṇa ('The Role of the Yajurveda': Chapter 7, *pp.* 118–

121), which are basically ritual-oriented even where the Vedas are not, and modern studies that started to flourish in the nineteenth century with Albrecht Weber (brother of the more well-known sociologist Max) and are now flourishing not only in India but wherever the Vedas are seriously studied. Dictionaries include Renou 1954 and more detailed: Sen, Chitrabhanu. 1978, 1982. *A Dictionary of the Vedic Rituals based on the Śrauta and Gṛhya Sūtras*. Delhi: Concept Publishing Company. Many of Mylius' articles and recensions (#149) deal with Vedic ritual, e.g.: Mylius, Klaus. 2000. *Das altindische Opfer*. Wichtrach: Institut für Indologie.—Rather than talk/write/think about ritual, one should participate in or witness one, and if that is not feasible (which in India it sometimes is), stay in one's armchair with Staal, CV and Itti Ravi 1983, Volume I until sleep prevails.

224. 'The other important component of *kalpa* are the Gṛhya or 'domestic' rites': Gonda 1980 called them 'non-solemn' because they exclude the Śrauta and are mainly the subject of the *Gṛhya Sūtras*. They belong to the home (*gṛha*). The Śrauta Sūtras have a more scientific structure than the Gṛhya Sūtras: Chapter 14, pp. 260–65. #263.—Gonda 1980 does not include the Pravargya which is generally looked upon as a Śrauta rite but boils down to boiling milk and is intermediate in some respects between Śrauta and Gṛhya: it is 'essentially independent,' sometimes 'placed at the end' or added later (Gonda 1977: 519, 522, 526). Special studies: Buitenen, J.A.B. van 1962. *The Pravargya*. Poona: Bhandarkar Oriental Research Institute; Houben 1991.

225. 'Lévi-Strauss could have made a contribution . . . because he had the basic background': Lévi-Strauss, Claude. 1955. *Tristes Tropiques*. Paris: Librarie Plon; English translation, 1961, New York: Athenaeum. Toward the end of that book (p. 397), he looked into the future: 'The world began with the human race and will probably end without it.' The truth of that thesis became evident in 2007 and it may now be added, that the end will be due to ourselves. Strenski 1993, 112, saw the original Levian sentence as 'a threat to humanism' but that was a decade and a half ago.—'Lévi-Strauss could have made a contribution . . .' because he knew that appearance and reality are not the same thing. He attributed that insight to his knowledge of geology and his familiarity with Marx. Recall that such a thesis is not metaphysical, but meta-phenomenological: like all theoretical science, it seeks true knowledge behind the phenomena (p. 186). It explains to some extent Lévi-Strauss' thesis that 'Theravāda Buddhism completed the material liberation of Marxism' but the Theravāda has to be placed in the wider context of Part V below.—'But he was also inspired by the distinctive features that the linguist Roman Jakobson had introduced in phonology': #183 and #294–5.—'That failure is surprising since the road was paved in 1899': Hubert and Mauss, discussed on the next page.

226. 'T. P. Mahadevan and I have studied such performances and not surprisingly': 2003 and 2005.—'However, they reflect belief systems with which the rituals have nothing to do'. Nothing or something? Let the reader decide: we describe how a small Dakṣiṇāmūrti shrine was erected immediately to the south of the ritual enclosure and touching it. It attracted popular attention, including that of the media, and a significant amount of donations. But Dakṣiṇāmūrti was not an alien presence there. The idol belonged to one of the Nambudiri priests who used to perform Vedic rituals in his home in its presence. Since the image is made of wood, he brought it with him without difficulty.

227. 'According to Renou 'Vedic religion is first . . .' and Dandekar 'in a similar vein . . .': Renou 1953: 29 and 16; Dandekar 1982:77. I have emphasized the essential correctness of these views but that does not imply that more traditional ideas about the relationships between myth and ritual are always invalid. They do appear in new garbs as in Jamieson 1991.—'Robert Sharf has studied a more radical development in the Japanese Shingon ritual': Sharf 2003.

228–33. 'Ritual exhibits another feature of recursiveness that ritual possesses and mantras in its wake: self-embedding:' Minkowski 1989b; Brereton 1997; Witzel 1992 and above #201. Minkowski and Brereton refer to *Darśapūrṇamāsa*, the 'Full- and New-Moon Rituals,' which illustrate elaborate self-embeddings (#202). Modern fire rituals such as the *Pavitreṣṭi*, an *iṣṭi* for purification (Tachikawa, Bahulkar and Kolbatkar 2001), exhibit simpler forms such as are illustrated on pp. 234–35 (and accompanying ##). Such structures have also been adopted in the study of the Shingon Tantric Fire Ritual of Japan by Payne 1989, 1997, 1999 and in that of the Roman Catholic Mass by Jucker 2006.

231. 'The advantage of the term 'self-embedding . . . embeds the work of Vedicists': see, e.g., Kadvany, John. 2008. 'Positional notation and linguistic recursion' in Staal, (ed.), 2008a. Divakaran, P.P. Forthcoming.

232. 'When Vedic stanzas declare that the layers of grass on which offerings are made constitute a nest': Gonda 1985, pp. 6–7 holds forth on 'the vital power inherent in grasses . . . brings the one who uses or wears them or has them ritually spread into contact with nature's energy and vitality, transfers it to him, makes him participate in it, purifies, wards off evil, or makes a place, a rite or other event auspicious. These phrases are followed by almost 250 pages of references and translations from the entire corpus of the Veda.—The Buddha (Chapter 16) also wanted to sit on grass: the grasscutter Svastika (called after *su-asti*, 'it is good,' and not a forerunner of Nazi ideology) handed grass to him as is often depicted in Buddhist art. It throws light on the structure of Borobudur (Staal. 1988. *Een wijsgeer in het Oosten*, Amsterdam: Meulenhoff: 30 with illustrations: see below Chapter 16: 327–9 with Figures 25 and 26.)

233. 'This is how Vedic rituals . . . such as the Royal Consecration or the famous *aśvamedha*': Heesterman 1957 and Dumont, P.-E. 1927. *L'Aśvamedha. Description du sacrifice solennel du cheval dans le culte védique d'après les textes du Yajurveda blanc*, Paris: Paul Geuthner, respectively.

234–35. 'There is a simple form of Vedic ritual in which only four priests take part': pp. 229–30 with ##.

238. 'In 1882, the learned translator of these texts, Julius Eggeling, had some worthwhile things to say on them': Eggeling, Julius, 1900, *The Śatapatha Brāhmaṇa* *according to the text of the Mādhyandina school,* Part V, Introduction: xl–xlv. Oxford: The Clarendon Press (Sacred Books of the East). Reprinted 1963, 1966. Motilal Banarsidas.

239. 'Its popularity survives in Varanasi where the central and most famous *ghāt*': Eck 1982: 68.

239–40. 'A final word about the terms 'ritual' and 'sacrifice. I have proposed to distinguish': the brief discussion that follows is not a quibble about words but is intended to assist the reader. The term 'sacrifice' has ethical and monotheistic overtones that should be avoided in the study of Vedic ritual because they are misleading. The OED distinguished its meanings very well: it lists first 'the ritual killing of an animal or person,' turns in **3** to *Theol.* **a** 'the Crucifixion as Christ's offering of himself in propitiation for human redemption', followed in **b** by the Eucharist, is then forced to take refuge in longer paraphrases and ends with chess, baseball and bridge.

240. 'According to Renou, the name of the Hotā priest must be connected with sacrifice, not invocation': Renou 1954: 157, referring implicitly to the verbal root *hu-*.—'J. C. Heesterman, from whom I learned a great deal about Vedic ritual': Heesterman 1985 and 1993, *Introduction*, 1.

241. 'I prefer Yājñavalkya's explanation of mantras, which may also apply to rituals': Chāndogya Upaniṣad 1.5.1: 'The *udgītha* is the sun and also OM for as it moves, it makes the sound OM.'

CHAPTER 13

242. 'All the larger Soma rituals are characterized by sequences of rites which I have called "Soma Sequences"': described in Staal, CV and Itti Ravi 1983, I, throughout the later chapters.—'You are the bed for coupling Rik and Sāman for the sake of procreation:' *p.* 183 with note.

243. 'The ritual has been, has been produced/It is born, it has grown': Staal, CV and Itti Ravi 1983, I: 625 and Taittirīya Saṃhitā 3.2.7.2m.

245. 'Sitting on the ground connects with the earth': Gonda, J. 1985. *The Ritual Functions and Significance of Grasses in the Religion of the Veda.* Amsterdam: North-Holland Publishing Company. #168.—'The king does more than sleeping with her: he is her husband': Hara, Minoru. 1973. 'The King as a Husband of the Earth (*mahī-pati*).' *Asiatische Studien/ Études Asiatiques* 27/2: 97–114.—'The Buddha sitting makes a vow by touching the earth in a similar spirit': the gesture (*mudra*) is *bhūmisparśamudra*, 'the gesture of touching (*sparśa*) the earth (*bhūmi*).'

246.—'To the east of the Ancient Hut a new enclosure is constructed . . . It points to Pirak': arrow 8 on the Frontispiece.

247. 'It is connected with Mount Mūjavat in the Pamirs, near the source of the Oxus': Frontispiece, north of arrow 5.

249. 'They mark the progressions of their chant on a piece of cloth with their sticks': the *viṣṭuti* markers of #171.

250. 'The case of the Sāmavedins is special as we have seen': Chapter 6. They were discriminated against and still are (#142).

CHAPTER 14

257. 'Science is universal, but the concept of science varies in different cultures': Staal. 1993, 1994. #195.

258. 'Imagine we want to transform a rectangle into a square with the same area': Staal 1999 and 2001a.

259. 'There may be links between that large unit and scientific developments in Africa, but not with Meso-American Cultures': Paz 1995: 91.

260. 'The Vedic sciences are not objects that moderns are at liberty to make up': Torella (ed.), 2001 treats the Vedic sciences as part of the history of Indic sciences by various authors in Section II, Part I. Flood (ed.), 2003 has a chapter on four Indian sciences in which the initial periods deal with Vedic sciences: Linguistics by Staal, Mathematics by Takao Hayashi, Calendar, Astrology and Astronomy by Michio Yano and Medicine by Dominik Wujastyk.—This was anticipated by a more adventurous list: freely after Olivelle 166–7.

261–2: 'The science of ritual is the first in which the notion of *sūtra* comes to the fore': Renou 1963. Staal. 1992. 'Sūtra,' in: Vatsyayan, Kapila (ed.), 1992: 303–14; Bäumer, Bettina, 'Sūtra in the Visual Arts': 314–21 and Tripathi, Radhavallabh, 'Sūtradhāra,': 321–32.

263. 'Other civilizations have been interested in the science of ritual . . . but it is unlikely that they attained the high level . . . we find in the Śrauta Sūtras': Caland 1903, 1966; Caland and Henry 1906–07; Heesterman 1957; Kashikar 1968; Gonda 1977; Einoo 1988. In Sanskrit and English: *Śrautakośa*. Poona: Vaidika Saṃśodhana Maṇḍala, an encyclopaedia in many volumes from 1958. # 224.

263–4. 'In the domain of *śrauta*, the road that led to these discoveries was paved . . .' Wezler 1972.

265. 'But brevity . . . expresses the most general solution to a particular problem': Kiparski, Paul. 1991, 'Economy and the Construction of the Śivasūtras,' in: Deshpande, Madhav M. and Saroja Bhate. 1991. *Pāṇinian Studies. Professor S.D. Joshi Felicitation Volume*. University of Michigan: Center for South and South-east Asian Studies; and Deshpande 1997b. #277.

267. 'The configuration of the thousand bricks in the offering altar': bricks and groups of bricks have their own names: Malamoud 2004 and throughout the latter parts of Staal, CV and Itti Ravi 1983, I.

268. 'But the relationships may be more complex': A. Seidenberg in Staal, CV and Itti Ravi 1983, II: 95–126, written in 1977, studied many of these complexities, also in other publications, and influenced B.L. van der Waerden, another well-known historian of early mathematics. Seidenberg could not take into account that the term *iṣṭakā* is not Indo-Iranian or Indo-European because

I, who had mentioned it to Seidenberg, did not know it: it comes from the BMAC as we have just seen (*p.* 267). More recently, Seidenberg's thesis has been discussed in Koetsier, Teun and Luc Bergmans. 2005. *Mathematics and the Divine: A Historical Study*. New York: Elsevier. Pp. 12–3, where the relations between Greek, Babylonian and Vedic are distorted.

270. 'Newton and Descartes still regarded algebra as a barbaric art': because it came from the Arabs.—'Leibniz had already seen that algebraic notations were the way of the future': Oaks, Jeffrey. 2008. 'Medieval Arabic Algebra as an Artificial Language' in Staal, (ed.), 2008a, discusses its earlier history.

273. 'My second observation is about the infinite': see #200–03 which discusses recursive structures and the infinite.

274. 'The infinite was loved throughout Indic civilization, but abhorred by the ancient Greeks, from Pythagoras onward': the list of ordered opposites, which is attributed to Pythagoras and includes good and bad, starts with finite and infinite. Indic numerals as an abstract notation for infinitely many numbers are discussed by Charles Burnett in Granoff, Phyllis, Michio Yano and Frits Staal (eds.), 2006. The Emergence of Artificial Languages. Proceedings of the 2002 Workshop. *Journal of Indian Philosophy* 34/1–2: 22: 'the first problem (of Arab, Greek and Latin writers about mathematics) was the difficulty in conceiving that a single symbol could be used to express an infinite range of numbers.' #200 and Whitehead in #300.

275. 'A few paragraphs should be added about': Bharati 1965. '*Vedic Mathematics* is neither mathematics nor Vedic:' Shukla, K.S. 1991. '*Vedic Mathematics*: The deceptive title of Swamiji's book,' in *Issues in Vedic Mathematics* (quoted by Wujastyk, D., 1998: 337 (#260), who aptly summarizes the discussion: 'It is quite definitely the Śaṅkarācārya's own discovery, and not Vedic.' #104 and Jayaram websites (end of Bibliography). For reliable information on Vedic mathematics: Hayashi 2003: 360–5. Scattered remarks on the connections between Vedic and later Indic mathematics: Hayashi, Takao. 1995. *The Bhakṣhālī Manuscript. An Ancient Indian Mathematical Treatise*. Groningen: Egbert Forsten.

276. 'In Europe': Oaks, Jeffrey. 2007. 'Medieval Arabic Algebra as An Artificial Language', *Journal of Indian Philosophy* 35: 543–75.

277. 'The Prātiśākhyas are attached to each of the Vedic schools (*śākhā*)': Renou 1960a.—'Scholars have long discussed whether the early Prātiśākhyas': Thieme 1931 and especially 1935. Since the methodology of the Prātiśākhyas is similar to that of Pāṇini, the reader may refer to the latter, e.g., Staal. 1962. 'A Method of Linguistic Description: The Order of Consonants According to Pāṇini', *Language* 38: 1–10; Kiparski, Paul. 1991 in #265.—'The Atharvaveda has two and the Sāmaveda possesses a number of compositions . . .: e.g., the *Puṣpasūtra*, 'Flower Sūtra.'

278. 'Surya Kanta called the Rik-Prātiśākhyas '*entirely* free from all oversights': Surya Kanta. 1970. *Ṛktantra*. Delhi: Mejar Chand Lachman Das. 'W.D. Whitney noted on a section of the Taittirīya Prātiśākhya, that he could not discover any case': Whitney, W.D. 1871. 'The Taittirīya Prātiśākhya with its Commentary the Tribhāshyaratna', *Journal of the American Oriental Society* 9:1–469.

280. 'They knew that its deeper source lies in the intention, that is the mind or heart': p. 67, pp. 291–2 and elsewhere: *vāc manasā*.

281. 'Modern linguistics uses distinctive features, but they would not exist': Jakobson in #183 and 294–5.

281–2. 'The discovery of the sound pattern of language was oral in two senses': the English word 'oral' is related to Latin *os,* which means 'mouth.'

282. 'The most recent work on *The World's Writing Systems*, a tome of almost a thousand pages': Daniels, Peter T. and William Bright (eds.), 1996. *The World's Writing Systems*. New York and Oxford: Oxford University Press, pp. 384 ff.

284. 'Kepler, Tycho Brahe and were all interested in astrology though Newton's real passion was alchemy': Staal. 1993, 1994. *Concepts of Science in Europe and Asia*. Leiden: International Institute for Asian Studies: 'Newton's Lesson.'—'I shall be brief on the entire subject and rely': mostly on Yano 2003. On Pingree: Conlon 2005.—'The only footnote in this book should be dedicated to . . . 43 books and 240 articles:' Pingree 1981, 1989, 1997 and 2001 are listed in the Bibliography.

286–7. 'Astronomy flourishes in sedentary civilizations which are able to concentrate on the skies . . .': Narasimha, Roddam. 2008. 'Epistemology and Language in Indian Astronomy and Mathematics' (in Staal 2008a) analyses three works of Nīlakaṇṭha Somayājī (1444–1545 CE) who during his long life observed the sky daily (and performed numerous Vedic rituals as his name Somayājī indicates).

286. 'It explains that later Indic astronomy was very different': Minkowski 2002.—'The demon myth was criticized by the astronomer Lalla': Subbarayappa, B.V. and K.V. Sharma (eds.), 1985. *Indian Astronomy: A Source-book (based primarily on Sanskrit texts). Bombay: Nehru Centre*, pp. 41–5 and discussed in Staal. 1998. 'Beyond Relativism', in Ariel, Yoav, Shlomo Biderman and Ornan Rotem. *Relativism and Beyond*: *Festschrift Ben-Ami Scharfstein*. Brill: Leiden: 37–66: 60.

CHAPTER 15

289–90. 'The phrase "narrowing religious outlook" comes from': Jawaharlal Nehru. 1946. *The Discovery of India*. New York: The John Day Company, 568 ff.

290. 'The Powers of Language': originally inspired by Renou 1955, 'Les pouvoirs de la parole dans le Ṛgveda' which emphasized *vāc manasā*, discussed throughout this book. Related notions include *pratibhā*, 'intuition' (Gonda 1963b and 1963a in general), *guru,* 'teacher' (Gonda 1965a), *upaniṣad* (p. 158), etc.

292. 'Where the sages fashioned language with their thought . . . filtering it like parched grain': Rigveda circle 9 deals with filtering the Soma liquid.

293. 'The Rigveda links language not only to thought but also to vision': #182 'interiorization' and Gonda 1963a.

294–95. 'According to Bhartṛhari, a philosopher as well as a linguist, there is no knowledge without language': Bhate 1994, Bhate and Bronkhorst 1994, Houben 1995.—'One is Wilhelm von Humboldt (1767–1835), whose numerous works': Humboldt 1836, 1988.—'The other is Roman Jakobson (1896–1982), who was equally prolific': #183, 281.

296. 'The *viśva* is easy or is it *viśvam*?' Kunhan Raja, C. 1956. *Asya Vāmasya Hymn (The Riddle of the Universe). Ṛgveda* 1.164. Madras: Ganesh and Co. follows Sāyaṇa but translates: 'that does not move.'

297. 'These are not later than 1.164 which maybe assigned to the tenth century BCE': Witzel 1989: 250 and 1997: 264–5.—'Another term is *anirvacanīya*, 'which cannot be expressed,' said of the world': put in a wider context by Bhattacharya 2001. Verhagen 1997 explains how Tibetan grammarians, having studied Sanskrit grammar for several centuries, speculated on how the ineffable should be pronounced.

298. 'Some are *upāṃśu*, "articulated (within the mouth) but inaudible"': Brereton 1988; Bhagwat 2004.—'As for rites, some are performed without mantras, that is *tūṣṇīm*': Renou 1949, Renou and Silburn 1954, Coomaraswamy 1937, 2000.—'I conclude that our ordinary, natural language is unable to express all that is true': On Whitehead's equivocation: #300.

299–300. More on the implications of the use of notations and artificial languages in the next chapter, *p.* 346.

299. 'The Ultimate Theory, the theory of everything if there will be one': Dyson 1985:21, 'the equations come first.' Also discussed in Dyson 1992, Chapters 24, 31, and Dyson 2007. Similar in Hawking 1996: 232: 'Even if there is only one unified theory, it is just a set of rules and equations.'

300. 'There is hope is we are willing to let languages expand': Whitehead, Alfred North: 'Philosophy is an attempt to express the infinity of the universe in terms of the limitations of language' in: Schilpp, Paul Arthur. 1941, 1951. New York: Tudor Publishing Company; Library of Living Philosophers. Autobiographical Notes: 14. Whitehead was almost omniscient and, of course, familiar with artificial languages such as the language of algebra but he was neither a linguist, nor a great writer and does not seem to have realized, unlike Pāṇini, Patañjali and Proust, that natural language itself is infinite too. #273, 298.

CHAPTER 16

303. 'A natural end might consist in the story of what happened to the Vedas after the Vedas': Renou 1960b did provide such a survey though 'he could not have mentioned more recent events' (p. 304).—'Much is now known about the arrival of Vedism in South India': Mahadevan, T.P. Forthcoming.

304. 'These periods are of special interest because they carried traces to:' South-east Asia, including on Thailand, with Khmer information Skilling 2007 (# 149) and on Bali: Hooykaas 1966, 1983 a. and b., all referring to other works by the same author. In Bali, an apparently post-Vedic version of the Taittirīya Upaniṣad was found.—'These and other contemporary developments': Arnold has remained unpublished; Kashikar and Parpola 1983; Knipe 1997 and 2004; Mahadevan and Staal 2003, 2005; Raghavan 1957. 'Present Position of Vedic Chanting and Its Future', *Bulletin of the Institute of Traditional Cultures* (Madras): 49–69; Smith 1984, 1994, 2000, 2001; Witzel 1992. Staal 1961, etc.; T.P. Mahadevan. Forthcoming. Staal, CV and Itti Ravi 1983. Galewicz 2004 should be added.

311. 'He hardly explained 'final redaction', but let us assume that he refers to': Olivelle, xxxiv: 'The issue of authorship is complicated by the fact that some of the earliest and largest Upaniṣads—at least the BĀU, the CU and the Kauṣītaki—are anthologies of material that must have existed as independent texts before their incorporation into these Upaniṣads by an editor or a series of editors . . . . leading us to believe that the editors at least partly drew upon a common stock of episodes and teachings.' These are the words of the leading translator and scholar of the Upaniṣads who was not concerned with Buddhism when he penned them down—though, a few pages later, he was: 311 with note.

312. 'My second illustration comes from Toshifumi Goto': Goto 2005.

313. Pre-Buddhist Upanisads: BĀU, CA, Taittirīya, Aitareya and Kauṣītaki. See above *p.* 162 and Olivelle, Introduction, xxxvi–vii and #311.

315. 'Note that *prajñā* contains the same verbal root *jñā* as does *jñāna* . . .': on Upaniṣadic *jñāna* and *prajñā*, see *p.*144 and note.

317. 'They also explain that, in due course, Buddhism returned': Snellgrove and Skorupski 1980 describe the Tibetan Buddhist culture of Ladakh and Zanskar. The area is depicted on the Frontispiece in eastern Kashmir, south of the Karakoram where the Indus flows through the valley of Ladakh, and immediately north of the western Himalayas which is the valley of Zanskar. Snellgrove and Skorupski's pioneering studies are complemented by many others, e.g., Khosla, Romi. 1979. *Buddhist Monasteries in the Western Himalaya.* Kathmandu: Ratna Pustak Mandar, which provides architectural drawings. Vedic Indians must have been in those valleys but the evidence (e.g., Iranian influence on Vairocana, the Resplendent Buddha) is of later date. The same holds for the Swat valley south of Chitral, between 5 and 7 on the Frontispiece which was also a Buddhist area: Stein, Aurel. 1972. *On Alexander's Track to the Indus. Personal Narrative of Explorations on the North-west Frontier of India.* New York: Benjamin Blom. Now being destroyed.

318–19. 'In partial response to that question I shall quote Etienne Lamotte': Lamotte 1958: 74–5, translated from the French. The present study of Buddhism covers so vast an area and has become so specialized that it is impossible for a non-specialist to keep up with it. I have often relied on Lamotte 1944–80, 1948, 1958, 1962 especially for the history of Buddhism. Supplemented on details by publications such as Bapat 1956, we would have to go back for more than a century before we find equally comprehensive surveys such as Oldenberg 1881, now dated but only in part.

319. 'The higher castes continued their demand for the great Vedic and Brahmanic deities': the cult of pagan gods survived throughout history until contemporary times, often in more remote areas, e.g., among the Rathvas of Central Gujarat: Jain 1979.

320. 'The Advaita philosopher Śrī Harṣa . . . wrote an epic poem . . . called "lusty"': Granoff 1978, p. 2, adding that the author was a deeply religious man and did not perceive any inconsistency (as a monotheist might).—'Here is how Śrī Harṣa presents Cārvāka, tucked away': Dasgupta, Surendranath. 1952. *A History of Indian Philosophy*, Vol. III. Cambridge: Cambridge University Press, p. 549.

321. 'Entering the Order, Women and Sexualities': Bechert and Gombrich 1984, 1991; Faure 1998; Findly 2002; Jamison 1996; Patton 2002.

322. 'The Mahāyāna challenged the distinction between monks and laymen': the greatest lay bodhisattva was Vimalakīrti. Of his Sanskrit teaching only a few fragments have been preserved, but many translations were made into other Buddhist languages. The fifth century CE translation into Chinese by Kumārajīva became an instant success and remains one of the best sources for the understanding of the Mahāyāna. Translated by Lamotte into French, here is an example (Lamotte 1962: 303): 'The ideas of pollution and purification are two. If one understands pollution, the notion of purification does not arise. Destroying every imagination (*vikalpa*) and the road which leads there is to penetrate the doctrine of non-duality.' Lamotte wrote in his Preface: 'Perhaps it scandalized the Indians . . . but it amused and charmed the Chinese.'—Little is known about Vimalakīrti's life in India though his house is supposed to have been in Vaiśāli, north of Pāṭaliputra, modern Patna. Snellgrove, David. 1987. *Indo-Tibetan Buddhism: Indian Buddhist and their Tibetan Successors*, II, Boston: Shambhala: 312.—On the life and works of Lamotte: Durt, Hubert. 1985. 'Etienne Lamotte 1903–1983', *Bulletin de l'école française d'éxtrême orient* 74: 1–28.—'(Forest monks) are still found in Myanmar and Thailand': Tambiah 1984. This continues to be true for Thailand at the time of writing these source notes (November 2007). I believe it continues to be true for Myanmar also though other monks have now risen against their dictators and been abused, imprisoned and killed.

323. 'They are *paṇḍakas*, often translated as 'eunuch' but in fact': Faure 1998.

324. 'I believe it reflects different periods of history . . . ferret out': the only publication which, to the best of my knowledge, has studied the geography of homosexuality in reasonable historical detail (*pace* Michel Foucault, Mahathir and so many others) is due to Richard Burton (not to be confused with the actor):

1886. *The Book of the Thousand Nights and a Night. Literal Translation from the Arabic*. Vol. X with *Terminal Essay*, 63–302, concluding on pp. 206–7: 'There exists what I shall call a 'Sotadic Zone,' bounded westwards by the northern and southern shores of the Mediterranean.' It includes, as I paraphrase freely, France, the Iberian Peninsula, Italy and Greece with the coast regions of Africa from Marocco to Egypte. Running east it narrows to Turkey, Mesopotamia, Afghanistan, Sind, the Punjab and Kashmir, and broadens again to Indo-China enfolding China, Japan and Turkistan, then the South Sea Islands and the New World. 'Within the Sotadic Zone, the Vice is popular and endemic, held at the worst to be a mere peccadillo, whilst the races to the North and South . . . practice it only sporadically.' Britain is not included because Burton was British and, at times, a civil servant. (Whether he practiced 'the Vice' himself remains controversial.)

324–26. 'Performances of large Vedic rituals were generally hidden but became public': several essays edited by Harris 2007 put the transition from private to public in Buddhism in a political context. Deeper connections have been explored by Shimoda 2006: 26–9 who explains how Mahākaśyapa, 'Great Turtle,' could have confirmed the teachings that had until then been contained in the private memories of individual disciples by collaborative recitation (*saṃgīti*). That development reflected an earlier transition from the wordless experience of the Buddha's meditation to his verbal expression by means of language. Though the Mahāyāna was familiar with the technology of writing, many of its adherents continued to give priority to hearing a teacher's voice. They are, therefore, worthy of the name *śrāvaka* or 'hearer.' The entire development should be related to the origins of writing in India. Falk, Harry. 1993. *Schrift im alten Indien. Ein Forschungsbericht mit Anmerkungen*. Tübingen: Gunter Narr and von Hinüber 1999.

328. 'This discovery inspired Jan Fontein, art historian, archeologist and museum director': Fontein 1989.

329. 'The Muṇḍaka Upaniṣad expresses the synthesis or identity that is the endpoint of the Vedic perspective': Muṇḍaka Up. 3.2.2. Śvetāśvatara Up. 1.8, 3.20, 4.16, etc. also discourse on freedom from sorrow and all fetters.

330. 'The distinction is obsolete because it cannot be expressed in Chinese': Graham's views are found in a series of studies discussed by Staal. 2001. 'Article One,' in Bronkhorst, Johannes (ed.), *La rationalité en Asie / Rationality in Asia* in *Etudes de Lettres*. Lausanne: Faculté des lettres: 59–95. Graham 1989 puts his own views in a wider perspective.

331. 'Kamaleswar Bhattacharyya has looked into similar problems': Bhattacharyya 1968, 1973, 1998.

333. 'Śaṅkara, to whom I referred as an Upaniṣadic philosopher, had his go at Buddhism *anusmṛteś ca*': *Brahmasūtra* 2.2.25.

334. 'It has even been adopted by the Bonpos of Tibet: Kvaerne 1981.—'The eleventh verse of the puzzle poem 1.164 of Chapter 15': excerpts quoted on p. 35.

335. 'In the Vedic instance, *dharma* is 'time,' but it is not a single thing: there are many *dharmas*': Olivelle, Patrick (ed.), 2004 for Dharma in Indic civilization from the Vedas onward: #54.

336. 'A Sāmavedic Brāhmaṇa, the Pañcaviṃśa, described a *sattra* ritual': a complex ritual that may be of infinite duration.—'Foremost among them are the decline of dharma through four ages': Hayashi, Takao. 1995. The *Bakhshālī Manuscript. An ancient Indian mathematical treatise*. Groningen: Egbert Forsten, 109–13 discusses measures of time and provides tables.

339. 'The University of Nālanda is the first university in the history of mankind': the literature is extensive from the Chinese travellers, via Dutt 1956, van Gulik 1980: 14 ff. to Sen 2005, Chapter 8 #340.

340. 'The first is Amartya Sen's book *The Argumentative Indian*': Sen 2005.

341. 'My only information is a letter of December 2006': Garten 2006.

342. 'Relevant facts about American universities': Kennedy 1987.—'It sheds much light on Nālanda: students kept going there': Bowring 2005 discusses implications for immigration.

343. 'It's the logic, stupid!' in Sanskrit: *ānvīkṣiky eva mūrkha*! *Ānvīkṣikī* is not Vedic but *mūrkha*, 'fool,' is an old Vedic and Indo-European word related to Old-Lithuanian *mulkis* (Burrow, see above #49: 391). On Indian logic there is a vast literature but one pioneer may be mentioned here: the Polish Sanskritist and logician Stanislaw Schayer (Balcerowitz and Mejor 2000).

344. 'The Leiden participants who knew Sanskrit did not know': the literature on Buddhist mediaeval logic is vast. It includes Bhattacharya 1973 and more recent articles by the same author. The birth of the New Nyāya or *Navya-Nyāya* logic has been most recently discussed by Wada, Toshihiro. 2007(earlier Wada in Hino and Wada (eds.), 2004 and Wada (ed.), 2006).—'A third international meeting, after Leiden and Hangzhou': *Strings 2006* deals with a theory which is said to be consistent though it is difficult to understand and there do not seem to be decisive experimental facts that support it—unlike Einstein's *Theory of General Relativity*.

346. 'One reason is related to the talk I had just given: the level of mathematical knowledge': the language faculty, which first appeared with humans, was in due time fused with the mathematical faculty thus leading to the birth of artificial languages. Pp. 299–300 with ##.

347. 'Should one delve into the matter, starting with the universe': Thapar 1996, Chapter 5, provides excellent reasons for rejecting these ideas which were prominent in the Purāṇas (i.e., 'the ancient'). #116. The Sanskrit proverb said already: 'something is not true just because it is ancient' (*purāṇam ity eva na sādhu sarvam*). Purāṇic cosmology is expressed by the four *yugas*, beginning with Satya, the 'Age of Truth', and ending with the Kaliyuga, an age that is characterized by *mleccha* rulers, corrupt *brāhmaṇas* and upstart *śūdras*. There are similar ideas in Theravāda Buddhism, where, over the *yugas*, life-expectancy is said to drop from 30,000 to one hundred years; and in Jainism, where man's height comes down from six miles (including 256 ribs) to about eighteen inches (with 16 ribs). I accept that these speculations should not be taken seriously, but stress on the remainder of this page that in the context of the cosmos, very large numbers make much sense.—'Even if they were thinking of cows, there is no need': the patron of the Agnicayana, above pp. 131–2.—'According to recent estimates, perhaps already outdated': Penrose, Roger. 1997, etc. *The Large, the Small and the Human Mind.* Cambridge: Cambridge University Press: p. 26.—'Contrast the story of creation ': *Genesis*, Chapter 1, *Qur'ān* 7: 54, 10: 3, 11: 7, 25: 59, 32: 4, 50: 38, 57: 4.—'But even monotheists have not failed to note': Pascal, Blaise. 1655–59 and later, never finished. *Pensées* ('Thoughts'). Many editions of which I used Paris: Garnier Fréres, 1957, 90. The original reads: *notre intelligence tient dans l'ordre des choses intelligibles le même rang que notre corps dans l'étendue de la nature.*

APPENDICES

348. Needham 1976: 22–4, 95–6; Chemla and Shuchun 2004, 'Présentation du Chapitre 9' especially pages 674 and following.

349. Heath 1956. Vol.I: 349–50.

READINGS

352. 'If I had to recommend a single general book about the Vedas . . . certainly outdated': Renou 1953. Half a century later and taking account of the enormous increases in knowledge and insight, but for those who read German: more than half of Witzel, Michael. 2003. *Das alte Indien* ('Ancient India'). München: C.H. Beck.—'For those who read German, Geldner remains the best guide:' Geldner, Karl Friedrich. 1951–57. *Der Rig-Veda aus dem Sanskrit ins Deutsche übersetzt und miet einem laufenden Kommentarversehen.* Cambridge, Mass.: Harvard University Press; London: Geoffrey Cumberledge, Oxford University Press; Leipzig: Otto Harrassowitz. Indices and Notes left by Geldner have been edited and completed by: Nobel, Johannes. 1957. *Namen-und Sach Register etc.,* same publishers.—'But (added in the proof) see the Preface': for those who read German, there was another surprise announcement on the Indology website of 25 October 2007: Witzel, Michael and Toshifumi Goto. 2007. *Rig-Veda. Das heilige Wissen. Erster und zweiter Liederkreis* ('The Rigveda. Sacred Knowledge. First and Second Circle'), Verlag der Weltreligionen, pp. 889.

353. 'For the Yajurveda': Keith's translation is mentioned in # 127. For the Śatapatha Brāhmaṇa, see #238, though the complete Eggeling consists of five volumes and was published between 1882 and 1900.—'The Artharvaveda has remained': in India, it is now somewhat more accessible thanks to Ghosh 2002.

~

BIBLIOGRAPHY

Anthony, David W. 1995. 'Horse, wagon and chariot: Indo-European languages and archaeology', *Antiquity* 69: 554–65.

———. 1998. 'The Opening of the Eurasian Steppe at 2000 BCE', in Mair 1998: I, 114–47.

Arnold, Harold F. (unpublished). 'The Hinduization of Vedic Ritual'.

Auden, W.H. 1948. 'The Greeks and Us', in *Forewords and Afterwords*. New York: Vintage Books, 1974: 3–32.

Bakker, Hans. 1989. *De leer van de wind. Een natuurfilosofie uit de Upanisaden*. Kampen: Kok Agora.

Balcerowicz, Piotr and Marek Mejor (eds.), 2000. *On the Understanding of Other Cultures*. Proceedings of the International Conference on Sanskrit and Related Studies to Commemorate the Centenary of the Birth of Stanislaw Schayer (1899–1941). *Studia Indologiczne* 7.

Bapat, P.V. (ed.), 1956. *2500 Years of Buddhism*. New Delhi: Publications Division, Government of India.

Basu, Jogiraj. 1969. *India of the Age of the Brāhmaṇas*. Calcutta: Sanskrit Pustak Bhandar.

Bechert, Heinz and Richard Gombrich. 1984, 1991. *Buddhism. Buddhist Monks and Nuns in Society and Culture*. London: Thames and Hudson.

Bhagwat, Bhagyashree. 2004. '*Upāṃśu*: Concept and Interpretation', in Maitreyee Deshpande (ed.), pp. 27–32.

Bharati Krishna Tirtha Maharaja, Shankaracarya of Govardhana Matha. 1965. *Vedic Mathematics or Sixteen Simple Mathematical Formulae from the Vedas (for one-line answers to all mathematical problems)*. Varanasi: Banaras Hindu University.

Bhate, Saroja. 1994. 'Bhartṛhari on Language and Reality', in Bhate and Bronkhorst (eds.), pp. 67–73.

Bhate, Saroja and Johannes Bronkhorst (eds.), 1994. *Bhartṛhari. Philosopher and Grammarian*. Proceedings of the First International Conference on Bhartṛhari. Delhi: Motilal Banarsidas.

Bhattacharya, Kamaleswar. 1968. '*Upādhi-*, *Upādi-* et *Upādana-* dans le canon bouddhique pali', in *Mélanges d'indianisme à la mémoire de Louis Renou*. Paris: Editions E. de Boccard, pp. 81–95.

———. 1973. *L'Atman-Brahman dans le bouddhisme indien*. Paris: Ecole française d'extrème orient.

______. 1998. *Some Thoughts On Early Buddhism with Special Reference to its Relation to the Upaniṣads*. Pune: Bhandarkar Oriental Research Institute.

______. 2001. '*Lakṣaṇa*, *Lakṣaṇā*, and Apophaticism in Śaṅkara's Commentary on *Taittirīyopaniṣad* II, 1,' in *Le parole e I marmi. Studi in onore di Raniero Gnoli nel suo 70 compleanno*. Roma: Istituto Italiano per l'Africa e l'Oriente, pp. 85–95.

Bowring, Philip. 2005. 'Facing the facts on migration', *International Herald Tribune*, 11 October.

Brereton, Joel P. 1981. *The Ṛgvedic Ādityas*. New Haven: American Oriental Society.

______. 1986. '*Tat Tvam Asi* in Context', *Zeitschrift der deutschen morgenländischen Gesellschaft*, 136: 98–109.

______. 1988. 'Unsounded Speech: Problems in the Interpretation of BU(M) 1.5.10 = BU(K) 1.5.3', *Indo-Iranian Journal*, 31: 1–10.

______. 1997. 'Why is a Sleeping Dog like the Vedic Sacrifice? The Structure of an Upaniṣadic *Brahmodya*', in Witzel (ed.), pp. 1–14.

______. 1999. 'Edifying Puzzlement: *Ṛgveda* 10.129 and the Uses of Enigma', *Journal of the American Oriental Society*, 119: 248–60.

______. 2004. 'On the Composition of the New and Full Moon Rites', in Maitreyee Deshpande (ed.), pp. 55–78.

Bronkhorst, Johannes. 1998. 'Did the Buddha believe in Karma and Rebirth?', *Journal of the International Association of Buddhist Studies* 21/1: 1–19/

Bronkhorst, Johannes and Madhav M. Deshpande (eds.), 1999. *Aryan and Non-Aryan in South Asia: Evidence, Interpretation and Ideology*. Proceedings of the International Seminar on Aryan and Non-Aryan in South Asia. Cambridge: Department of Sanskrit and Indian Studies. Harvard Oriental Studies. Opera Minora, Vol. 3.

Brough, John 1959. 'The Tripartite Ideology of the Indo-Europeans: an Experiment in Method', *Bulletin of the School of Oriental and African Studies*, 22/1: 69–85. Reprinted in Brough, 1996, pp. 180–202.

______. 1971. 'Soma and *Amanita muscaria*', *Bulletin of the School of Oriental and African Studies*, 34/2: 331–62. Reprinted in Brough, 1996, pp. 366–97.

______. 1996. *Collected Papers* (eds.), Minoru Hara and J.C. Wright. London: School of Oriental and African Studies.

Buitenen, J.A.B. van. 1968. *The Pravargya. An Ancient Indian Iconic Ritual.* Poona: Bhandarkar Oriental Research Institute.

Burmeister St. 2004. 'Der Wagen im Neolithikum und in der Bronzezeit', in *Rad und Wagen*, pp. 13–39.

Burnett, Charles. 2003. 'Fibonacci's "Method of the Indians"', *Bolletino di Storia delle Szienze Mathematiche*, 23/2: 87–97.

______. 2006. 'The Semantics of Indian Numerals in Arabic, Greek and Latin', *Journal of Indian Philosophy*, 34/1–2: 15–30.

Caland, W. 1896, 1967. *Die Altindischen Todten- und Bestattungsgebräuche*. Wiesbaden: Dr. Martin Sändig.

_____. 1903, 1966. *Über das rituelle Sūtra des Baudhāyana*. Leipzig: Brockhaus.

Caland, W. and V. Henry. 1906–07. *L'Agniṣṭoma. Description complète de la forme normale du sacrifice de Soma dans le culte védique*. Vols. 1–2, Paris: Ernest Leroux.

Cardona, George. 2005. 'Arapacana and Indian Phonological Traditions', Indo-European_research@yahoogroups.com, 13 August.

Carpelan, Christian, Asko Parpola and Petteri Koshikikallio (eds.), 2001. *Early Contacts between Uralic and Indo-European: Linguistic and Archaeological Considerations*. Helsinki: Suomalais-Ugrilainen Seura.

Carvalho-Silva, R. Denise, Tatiana Zerjal and Chris Tyler-Smith. 2006. 'Ancient Indian Roots?' *Journal of Biosciences*, 31/1, March, 101–2. epublication: 20 February 2006, (email: cts@sanger.ac.uk).

Catchpole, C.K. and P.J.B. Slater. 1995. *Bird Song: Themes and Variations*. Cambridge: Cambridge University Press.

Chakrabarti, Samiran Chandra. 1980. *The Paribhāṣās in the Śrautasūtras*. Calcutta: Sanskrit Pustak Bhandar.

Chandra, Vikram. 2000. 'The Cult of Authenticity', *Boston Review*, February–March: 42–9.

Chemla, Karine and Guo Shuchun. 2004. *Les neuf chapitres. Le Classique mathématique de la Chine ancienne et ses commentaries*. Paris: Dunod.

Conlon, Frank. 2005. 'Professor David Edwin Pingree, 1933–2005', INDOLOGY WEBSITE, 16 November.

Coomaraswamy, Ananda K. 1937, 2000. 'The Vedic Doctrine of "Silence"', *Indian Culture*, 3, republished in Coomaraswamy, 2000, pp. 226–34.

Coward, Harold and Krishna Sivaraman (edṣ.), 1977. *Revelations in Indian Thought. A Festschrift in Honour of Professor T.R.V. Murti*. Emeryville, California: Dharma Publishing.

Crouwel, J. 2004. 'Der alte Orient un seine Rolle in der Entwicklung von Fahrzeugen', in *Rad und Wagen*, pp. 68–9.

Dandekar, R.N. 1964. *Vedic Bibliography*. Ongoing volumes, Poona: University of Poona.

_____. 1982. 'Some Aspects of Vedic Exegesis', *Indologica Taurinensia*, 10: 71–81.

_____. 1997. 'Vedic Mythology: A Rethinking,' in Witzel (ed.): 39–48.

Daniels, Peter T. and William Bright (eds.), 1996. *The World's Writing Systems*. New York and Oxford: Oxford University Press.

Dasgupta, Surendranath. 1922. *A History of Indian Philosophy*, Vol. I. Cambridge: Cambridge University Press.

Dejenne, Nicolas. 2003. '"Do you enjoy the Somayaagam?" A propos d'un agniṣṭoma célébré `a Trichur (Kerala) en avril 2003', *Bulletin des Etudes Indiennes*, 21/1: 225–38.

Deshpande, Madhav M. 1997a. *Śaunakīyā Caturādhyāyikā. A Prātiśākhya of the Śaunakīya Atharvaveda*. Cambridge, Mass.: Harvard Oriental Series.

_____. 1997b. 'Who inspired Pāṇini? Reconstructing the Hindu and Buddhist Counter-Claims', *Journal of the American Oriental Society*, 117/3: 444–65.

_____. 1999. 'What to do with the Anāryas? Dharmic Discourse of Inclusion and Exclusion', in Bronkhorst and Deshpande (eds.), pp. 107–27.

_____. 2002. *Recitational Permutations of the Śaunakīya Atharvaveda*. Cambridge, Mass.: Harvard Oriental Series.

Deshpande, Maitreyee (ed.), 2004. *Problems in Vedic and Sanskrit Literature. Presented to Ganesh Umakant Thite on his 60th Birthday*. Delhi: New Bharatiya Book Corporation.

Doniger O'Flaherty, Wendy. 1968. 'The Post-Vedic History of the Soma Plant', in Wasson (ed.), 1968, Part II, pp. 95–147.

Doniger, Wendy. 1981. *The Rig Veda: An Anthology*. Harmondsworth: Penguin Books Ltd.

_____. 1992. 'The Deconstruction of Vedic Horselore in Indian Folklore', in van den Hoek, Kolff and Oort (eds.), pp. 76–101.

_____. 1998. 'From Great Neck to Swift Hall: Confessions of a Reluctant Historian of Religions', in Stone, Jon R. (ed.), pp. 36–51.

Dumézil, Georges. 1958. *L'idéologie tripartite des Indo-Européens*. Brussels: Coll. Latomus.

Dutt, S., 1956. 'Monastic Universities', in Bapat (ed.), pp. 185–92.

Dyson, Freeman. 1981. 'Unfashionable Pursuits', in *From Eros to Gaia*. Pantheon Books (1992) and Penguin Books (1993).

_____. 1985. *Infinite in All Directions*, Gifford Lectures given at Aberdeen, Scotland. Edited by the author.

_____. 2007. *The Scientist as Rebel*. The New York Review of Books.

Eck, Diana L. 1982. *Banaras: City of Light*. Princeton, New Jersey: Princeton University Press.

Einoo, Shingo. 1988. *Die Cāturmāsya oder die Altindischen Tertialopfer dargestellt nach den Vorschriften der Brāhmaṇas und der Śrautasūtras*. Tokyo: Institute for the Study of Languages and Cultures of Asia and Africa.

Elizarenkova, Tatiana Y. 1997. 'Problems of Synchronic Description of Language and Style in the *Ṛgveda*', in Witzel (ed.), pp. 49–59.

Falk, Harry. 1981. 'Vedisch arma', *Zeitschrift der deutschen morgenländischen Gesellschaft*, 131: 160–171

_____. 1989. 'Soma I and II', *Bulletin of the School of Oriental and African Studies*, 52: 77–90.

Farmer, Steve, Richard Sproat and Michael Witzel. 2004. *The Collapse of the Indus-Script Thesis: The Myth of a Literate Harappan Civilization*. Electronic Journal of Vedic Studies (EJVS), 11/2: 19–58.

Faure, Bernard. 1998. *The Red Thread. Buddhist Approaches to Sexuality*. Princeton, New Jersey: Princeton University Press.

Feferman, Anita Burdman and Saul Feferman. 2004. *Alfred Tarski. Life and Logic*. Cambridge: Cambridge University Press.

Findly, Ellison Banks. 2002. 'The Housemistress at the Door: Vedic and Buddhist Perspectives on the Mendicant Encounter', in Patton (ed.), pp. 21–31.

Flattery, David Stophlet and Martin Schwartz. 1989. *Haoma and Harmaline: The Botanical Identity of the Indo-Iranian Sacred Hallucinogen 'Soma' and Its Legacy in Religion, Language, and Middle Eastern Folklore*. Berkeley: University of California Press.

Flood, Gavin (ed.), 2003. *The Blackwell Companion to Hinduism*. Oxford: Blackwell Publishing.

Fontein, Jan. 1989. *The Law of Cause and Effect in Ancient Java*, Amsterdam etc.: North-Holland. Koninklijke Nederlandse Akademie van Wetenschappen. Afdeling Letterkunde, n.r. *140*.

French, Patrick. 1994. *Younghusband. The Last Great Imperial Adventurer*. Hammersmith: Flamingo.

Galewicz, Cezary. 2004. 'Kaṭavallūr Anyonyam: a Competition in Vedic Chanting?', in Griffiths and Houben (eds.), pp. 361–84.

Gardner, Robert. 1992. 'The More Things Change', *Transition*, 58: 33–66.

Garten, Jeffrey E. 2006. 'Really Old School: Higher Education in Asia', *International Herald Tribune*, 11 December.

Geldner, Karl Friedrich. 1951. *Der Rig-veda*. Vols. I–III. Cambridge, Mass.: Harvard Oriental Series.

_____. 1957. *Register, Nachträge und Verbesserungen*. Cambridge, Mass.: Harvard Oriental Series.

Ghosh, Abhijit. 2002. *Ātharvaṇa* (*a collection of essays on the AtharvaVeda with special reference to its Paippalāda tradition*). Kolkata: Sanskrit Book Depot.

Gonda, Jan. 1960. *Die Religionen Indiens*. Vol. I: *Veda und älterer Hinduismus*. Stuttgart: W. Kohlhammer.

_____. 1963a. *The Vision of the Vedic Poets*. The Hague: Mouton and Co.

_____. 1963b. 'Pratibhā', in Gonda 1963a, pp. 318–48.

_____. 1965a. 'The Guru', in Gonda 1965b, pp. 229–83.

_____. 1965b. *Change and Continuity in Indian Religion*. London. The Hague, Paris: Mouton and Co.

_____. 1976. *Triads in the Veda*. Amsterdam, Oxford, New York: North-Holland Publishing Company.

_____. 1977. *The Ritual Sūtras*. Wiesbaden: Otto Harrassowitz.

_____. 1980. *Vedic Ritual: The Non-Solemn Rites*. Leiden, Kỏln: E.J. Brill.

_____. 1985. *The Ritual Functions and Significance of Grasses in the Religion of the Veda*. Amsterdam etc.: North-Holland Publishing Company. Koninklijke Nederlandse Akademie van Wetenschappen, Afdeling Letterkunde, n.r., 132.

Goto, Toshifumi. 2005. 'Yājñavalkya's Characterization of the Ātman and the Four Kinds of Suffering in Early Buddhism', *Electronic Journal of Vedic Studies* (EJVS), July: 71–85.

Graham, A.C. 1989. *Disputers of the Tao. Philosophical Argument in Ancient China*. As Salle, Ill: Open Court.

Granoff, Phyllis. 1978. *Philosophy and Argument in Late Vedānta: Śri Harṣa's Khaṇḍanakhaṇḍakhādya*. Dordrecht etc.: D. Reidel.

Grapard, Allan G., Burton L. Mack, Ivan Strenski and Frits Staal. 1991. 'Symposium: Ritual as Such', *Religion*, 21: 205–34.

Griffiths, Arlo. 2002. 'Aspects of the Study of the Paippalāda Atharva Vedic Tradition', in Ghosh, A. (ed.), pp. 35–54.

_____. 2003. 'The Orissa Manuscripts of the Paippalāda Saṃhitā', *Zeitschrift der deutschen morgenländischen Gesellschaft*, 153/2: 333–70.

_____. Forthcoming. *The Paippalādasaśṃhitā of the Atharvaveda Kāṇḍas 6 and 7. A New Edition with Translation and Commentary*. Groningen: Egbert Forsten.

Griffiths, Arlo and Jan E.M. Houben (eds.), 2004. *The Vedas. Texts, Language and Ritual*. Proceedings of the Third International Vedic Workshop, Leiden 2002. Groningen: Egbert Forsten.

Grimes, Ronald L. (ed.), 1996. *Readings in Ritual Studies*. New Jersey: Prentice Hall.

Gulik, R.H. van. 1980. *Siddham. An Essay on the History of Sanskrit Studies in China and Japan*. Śata-piṭaka Series. Vol. 247, New Delhi: International Academy of Indian Culture, Mrs. Sharada Rani.

Hamp, Eric P. 1998. 'Whose were the Tocharians?—Linguistic Subgrouping and Diagnostic Idiosyncrasy', in Mair 1998: I, 307–46.

Hanneder, Jürgen. 1998. 'Vedic and Tantric Mantras', *Rivista degli studi orientali*, 71: 147–68.

Hara, Minoru. 2000. 'Two notes on the word *upaniṣad* in the *Mahābhārata*', in Balcerowicz and Mejor (eds.), pp. 157–67.

Harris, Ian (ed.), 2007. *Buddhism, Power and Political Order*. London: Routledge.

Hawking, Stephen. 1996. *The Illustrated A Brief History of Time*. Updated and expanded. New York: Bantam Books.

Hayashi, Takao. 2003. 'Indian Mathematics', in Flood (ed.), pp. 360–75.

Heath, Thomas L. 1956. Many reprints. *The Thirteen Books of Euclid's Elements*. Cambridge: Cambridge University Press, New York: Dover Publications.

Heesterman, J.C. 1957. *The Ancient Indian Royal Consecration. The Rājasūya Described According to the Yajus Texts and Annotated*. Utrecht: Disputationes Rheno-Trajectinae.

_____. 1985. *The Inner Conflict of Tradition. Essays in Indian Ritual, Kingship, and Society*. Chicago and London: The University of Chicago.

_____. 1993. *The Broken World of Sacrifice. An Essay in Ancient Indian Ritual*. Chicago and London: The University of Chicago.

Hino, Shoun and Toshihiro Wada (eds.), 2004. *Three Mountains and Seven Rivers. Prof. Musashi Tachikawa's. Felicitation Volume*. Delhi: Motilal Banarsidas.

Hinüber, Oskar von. 1989. *Der Beginn der Schrift und frühe Schriftlichkeit in Indien*. Stuttgart: Franz Steiner. Akademie der Wissenschaften und der Literatur, Mainz.

Hock, Hans Heinrich. 1999. 'Out of India? The Linguistic Evidence', in Bronkhorst and Deshpande (eds.), pp. 1–18.

Hoek, van den, D.H.A. Kolff and M.S. Oort (eds.), 1992. *Ritual, State and History in South Asia. Essays in Honour of J.C. Heesterman*. Leiden etc.: E.J. Brill.

Hoogt, J.M. van der. 1929. *The Vedic Chant Studied in its Textual and Melodic Form*. Wageningen: H. Veenman & Sons.

Hooykaas, C. 1966. *Surya-Sevana. The Way to God of a Balinese Priest*. Verhandelingen der Koninklijke Nederlandse Akademie van Wetenschappen, Afdeling Letterkunde, n.r., LXXII, No. 2, Amsterdam: Noord-Hollandsche Uitgevers Maatschappij.

_____. 1983a. 'Agni Offerings in Java and Bali', in Staal et al., Vol. II, pp. 382–402.

_____. 1983b. 'Homa in India and Bali', in Strickmann (ed.), Vol. II, pp. 512–91.

Hopkins, Thomas J. 1966. 'The Social Teaching of the *Bhāgavata Purāṇa*', in Singer, (ed.), pp. 3–22.

Houben, Jan E.M. 1955. *The Pravargya Brāhmaṇa of the Taittirīya Āraṇyaka. An Ancient Commentary on the Pravargya Ritual*. Delhi: Motilal Banarsidas.

_____. 1995. *The Saṃbandha-samuddeśa (Chapter on Relation) and Bhartṛhari's Philosophy of Language*. Groningen: Egbert Forsten.

Howard, Wayne. 1977. *Sāmavedic Chant*. New Haven and London: Yale University Press.

_____. 1983. 'The Music of Nambudiri Unexpressed Chant (*aniruktagāna*)', in Staal et al., Vol. II, pp. 311–42.

_____. 1986. *Veda Recitation in Varanasi*. Delhi: Motilal Banarsidas.

_____. 2001. '*Prācīna* Kauthuma Traditions of South India: Letters from L.S. Rajagopalan, 1985–1988', in Kartunen and Kokikallio (eds.), pp. 291–302.

Høyrup, Jens. 1998. 'On a Collection of Geometrical Riddles and their Roles in Shaping Four to Six Algebras', *Filosofi og Videnskabsteori pe Roskilde Universitetscenter*, 3/2: 1–68.

Hubert, H. and M. Mauss. 1899. 'Essai sur la nature et la fonction sociale de sacrifice', *Année sociologique*, 2: 29–138.

Humboldt, Wilhelm von. 1836, 1988. *Introduction* to *The Diversity of Human Language-Structure and its Influence on the Mental Development of Mankind*, tr. Peter Heath. Cambridge: Cambridge University Press.

Ikari, Yasuke. 1989. 'Some Aspects of the Idea of Rebirth in Vedic Literature', *Studies in the History of Indian Thought*. Kyoto University, pp. 155–64.

Ingalls, Daniel H.H. 1971. 'Remarks on Mr. Wasson's Soma', *Journal of the American Oriental Society*, 91: 188–91.

Insler, Stanley. 1998a. 'On the Recensions of the Atharvaveda and Atharvan Hymn Composition', *Wiener Zeitschrift für die Kunde Südasiens*, 42: 5–21.

_____. 1998b. 'The Scattered Head Split and the Epic Tale of Śakuntalā', *Bulletin des Etudes Indiennes*, 7/8: 97–140.

Jain, Jyotirindra. 1979. *Painted Myths of Creation: Art and Ritual of an Indian Tribe*. New Delhi: Lalit Kala Akademi.

Jaini, Padmanabh S. 1966. 'The Story of Sudhana and Manoharā: An Analysis of the Texts and the Borobudur Reliefs', *Bulletin of the School of Oriental and African Studies*, 29: 533–58.

Jakobson, Roman. 1962. 'Why "Mama" and "Papa"?' *Selected Writings*, Vol. I, pp. 538–545. The Hague: Mouton.

_____. 'The Slavic God Veles and his Indo-European Cognates', *Studi Linguistici in Onore di Vittore Pisani*. Brescia: Paideia, 579–99.

Jamison, Stephanie. 1991. *The Ravenous Hyenas and the Wounded Sun: Myth and Ritual in Ancient India*. Ithaca and London: Cornell University Press.

_____. 1996. *Sacrificed Wife, Sacrificer's Wife*. New York: Oxford University Press.

Jarrige, Jean-François. 1985. *L'archéologie de la Bactriane ancienne*. Paris: Diffusion de Boccard.

Jarrige, Jean-François, Marielle Santonie et Jean-François Enault. 1979. *Fouilles de Pirak*, Vols. I–II. Paris: Diffusions de Broccart.

Jha, V.N. 1976. 'Stages in the Composition of the Ṛgveda-Padapāṭha', *Bulletin of the Deccan College Research Institute*, 25/3–4: 47–50.

Jucker, Jean-Luc. 2006. *Dites-le et Faites-le. Le rituel religieux considéré comme un enchainement de paroles et d'actes codifiés en parti d'un enquête ethnographique menée auprès d'une communité chrétienne de type traditionaliste pratiquant la messe tridentine*. Lausanne: Jean-Luc Jucker.

Kane, Pandurang Vaman. 1930. *History of Dharmaśāstra*, Vol. I. Poona: Bhandarkar Oriental Institute.

Kartunen, Klaus and Kokikallio, Petteri (eds.), 2001. *Vidyārṇavavandanam. Essays in Honour of Asko Parpola*, Helsinki: Studia Orientalia, Vol. 94.

Kashikar, C.G. 1968. *A Survey of the Śrautasūtras*. University of Bombay.

Kashikar, C.G. and Parpola, Asko. 1983. 'Śrauta Traditions in Recent Times', in Staal et al., Vol. II, pp. 192–3.

Kennedy, Paul. 1987. *The Rise and Fall of the Great Powers. Economic Change and Military Conflict from 1500 to 2000*. New York: Random House.

Kenoyer, M. 2004. 'Die Karren der Induskultur Pakistans und Indiens', in *Rad und Wagen*, pp. 87–106.

Knipe, David. M. 1997. 'Becoming a Veda in the Godavari Delta', in Meij, Dick van der (ed.), pp. 306–32.

_____. 2004. 'Ritual Subversion: Reliable Enemies and Suspect Allies', in Griffiths and Houben (eds.), pp. 433–48.

Kolver. B. (ed.), 1997. *Recht, Staat und Verwaltung im Klassischen Indien. The State, the Law, and Administration in Classical India*. München: R. Oldenbourg.

Kuiper, F.B.J. 1991. *Aryans in the Ṛgveda*. Amsterdam and Atlanta: Rodopi.

Kulke, Hermann and Dietmar Rothermund. 1998. *A History of India*. London and New York: Routledge.

Kvaerne, Per. 1981. 'A Bonpo Version of the Wheel of Existence', in Strickmann (ed.), Vol. I, pp. 274–89.

Lamotte, Étienne. 1944–80. *Le traité de la grande vertu de sagesse de Nāgārjuna* (*Mahāpajñāpāramitāśāstra*), Vols. I–V. Louvain: Bureau du *Muséon*.

_____. 1948, 1991. 'The Buddha, His Teachings and His Sangha', and 'Mahāyāna Buddhism', in Bechert and Gombrich (eds.), pp. 41–58 and 90–93.

_____. 1958, 1967. *Histoire du bouddhisme indien*. Louvain/Leuven: Institut Orientaliste/Instituut voor Orientalistiek.

_____. 1962. *L'Ensignement de Vimalakīrti* (*Vīmalakīrtinirdeśa*). Louvain/Leuven: Publications Universitaires/Institut Orientaliste.

Levine, Marsha, Colin Renfrew and Katie Boyle (eds.), 2003. *Prehistoric Steppe Adaptation and the Horse*. Cambridge: McDonald Institute for Archaeological Research.

Levy, John and Frits Staal. 1969. *The Four Vedas*. Record Album. New York: Asch Mankind Series, AHM 4126.

Lindquist, Stephen E. 2004. '*Yājñavalkya's Riddle* (*BĀU* 3.9.28K)', in Maitreyee Deshpande (ed.), pp. 192–211.

Lubotsky, Alexander. 1998. 'Tocharian Loanwords in Old Chinese: Chariots, Chariot Gear and Town Building', in Mair 1998: I, pp. 379–90.

_____. 2001. 'The Indo-Iranian Substratum', in Carpelan, Parpola and Koshikikallio (eds.), pp. 301–17.

Macdonell, A.A. 1917. *A Vedic Reader for Students*. Oxford: Oxford University Press.

Mâche, François-Bernard. 1983. *Musique, Mythe, Nature: ou les Dauphins d'Arion*. Paris: Klincksieck.

Mahadevan, I. 1977. *The Indus Script: Texts, Concordance, and Tables*. Calcutta and Delhi: Memoirs of the Archaeological Survey of India.

Mahadevan, T.M.P. 1957. *The Philosophy of Advaita with Special Reference to Bhāratītīrtha-Vidyāraṇya*. Madras: Ganesh and Co.

Mahadevan, T.P. Forthcoming. *The Arrival of Vedism in South India, The* Pūrvaśikhā *and* Aparaśikhā *Brahmans*.

Mahadevan, T.P. and Frits Staal. 'The Turning Point in a Living Tradition: Somayagam 2003', Electronic Journal of Vedic Studies (EJVS), Vol. 10. Revised version in *Indische Kultur im Kontext: Rituale, Texte und Ideen aus Indien und der Welt. Festschrift für Professor Klaus Mylius*, (ed.) Lars Göhler, Wiesbaden: Otto Harrassowitz, 2005, pp. 365–89.

Mair, Victor H. 1998. *The Bronze Age and Early Iron Age Peoples of Eastern Central Asia*, Vols. I–II. Washington: Institute for the Study of Man Inc., and Philadelphia: The University of Pennsylvania Museum Publications.

_____. 2003. 'The Horse in Late Prehistoric China: Wrestling Culture and Control from the "Barbarians",' in Levine, Renfrew and Boyle (eds.), Chapter 12, pp. 163–87.

Malamoud, Charles. 1976. 'Village et forêt dans l'idéologie de l'Inde brahmanique', *Archives européennes de sociologie*, 17: 6–26. Reprinted in 1989. *Cuire le monde. Rite et pensée dans l'inde ancienne*. Paris: Editions la Découverte, pp. 93–114. English translation by David White, 1996, 'Village and Forest in the Ideology of Brahmanic India,' in *Cooking the World. Ritual and Thought in Ancient India*. Delhi: Oxford University Press, pp. 74–91.

_____. 2004. 'A Note on abīṣṭakā (Taittirīya Āraṇyaka I)', in Griffiths and Houben (eds.), pp. 449–55.

Mallory, James P. 1989. *In Search of the Indo-Europeans: Language, Archaeology and Myth*. London: Thames and Hudson.

Masson, J.L. and M.V. Patwardhan. 1970. *Aesthetic Rapture. The Rasādhyāya of the Nāṭyaśāstra*, Vols. I–II. Poona: Deccan College.

Meij, Dick van der (ed.), 1997. *India and Beyond. Aspects of Literature, Meaning, Ritual and Thought. Essays in Honour of Frits Staal*. London and New York: Kegan Paul International, Leiden and Amsterdam: International Institute for Asian Studies.

Minard, Armand. 1949, 1956. *Trois Enigmes sur les Cent Chemins*, Vols. I–II, Paris: Les Belles Lettres and E. de Boccard.

Minkowski, Christopher Z. 1989a. 'The Rathakāra's Eligibility to Sacrifice', *Indo-Iranian Journal*, 32: 177–94.

_____. 1989b. 'Janameyaja's *Sattra* and Ritual Structure', *Journal of the American Oriental Society*, 109/3: 401–20.

_____. 2002. 'Astronomers and Their Reasons: Working Paper on *Jyotiḥśāstra*', *Journal of Indian Philosophy*, 30: 495–515.

Misra, Vidya Nivas (ed.), 2000. *Perception of the Vedas*. New Delhi: Indira Gandhi National Centre for the Arts and Manohar.

Mukherjee, Meenakshi. 1993. 'The Anxiety of Indianness—Our Novels in English', *Economic and Political Weekly*, 27 November: 2607–11.

Murti, T.R.V. 1955. *The Central Philosophy of Buddhism*. London: George Allen and Unwin.

_____. 1963. 'Some Thoughts on the Indian Philosophy of Language', *Presidential Address. Indian Philosophical Congress*, 37th Session (Chandigarh).

Needham, Joseph. 1976. *Science and Civilisation in China*, Vol. 3: *Mathematics and the Sciences of the Heavens and the Earth*. Cambridge: Cambridge University Press.

Nilakanta Sastri, K.A. 1955. *A History of South India from Prehistoric Times to the Fall of Vijayanagar*. London: Oxford University Press.

Obeyesekhere, Gananath. 2002. *Imagining Karma. Ethical Transformation in Amerindian, Buddhist and Greek Rebirth*. Berkeley: University of California Press.

Oldenberg, Hermann. 1881. *Buddha, Sein Leben, Seine Lehre, Seine Gemeinde*.

Berlin: Wilhelm Hertz. Often reprinted and translated into English (London, 1882).

Olivelle, Patrick. 1992. *Saṃnyāsa Upaniṣads: Hindu Scriptures on Ascetism and Renunciation*. New York: Oxford University Press.

———. 1996. *Upaniṣads*, translated from the original Sanskrit. Oxford: Oxford University Press.

———. 1999. *Dharmasūtras: The Law Codes of Ancient India*, A New Translation. Oxford: Oxford University Press.

———. 2004. *The Law Code of Manu*, A New Translation. Oxford: Oxford University Press.

Padoux, André. 2001. '*Mantra, Devatā, "Mantradevatā"*: Quelques observations sur les mantra tantriques', in *Vidyārṇavandanam: Essays in Honour of Asko Parpola* (eds.), Klaus Karttunen and Petteri Koskikallio, *Studia Orientalia*, Vol. 94, pp. 397–403.

Parpola, Asko. 1998. 'Aryan Languages, Archaeological Cultures and Sinkiang: Where did Proto-Iranian Come into Being and How did it Spread?', in Mair 1998: I, pp. 114–47.

———. 2005. 'The Nāsatyas, The Chariot and Proto-Aryan Religion', *Journal of Indological Studies* (Kyoto), 16/17: 1–63.

Patton, Laurie L. 2002. *Jewels of Authority: Women and Texts in the Hindu Tradition*. New York: Oxford University Press.

Payne, Richard. 1989. *The Tantric Ritual of Japan. Feeding the Gods: The Shingon Fire Ritual*. New Delhi: International Academy of Indian Culture and Aditya Prakashan.

———. 1997. 'The Tantric Transformation of Puja: Interpretation and Structure in the Study of Ritual', in Meij, Dick van der (ed.), pp. 384–404.

———. 1999. 'The Shingon *Ajikan*: Diagrammatic Analysis of Ritual Syntax', *Religion*, 29: 215–29.

———. Forthcoming. 'Ritual Syntax and Cognitive Theory'.

Paz, Octavio. 1995. *In Light of India* ('*Vislumbres de la India*'), Orlando, Florida: Harcourt Brace and Company.

Penrose, Roger. 1997. *The Large, the Small and the Human Mind*. Cambridge: Cambridge University Press.

Pingree, David. 1981. *Jyotiḥśāstra. Astral and Mathematical Literature*. Wiesbaden: Otto Harrassowitz.

———. 1989. 'MUL.APIN and Vedic Astronomy', *Studies in Honor of Ake Sjoberg*. Philadelphia: University Museum. Pp. 439–45.

———. 1997. *From Astral Omens to Astrology, from Babylonia to Bikaner*. Roma: Istituto Italiano per l'Africa e l'Oriente.

———. 2001. 'Astronomy in the Vedas', (partly published in Torella (ed.), 2001, pp. 729–33).

Pinnault, Georges-Jean. 1998. 'Tocharian Languages and Pre-Buddhist Culture', in Mair 1998: I, pp. 358–71.

_____. 2002. 'Tokh. B KuCanne, A KuCim et Skr. Tokharika', *Indo-Iranian Journal*, 45: 311–45.

Rad und Wagen. Der Ursprung einer Innovation: Wagen im Vordern Orient und Europa. Landesmuseum für Kultur und Mensch. Mainz am Rhein: Philipp von Zabern.

Raghavan, V. 1957. 'Present Position of Vedic Chanting and its Future', *Bulletin of the Institute of Traditional Cultures*, 1: 48–69.

Rau, Wilhelm. 1957. *Staat und Gesellschaft im Alten Indien nach den Brāhmaṇa-Texten dargestellt*. Wiesbaden: Otto Harrassowitz.

_____. 1969. 'Index zu Renou *Etudes védiques et pāṇinéennes* I–XVI', *Orientalistische Literaturzeitung*, 64: 74–84.

_____. 1970. *Weben und Flechten im vedischen Indien*. Wiesbaden: Otto Harrassowitz.

_____. 1976. *The meaning of* pur *in Vedic Literature*. München: W. Winck. Abhandlungen der Marburger Gelehrten Gesellschaft III/1.

_____. 1997. 'The Earliest Literary Evidence for Permanent Vedic Settlements', in Witzel (ed.), pp. 203–206.

Raulwing, P. und Hainz Meyer. 2004. 'Der Kikkuli-Text. Hippologische und Methodenkritische Überlegungen zum Training von Streitwagenpferden im Alten Orient', in *Rad und Wagen*, pp. 491–506.

Renou, Louis. 1937. 'Les *yājyānuvākyā* du Yajurveda', *Journal of the American Oriental Society*, 69: 11–18.

_____. 1939. 'La maison védique', *Journal asiatique*, 481–504.

_____. 1947. *Les écoles védiques et la formation du Veda*. Paris: Imprimerie Nationale.

_____. 1949. 'La valeur du silence dans le culte védique', *Journal of the American Oriental Society*, 69: 11–18.

_____. 1952. 'Les vérsets du Sāmaveda d'origine non-ṛvédique', *Journal asiatique*, 133–41.

_____. 1953. *Religions of Ancient India*. London: The Athlone Press.

_____. 1953a. 'Le Passage des Brāhmaṇa aux Upaniṣad', *Journal of the American Oriental Society*, 73: 138–44.

_____. 1954. *Vocabulaire du rituel védique*. Paris: Librarie C. Klincksieck.

_____. 1955. 'Les pouvoirs de la parole dans le Ṛgveda', in *Etudes védiques et pāṇinéennes 1955–69*, Vol. 1, pp. 1–27.

_____. 1955–69. *Etudes védiques et pāṇinéennes*, Vols. 1–17. Paris: Editions E. de Boccard.

_____. 1958. *Etudes sur le vocabulaire du Rgveda* I. Pondichéri: Institut Français d'Indology.

_____. 1960a. 'La forme et l'arrangement interne des Prātiśākhya', *Journal asiatique*, 1–40.

_____. 1960b. 'Le destin du Véda dans l'Inde', *Etudes védiques et pāṇinéennes*, Vol. 6. Paris: Editions E. de Boccard.

———. 1963. 'Sur le genre du sūtra dans la litérature sanskrite', *Journal asiatique*, 165–216.

Renou, Louis and Liliane Silburn. 1954. 'Nirukta and anirukta in Vedic', *Lakshman Sarup Memorial Volume*. Hoshiarpur: Vishveshvaranand Institute Publications, pp. 68–79.

Richter, Th. 2004. 'Der Streitwagen im alten Orient im 2. Jahrtausend v. Chr.—eine Betrachtung Anhand der keilschriftlichen Quellen', in *Rad und Wagen*, pp. 507–14.

Sahoo, P.C. 2004. '*Meditation Through the Vedic Ritual*', in Maitreyee Deshpande (ed.), pp. 27–32.

Salomon, R. 1981. 'A Linguistic Analysis of the Muṇḍaka Upaniṣad', *Wiener Zeitschrift für die Kunde Südasiens und Archiv für indische Philosophie*, 25: 91–105.

Schmidt, Hanns-Peter. 1968. *Bṛhaspati und Indra. Untersuchingen zur vedischen Mythologie und Kulturgeschichte*. Wiesbaden: Otto Harrassowitz.

———. 1987. *Some Women's Rites and Rights in the Veda*. Poona: Bhandarkar Oriental Research Institute.

Schwab, Raymond. 1950. *La Renaissance Orientale*. Paris: Payot.

Sebeok, Thomas A. (ed.), 1969. *Current Trends in Linguistics, Vol. 5: Linguistics in South Asia*. Mouton: The Hague—Paris.

Sen, Amartya. 2005. *The Argumentative Indian. Writings on Indian Culture, History and Identity*. London: Penguin Books Ltd.

Sengupta, S., L.A. Zhivotovsky, R. King, S.Q. Mehdi, C.A. Edmonds, C.E. Chow, A.A. Lin, M. Mitra, S.K. Sil, A. Ramesh, M.V. Usha Rani, C.M. Thakur, L.L. Cavalli-Sforza, P.P. Majumdar and P.A. Underhill. 2006. 'Polarity and temporality of high-resolution Y-chromosome distributions in India identify both indigenous and exogenous expansions and reveal minor genetic influence of Central Asian pastoralists', *American Journal of Human Genetics*, 78: 202–221.

Sharf, Robert H. 2003. 'Thinking Through Shingon Ritual', *Journal of the International Association of Buddhist Studies*, 26/1: 51–93.

Shimoda, Masahiro. 2006. 'An Essay on the Formation Process of Buddhist Scriptures in Ancient India', in Toshihiro Wada, (ed.), pp. 23–35.

Singer, Milton (ed.), 1966. *Krishna: Myths, Rites and Attitudes*. Honolulu: East-West Centre Press.

Skilling, Peter. 2007. 'King, Sangha and Brahmins: Ideology and Ritual in Pre-Modern Siam', in Harris (ed.), pp. 182–215.

Smith, Frederick M. 1984. *The Vedic Sacrifice in Transition: A Translation and Study of the Trikaṇḍamaṇḍana of Bhāskara Miśra*. Ann Arbor and London: University Microfilms International. Updated but not seen: (1987). Poona: Bhandarkar Oriental Research Institute.

———. 1994. 'Purāṇaveda', in Laurie Smith (ed.), pp. 97–138.

_____. 2000. 'Indra goes West: Report on a Vedic Soma sacrifice in London in July 1996', *History of Religions*, 40/3: 247–67.

_____. 2001. 'The Recent History of Vedic Ritual in Maharasthra', in Kartunen and Kokikallio (eds.), pp. 443–63.

Smith, Laurie (ed.), 1994. *Authority, Anxiety and Canon*. Albany: SUNY Press.

Snellgrove, David L. and Tadeusz Skorupski. 1980. *The Cultural Heritage of Ladakh*, Vols. I–II, Warminster, England: Aris and Phillips.

Somayajipad, C.V., M. Iti Ravi Nambudiri and Erkkara Raman Nambudiri. 1983. 'Recent Nambudiri Performances of Agniṣṭoma and Agnicayana', in Staal et al., Vol. II: 252–55.

Sparreboom, Max. 1985. *Chariots in the Veda*. Leiden: E.J.Brill.

Sprockhoff, Joachim F. 1981. 'Āraṇyaka und Vanaprastha in der vedischen Literature', *Wiener Zeitschrift für die Kunde Südasiens und Archiv für indische Philosophie*, 25: 19–90.

Staal, Frits. 1961. *Nambudiri Veda Recitation*. The Hague: Mouton.

_____. 1963. 'Sanskrit and Sankritization', *Journal of Asian Studies*, 22: 261–75. Reprinted in *South and South-east Asia: Enduring Scholarship*, (ed.) J.A. Harrison, Tucson, pp. 213–17.

_____. 1964. 'Report on Vedic Rituals and Recitations', *Yearbook of the American Philosophical Society*, 607–11.

_____. (ed.) 1972. *A Reader on the Sanskrit Grammarians*. Cambridge and London: MIT Press, reprint, Delhi: Motilal Banarsidas.

_____. 1975 etc. *Exploring Mysticism. A Methodological Essay.* Berkeley: University of California Press and Harmondsworth: Penguin Books.

_____. 1977. 'Ṛgveda 10.71 on the Origin of Language', in Harold Coward and Krishna Sivaraman (eds.), pp. 3–14.

_____. 1979. 'The Meaninglessness of Ritual', *Numen. International Journal of the History of Religions*, 26: 2–22. Reprinted in Grimes (ed.), 1996, pp. 483–94.

_____. 1981. 'Vedic Religion in Kerala', *The Adyar Library Bulletin*, 44/5: 74–89.

_____. 1986. *The Fidelity of Oral Tradition and the Origins of Science*. Amsterdam: Royal Netherlands Academy of Arts and Sciences.

_____. 1987. 'Professor Schechner's Passion for Goats', *Journal of Asian Studies*, 86: 206–9.

_____. 1988. *Universals. Studies in Indian Logic and Linguistics*. Chicago and London: The University of Chicago Press.

_____. 1989. 'The Independence of Rationality from Literacy', *European Journal of Sociology*, 30: 301–10.

_____. 1989, 1993. *Rules without Meaning: Ritual, Mantras and the Human Sciences*. New York: Peter Lang. Reprint 1996. *Ritual and Mantras: Rules without Meaning*. Delhi: Motilal Banarsidas. See also Grapard et al. (1991).

——. 1992a. 'Agni 1990. With an Appendix by H.F. Arnold', in van den Hoek, Kolff and Oort (eds.), pp. 650–76.
——. 1992b. 'Sūtra,' in Vatsyayan, pp. 303–14.
——. 1993. 'From Meanings to Trees', *Journal of Ritual Studies*, 7/2: 11–32.
——. 1995a. *Mantras between Fire and Water. Reflections on a Balinese Rite.* With an Appendix by Dick van der Meij. Amsterdam etc.: North-Holland. Koninklijke Nederlandse Akademie van Wetenschappen. Afdeling Letterkunde, n.r. 166.
——. 1995b. 'The Sanskrit of Science', *Journal of Indian Philosophy*, 23: 73–127
——. 1998. 'There Is No Religion There', in Stone, Jon R. (ed.), 52–75.
——. 1999. 'Greek and Vedic Geometry', *Journal of Indian Philosophy*, 27: 105–127.
——. 2000. 'A Breakthrough in Vedic Studies', *IIAS Newsletter*, October, Leiden: International Institute of Asian Studies.
——. 2001a. 'Squares and Oblongs in the Veda', *Journal of Indian Philosophy*, 29: 258–273.
——. 2001b. 'How a Psychoactive Substance Becomes a Ritual: The Case of Soma', *Social Research*, 68/3: 745–778.
——. 2001c. 'La Scienza nella Cultura Indiana', in Torella (ed.), pp. 611–38.
——. 2003a. 'The Science of Language', in Flood, (ed.), pp. 348–59.
——. 2003b. 'The Future of Asian Studies', *Newsletter of the International Institute for Asian Studies*, November, no. 32, pp. 6–7.
——. 2004. 'From *prāṅmukham* to *sarvatomukham*: A Thread through the Śrauta Maze', in Griffiths and Houben (eds.), pp. 521–55.
——. 2004. 'Three Mountains and Seven Rivers', in Hino and Wada (eds.), *Three Mountains and Seven Rivers. Prof. Musashi Tachikawa's Felicitation Volume*, pp. 3–24.
——. 2006. 'Artificial Languages across Sciences and Civilizations', *Journal of Indian Philosophy*, 34: 89–141.
——. 2006a. *What Euclid is to Europe, Pāṇini is to India—Or Are They?* Bangalore: National Institute of Advanced Studies.
——. 2006b. 'The Sound Pattern of Sanskrit in Asia', *Sanskrit Studies Centre Journal* (Silpakorn University, Bangkok), 2: 193–208.
——. 2007. '*Secrets Behind Walls*', *JOSA. The Journal of the Oriental Society of Australia*. A.R. Davis Memorial Lecture.
——. 2008a. 'Artificial Languages between Innate Faculties', Proceedings of the Workshop on 'Asian Contributions to the formation of modern science II: The Generosity of Artificial Languages in an Asian Perspective', Amsterdam: May 18–20, 2006. *Journal of Indian Philosophy*.
——. 2008b. 'Formalizing Logic with Special Reference to *Hetuvidyā*', Proceedings of the International Conference on Hetuvidyā, Hangzhou: Hangzhou Buddhist Academy. Website: http//philosophy.berkeley.edu/staal

_____. Forthcoming. 'Nature, Culture and Language', in Roddam Narasimha and Sangeetha Menon (eds.), *Nature and Culture*. Bangalore: National Institute of Advanced Studies.

Staal, Frits, in collaboration with C.V. Somayajipad and M. Itti Ravi Nambudiri. 1983. *AGNI. The Vedic Ritual of the Fire Altar*, Vols. I–II. Berkeley: Asian Humanities Press. Reprint 2001, Delhi: Motilal Banarsidas.

Stein, Burton. 1998. *A History of India*. Oxford and Malden, Mass.: Blackwell Publishing.

Stone, Jon R. (ed.), 1998. *The Craft of Religious Studies*. Macmillan: Hampshire and London and New York: St. Martin.

Strenski, Ivan. 1997. 'The Social and Intellectual Origins of Hubert and Mauss's Theory of Ritual Sacrifice', in Dick van der Meij (ed.), pp. 511–37.

_____. 1993. *Religion in Relation: Method, Application and Moral Location*. Columbia: University of South Carolina Press.

Strickmann, Michel (ed.), 1981, 1983. *Tantric and Taoist Studies in Honour of R.A. Stein*, Vols. I–II. Bruxelles: Institut Belge des Hautes Etudes.

Tachikawa, Musashi. 1985. *An Ancient Indian Homa Ritual. Pavitreṣṭi, a Modified Form of Darśapūrṇamāsa*. Nagoya: Department of Indian Philosophy.

Tachikawa, Musashi, Shrikant Bahulkar and Madhavi Kolhatkar. 2001. *Indian Fire Ritual*. Delhi: Motilal Banarsidas.

Tambiah, Stanley Jeyaraja. 1984. *The Buddhist Saints of the Forest and the Cult of Amulets*. Cambridge: Cambridge University Press.

Thapar, Romila. 1996. *Time as a Metaphor of History: Early India*. Delhi: Oxford University Press.

_____. 2002. *Early India from the Origins to 1300*. Berkeley and Los Angeles: University of California Press and London: Penguin Books Ltd. Reprint, New Delhi: Penguin Books India (2003).

Thieme, Paul. 1931. 'Grammatik und Sprache, ein Problem der altindischen Sprachwissenschaft', *Zeitschrift für Indologie und Iranistik*, 8: 23–32.

_____. 1935. *Pāṇini and the Veda. Studies in the Early History of Linguistic Science in India*. Allahabad: Globe Press.

Thite, G.U. 2004. 'Vicissitudes of Vedic Ritual', in Griffiths and Houben (eds.), pp. 557–63.

Thompson, George. 1997. 'On Mantras and Frits Staal', in Dick van der Meij (ed.), pp. 574–97.

_____. 2003. 'Ṛgveda 10.119', *Electronic Journal of Vedic Studies* (EJVS) 9.1 *www.shore.net/~india/ejvs*

Torella, Raffaele. (ed.), 2001. '*La Scienza Indiana*', in *Storia della Scienza*. Rome: Treccani, pp. 609–949.

Vatsyayan, Kapila. (ed.), 1992. *Kalātattvakośa. A Lexicon of Fundamental Concepts in the Indian Arts*. New Delhi: Indira Gandhi National Centre for the Arts and Delhi: Motilal Banarsidas.

Verhagen, P.C. 1997. 'Tibetan Expertise in Sanskrit Grammar (3): On the Correct Pronunciation of the Ineffable', in Dick van der Meij (ed.), pp. 598–619.

Wada, Toshihiro. (ed.), 2006. *Conflict Between Tradition and Creativity in Indian Philosophy: Text and Context.* Nagoya University: Graduate School of Letters.

Wasson, R. Gordon. 1968. *SOMA. Divine Mushroom of Immortality*. New York: Harcourt Brace Jovanovich.

———. 1978. *Soma and the Fly-Agaric; Mr. Wasson's Rejoinder to Professor Brough*. Cambridge: Botanical Museum of Harvard University.

———. 1979. 'Soma brought Up-to-Date', *Journal of the American Oriental Society*, 99: 100–4.

Wezler, Albrecht. 1972. 'Marginalien zu Pāṇini's I: *sthānin*', *Zeitschrift für vergleichende Sprachforschung*, 86: 7–20.

Wilson, Angus. 1979. *The Strange Ride of Rudyard Kipling. His Life and Works.* Harmondsworth: Penguin Books.

Witzel, Michael. 1980. 'Early Eastern Iran and the Atharvaveda', *Persica*, 9: 86–128.

———. 1984. 'The Earliest Form of the Idea of Rebirth in India', Proceedings of the Thirty-First International Congress of Human Sciences in Asia and North Africa. Tokyo–Kyoto 1983. Tokyo: Toyo Gakkai.

———. 1989. 'Tracing the Vedic Dialects', in Colette Caillat (ed.), *Dialectes dans les litteratures indo-ariennes*. Paris: Institut de Civilisation Indienne.

———. 1992. 'Meaningful Ritual. Vedic, Medieval and Contemporary Concepts in the Nepalese Agnihotra Ritual', in van den Hoek et al. (eds.), pp. 774–827.

———. (ed.), 1997. *Inside the Texts/Beyond the Texts: New Approaches to the Study of the Vedas*. Cambridge: Department of Sanskrit and Indian Studies. Harvard Oriental Studies. Opera Minora, Vol. 2.

———. 1997a. 'Early Sanskritization. Origins and Development of the Kuru State', in Kolver (ed.), pp. 27–52.

———. 1997b. 'The Development of the Vedic Canon and its Schools: The Social and Political Milieu', in Witzel (ed.), 1997: pp. 257–345.

———. 1999a. 'Aryan and Non-Aryan Names in Vedic India', in *Aryan and Non-Aryan in South Asia: Evidence, Interpretation and Ideology.* Proceedings of the International Seminar on Aryan and Non-Aryan in South Asia (see Bronkhorst and Deshpande (eds.)), pp. 337–404. Harvard Oriental Studies. Opera Minora, Vol. 3.

———. 1999b. 'Substrate Languages in Old Indo-Aryan', *Electronic Journal of Vedic Studies* (EJVS) 5–1. www.shore.net/~india/ejvs

———. 2000. 'The Home of the Aryans', *Festschrift für Johanna Narten zum 70. Geburtstag* (ed.), A. Hintze and E. Tichy. Dettelbach: J.H. Roll, pp. 283–338.

———. 2001. 'Autochthonous Aryans? The Evidence from Old Indian and Iranian Texts', *Electronic Journal of Vedic Studies* (EJVS) 7–3. www.shore.net/~india/ejvs

_____. 2003a. *Das alte Indien*. Munchen: C.H. Beck.
_____. 2003b. 'Vedas and Upaniṣads', in Flood (ed.), pp. 68–98.
_____. 2003. 'Linguistic Evidence for Cultural Exchange in Prehistoric Western Central Asia', *Sino-Platonic Papers* 129, Philadelphia: Department of East Asian Languages and Civilizations, University of Pennsylvania.
_____. 2004a. 'The Ṛgvedic Religious System and its Central Asian and Hindukush Antecedents', in Griffiths and Houben (eds.), pp. 581–636.
_____. 2004b. 'F.B.J. Kuiper (1907–2003)', *Indo-Iranian Journal*, 47: 173–91.
Witzel, Michael and Steve Farmer. 2000. 'Horseplay in Harappa. The Indus Valley Decipherment Hoax', *Frontline*, 13 October: 4–14.
Yano, Michio. 2003. 'Calendar, Astrology and Astronomy', in Flood (ed.), pp. 376–92.
www.imsc.res.in/~jayaram/
www.imsc.res.in/~jayaram/Articles/lfrontline/lfrontline.html

~

COPYRIGHT ACKNOWLEDGEMENTS

Every effort has been made to contact copyright holders. The publishers shall be happy to make good in future editions any errors or omissions brought to their attention. The author would like to thank the following for permission to use copyright material in this book:

For extracts from *Taittiriya Samhita*, vols I–II by A.B. Keith, used by permission Editor, Harvard Oriental Series, published by Harvard University Press; quotes from The *Upanisads*, translated and edited by Patrick Olivelle, by permission of Oxford University Press and Olivelle; extracts from the *Rig Veda: An Anthology* translated and edited by Wendy Doniger, used by permission of Penguin Books Ltd., and Doniger; for extracts from *Paippalada Samhita* translated by Arlo Griffiths and Lubotsky, used by permission of Griffiths and Egbert Forster, Groningen; for quotation from 'On Mantras and Frits Staal' by George Thompson in *India and Beyond: Aspects of Literature, Meaning and Ritual and Thought: Essays in Honour of Frits Staal*, by permission of George Thompson; for quotation from 'Edifying Puzzlement: The Rigveda 10.12 and the Uses of Enigma', *Journal of the American Oriental Society*, by permission Joel Brereton;

For illustrations: Michael Witzel for 'Geography of the Vedas: Rivers' and 'The Rigveda and the Other Three Vedas: Tribes' from 'Tracing the Vedic Dialects' in Caillat Colette (ed.), *Dialectes dans les litteratures indo-ariennes*; Regents of the University of Minnesota for 'The Indus Civilization between 2100 and 1600 BCE' from *A Historical Atlas of South Asia*, (ed.), Joseph E. Schwartzberg, University of Chicago Press; the Landesmuseum for Kultur and Mensch, Oldenburg, for 'Two Pages of Kikkuli's Treatise', 'Carts from Harappa (2100–1600 BCE)', 'Wheels from Harappa (2600–1900 BCE)', all from *Rad und Wagen. Der Ursprung einer Innovation: Wagen im Vordern Orient and Europa*; Viktor Sarianidi for Togolok-21, BMAC, in *Information Bulletin of the International Association for the Study of the Cultures of Central Asia*; Archeological Survey of India for 'Panel from Sanchi With Spoked Wheel', Spoked Wheel from the Sun Temple at Konarak' and 'Ceiling Panel of Sage Vidyaranya from Hampi'; the National Museum, New Delhi, for 'Procession Cart with Solid Wheels from a Temple at Kumbakonam'; South Ural State University Press for 'Sintashta Grave (between 2200 and 1800 BCE); Adelaide de Menil for 'Looking East into the Sadas'; Cambridge University Press for 'The History of Ancient and Medieval Science' by Otto Neugebauer in *Science and Civilization in China*, vol. 3, by Joseph Needham; Royal Netherlands Academy of Arts and Sciences for 'Karmic Arithmetic or Tit-for-tat I: Ridiculing Ugly People' and 'Karmic Arithmetic or Tit-for-tat II: Despising Low-class Musicians' by Jan Fontein; Wayne Howard for the Tables 'The Excellent Chariot with *bha* Syllables I and II'.

~

INDEX

Having argued (especially pages 277–80 with Figure 24), that there is no rhyme or reason to the ABC alphabet, the chief names, concepts and topics discussed in this book are listed here in alphabetical order. Many names of modern scholars and scientists are included.